ISLAM: ESSAYS ON SCRIPTURE, THOUGHT AND SOCIETY

ISLAMIC PHILOSOPHY THEOLOGY AND SCIENCE

Texts and Studies

EDITED BY

H. DAIBER and D. PINGREE

VOLUME XXVIII

Anthony H. Johns

ISLAM: ESSAYS ON SCRIPTURE, THOUGHT AND SOCIETY

A Festschrift in Honour of Anthony H. Johns

EDITED BY

PETER G. RIDDELL AND TONY STREET

BRILL
LEIDEN · NEW YORK · KÖLN
1997

This book has been printed on acid-free paper.

Library of Congress Cataloging-in-Publication Data

Islam : essays on scripture, thought, and society : a festschrift in honour of Anthony H. Johns / edited by Peter G. Riddell and Tony Street
p. cm. — (Islamic philosophy, theology, and science, ISSN 0169-8729 : v. 28)
Includes bibliographical references (p.) and index.
ISBN 9004106928 (cloth : alk. paper)
1. Johns, Anthony H. (Anthony Hearle) 2. Islam–Essence, genius, nature–Miscellanea. I. Riddell, Peter G. II. Street, Tony. III. Johns, Anthony H. (Anthony Hearle) IV. Series.
BP163.J64I85 1997 97-9661
297–dc21 CIP

Die Deutsche Bibliothek – CIP-Einheitsaufnahme

Islam - Essays in scripture, thought and society : a Festschrift in honour of Anthony H. Johns / ed. by Peter G. Riddell and Tony Street. – Leiden ; New Yorl ; Köln : Brill, 1997
(Islamic philosophy, theology, and science ; Vol. 28)
ISBN 90-04-106928 Gewebe

ISSN 0169-8729
ISBN 90 04 10692 8

PRINTED IN THE NETHERLANDS

CONTENTS

PREFACE

A conference called "Transmissions of Islam" was held from the 17th to the 19th of September, 1993 at the Australian National University (ANU) to mark the retirement of Professor Anthony Hearle Johns, now a Professor Emeritus of the University. The conference, jointly organised and chaired by Professor Anthony Reid, Dr Virginia Hooker and Dr Tony Street, all of the ANU, attracted the participation of established and emerging scholars from all over the world, including North America, Southeast Asia, the Middle East and Australia. The participation of scholars from such diverse locations was made possible by funding support obtained by the participants from various sources. Moreover, the organisers received funding support from the Australia-Indonesia Institute to enable the participation of Dr Nurcholish Madjid and Dr Taufik Abdullah, leading Indonesian scholars of Islam.

With the conclusion of a very successful conference, the organisers turned their attention to the production of a volume arising from conference papers. A process was thereby initiated, which involved various stages and which culminated in this present volume. This process included discussions with potential publishers about matters relating to theme and focus, the involvement of academic referees who advised the editors on the consolidation of core themes for the volume, and the enlisting of additional contributions which had not been presented at the original conference. The result of this process was that this present volume represents a somewhat distant descendant of the original conference, drawing on it in significant respects, but having evolved considerably in terms of participants and thematic considerations.

With regard to the physical format of the volume, the reader's attention is drawn to several points. Firstly, in the interests of clarity, all dates have been given in C.E. only. Similarly, to leave the text as uncluttered as possible, all honorifics have been omitted. Thirdly, readers will observe differences in the use of Arabic diacritics between Parts I and II of the volume. Arabic terminology in Part I has been rendered with the full diacritical machinery. By contrast, Part II is concerned not with Middle Eastern Islam, but with Islam in Southeast Asia. Since many Arabic terms have been taken up into the broader Indonesian/Malay language vocabulary and are normally rendered in that language without diacritical symbols, the diacritics are largely absent from Part II of the volume. Finally, with regard to the format of the bibliography, the editors have been guided in the presentation of information by the library catalogues which they have consulted during the process of editing.

A debt of gratitude is owed to many people for having made the publication of this volume possible. Firstly, the original conferees of "Transmissions of Islam"; secondly, the referees for the contributions to this volume; and finally, the contributors themselves. All have committed themselves to the production of this volume in honour of Professor A.H. Johns and have patiently participated in the lengthy process between original conference and finalisation of this volume.

The September 1993 conference was held at John XXIII College of the Australian National University, and thanks are expressed to that College for the provision of its facilities. It is fitting that John XXIII was the venue for the conference, because it is the Dominican college of the ANU, and Professor Johns has had a long and fruitful scholarly relationship with the Dominican Order, both in Australia and in Cairo. Thanks are also expressed to the Faculty of Asian Studies at the ANU for having provided resources in support of the original conference and preparation of this volume. Moreover, the editors wish to acknowledge the University, with thanks, for access to the ANU Indian font for the preparation of this volume.

The editors also wish to record their thanks to the London Bible College (LBC) for provision of wide-ranging resources in the preparation of this volume. Particular thanks are due to Miss Jenny Davies for her patient and meticulous work on the detailed preparation and presentation of this volume in support of the editors. Without her assistance this volume would not have reached fruition. Thanks are also due to Dr Conrad Gempf, who developed and provided the Corinth Greek font used in the paper contributed by Professor Frank, and Ian McNair, who proof-read the final Greek text. The editors also wish to thank Mark Henley, who provided valuable support with the inclusion of the graphics in the paper contributed by Professor Fox.

Finally, thanks are due to the Oxford Centre for Islamic Studies, whose Visiting Fellowship program enabled Dr Tony Street to be in England for the collation and finalisation of the document.

Peter G. Riddell and *Tony Street* *London, 12 December 1996*

CONTRIBUTORS

Jutta Bluhm-Warn is a public servant with the Australian Government, and dealt for some years with concerns of Muslim migrants to Australia. She published "A Preliminary Statement on the dialogue established between the Reform magazine al-Manār and the Malayo-Indonesian World" in *Indonesia Circle* (SOAS, University of London, 1983). Her continuing research is on the development of the Muḥammad ʿAbduh Reform movement in the Malay-Indonesian World from the turn of the century, as exemplified in the work of Ahmad Soorkattie.

David Burrell, C.S.C. is Theodore M. Hesburgh Professor in Philosophy and Theology at the University of Notre Dame (Indiana, USA). His work has focused on comparative study of Jewish, Christian, and Islamic philosophical theology, especially in the medieval period. His publications include *Knowing the Unknowable God: Ibn Sīnā, Maimonides, Aquinas* (1986); *Voices from Jerusalem* (edited with Yeheskel Landau, 1991), an anthology on Jerusalem as an interfaith reality; *Freedom and Creation in Three Traditions* (1993); and translations of *Al-Ghazālī on the Ninety-Nine Beautiful Names of God* (with Nazih Daher), and *The Book of Faith in Divine Unity and Trust in Divine Providence* (from al-Ghazālī's *Iḥyāʾ ʿUlūm al-Dīn*).

Michael Carter is Senior Lecturer in the Department of East European and Oriental Studies of the University of Oslo. He specialises in the history of Arabic grammar. His publications include *Arabic Linguistics: An Introductory Classical Text with Translation and Notes* (J. Benjamins, 1981), and *Studies in the History of Arabic Grammar II, Proceedings of the 2nd Symposium on the History of Arabic Grammar, Nijmegen, 27 April–1 May 1987* (edited with Kees Versteegh, John Benjamins, Phil. and Amsterdam, 1990). He is currently preparing to produce a hypertext edition of the *Kitāb* of Sībawayhi, and a Reference Grammar of Modern Written Arabic.

Christine Dobbin is currently a Visiting Fellow in the Division of Pacific and Asian History, Research School of Pacific and Asian Studies at the Australian National University. Her publications include *Islamic Revivalism in a Changing Peasant Economy: Central Sumatra, 1784–1847* (Curzon, London, 1983); and *Asian Entrepreneurial Minorities: Conjoint Communities in the making of the world economy 1570–1940* (Curzon, London, 1996). Her current research interest are concerned with the Islamic and Asian Trade Diaspora.

James J. Fox is Professor of Anthropology at the Research School of Pacific and Asian Studies of the Australian National University. His most recent books include *Balanced Development: East Java in the New Order* (edited with H. Dick and J.A.C. Mackie, Oxford University Press, Singapore, 1993); *Inside Austronesian Houses: Perspectives on Domestic Designs for Living* (ANU-RSPAS, Canberra, 1995); *The Austronesians: Historical and Comparative Perspectives* (edited with P. Bellwood and D. Tryon, ANU-RSPAS, Canberra, 1995); and *Origin, Ancestry and Alliance: Explorations in Austronesian Ethnography* (edited with C. Sather, ANU-RSPAS, Canberra, 1996). His current research interests include the historical ethnography of Java and eastern Indonesia, as well as foundations of Islam in Indonesia.

Richard Frank is Professor Emeritus at the Catholic University of America (Washington, D.C.). His published works include *Beings and Their Attributes: The Teachings of the Basrian School of the Muʿtazila in the Classical Period* (SUNY Press, Albany, 1978); *Creation and the Cosmic System: Al-Ghazālī and Avicenna* (Heidelberg, 1992); and *Al-Ghazālī and the Ashʿarite School* (Duke University Press, Durham, NC, 1994). His current research interests include the history of Islamic philosophy and theology.

Raphael Israeli, Chair of the Department of East Asian Studies at the Hebrew University of Jerusalem, is a specialist on Islam, Middle-Eastern Studies and Chinese History. He has published some 15 books and 80 articles on these topics, the most relevant to this volume being: *Muslims in China* (Curzon, 1980); *Muslim Fundamentalism in Israel* (Brasseys, 1993); and *A Critical Bibliography of Chinese Islam* (Greenwood, 1994).

Clive S. Kessler is Professor of Sociology at the University of New South Wales in Sydney, Australia, a position he has held since 1980. Before that he taught at the London School of Economics and Political

Science and at Barnard College, Columbia University, New York. Since the mid-1960s he has been pursuing research on the involvement of Islam, both ideologically and institutionally, in shaping responses to socio-economic change and the cultural dilemmas that it occasions in modern Malaysia. He is the author of numerous works in this field including *Islam and Politics in a Malay State: Kelantan 1838–1969* (Cornell U.P., Ithaca, 1978).

Ann Kumar is Reader in the Asian History Centre of the Australian National University. Her major publications include *Surapati, Man and Legend: a Study of Three Babad Traditions* (E.J. Brill, Leiden, 1976); *The Diary of a Javanese Muslim: Religion, politics and the pesantren 1883–1886*, (Faculty of Asian Studies Monographs: New Series No. 7, Canberra, 1985); and *Java and Modern Europe: Ambiguous Encounters*, (Curzon, London, 1996). Her current research interests are Islam and modernity in Indonesia.

Nehemia Levtzion is Professor of the History of the Muslim Peoples, The Hebrew University of Jerusalem, and Executive Director, the Van Leer Jerusalem Institute. His publications include *Eighteenth Century Renewal and Reform in Islam* (edited with John O. Voll, Syracuse University Press, 1987) and *Islam in West Africa: Religion, Society and Politics Before 1800* (Variorum, London, 1994). His current research projects include Structural, Organisational and Ritual Changes in Sufi Brotherhoods in the Eighteenth Century; the Development of Islamic Vernacular Literature in the Eighteenth Century; Renewal and reform in Islam in the Eighteenth Century.

Wendy Mukherjee specialises in and publishes on the Sundanese literature of West Java. She recently completed her doctoral work on the early Sundanese novel under the supervision of Emeritus Professor A.H. Johns at the Australian National University. Her present research interest is in women's ethics in the Islamic manuscript traditions of the Malay-Indonesian archipelago.

Ian Proudfoot is Senior Lecturer in Asian History at the Australian National University. His recent publications include *Early Malay Printed Books* (Kuala Lumpur: Academy of Malay Studies and the Library, University of Malaya, 1993). He is currently investigating print literacy in nineteenth century Indonesia and Malaysia.

Anthony Reid is Professor of Southeast Asian History at the Research School of Pacific and Asian Studies at the Australian National University. Recent publications include *Southeast Asia in the Age of Commerce, c. 1450–1680* (2 vols., New Haven, Yale University Press, 1988–93) and (as editor) *The Making of an Islamic Political Discourse in Southeast Asia* (Clayton, Victoria, Monash University Centre of Southeast Asian Studies, 1993). His current research interests include investigating shifts in religious and political identity in Indonesia and Malaysia.

Merle Ricklefs is Director of the Research School of Pacific and Asian Studies at the Australian National University. Among his publications are "Unity and Disunity in Javanese Political and Religious Thought of the 18th Century" in *Modern Asian Studies*, 26:4 (1992); *War, Culture and Economy in Java, 1677–1726* (1993); and his translation into English of *Pantheism and Monism in Javanese Suluk Literature by P.J. Zoetmulder* (Leiden, 1995). His new book *The Seen and Unseen Worlds in Java, 1726–49* is currently awaiting publication. He is now writing a book on Islam and Identity in Java from the 14th to the 19th centuries.

Peter G. Riddell is Senior Lecturer in Islamic Studies and Linguistics, and Director of the Centre for Islamic Studies and Muslim-Christian Relations, at the London Bible College (Brunel University). His PhD thesis was published as *Transferring a Tradition* (Berkeley, 1990: Centers for South and Southeast Asian Studies, University of California). He is currently preparing a book on the sources and development of Islamic thought in the Malay-Indonesian world c. 1300–c. 1990.

Tony Street is Lecturer in Arabic and Islamic Studies at the Australian National University. He works on medieval Arabic logic, and is currently a Visiting Fellow at the Oxford Centre for Islamic Studies.

S. Supomo is Reader in the Southeast Asia Centre at the Australian National University. His publications include *Arjunawijaya: a kakawin of Mpu Tantular* (Bibliotheca Indonesica, vol. 14. The Hague, Martinus Nijhoff, 1977) and *Bhāratayuddha: an Old Javanese poem and its Indian sources* (International Academy of Indian Culture and Aditya Prakashan, New Delhi, 1993). He is currently working on an English translation of an anthology of Old Javanese poems.

INTRODUCTION

A distinguished scholar of tremendous breadth, Professor Anthony Johns has worked on Islam in Southeast Asia, and on Islam in the primary Middle Eastern centres of learning. The work of Professor Johns offers a profound insight into the way Islam has been transmitted across the Muslim world, ending forever the theory that cultural and scholarly movement was in one direction, from the Middle East to Southeast Asia. It is only natural, then, that a celebration of the scholarly contribution of Professor Johns should look, firstly, at the dynamics of the transmission of Islam, and secondly, at the manifestations of Islam in Southeast Asia. These two emphases have served to divide the contributions which make up this volume.

The Qur'ān lies at the heart of Islam, and when we consider the dynamics of the transmission of Islam, we must first look to the way Muslims have responded to the Qur'ān. The first article presented in this volume is by Professor Johns, and it is a magisterial study of an important Southeast Asian Arabic commentary on the Qur'ān, and its antecedents. By minute source-critical analysis of the text, we are led to see just how interactive Qur'anic commentaries from different times and places can be. Further, literary sensitivity to the text and context of logia in the Qur'ān and the way in which they are treated in the various commentaries enables us to get a sense of what things are heard for all time in the Qur'ān, and what things are heard only in specific cultural contexts.

Clearly, the methods a non-Muslim has to follow to produce this kind of scholarship must be reflective. Above all else, one has to guard against the danger of generalising too quickly about interpretations of the Qur'ān on the basis of expectations imported from another cultural context. The second article, by Professor Burrell, deals with the dangers inherent in non-Muslim study of the Qur'ān.

The third article, by Dr Riddell, looks at one approach to the Qur'ān, that of narrative based exegesis. By concentrating on the treatment of one narrative pericope from the Qur'ān in a number of commentaries, Dr Riddell is able to examine different receptions of that style of exegesis in the Middle East and Central Asia on the one hand, and Southeast Asia on the other. In the fourth article, Professor

Israeli looks at the translation of the Qur'ān into Chinese, and the problems of interpretation involved in giving accurate renderings in ideographs of key Arabic terms. Professor Israeli's article throws light on a fascinating problem, that of preparing an interpretative translation of the Qur'ān that is comprehensible in a vastly different cultural context, yet which maintains some sense of the dignity and grandeur of the original.

Also central to Islam are the basic doctrines—God, prophets, judgement—presented in the Qur'ān, the methods for extending these doctrines in various ways, and the differentiation of these doctrines from those of other religions. The next group of papers address these doctrines and methods.

Substantive doctrine has to be supported and extended by coherent methods and consistent speculative theology. Professor Carter examines two methods of reasoning in the Islamic sciences, the analogical and the analytical, the spheres in which each operates, and their interdependence. Professor Frank has contributed a study of the major themes and assumptions of three important systems of speculative theology: the Muʿtazilites, the early Ashʿarites, and that of al-Ghazālī. The analysis of a sharp cluster of central problems is at once helpful for understanding each of these systems, and for exhibiting the most basic theological differences that characterise the three schools of thought. Too often these matters are overlooked, simply because they no longer occupy centre stage in modern philosophical discussions. Dr Street presents a paper which looks at the biographical tradition of medieval Islam, and shows how this biographical tradition is more intertwined with doctrinal disputes than is sometimes thought. The particular focus of Dr Street's paper is Fakhr al-Dīn al-Rāzī, a commentator on the Qur'ān whom Professor Johns has studied extensively.

In the efforts of transmitting Islam, of propagating the Qur'ān and Islamic doctrine, certain of the institutions generated by the Sufi movement have been of paramount importance, particularly subsequent to the fall of Baghdad to the Mongols. Professor Levtzion looks at the centralisation of three major Sufi orders in recent times, and the consequences this had for intellectual interchange throughout the Muslim world. Not only are certain institutions vital for the dissemination of scripture and doctrine; so also is the technology of printing. Dr Proudfoot examines this strangely neglected topic, and concentrates especially on the reason that lithography was preferred to typography. This study turns out to be important not only as a contribution to the history of printing, but also as a cautionary tale for studies of Islam and the need to avoid ascribing to "conservatism" decisions which have to do with deeper perceptions of what is aesthetic.

In Part II of this volume, the focus moves to the Malay-Indonesian world and the manifestations of Islamic belief and practice in that region. The adoption of Islam by the residents of the Malay world led to another layer being added to the mosaic of religious experience of the Malay peoples during the past two millennia. In its interaction with previous belief systems, Islam in the Malay world assumed certain characteristics of those earlier faiths and this was manifested in the literature and religious thought of that region, as well as in its popular forms.

The first five papers in Part II concern themselves in various ways with Central Java and with the form of Islam practised in that area. The paper by Professor Fox serves as an effective bridge between the two parts of this volume. It focuses upon a detailed genealogical study of the *Babad Tanah Jawi*, a monumental work whose pages can be seen from a myriad of perspectives. Professor Fox demonstrates how the *Babad* uses the device of narrative context for presenting wide-ranging Islamic themes, including the spread of Islamic teaching, the lives and deeds of the Muslim saints of Java, and the importance of asceticism and mystical practice in Javanese Islam in the early period.

The papers by Dr Supomo and Professor Ricklefs are significant in that they connect the pre-Islamic and the Islamic streams in the early 18th century, and show the importance of texts in defining the Javanese Islamic world. Dr Supomo presents significant observations on the re-interpretation and localisation of Islamic culture into earlier Javanese streams of thought. The paper by Professor Ricklefs points to the self-conscious use of Islam as a political force in the kraton world, as well as presenting a reconsideration of the stereotypical tenets of the history of Javanese Islamisation. The examination of the reign of Pakubuwana II (1726–49) by Professor Ricklefs is innovative in its division of this period into two distinct parts, the first prior to the Chinese war (1740–42) when the monarch was supposedly an aspiring Sufi, and the second following the war when he adopted a more obviously Javanese approach to religion.

The contribution by Dr Kumar is complementary in presenting a detailed examination of a little-studied text which contains indicators of the adaptive nature of Javanese Islam, representing new and valuable material about 19th century Islam in Java. Dr Kumar sets this study in the changing perspectives on modern Indonesian political thought, thus producing a diachronic study of Javanese Islam of considerable importance in the field.

In contrast to the aforementioned internal studies of Javanese Islam, Dr Dobbin contributes comparative study of three Muslim minorities, one of which, based in Java, made use of the economic opportunities opened up by European colonial expansion. This paper serves as a bridge to the study of reformism in the Malay world, because it shows clearly the effect that European capitalism exerted upon local Muslim communities in 19th century Java.

Thus, the audience has so far been presented with a profile of Javanese Islam which is impregnated with influences of other systems of belief and culture, be they religious or commercial. The adaptive nature of Javanese Islam, supplemented by the influence upon Javanese Islam of Western capitalism, made it an ideal candidate for redefinition along the lines of the reformist ideology emerging from the Middle East at the turn of the 19th century.

The reformist ideas, which owe so much to the figure of Muḥammad ʿAbduh (1849–1905)—scholar, writer and Grand Mufti of Egypt—were to make their mark on all corners of the Islamic world, including the Malay-Indonesian world. After 250 years of subjugation to European domination, it was inevitable that Southeast Asian Muslims, like their Middle Eastern co-religionists, would be thirsting for new ideologies which would offer a promise of deliverance and self-determination. The teachings of the reformists, based upon the twin focus of returning to the fundamentals of Islam in the form of the Qur'ān and Sunnah, combined with the use of modern rationalist criticism to reinterpret those primary sources, found fertile ground in Southeast Asia.

The final three papers in this volume address the manifestations of Islamic reformism in Southeast Asia. In an attempt to place signposts on the landscape of Southeast Asian reformism, these papers at times use the terms "reformism" and "modernism" interchangeably. The editors have deliberately avoided tampering with this usage by the authors concerned, in order to maintain the authentic style of the contributions. However, it should be noted that Professor Johns has signalled the danger inherent in this interchangeable usage, and writes:

> "Modernism" is not a term in the Islamic tradition. Muḥammad 'Abduh struggled for *Islāḥ* . . . *Islāḥ* in 'Abduh's use of the term means reformation, or perhaps better re-formation of the practice of Islam in the sense of making it true to itself. The movement was to be a matter of purification, and re-establishing of proper balance . . . "Reformist" is a term that has a historical context to give it some kind of a definition. The ideas of an Ahmad Wahib or a Nurcholish deserve better than to be subsumed by the term "modernist".

The ideas of the Arab reformists were to be disseminated among Southeast Asian Muslims in a variety of forms. In her contribution, Mrs Bluhm-Warn demonstrates that the newsprint—magazines and newspapers—served as an effective vehicle in transmitting reformist ideas from the Middle East to Southeast Asia. Mrs Bluhm-Warn has collected important data on correspondence between individual Southeast Asian Muslims and reformist journals in the Middle East addressing a range of issues pertinent to Islam in early 20th century Southeast Asia. In addition, she shows the way local journals produced in Southeast Asia and based upon Middle Eastern journals for their format and goals transmitted reformist ideas.

Dr Mukherjee addresses the issue of the transmission of Islamic reformism through a different but equally powerful medium: namely, fictional literature. In her ongoing research, Dr Mukherjee devotes attention to the literature of the Sundanese region of West Java, focusing upon the clash between conservative elements and youthful reformist zealots, and the manifestation of these clashes in the local literary context.

In the final paper in Part II, Professor Kessler links the activities of modernist reformists in Southeast Asia in the early part of the 20th century to contemporary political trends within the region, with special reference to Malaysia. Professor Kessler demonstrates that reformist ideas dating back to the teachings of Muḥammad 'Abduh are still a force within contemporary Southeast Asia, though with the passage of time they have in turn come to be regarded as traditionalist by certain opposing ideologies. In conflict with Islamic reformism in the region, one finds the politically marginalised yet still important groups, such as the *Al-Arqam* movement, which opt out of modern life and development in favour of attempting to recreate an idealised social paradigm supposedly existing during the life of the

Prophet Muḥammad in Mecca and Medina. Alongside this group are the two principal players on the Islamic political stage in Malaysia: UMNO, traditionally representing those Muslims who wish to focus upon renewing Islamic values, and PAS, which has a more aggressive policy aiming at instituting the *Sharīʿah*. Professor Kessler also demonstrates a significant resurgence of earlier modernist thinking in modern Malaysia.

Thus Part II has demonstrated the mosaic of Islam in the Malay world. Initially Islam encountered and borrowed characteristics from its religious predecessors in the region, producing a degree of syncretism. At the same time, the expansion of European power led to another colour being added to the kaleidoscope of Southeast Asian Islam which made it an obvious candidate, because of what the reformists regarded as accretions, for the purifying zeal of the Islamic reformists. In the process of the reformist reaction, yet another layer was added, contributing to the multi-cultural, multi-religious, multi-ideological nature of Southeast Asian Islam in the modern world.

Peter G. Riddell and *Tony Street* *London, 12 December 1996*

ANTHONY HEARLE JOHNS

A Vocation[1]

Anthony Reid

It was said of Corporal Johns in the British Army that he was the sort of fellow who might win a V.C., not because he was courageous but because he never recognised there was a danger there. He has pursued life with wonderful vigour but also a kind of innocence, restlessly pursuing one idea, one language, one lead after another. Despite the distinction he has achieved, and the scholarly mountains he has climbed, he has had the courage to prefer the role of a student always struggling to come to terms with some new insight, persuaded that what he had painfully discovered others had always known. He later described his experience in Indonesia as,

> like being blind and deaf, and then the shock of experience that relates to something known opens a chink in the mind encased in ignorance, and fragments of what is seen and heard leads to a quest for what has not yet been seen or heard.[2]

Looking back now, we can see it was just the kind of open mind and heart to discover dimensions of life and thought long stifled by colonial scholarly conventions.

Tony Johns was born in London in 1928. His Englishness was fundamental—particularly his love for English literature—but his Catholicism, his faintly continental origins and his musical and artistic nature must nevertheless have prevented him taking that Englishness for granted. His paternal grandfather had made the fateful move from Hungary to London in the 1880s, and submerged his Polish roots by exchanging the surname Nasinszky for the patronymic Johns. He, and his son, Tony's father, had been master tailors in London.

Tony Johns' romanticism and love of books may have come from his mother's side, and particularly from her father in Plymouth. As

---

[1] I am most grateful to Tony Johns for consenting to be interviewed in the preparation of this article, though it remains, of course, my responsibility.

[2] Johns 1991:3.

the Luftwaffe rained bombs on London Tony was sent to stay with these grandparents, though Plymouth was hardly safer, and to attend St Boniface's College run by Irish Christian Brothers there. The brothers clearly allowed his individuality to develop, especially the sixth form English master who inspired him "to love Keats, Spenser and Chaucer with a genuine enthusiasm", and to sample the novel delights of Hopkins and Eliot.[3] Two other experiences stay in his mind as helping to explain some of his intellectual restlessness. One was the Benedictine monks, many of them German, at Buckfast Abbey, on the edge of Dartmoor, to which St Boniface's moved as the bombing grew more intense. Tony Johns was billeted for a time with other boys in the pre-reformation abbey. It gave him, he remembers, "a sense of the wider dimension of things, and set life in a European rather than simply an English or Devonian context".[4] The other was the "book room" of his self-educated Plymouth grandfather, where he devoured everything he could in the brief interval between School and Army, including T.E. Lawrence's heady introduction to the Arab world, *The Seven Pillars of Wisdom.*

It was however the British Army which deposited Corporal Johns in the Malay World. Drafted at age 18 in 1946, he spent a year as a clerk at an Army base near Newbury, before being sent to Malaya late in 1947. The Emergency was not to break out for another year, so the proportion of his intake which went to this remote imperial outpost was very small. Of the group half remained in Singapore and learned little of Islam or Malay. Corporal Johns was trucked across the causeway to a barracks a few miles up the Kota Tinggi road out of Johor Baru, where he would remain for two years.

Fortunately his education and studious temperament directed him to the Army education service rather than more gruesome tasks. His assignment was to teach English to the young Malays who were recruited to serve the military in various ways. They in turn introduced him to their language, life and faith. He remembers especially the last days of *puasa* (fasting) before *Idulfitri.*

> the sight of torches burning during the nights in front of the houses, the scent of incense, the atmosphere of expectation until the first sliver of the new moon appeared held me enthralled. At the [*Idulfitri*] celebrations, the Malays took me to watch the service at the Abu Bakr

[3] Ibid. 3.
[4] Ibid. 3.

> mosque, and to their homes to eat snacks and sweetmeats. It was intoxicating.[5]

So he resolved to study Malay and Islam on his return to England at Christmas 1949, not the English literature which had been his passion at school. SOAS was all there was; but its inadequacies at this time seemed less a constraint for young Johns than a challenge to go his own original way. He took less than three years for his BA under the unimaginative C.C. Brown, followed by little more than two years for his PhD (1953 & 1954). He was the only student of Malay in this time except for Cyril Skinner, a year his senior. In his last year he was president of the SOAS Students' Association.

Despite this unpromising environment, he blazed a number of new paths. Though colonial officials like Winstedt, Wilkinson, Brown and Hamilton had produced a considerable semi-scholarly corpus, A.H. Johns was the first to write a doctoral dissertation in English on Malay literature. Equally he was the first in Britain to tackle Islamic writing in Malay with the seriousness with which it was written. Sir Richard Winstedt, in retirement from the colonial service, was the reigning eminence on all things Malay, and for those who did not read Dutch his was almost the only opinion available. He encouraged the young Johns, of course, but his writing exuded patronising disapproval of the vast body of Malay religious writing, on the grounds that it was firstly derivative, and secondly took Malay syntax away from the model of his beloved *Sejarah Melayu* (Malay Annals). Tony Johns must have found these attitudes painfully restrictive as a student, and he would later write and speak persuasively against them.[6]

The Malay teaching at SOAS, he remembers:

> many times reduced me to near despair. . . . There were no set texts written after 1848; there were no critically edited texts (or even accurately transcribed or carefully printed ones). Not a single analytic idea was proffered for consideration. The conceptual framework for the course was provided by six books by R.O. Winstedt.[7]

This situation encouraged Tony Johns to turn to the Lebanese scholar Majid Fakhri for Islamic philosophy, and to Hooykaas, who arrived at SOAS towards the end of his time there, for the beginnings of Javanese. Above all he pursued his own agenda of reading. He

---

[5] Ibid. 6.
[6] Johns 1964:8–10.
[7] Johns 1991:7.

was fascinated by the mysticism of Ibn ʿArabī and al-Ḥallāj, encountered particularly through the writing of R.A. Nicholson and Louis Massignon.

More serious scholarly work on Malay and Indonesian studies was going on across the Channel in Leiden, where he paid several visits. It was P. Voorhoeve who suggested the topic of his doctoral thesis, editing some of the earliest Malay Sufi texts derived from Aceh and resting in the Marsden collection. In 1953 he stayed with G.W.J. Drewes for a week, and the great Islamicist went through a chapter of his thesis each day. Tony is not especially proud of his thesis today, but when it was published in 1957,[8] it signalled a new trend in scholarship in English, at last taking seriously the Islamic ideas of the texts in their own terms.

He was still more excited by the extraordinary events which led the Netherlands Indies through to independence as Indonesia. He had first sensed the drama of the Indonesian revolution through his Malay friends in Johor, and then from some Indonesian students met in Holland. He read avidly George Kahin's *Nationalism and Revolution* when it came out in 1952, and determined that he would go there if chance arose, rather than back to Malaya—least of all in the Colonial Service.

1. *Indonesia, 1954–58*

As it happened John Echols, the linguist of Cornell's Southeast Asia Program, came to London in 1954 and met Tony Johns. His mission was to recruit six teachers of English for a Ford Foundation project to improve the capacity of Indonesian tertiary lecturers in English, and he had taken the view that two of the six should have English rather than American accents. Since Tony had not only taught English for the Army, but had earned some pocket money during his doctorate by teaching at Davies' School of English in London, he was outstandingly well qualified. More surprisingly, no other appropriate Englishman could be found, despite the then handsome U.S. $5,000 a year salary.

Dr Johns was especially keen to teach in Yogyakarta, to build on the Javanese he had begun to learn from Hooykaas. After a briefing

[8] Johns 1957.

from the Ford Foundation in Jakarta and only a few weeks at the IKIP in Yogyakarta, however, he was sent in September 1954 to Bukittinggi, where a group of about 30 schoolteachers had been assembled to learn English and provide the kernel of the future IKIP (Teacher's College) there. So he moved to the Islamic society of Minangkabau. There was the opportunity "to grow out of the part bucolic, part outdated style of Malay language that I had brought with me from SOAS",[9] but still more to experience a functioning Muslim community which had only limited use for the esoteric mysticism he had studied in his thesis.

> I had learned nothing of the central role of Jurisprudence in any Malay community, of the basic creeds about the nature of God and his attributes, of what was possible and impossible of Him, nothing of the Qur'anic exegesis, or the elaboration of the Qur'anic stories of the prophets that every Muslim child knew—all of those things which come before mysticism.[10]

The way Tony Johns himself describes this sense of being "an intellectual cripple", with every local *Qadi* having better Arabic than he did, is an astonishing reversal of the colonial pretence of omniscience. One sees why he learned quickly, because he conceded he had everything to learn.

Yohanni was one of six women among his English class of some thirty students. In the course of classes on Applied Linguistics and Educational Testing something clicked. But the two youngsters could never be seen alone in the climate of Bukittinggi. If they wanted to go out together, all the other five girls in the class had to be invited along. Nevertheless somehow, with the same sublime or foolhardy courage we noted in Corporal Johns, he arranged with Yohanni to elope with him by going by separate routes to the airport in Padang, and flying off to Singapore and then England to marry. Every respectable English Catholic, and every respectable Sumatran Muslim, would have told them this was madness which could only lead to disaster. Forty years later, they continue to sustain each other in a model marriage, blessed with five accomplished and devoted children. The commitment of each to their respective traditions of faith is undiminished, indeed enriched—bound to each other but distinct and parallel, like the separate tracks of a railway, as Yohanni once put it.

[9] Johns 1991:10.
[10] Ibid. 9.

Though only twenty months in Bukittinggi, Tony began there his encounter with modern Indonesian literature. The language and literature of Minangkabau presented another challenge which he accepted with alacrity. Though there was then little scholarly tradition to build on in respect to Minangkabau literature, he began a study of a popular *kaba*, the *Rancak di Labueh*, as "an experiment: an attempt to render a specimen of Minangkabau dialect literature into English as literature in its own right, and to probe its value as a guide to the sociology and history of Minangkabau".[11] The translation and text was published by Cornell in 1958. It tells the story of a profligate son and his eventual redemption as a valued member of society. Hence it offers a kind of mirror of the values of Minangkabau society on the eve of its twentieth century transformation. Tony generously insists that any merit the translation has is due to Yohanni's understanding of her own culture, as they worked over the text during the first two years of their marriage. His own, however, is the eagerness to make Minangkabau culture explicable to outsiders, and help them to share his fascination with it. Among the tools he uses is the analogy with Christian puritanism in many of the values of the *kaba*—condemnation of self-indulgence, and the idea that prosperity is the visible reward for virtue.[12]

After two academic sessions in Bukittinggi, and a spell of leave in England introducing Yohanni to people and places, he returned for a second contract with the Ford Foundation, this time in Yogyakarta. There he was able to pursue his interests: in Javanese, in modern Indonesia and its literature, in Muslim life and thought. Once more he seized upon a text to edit.

2. *Indonesian Studies at the ANU*

In June 1955 the Director of the Australian Commonwealth Office of Education (then still a minuscule operation, in Sydney) wrote to the Canberra University College, as well as to the Universities of Sydney and Melbourne, offering funds "for the teaching of Indonesian and Malayan Studies". The Government hoped that teaching

---

[11] Johns 1958:v. The text as published has "to *prove* its value", a mistake of the typist at Cornell.

[12] Ibid. xiii–xv.

could begin in the 1956 year, that Bahasa Indonesia would be the major study, as part of degree courses in Arts, but that "possibly provision could be made for teaching something of the culture of the region".[13]

The Canberra College, despite misgivings about the dangers of spreading Indonesian Studies over a number of centres, was quick to advertise a lectureship in Indonesian and Malayan Studies. Somebody sent the advertisement from England to Tony in Bukittinggi, and he applied in September. The College was impressed with his record and his references. D.G.E. Hall described him as "a young man of extremely pleasant personality", and "a teacher of immense enthusiasm", while Voorhoeve emphasised that he was "an enthusiastic and gifted Malay scholar".[14] But before moves were completed to have him interviewed in Jakarta, he withdrew his application. His Ford contract had been extended, with two more years teaching English, and this time in Yogyakarta, and he wanted to give priority to gaining experience in Indonesia.

The College had been impressed with what they heard about Dr Johns, and relatively unimpressed by the other candidates who applied. They kept looking for their candidate while teaching began in 1956 through the agency of the Indonesian cultural attaché in Canberra, Supangkat. About twenty students enrolled in that initial course, a remarkable sign of interest when compared with the three students then enrolled in Chinese and Japanese.[15]

Meanwhile the foundation Professor of Oriental Languages, Hans Bielenstein, made a four month tour of centres of Southeast Asian Studies, notably Cornell, Berkeley, Columbia, SOAS, Cambridge, Leiden and the University of Indonesia. Everywhere he enquired how Bahasa Indonesia was taught, what other subjects were combined with it, and who were the outstanding scholars who might be attracted to Canberra. Nowhere except in Jakarta did he find a degree program exclusively in Indonesian studies, and he concluded that a modified version of the University of Indonesia program, with its classical Malay, Javanese, Arabic and Sanskrit as well as modern Indonesian, should be the model for Canberra. Everywhere he heard good things about Dr Johns. Echols pointed out that no Americans

---

[13] Weedon to Burton 24 June 1955, Johns file, ANU Archives—henceforth ANUA.
[14] Johns file, ANUA.
[15] School of Oriental Studies Report, 1955, ANUA.

had comparable language and literature qualifications. In London, however, D.G.E. Hall ventured the opinion,

> that no foreign scholars would stay in Australia for any considerable length of time. He suggests that the School . . . should train a post-graduate Australian student for our position. The requirement would be that this student must have first class honours in classics or modern languages.

Fortunately this advice did not impress Bielenstein. On the contrary he recommended that "We should go to any length in trying to obtain the services of Dr Johns or of the other scholars recommended by Hall"—Lesley Palmier (later recruited to Wellington) and Cyril Skinner (to Monash). In order to compete with Sydney University, which had decided to use its Commonwealth funds to advertise a readership, the College should raise its post to a Senior Lectureship at least.[16]

In March 1956, therefore, the Principal wrote again to Dr Johns in Bukittinggi, to say that the College had not filled the earlier position but now wished to appoint at the Senior Lecturer level, and wondered whether Johns might be interested. He wrote back from the Hotel des Indes in Jakarta in April, at the end of his Bukittinggi contract, to explain his decision to take the Ford Foundation offer of another one or two years in Yogyakarta. "I feel that to a great extent the value of one's work as an orientalist depends on living in a community as an accepted member of it."[17]

By this time the College was convinced it wanted Tony Johns and should do its utmost to outbid Sydney and Melbourne to get him. The Principal, Joe Burton, agreed to wait for him to the end of his Ford contract, and meanwhile to accept the Indonesian government offer of "Colombo Plan aid in reverse" in the form of a visiting lecturer, Amir Hamzah Nasution, who began teaching in 1957 and continued past the Johns appointment to 1960. In 1957 the contract with Tony Johns was sealed when the young Englishman made his first visit to Australia, where "the warmth of Joe Burton, his wife and many others made it clear that this was a good place to be".[18] The Johns family (by now with a five-month son), did not finally reach Canberra to take charge of the Indonesian programme until

---

[16] Bielenstein memorandum, 19 March, 1956, ANUA.
[17] Johns to Burton 25 April, 1956, ANUA.
[18] Johns 1991:12.

1 August 1958, with Tony a few weeks short of his thirtieth birthday.

In reality the chief rival for his services had not been Sydney and Melbourne but the Islamic Studies Centre of McGill University in Montreal. The three Australian universities had all responded to the government's proposal for "Indonesian and Malayan Studies" by setting up departments of exactly that name, but the content of each was very different. Sydney appointed an established Dutch Javanist, F.H. van Naersson, who built a "Studies" department around the highly developed Leiden tradition of Indology. Melbourne hired the political economist Jamie Mackie, who also built a multidisciplinary department but centred around contemporary politics. Dr Johns was determined that his enterprise would not be of that type, and quickly changed the original Studies name of his Department to "Indonesian Languages and Literatures", analogous to the established Departments of Chinese and Japanese in the Oriental Faculty, and of French and German elsewhere. Indonesian, he insisted, was a language and literature as deserving of study in its own right as any other, and should not be patronised by assumptions that only Indonesia's turbulent politics were of serious interest. He was equally scathing about "the humbug which needs to be excised from the concept of the Oriental Language", as somehow opposed to "modern languages", or necessarily arcane and difficult.[19] In his inaugural lecture as Professor in 1964 he made no apology for turning the Malay syllabuses of London and Leiden on their head, "devoting the greater part of the three-year major my department offers in Bahasa Indonesia and Malay to the study of modern language and literature, gradually in the third year deepening and enriching it by the introduction of older and more traditional works."[20] Enrolments grew rapidly until by 1966 there were 68 students in the first year and 25 in the third. In the long term the Department Johns built (though now called the Centre for Southeast Asian Studies) has fared rather better than its two counterparts, and shown that Canberra was particularly fortunate in its choice of a scholar who was an heir to the best traditions of European orientalism without being in any sense limited by them; a man who took Indonesian and Islamic ideas with immense seriousness, and never let his students imagine that there was anything easy about them. Tony Johns was in turn fortunate in coming to a pio-

[19] Johns 1964:5–6.
[20] Ibid. 15–16.

neering post where everything was to be built, and where his enthusiasm for teaching and communicating had every encouragement. Later he had wider responsibilities during two periods as Dean of Asian Studies.

The Department was also very well served by the Indonesians whom Dr Johns (Professor from 1964) recruited in the 1960s—Soebardi, the novelist Achdiat Kartamihardja, Supomo, Soewito-Santoso and Yohanni herself, who laid the foundation of the modern Indonesian language programme. All were outstanding scholars and teachers, but all except Achdiat developed their international reputations after coming to the ANU, encouraged by the Department head to take their PhDs there. The intensity with which he sought out the best in Indonesian literature did much to encourage the best in his colleagues. He spelled out in 1970 the aims he then had for the Department: "To contribute to understanding and mutual respect between Australians and the peoples of Malaysia and Indonesia by adding to and making more accessible the corpus of knowledge relating to this region of the world."[21] It has been and remains a dedicated professional enterprise, producing graduates who have graced the scholarly world from Auckland to Amsterdam, and represented Australia at the highest diplomatic levels.

3. *Modern Indonesian Literature*

In his Malay training at SOAS the most modern text offered for study was written in 1848, "and Bahasa Indonesia was regarded with contempt when it was not disregarded".[22] It was during his initial baptism of teaching in Bukittinggi that Tony began to read and collect Indonesian novels, including Achdiat's *Atheis*, first published only five years earlier. He began his first writing about it on the ship travelling from Jakarta to Sydney in 1958, a paper for the ANZAAS conference in Adelaide later that year which represented his introduction to Australian academic life. Taking as his theme three novels, by Marah Rusli, Armijn Pane and Achdiat, he took issue with characterisations of Indonesian literature as purely derivative, insisting that in Armijn Pane's *Belenggu*, in particular, "the singularly delicate treat-

[21] Johns 1970–71:36.
[22] Johns 1964:15.

ment of the theme and its environment are purely Indonesian".[23]

This was followed by numerous other thoughtful studies of modern Indonesian literature, including the influential survey in McVey's *Indonesia*, the translation of Mochtar Lubis' novel *Djalan tak ada Udjung*, and articles on Chairil Anwar, Sitor Situmorang, Pramoedya, Amir Hamzah and the Malaysian Shahnon Ahmad.[24] A.H. Johns was one of the first writers in English to treat contemporary Indonesian writing as an authentic modern literature, and to write about it in an analytical way. He introduced the subject to a broader public who did not read Indonesian or Dutch. In the 1960s he was unrivalled as a sophisticated commentator on this literature. At a time when older European scholars were still patronising or dismissive about the efforts to build a literature both modern and Indonesian, he insisted that "the best Indonesian writers are—and in fact have long been—expressing and developing an Indonesian personality".[25]

4. *Indonesian Mysticism*

Meanwhile he had been steadily making a name for himself as a student of Islamic literature in the Malay World. The publication of his thesis in 1957 signalled the arrival of a new talent writing in accessible English on this seemingly arcane subject. In it one already sees his characteristic eagerness to show the relevance of his passions to contemporary concerns. He made the point that there is a striking parallel between the seventeenth century and our own times in "the sudden influx of new ideas and vocabulary . . . the effort to express something new".[26] Three articles associated with the thesis had already appeared between 1953 and 1955.[27]

As a result of Hooykaas' inspiration at SOAS, Tony had begun to learn Javanese. As we have seen this contact had already interested him in the cultural heartland of central Java, and he had initially

[23] Johns 1959; 1979a:12.

[24] Johns 1963 and 1968. The articles on specific writers are conveniently brought together in *Cultural Options*. Those on the four Indonesian authors all appeared originally between 1963 and 1966, while "Man in a Merciless Universe: The Work of Shahnon Ahmad" first appeared in a 1974 collection.

[25] Johns 1979a:56.

[26] Johns 1957:6. I made a similar point about this parallel 35 years later, unaware of just how far I had been preceded—Reid 1993b:329–30.

[27] Johns 1953, Johns 1955b, Johns 1955a.

turned down the ANU for the chance to spend two years in Yogyakarta as a Ford Foundation English teacher. There he worked hard on his Javanese, sitting at Fr Zoetmulder's feet as well as working with a private tutor. He put this new skill to work at once in editing and translating an Islamic mystical text.

The choice fell on a Javanese rendition in *macapat* verse of a mystical text in the Ibn ʿArabī tradition, *al-Tuḥfa al-mursala ilā rūḥ al-nabī* (The Gift addressed to the Spirit of the Prophet), written in 1590 by the north Indian scholar Muḥammad ibn Faḍl Allāh. His painstaking work to edit and translate this Javanese text, together with the Arabic on which it was based, was "in broad outline" complete by 1960, but was only published four years later in Canberra.[28] Johns' foreword notes that "Its path towards publication has been chequered to say the least"[29]—a comment which appears to refer not only to the extreme difficulty of transliterating the varied metres of *macapat* verse, of comparing the Javanese to the Arabic original, of identifying quotations from other Javanese, Malay and Arabic works, and of rendering comprehensible to the modern mind the Islamic mystical debates of which it formed a part. Despite Johns' acknowledgement of the help of the established scholars P. Voorhoeve, G.W.J. Drewes and Th. Pigeaud, Leiden remained sceptical of this brash Englishman who had thrown himself so energetically into a field hitherto monopolised by the damp Dutch citadel of Indology. When the book finally appeared not in Leiden, nor even in Europe, but in Canberra (where was that?), the critical rumbles were harsh and hurtful to a career which might otherwise have gone further into Javanese and Malay texts. Nevertheless the *Gift* was a remarkable first step for Javanese Islamic scholarship in English. Subsequent steps were taken by a number of Professor Johns' outstanding students—Soebardi, Supomo and Ann Kumar—in the first generation, and by their students in a second generation.

Tony Johns would write a number of other illuminating papers on Indonesian mystical literature from this period onward. Probably the most widely read was an article prepared for what proved a seminal conference on Southeast Asian history convened by Ken Tregonning in Singapore, in 1961. "Sufism as a Category in Indonesian Literature and History", published the same year in Tregonning's new

[28] Johns 1965:3.
[29] Ibid. 3.

journal,[30] brought this tradition of scholarship on the Islamic texts of seventeenth century Southeast Asia for the first time to the broader new generation of historians and social scientists working in English. It made a strong case, subsequently incorporated into all classroom discussions of the Islamization of the Malay World, that it was the attraction of Sufi mystical doctrines to established ways of thinking in the region that primarily accounted for conversion. It was an eye-opener for my generation in showing how extremely relevant that scholarship was to any understanding of modern Indonesian reality.

This was Tony Johns' unselfconscious achievement. He brought the analytic skills and scholarly traditions of an old, somewhat discredited Europe to a vibrant if troubled new Indonesia and showed how they fitted together.

5. *Muslim and Christian Approaches to God*

The Johns' sabbatical in Cairo in 1964–65 marked another step into the unknown. At a stage when most of us struggle to preserve what little dignity our writings have endowed us with by sticking to familiar paths, Tony Johns became again the eager student, relentlessly beating his head against another very difficult language. Having studied Arabic as a subsidiary subject at SOAS in 1950–52, he now engaged intensively with it for five months at the American University, and committed himself to navigating yet deeper waters:

> This was an experience that utterly changed my world. It gave me a new vision of the Islamization of Indonesia, and a major step towards acquiring the language competency sufficient to use Arabic sources relevant to Indonesia. . . . It has dominated my development ever since . . . for the Indonesian . . . use of Arabic sources over the centuries led to a discovery of authors in the main stream of the Islamic tradition that were to inspire a new emphasis in my research: the treatment of Qur'anic story telling in the Exegetical tradition, and the role of

[30] Johns 1961. These pioneering thoughts were extended in "Islam in Southeast Asia: Problems of Perspective", in Johns 1976 and Johns 1981b. Professor Johns reflected on his influential 1961 article much later in Johns 1993a, conceding that he was predisposed to perceive the relevance of Sufism, "because I had at that time an enthusiasm for the theosophy of Ibn 'Arabī, doubtless imperfectly understood . . . and was intoxicated by the writings of Nicholson and Massignon". His final rethinking of this issue with reference to much newer Arabic material he has now located is in Johns 1995.

> story telling in creating the universalistic dimension of Islamic salvation history.[31]

In addition to his study of Arabic, he discovered two other important things in Cairo—the friendship of Fr Georges Anawati and his fellow Dominicans devoted to the study of Islam; and the eastern (Melekite) rite Church, in which the great French scholar and visionary Louis Massignon had been ordained a Catholic priest (though married), where Tony Johns relished the liturgy of St John Chrysostom in Arabic. He returned frequently to Cairo thereafter, and gradually transferred his teaching and research interests to Arabic and "mainstream" Islamic theology, though never ceasing to publish on Indonesia.

It was largely due to his ceaseless efforts that the ANU introduced, in the period 1971–75, a first-rate major in Arabic. Among its products were the graduate students who were the pride of his last decade as Professor at the ANU—Tony Street and Laurie Fitzgerald, OP, both writing on aspects of the thought of Fakhr al-Dīn al-Rāzī, and Peter Riddell and Jutta Bluhm, who both used their Arabic to work on the vernacularization of Islamic ideas in Southeast Asia. Tony liked to say that he aimed not to build an empire but to plant trees, and with these trees it can be said that the Islamic dimension of western scholarship on Indonesia has been assured another generation, at a time when it seemed to be dying.

During the 1970s Tony Johns was still expanding his reach into Malay literature and its connections with Islamic and Indian models, as witness his influential paper on historical writing—"The Turning Image".[32] By the 1980s, however, it was primarily the Islamic tradition per se which interested him. He came increasingly to be regarded as Australia's leading commentator on Islamic theology, especially from a Christian standpoint. In 1980 he convened an international conference on "The Qur'ān through Fourteen Centuries" at ANU to mark the commencement of the fifteenth century of the Hijra. In 1983 he was invited by the Egyptian Government to represent Australia at a seminar to mark the millennium of al-Azhar University in Cairo. He was called upon to lecture and write frequently on the Islamic view of Moses, Joseph, David and Solomon

[31] Johns 1991:12–13.
[32] Johns 1979b.

and to explicate Islamic ideas to Christians. In this period his academic writing focused on the presentation of the prophetic figures of Judaism and Christianity in the Islamic tradition of salvation history, with two papers making major advances in understanding the Qur'anic Joseph.[33] Among his contacts in this period was the liberal Catholic theologian Hans Küng, whose passion he shared (if not his theology) for an open Christianity engaged with other faiths.

In the midst of these new challenges Tony Johns left behind, to the regret of many Indonesianists, the studies of modern Indonesian literature which he had pioneered. This followed his disappointment that the humanistic "nobility of utterance" and "conscious rejection of chauvinism that characterised the first years of the revolution . . . was a tradition which by 1955 had spent its force".[34] He felt it was a field in which he had nothing more to say, and could find no renewed stimulus in the theories of literary criticism which became fashionable in the 1980s.

Once again, however, he was ahead of us in looking for the roots of the most important contemporary ideas (as his 1976 paper on the "Satanic Verses" prophetically showed!).[35] While many in Australia and the West have seen Southeast Asia in terms of political and economic challenges, Tony Johns has shared the enthusiasm of younger Indonesians to take the ideas of Islam as seriously as they were ever taken.

He has never doubted that the relation between the human and the divine is what matters, more fundamentally than "national priorities" or academic trends. That conviction has provided the common ground with the Muslims whose ideas he has studied. It has also fuelled the wonderful enthusiasm for ideas and for people that has marked his career.

---

[33] Johns 1981a and 1993b.
[34] Johns 1968:5.
[35] Johns 1982.

PUBLICATIONS BY A.H. JOHNS

1. *Relating to Islamology*

1.1 *Chapters in Books*

(1978) "Friends in Grace: Ibrahim al-Kurani and Abd al-Ra'uf al-Singkeli" in: *Spectrum—Essays presented to Sutan Takdir Alisyahbana on his seventieth birthday*, (S. Udin ed.), Dian Rakyat, Jakarta, pp. 469–485.

(1979) *Ḳiṣṣa* in: *EI*[2] vol. 5, p. 205.

(1981) *al-Kūrānī* in: *EI*[2] vol. 5, pp. 432–433.

(1982) "The Incident of the 'Satanic Verses' allegedly interpolated into sura al-Najm: a psychological interpretation" in: *Middle East I*, (G. de la Lama ed.), Proceedings of the 30th International Congress of Human Sciences in Asia and North Africa, 1976, El Colegio de Mexico, Mexico, pp. 145–152.

(1986) "Islam as a Challenge to Christianity" in: *Concilium Christianity Among World Religions*, (Hans Küng and Jürgen Moltmann ed.), no. 1, Edinburgh, pp. 13–21.

(1987) "Ṭarīqah" in: *The Encyclopedia of Religion*, (Mircea Eliade et al. eds.), Macmillan Publishing Co., New York, vol. 14, pp. 342–352.

(1987) "Moses in the Qur'an: Finite and Infinite Dimensions of Prophecy" in: *The Charles Strong Lectures 1972–1984*, (Robert B. Crotty ed.), E.J. Brill, Leiden, pp. 123–138.

(1991) "Moses in koran en moslimse mystiek" in: *Islam. Een nieuw geloof in Nederland*, (P. Reesink redactie), Ambo/Baarn, pp. 229–234.

(1993) "The Quranic presentation of the Joseph story: Naturalistic or formulaic language?" in: *Approaches to the Study of the Qur'an*, (G.R. Hawting and A.K.A. Shareef eds.), Routledge, London and New York, pp. 37–70.

(1994) *Shams al-Dīn al-Sumaṭrānī* in: *EI*[2] vol. 9.

1.2 *Articles*

(1978) "Qur'anic 'Translation': Some Remarks and Experiments" in: *Milla wa Milla*, (The Australian Bulletin of Comparative Religion), no. 18, pp. 37–51.

(1981) "The Koran, Part I" in: BCA: *Bulletin of Christian Affairs*, Melbourne, no. 112, June, pp. 2–16.

(1981) "The Koran, Part II" in: BCA: *Bulletin of Christian Affairs*, Melbourne, no. 113, July, pp. 2–20.

(1981) "Joseph in the Qur'ān: Dramatic Dialogue, Human Emotion and Prophetic Wisdom" in: *Islamochristiana*, Rome, vol. 7, pp. 29–55.

(1982) "The Qur'an on the Qur'an" in: *Journal of the International Congress for the Study of the Qur'an*, Series 1, Canberra, pp. 1–6.

(1982) "Moses in the Qur'an: Finite and Infinite Dimensions of Prophecy", Charles Strong Memorial Trust, Adelaide, pp. 1–15.

(1986) "Solomon and the Queen of Sheba: Fakhr al-Dīn al-Rāzī's Treatment of the Qur'anic Telling of the Story" in: *Abr Nahrain*, no. 24, E.J. Brill, Leiden, pp. 58–82.

(1986) "Al-Rāzī's Treatment of the Qur'anic Episodes Telling of Abraham and His Guests. Qur'anic Exegesis with a Human Face", in: *MIDEO* (*Mélanges de l'Institut Dominicain d'Etudes Orientales du Caire*), vol. 17, Librairie du Liban, pp. 81–114.

(1987) "Islam: Genesis, Doctrines and Character" in: *The Australasian Catholic Record*, vol. LXIV, no. 1, Sydney, pp. 3–19.

(1989) "David and Bathsheba. A Case Study in the Exegesis of Qur'anic Story-telling" in: *MIDEO* (*Mélanges de l'Institut Dominicain d'Etudes Orientales du Caire*), vol. 19, Editions Peeters, Louvain and Paris, pp. 225–266.

(1989) "Let My People Go! Sayyid Qutb and the Vocation of Moses" in: *Islam and Christian Muslim Relations*, vol. 1, no. 2, December, Centre for the Study of Islam and Christian-Muslim Relations (CSIC), Birmingham UK, pp. 143–170.

(1991) "Hopes and Frustrations: Islamic and Middle Eastern Studies in Australia" in: *Middle East Studies Association Bulletin*, vol. 25, no. 2, pp. 173–180.

(1993) "The Qur'an: Some Literary Perspectives" in: *Australian Religion Studies Review*, vol. six, no. 1, Autumn, pp. 24–37.

(1993) "In Search of Common Ground: The Qur'ān as Literature?" in: *Islam and Christian Muslim Relations*, vol. 4, no. 2, December, CSIC, Birmingham UK, pp. 191–209.

(1995) "Ellipsis in the Qur'ān: A Response to Salah Salim Ali" in: *Hamdard Islamicus*, vol. XVIII, no. 2. pp. 15–23.

1.3 *Review Articles*

(1963) "Islamology, Political Science and History" in: *Australian Outlook*, vol. 17, pp. 339–341.

(1979) *The Qur'anic Sufism*, by Dr Mir Valiuddin, Motilal Banarsidass, Delhi, 1977, second revised edition, in: *The Muslim World*, vol. 69, pt. 3, pp. 198–200.

(1979) *The Collection of the Qur'an*, by John Burton, Cambridge University Press, New York, 1977, first paperback, 1979, in: *The Muslim World*, vol. 69, pt. 4, pp. 269–272.

(1979) *The Rose and the Rock: Mystical and Rational Elements in the Intellectual History of South Asian Islam*, (B.B. Lawrence ed.), Duke University Programs in Comparative Studies on Southern Asia, no. 15, in: *The Muslim World*, vol. LXXII, no. 1, Jan. 1982, pp. 57–59.

(1982) *Intellectual Modernism of Shibli Nuʿmani: An Exposition of His Religious and Political Ideas*, by Mehr Afroz Murad, Institute of Islamic Culture, Lahore, 1976, *Sayyid Ahmad Khan: A Reinterpretation of Muslim Theology*, by Christian W. Troll, Viking Publishing House, Delhi, 1978, in: *The Muslim World*, April 1982, vol. LXXII, pp. 149–153.

(1983) *Islamic Life and Thought*, by Sayyed Hossein Nasr, Allen & Unwin, 1981, in: *Hamdard Islamicus*, vol. VI, no. 2, Summer, pp. 123–125.

(1987) *Creation and the Teaching of the Qur'an*, by Th.J. O'Shaughnessy [Biblica el Orientalia, 40], Biblical Institute Press, Rome, 1985, in: *Abr-Nahrain* (T. Muraoka ed.), vol. XXV, E.J. Brill, Leiden, pp. 113–117.

(1993) *The History of al-Ṭabarī, Volume XXIII. The Zenith of the Marwanid House* (Martin Hinds trans.), State University of New York Press, Albany 1990, in: *Journal of Islamic Studies*, Oxford University Press, vol. 4, no. 1, pp. 90–92.

(1994) *Paths to the Middle East: Ten Scholars Look Back*, (Thomas Naff ed.), State University of New York Press, Albany, 1993, in: *Journal of Semitic Studies*, Manchester, September, pp. 190–193.

2. *Relating to Islam in the Indonesian Archipelago*

2.1 *Books*

(1957) *Malay Sufism as illustrated in a Collection of Anonymous Malay Tracts*, (Doctoral dissertation), in: JMBRAS, no. 178, vol. XXX, part 2, complete number.
(1965) *The Gift Addressed to the Spirit of the Prophet*, Oriental Monograph Series No. 1, Australian National University, Canberra.
(1984) *Islam in Asia, Volume II, Islam in Southeast and East Asia*, (with R. Israeli eds.), Magnes Press, Jerusalem.

2.2 *Chapters in Books*

(1961) "Muslim Mystics and Historical Writing" in: *Historical Writing on the Peoples of Asia*, OUP, London, vol. II, pp. 37–49.
(1976) "Islam in Southeast Asia: Problems of Perspective" in *Southeast Asian History and Historiography, Essays Presented to D.G.E. Hall*, (C.D. Cowan & O.W. Wolters eds.), Cornell University Press, Ithaca, pp. 304–320.
(1978) "Friends in Grace: Ibrahim al-Kurani and Abd al-Ra'uf al-Singkeli", in: *Spectrum—Essays presented to Sutan Takdir Alisyahbana on his seventieth birthday*, (S. Udin ed.), Dian Rakyat, Jakarta, pp. 469–485.
(1981) "Modes of Islamization in Southeast Asia", in: *Religious Change and Cultural Domination*, (David N. Lorenzen ed.), Colegio de Mexico, Mexico, pp. 61–77.
(1984) "Islam in the Malay World, An Exploratory Survey with some reference to Qur'anic Exegesis", in: *Islam in Asia, Volume II, Islam in Southeast and East Asia*, (A.H. Johns and R. Israeli eds.), Magnes Press, Jerusalem, pp. 115–161.
(1985) "Islam in Southeast Asia: Problems of Perspective" in: *Readings on Islam in Southeast Asia*, (Ahmad Ibrahim, Sharon Siddique, Yasmin Hussain Compilers), Institute of Southeast Asian Studies, Singapore, pp. 20–24.
(1987) "Indonesia: Islam and Cultural Pluralism", in: *Islam in Asia: Religion, Politics and Society*, (John L. Esposito ed.), Oxford University Press, New York, pp. 202–229.
(1987) "An Islamic System or Islamic Values? Nucleus of a Debate in Contemporary Indonesia", in: *Islam and the Political Economy*

of Meaning: Comparative Studies of Muslim Discourse, (William R. Roff ed.), Croom Helm, London and Sydney, pp. 254–280.

(1987) "Islam in Southeast Asia", in: *The Encyclopedia of Religion*, (M. Eliade et al. eds.), Macmillan Publishing Co., New York, vol. 7, pp. 404–422.

(1988) "Qur'anic Exegesis in the Malay World: In Search of a Profile" in: *Approaches to the History of the Interpretation of the Qur'an*, (A. Rippin ed.), Clarendon Press, Oxford, pp. 257–287.

(1993) "Political Authority in Islam: Some Reflections Relevant to Indonesia", in: *The Making of an Islamic Political Discourse in Southeast Asia*, (A. Reid ed.), Monash Papers on Southeast Asia, no. 27, Melbourne, pp. 17–34.

(1996) "In the Language of the Divine: The contribution of Arabic" in: *Illuminations: The Writing traditions of Indonesia*, (A. Kumar & J.H. McGlynn eds.), The Lontar Foundation, Jakarta and Weatherhill Inc., New York and Tokyo, pp. 33–48.

2.3 *Articles*

(1953) "Nūr al-Daḳā'iḳ by Shams al-Dīn of Pasai" in: *JRAS*, pp. 137–151.

(1955) "Daḳā'iḳ al-Ḥurūf by 'Abd al-Ra'ūf of Singkel", in: *JRAS*, pp. 55–73, pp. 139–158.

(1955) "Aspects of Sufi Thought in India and Indonesia at the Beginning of the 17th Century" in: *JMBRAS*, vol. 28, no. 1, pp. 70–77.

(1961) "Sufism as a Category in Indonesian literature and history", in: *Journal of Southeast Asian History*, Singapore, vol. 2, no. 2, pp. 10–23.

(1961) "The role of Sufism in the Spread of Islam to Malaya and Indonesia", in: *Journal of the Pakistan Historical Society*, vol. 9, pp. 143–161.

(1961) "Muslim Mystics and Historical Writing" in: *Historical Writing on the Peoples of Asia*, OUP, London, vol. II, pp. 37–49.

(1964) "The Role of Structural Organisation and Myth in Javanese Historiography", in: *The Journal of Asian Studies*, vol. XXI no. 1, pp. 91–99.

(1966) "From Buddhism to Islam: An Interpretation of the Javanese Literature of the Transition", in: *Studies in Comparative History and Culture*, vol. IX.

(1975) "Islam in Southeast Asia: Reflections and New Directions", in: *Indonesia* (Cornell Modern Indonesia Project), no. 19, pp. 33–55.

(1981) "From Coastal Settlement to Islamic School and City: Islamization in Sumatra, the Malay Peninsula and Java", in: *Hamdard Islamicus*, vol. IV, pp. 3–28.

(1988) "Coming to terms with the Qur'an. A Challenge for Indonesianists", in: *RIMA* (Review of Indonesian and Malaysian Studies), University of Sydney, vol. 22, no. 1, pp. 69–92.

(1991) "Traps for the Unwary: A causerie on the place of Islam in Indonesian Studies", in: *Research Project "Urbanism in Islam"*, Monograph Series No. 19, pp. 1–17.

(1991) "Islam and Indonesia: Perceptions and Misconceptions" in: *Newsletter of the World Conference on Religion and Peace*, May, pp. 1–5.

(1992) "Tuhfat al-Nafis: Not a Precious Gift?", in: *Bijdragen tot de Taal-, Land- en Volkenkunde*, vol. 148, pt. 2, pp. 317–321.

(1995) "Sufism in Southeast Asia: Reflections and Reconsiderations", in: *Journal of Southeast Asian Studies*, Singapore, vol. 26, no. 1, March, pp. 169–183.

2.4 *Review Articles*

(1969) *Islam Observed, Religious Development in Morocco and Indonesia*, by C. Geertz, Yale University Press, in: *Journal of Southeast Asian History*, vol. 10, pp. 378–381.

(1972) *The Admonitions of Seh Bari*, re-edited and translated with an introduction by G.W.J. Drewes, in: *Journal of Southeast Asian Studies*, vol. III, no. 2, September, pp. 341–344.

(1978) *Indonesien, Malaysia und die Philippinen Unter Einschluss der Kap-Malaien in Sudafrica. Volume I Geschichte*, by H. Kahler, E.J. Brill, Leiden, 1976, in: *Pacific Affairs*, vol. 51, no. 3, pp. 531–532.

(1981) *Arabic Loan-Words in Malay: A Comparative Study*, second edition by Dr Muhammad Abdul Jabbar Beg, Kuala Lumpur, 1979, in: *The Muslim World*, vol. LXXI, no. 2, pp. 143–144.

(1981) *Purifying the Faith. The Muhammadijah Movement in Indonesian Islam*, by James L. Peacock, The Benjamin/Cummings Publishing Co., Menlo Park California, 1979, in: *Pacific Affairs*, vol. 54, no. 3, pp. 567–569.

(1990) *The Poems of Hamzah Fansuri*, translated, edited and with commentary by G.W.J. Drewes and L.F. Brakel, Dordrecht, Foris, 1986, Bibliotheca Indonesica 26, Koninklijk Instituut voor Taal-, Land- en Volkenkunde, in: *Bijdragen tot de Taal-, Land- en Volkenkunde*, vol. 146, pp. 325–331.

3. *Relating to Literature in Indonesia and Malaysia*

3.1 *Books*

(1958) *Rantjak di Labueh, a specimen of the traditional literature of Central Sumatra, comprising introduction, text and translation*, Data paper no. 32, S.E. Asia Program, Cornell.

(1968) *A Road with No End*, Translation of *Djalan Tak Ada Udjung* by Mochtar Lubis with an introduction, Djakarta, 1951, Hutchinson, London.

(1972) *Indonesia* (with Y. Johns and Richard Woldendorp), Thomas Nelson Pty. Ltd. (Australia).

(1981) *Cultural Options and the Role of Tradition. A Collection of Essays on Modern Indonesian and Malaysian Literature*, ANU Press in Association with Faculty of Asian Studies, Canberra.

3.2 *Chapters in Books*

(1963) "The Genesis of a Modern Literature" in: *Indonesia*, (R. McVey ed.), Southeast Asia Studies, Yale University, New Haven, pp. 410–554.

(1964) "Amir Hamzah: Malay Prince, Indonesian Poet" in: *Malayan and Indonesian Studies*, (J. Bastin and R. Roolvink eds.), Clarendon Press, Oxford, pp. 303–319.

(1973) "Indonesia and Malaysia" in: *Encyclopaedia of World Literature*, Cassel's New Edition.

(1974) "Man in a Merciless Universe: the work of Shahnon Ahmad" in: *Search for Identity: Modern Literature and the Creative Arts in Asia*, (A.R. Davis ed.), Sydney, pp. 59–75.

(1975) "From Caricature and Vignette to Ambivalence and Angst: Changing perceptions of character in the Malay World" in: *Self and Biography: Essays on the individual & Society in Asia*, (W. Gungwu ed.), Sydney University Press, pp. 29–54.

(1976) "Cultural Options and the Role of Tradition: Fecundation of a new Malay Poetry" in: *Bahasa Kesusasteraan dan Kebudayyan Melayu-Essei-essei penghormatan Kepada Pendita Za'ba* (Malay Literature, Language and Culture—Essays in honour of Pendita Za'ba), Kuala Lumpur, pp. 93–135.

(1979) "The Turning Image: Myth and Reality in Malay Perceptions of the Past" in *Perceptions of the Past in Southeast Asia*, (A. Reid and D. Marr eds.), Singapore, pp. 43–67.

(1981) "In Search of the Lost Chord: Adventures in New Literatures" in: *Society and the Writer: Essays on Literature in Modern Asia*, (W. Gungwu, M. Guerrero and D. Marr eds.), RSPacS, Canberra, pp. 199–220.

(1982) "In Search of Tradition: Reflections on Chairil Anwar's Translations and Adaptations" in: *Gavac Studies in Austronesian Languages and Cultures dedicated to Hans Kahler*, (Rainer Carle ed.), Berlin, pp. 647–671.

(1982) "In Search of the Lost Chord: Adventures in New Literatures" in: *Austrina—essays in commemoration of the 25th anniversary of the founding of the Oriental Society of Australia*, (A.R. Davies & A.D. Stefanowska eds.), Oriental Society of Australia, Sydney, pp. 557–577.

3.3 *Articles*

(1959) "The Novel as a Guide to Indonesian Social History" in: *Bijdragen tot de Taal-, Land- en Volkenkunde*, vol. 115, pt. 3, pp. 232–248.

(1959) "Indonesian Literature and the Social Upheaval" in: *Australian Outlook*, vol. 13, pp. 293–303.

(1960) "Towards a Modern Indonesian Literature" in: *Meanjin*, pt. 4, pp. 380–387.

(1960) "Sensation at Top of Coconut Palm! a short story by Achdiat Karta Mihardja" (Translation) in: *Meanjin*, pt. 4, pp. 388–399.

(1961) "Indonesian Tensions—The Literary Record" in: *Quadrant*, pp. 51–60.

(1963) "Devarucci, or the Divine Splendour: A Javanese Presentation of an Indian Religious Concept" in: *Vivekananda: The Cosmic Conscience*, Prafulla Candra Das, Calcutta.

(1963) "Pramudya Ananta Tur: The Writer as an outsider—An Indonesian example" in: *Meanjin*, pt. 4, pp. 354–363.

(1963) "Pramudya's Inem" (Translation) in: *Meanjin*, pt. 4, pp. 365–374.

(1964) "Indonesian Studies in Australia: An Open Horizon" (Inaugural Lecture) Australian National University.

(1964) "Herdjan's Way" (Translation) in: *Hemisphere*, December.

(1964) "Translating Modern Indonesian Literature" in: *Hemisphere, Asian-Australian Viewpoints and Ideas*, Cheshires, pp. 161–166.

(1964) "Chairil Anwar: An Interpretation" in: *Bijdragen tot de Taal-Land-en Volkenkunde*, vol. 120, pt. 4, January, pp. 393–405.

(1966) "On Translating the Nagarakrtagama" in: *Indo-Pacific Linguistic Studies II*, North Holland Publishing Company Special Edition, no. 15, pp. 531–563.

(1969) "Through Myth and Dream: The Indonesian Quest for Reality" in: *Quadrant*, Indonesia Special Issue, pp. 25–34.

(1969) "The Indian Influence in Southeast Asia" in: *Hemisphere*, March, pp. 10–17.

(1970–71) "Bahasa Indonesia and Malay Studies at the Australian National University" in: *Abr-Nahrain* X, pp. 26–36.

(1971) "The Educational Value of Asian Studies in Australian Schools" in: *Teaching about Asia in Australian Schools*, ANU Centre for Continuing Education, pp. 1–7.

(1986) "Professor A.L. Basham" (obituary) in: *The Journal of the Asiatic Society*, vol. XXVIII, no. 3, Calcutta, pp. 81–85.

3.4 *Review Articles*

(1966) *Selected Poems: Chairil Anwar*, by B. Raffel, in: *Journal of the American Oriental Society*, vol. 86, no. 2, pp. 258–261.

(1970) *A Short History of Indonesia*, by A. Zainu'ddin, Cassel, Australia, 1968. *A History of Modern Southeast Asia*, by J. Bastin and H.J. Benda, Prentice-Hall Inc., London, 1968, in: *Historical Studies*, University of Melbourne, vol. 14, no. 55, pp. 445–449.

(1970) *Indonesian Political Thinking, 1945–1965*, (H. Feith and L. Castles eds.), Cornell University Press, 1970, in: *Australian Journal of Politics and History*, vol. XVI, no. 3, pp. 456–458.

(1978) *Sumatran Contributions to the Development of Indonesian Literature 1920–1942*, by A.J. Freidus, University Press of Hawaii, Honolulu, 1977, in: *Pacific Affairs*, vol. 51, no. 3, pp. 536–537.

PART I

ON QUR'ANIC EXEGETES AND EXEGESIS

*A Case Study in the Transmission of Islamic Learning**

To my students, friends and colleagues over the years,
with thanks and appreciation.

A.H. Johns

1. *Introduction*

The Qur'ān is the prime instrument of unity of the Muslim world, and the transmission and diffusion of Islam is inconceivable without it. Yet the Qur'ān is never present in a vacuum. The first Muslims experienced it as illumined, supplemented and explained by the presence and charisma of Muḥammad. After Muḥammad's death, this primal encounter was continued through the Companions, with all the further experience in interpreting and applying its teaching acquired during the early expansion of the Islamic commonwealth, which, transmitted and developed by the *ʿulamāʾ*, laid the foundations of the great branches of Islamic learning. Foremost among them were jurisprudence, exegesis and dogmatics, and these, supported by grammar and rhetoric were to come into full flower by the ninth century alongside the secular traditions of learning in the sciences and belles-lettres.

The Qur'ān then, is presented and experienced through the implementation of these disciplines, thanks to the efforts of the *ʿulamāʾ*, those who devote their lives in every corner of the Islamic world to the study and teaching of the Qur'ān. They pass on their understanding of it in ways suited to every level of society, concerning matters of all kinds, ranging from jurisprudence to the retelling and interpretation of the stories of the prophets, the foundation of the universalised structure of salvation history shared among the peoples of Islam.

The teaching of the *ʿulamāʾ* is mediated through the *madrasa*, or

---

* This chapter in embryonic form was first presented as a paper to the International Seminar on Islamic Civilisation in the Malay World held at Brunei, Darussalam, 1–5 May 1989.

whatever local name by which the institution is known. The *madrasa* offer normative, although not necessarily identical training in the disciplines they teach. For the most part, they are independent bodies, and each has its own mix of emphases reflecting the varying personalities and standing of its individual teachers, their spiritual taste and the traditions to which they are affiliated. It is the *madrasa* which preserve and ensure the transmission and diffusion of the core works of Islamic learning. Collectively, they generate a critical mass of secondary texts which are extended and vernacularised so as to serve the formation of future generations of *ʿulamāʾ* as leaders and guides to local communities in their turn. Such institutions, though in the first instance often established as individual responses to local needs, soon become associated with wider networks of schools and teachers. It is the study of such schools, the teachers who staff them, the handbooks and treatises they compile, the wider networks to which they belong—ultimately extending to Mecca and Medina and other centres of learning in the Middle East, that serves as a key source for an understanding of the intellectual and spiritual history of Islam.

From the late 16th century on, there is documentary evidence of the prosecution of the various Islamic disciplines in the Indonesian archipelago, whether in Arabic, or vernacularised into various of the local languages. The survival, collection, cataloguing and study of such materials has been haphazard at best, but there exists a critical mass of documentation sufficient to establish the existence of a number of centres of reception and diffusion of Islamic learning throughout the archipelago—such as Acheh, Palembang, Patani, Banten, Cheribon, Banjar, and Makasar—reflecting a variety of traditions of jurisprudence and mysticism, and yielding treatises on these disciplines alongside numerous stories of the prophets, kings, saints and military heroes of Islamic history. As the years passed, such centres waxed and waned in relative importance. Their interest is all the more enhanced when it is possible to uncover and trace the traditional networks to which the teachers, local and foreign, who established themselves there belonged.

There are extant a significant number of MSS of the better known Arabic works of Qurʾanic exegesis, most popular among them being the *Tafsīr al-Jalālayn*. At first sight, however, it is something of a paradox that the region itself has yielded so little on *tafsīr*. Between 1600 and the late 1920s, although there survive fragments of Qurʾanic renderings in Malay, whether original or translations, there are only two works by local authors which deal with the Qur'ān as a whole. One is the *Tarjumān al-mustafīd* by 'Abd al-Ra'ūf of Singkel (d. 1693), essentially a Malay rendering of the *Tafsīr al-Jalālayn*, and the other, *Marāḥ labīd*, a two volume Arabic commentary of the Qur'ān by Nawawī of Banten (d. 1897). This latter is a work on a large scale. It was and still is popular. It has been reprinted many times in Indonesia, Malaysia and Egypt, and is still readily available.

There is in addition a wide range of renderings in Malay and other regional languages of individual verses of the Qur'ān in vernacular works devoted to the various Islamic disciplines. It could be a useful study to work out how much of the Qur'ān in these languages could be compiled from quotations in other works up to the end of the 19th century. Given that the Qur'ān was studied in Arabic, and the dominant role of the oral tradition, there was perhaps little need felt to put in written form the explanations given orally in local languages such as Malay, Javanese or Sundanese in the myriad of Qur'ān schools that dot the archipelago. It need hardly be mentioned there are special problems in studying the religious traditions of a society without a strong written tradition, when there is virtually no way in which it is possible to document those elements of cultural behaviour expressed only in social interaction, of which by the very nature of the case, there is no written record. This paucity of written works dedicated to the Qur'ān then, should not be misunderstood.

Even so, such a corpus of work on the Qur'ān in the region after a documented period of over 400 years participation in the Muslim world appears meagre. And scholarly attention to it, despite its importance, has been even less. In *The Achehnese*, Snouck Hurgronje in fact refers rather slightingly to 'Abd al-Ra'ūf's *Tarjumān al-mustafīd*[1] the title given to this Malay rendering of the Jalālayn *tafsīr*, and in any case mistakenly believed it to be a rendering of al-Bayḍāwī's *Anwār al-tanzīl*. The first serious study of this work and a correct attribution of authorship was not completed until 1984.[2] To the best of my knowledge, no study has yet been made of Nawawī's *tafsīr*.

---

[1] "Another famous work of this same Abdurra'uf is his Malay translation of Baidhawi's commentary on the Qur'an, published in A.H. 1302 at Constantinople in two handsomely printed volumes. On the title page Sultan Abdulḥamid is called "the king of all Mohammedans"! From this work we perceive among other things that the learning of our saint was not infallible; his translation for instance of chap. 33 verse 20 of the Qurān (sic) is far from correct." Snouck Hurgronje 1906: vol. II, 17 f.n.

[2] Riddell 1984; 1990a.

2. *Nawawī al-Bantanī*

Nawawī was one of the single most important figures in the religious history of the region in the 19th century. In addition to the *Marāḥ labīd*, his works include treatises on a wide range of the Islamic disciplines: *fiqh*, dogmatics, mysticism and *ḥadīth*, grammar, rhetoric. They are all clarifications of works by authors of greater authority than he dares claim for himself. In fact in none of his writings does he lay claim to originality. He is in fact the exemplary *ʿālim*, one who does not set out to write masterpieces to immortalise his own name, but to continue a patient and continuing elaboration and distillation of a living tradition of learning to meet the needs of the community he serves. The *tafsīr Marāḥ labīd* however, in two volumes totalling 600 pages, is his most extensive work.[3] He wrote exclusively in Arabic and most of his writings were first published in the Middle East. His life and work is a testimony to the central role of Mecca in the diffusion of Islamic learning.

Snouck Hurgronje, who met Nawawī in Mecca in 1884, comments on the high proportion of Bantenese among the religious scholars from the Indies in Mecca, and notes that of them, at the time of his visit, Nawawī was the most outstanding, describing him as the acknowledged head of the Jāwī community in Mecca. He refers to this *tafsīr* as "a large commentary on the Qurʾān", among a number of other of his works, remarking that it had been printed at the newly established Mecca Press,[4] but does not identify the book by name, or offer any comment on its content. He provides a modicum of biographical information on Nawawī: that his father was a religious scholar at Tanara (Banten) and that he received his first religious instruction from him. He made the pilgrimage while "quite young" and stayed three years in Mecca before returning home. He then decided to return to the Middle East, and to spend the remainder of his life there.

Snouck Hurgronje adds that when he met him, he had been active for thirty years, and gives the names of some of his teachers, ". . . the now departed great ones of the previous generation, Khatīb Sambas, Abdulghāni Bima etc., but his real teachers were the Egyptian Yūsuf

[3] Johns 1988:267.
[4] Snouck Hurgronje 1931:271.

Sumbulawēnī and Nahrāwī besides Abd el-Hamīd Daghestānī."[5]

Chaidar, in a work published in 1978 gives further biographical information about him. He was born in Banten, West Java, in 1813 and died in Mecca in 1897. At the age of eight, he was sent to study in East Java. After returning to Banten, at the age of fifteen, i.e. in 1828, in the midst of the Java War (1826–30) inspired and led by Diponegoro, he went to Mecca where he was to remain for the rest of his life, apart from travels in the Middle East. His teachers, in addition to those mentioned by Snouck Hurgronje included "Aḥmad Dimyātī and Aḥmad Zaynī Daḥlān in Mecca, and in Medina, Muḥammad Khaṭīb al-Ḥanbalī."[6] Chaidar notes further that he studied in Egypt and Syria, although unfortunately gives no details as to the identity of his teachers there.

Given his departure from Banten in the disturbed conditions of this period, without doubt he was aware of events in Sumatra and Java. While in the Holy Land he surely followed the course of the Padri War and heard the grievous news of the Dutch capture of Bonjol in 1837. He knew of the outbreak of the Acheh War, and the problems it was causing the Dutch Colonial Government (see below). Not that he had to look as far afield as Sumatra and Java to see the increasing encroachment of European powers on the Islamic world. News would have reached Mecca very swiftly of the Indian Mutiny in 1857, with the influx to the Holy Land of Indian Muslims in its wake. Likewise reports of the ferment created by al-Afghānī's study circle (which included Muḥammad ʿAbduh), founded after al-Afghānī arrived in Cairo in 1871 and the vigorous journalism that he encouraged would soon have been common knowledge. He would have been aware of the rise of Egyptian nationalism, the expulsion of al-Afghānī from Egypt in 1879, the Urabi Pasha revolt which led to the British bombardment of Alexandria and the occupation of Egypt in 1882 and the arrest and exiling of Muḥammad ʿAbduh in 1883. He may well have heard of the publication of the journal *al-ʿUrwa al-Wuthqā* in Paris, and given his association with Aḥmad Zaynī Daḥlān[7]—mentioned by Chaidar as one of his teachers he may have been well aware of the revolt of the Mahdi in the Sudan, and perhaps even of the death of Gordon. There is no direct reference to

[5] Ibid. 268–9.
[6] Chaidar 1978:85–91.
[7] Born early 19th century, died Medina 1886, Muftī of the Shāfiʿites and head of the corporation of scholars of the Haram (Mekka) from 1871; cf. Schacht 1965:91.

any of these events in his writings, but given his perception of his role as an *ʿālim*, one would expect his response to be to write and teach with all the more vigour, in the conviction that the better understanding and practice of Islam as a religion and way of life would create the necessary moral basis for the eventual overthrow of the unbelievers. That this was indeed the case is confirmed by Snouck Hurgronje. In referring to Nawawī's position as leader of the Jāwī community, he speaks both of his deep personal modesty, and the inspiration he gave them to the deeper study of Islam. Snouck Hurgronje's subsequent remarks are highly relevant:

> Under his inspiration, more and more Sundanese, Javanese and Malays turn to the thorough study of Islam, and the politico-religious ideals of Islam gain, in their most highly developed form, increased circulation. But Nawawī is no man's father-confessor. It is only natural that the man should rejoice in the difficulties caused by Acheh to the Government, and, in conversation, disagree with those pensioned officials who hold that the Jawah lands must necessarily be governed by Europeans. The resurrection of the Banten sultanate, or of an independent Moslim state, in any other form would be acclaimed by him joyously, whether or not the insurrection followed according to the Holy Law or took the form of undisciplined fanatical bands. For himself, however, he would seek no political role, nor counsel such to others. It would however be impossible for him to do as was once done by his father, and is now done by his brother Hajj Ahmad in succession to his father, serve the infidel government even as penghulu.[8]

The personal modesty Snouck Hurgronje refers to is manifest from the first page of the *Marāḥ Labīd* where Nawawī refers to the saying attributed to Muḥammad reproving those who interpret the Qur'ān according to personal opinion. To do such is not his intention. Rather it is to preserve and re-present knowledge, not add to it. He accordingly lists five authors of the exegetical tradition on whose work he draws. They are Fakhr al-Dīn al-Rāzī's (d. 1210) *Mafātīḥ al-ghayb*; Muḥammad b. Muḥammad al-Khaṭīb al-Shirbīnī's (d. 1570) *al-Sirāj al-munīr fī 'l-iʿāna ʿalā maʿārif baʿḍ maʿānī kalām rabbinā 'l-ḥakīm al-khabīr*; Abū 'l-Suʿūd Muḥammad b. Muḥammad al-Āmadī's (d. 1544) *Irshād al-ʿaql al-salīm ilā mazāyā 'l-Qur'ān al-karīm*; Muḥammad ibn Yaʿqūb al-Fīrūzābādī's (d. 1415) *Tanwīr al-miqbās min tasfīr ibn ʿAbbās*; Sulaymān b. ʿUmar al-ʿUjaylī al-Azharī's (d. 1790) *al Futūḥāt al-ilāhiyya bi-tawḍīḥ tafsīr al-Jalālayn liʾl-daqāʾiq al-khāfiya*, and finally Jalāl al-Dīn al-Maḥallī

[8] Snouck Hurgronje 1931:270–271.

(d. 1459) and Jalāl al-Dīn al-Suyuṭī's (d. 1505) *Tafsīr al-Jalālayn*, this being the *matn* of al-ʿUjaylī's work.[9]

Abū ʾl-Suʿūd and al-Shirbīnī are highly respected figures. The *Tafsīr al-Jalālayn* is a popular word by word *tafsīr* well-known in the Indies, and as mentioned above, rendered into Malay by ʿAbd al-Ra'ūf of Singkel. Al-ʿUjaylī's *al-Futūḥāt al-ilāhiyya*, a massive commentary on it, is not frequently referred to, but he is mentioned in al-Jabartī, and Brockelmann remarks that he belonged to a group that developed the use of tradition to counter the use of personal opinion in religious matters.[10] The *Tanwīr al-miqbās* is frequently quoted. Al-Rāzī, however, is one of the greatest figures, not only in the history of exegesis but in Islamic thought. Nawawī's work may be regarded as a mosaic of selections from these authors. Only occasionally does he identify a citation from any of them by name. To discover how Nawawī has selected from and combined them it is necessary to read each of them closely alongside Nawawī's work, and to distinguish what originates from each of them by judicious underlining in different colours. This exercise shows beyond reasonable doubt that al-Rāzī is Nawawī's principal source, almost 70% of his work being taken from al-Rāzī's *Mafātīḥ al-ghayb*, and perhaps only 10% or less being unattributable, or presumably Nawawī's own. Given the number of Nawawī's students over his long life-time in Arabia, and the constant popularity his *tafsīr* has enjoyed, and enjoys up to the present,—it is today widely available in Indonesia and Malaysia, and the most recent edition I have seen from Cairo is dated 1967,—one would expect that many of the emphases and concerns that were important to al-Rāzī, through Nawawī have been absorbed into numerous centres of religious education in the Indonesian archipelago and become established in attitudes to and understanding of the Qur'ān.

3. *Fakhr al-Dīn al-Rāzī*

Fakhr al-Dīn al-Rāzī was a Persian who wrote in Arabic. He was born in Ray in around 1149. While still young he established himself as a preacher and debater. He travelled widely, teaching and establishing a reputation in eastern Persia and Oxiana, gaining patronage

[9] Nawawi *Marāḥ labīd*: vol. 1, 1, and for further details, see Johns 1988:268–269.
[10] *GAL* II, 465–466/353–354.

at the courts of the Ghūrids and Khwarezmshah. In Herat, between 1196 and 1198 he met the sufi Najm al-Dīn Kubrā (d. 1221) and began the study of mysticism. It was at this time that he began to write his commentary on the Qur'ān *Mafātīḥ al-ghayb*. In 1199 he quarrelled with the Karrāmites, and was driven out of town. He died in 1210. He is attributed the words: "I tried the paths of *kalām* and philosophical curricula, but I did not find there any benefit equal to that found in reading the Qur'ān."[11]

Al-Rāzī was familiar with the breakdown of law and order. He lived, after all, in the late twilight of the Abbasid Caliphate, a period full of political and social uncertainties, a "time of troubles", in al-Rāzī's terms *harj wa-marj* (confusion and disturbance) of which he too was at times a victim. Bernard Lewis retells the following anecdote, which even if apocryphal, gives some idea of the period in which he lived:

> In his lectures to theological students in Rayy, Fakhr al-Dīn made a special point of refuting and reviling the Ismailis. Hearing of this the lord of Alamut decided to put a stop to it and sent a fidā'ī to Rayy. There he enrolled himself as a student, and attended Fakhr al-Dīn's lectures daily for seven months, until he found an opportunity of seeing his teacher alone in his room, on the pretext of discussing a knotty problem. The fidā'ī at once drew a knife, and menaced the theologian with it. Fakhr al-Dīn jumped aside, and said: "Man, what do you want?" The fidā'ī replied: "I want to slit your honour's belly from the breast to the navel, because you have cursed us from the pulpit." After a tussle, the fidā'ī threw Fakhr al-Dīn to the ground, and sat on his chest. The terrified theologian promised to repent, and to refrain from such attacks in the future. The fidā'ī allowed himself to be persuaded, and, accepting a solemn undertaking from Fakhr al-Dīn to mend his ways, produced a bag containing 365 gold dinars. This, and a similar amount every year, would be paid to him in return for his compliance. Thenceforth, in his lectures on the sects of Islam, Fakhr al-Dīn took good care to avoid expressions offensive to the Ismailis. One of his students, noting this change, asked the reason for it. The professor replied: "It is not advisable to curse the Ismailis, for they have both weighty and trenchant arguments."[12]

Now al-Rāzī is one of the greatest figures in the history of exegesis; in stature he stands beside al-Ṭabarī. In fact it is hardly possible to exaggerate his importance in the history of Muslim learning. In his great work of *tafsīr Mafātīḥ al-ghayb* are to be found theology, phi-

[11] Al-Subki *Ṭabaqāt*: 5, 37.
[12] Lewis 1967:75–76.

losophy, evidence of a marvellous spirituality, extraordinary dialectic skill, Shāfiʿite *fiqh*, and a love of stories and story-telling. Even when he rejects stories he regards as showing the prophets or angels in an unworthy light, alongside the reasons he gives why they should be rejected, he re-tells them with panache.

There is a strong rationalist element in his thought. He appeals to intellectual criteria to assess the validity of information passed on by tradition, constructs a strong intellectual defence for the impeccability of the prophets, and argues for the acceptance of an allegorical interpretation for anthropomorphic verses in the Qur'ān. In the range of his intellectual inquiry, on a number of points he anticipates the great reformist ʿAbduh (d. 1905). Effat al-Sharqawi's summation of at least part of his achievement is particularly felicitous: "He was a man of an Ashʿarī heart and Avicennian mind, and in practice he tried to put the Ashʿarī traditions into a philosophical system that could appeal to the intellectual Muslim."[13]

The *Mafātīḥ al-ghayb* is a work on a monumental scale. It is so encyclopaedic that Ibn Taymiyya acidly remarks that it contains everything but *tafsīr*.[14] In sheer intellectual range, it stands alone, and the issues it raises and the difficulties it faces give it a character that in many places addresses concerns that are felt as modern.

4. *Al-Rāzī and Nawawī*

It is of significance that Nawawī should have taken so much of his work directly from Fakhr al-Dīn al-Rāzī, giving the other authorities he cites only a supporting role, blending them in a way that must, in the first instance, have occurred in oral delivery. Not all of al-Rāzī's excursuses are appropriate to Nawawī's concerns. Nawawī has, as we shall see, his own more limited agenda. Al-Rāzī, after all, interprets the Qur'ān at different levels and in different ways, almost as though he was writing a number of commentaries simultaneously with different concerns. That level represented by the telling of stories, complementary and explicative in character, well described as haggadic, is something that al-Rāzī does superbly, not withstanding his profound theological concerns. He retells and expands the stories

[13] Al-Sharqawi 1987:222.
[14] Al-Ṣafadī *al-Wāfī*: 4, 254.

told by the Qur'ān into vivid mini-dramas in a way that can hold a class or a congregation spellbound. This haggadic emphasis is clearly primary in Nawawī's work too, but there are theological issues important for al-Rāzī that Nawawī also takes up, frequently quoting al-Rāzī verbatim, albeit without explicit acknowledgement of his source. There are also concerns to which Nawawī does not explicitly refer, but which leave their imprint on his work. One is al-Rāzī's elaboration of the concept of coherence (*naẓm*) in the Qur'ān—drawing attention to a network of linkages binding the parts of the Qur'ān which serve to confirm not only the revelatory status of the prophetic logia, but their order and arrangement. On the other hand he does not take up or refer to a large number of excursuses condemning particular schools of thought, from that of the *ḥashwī* literalists and Muʿtazilites to the *ghulāt* among the Shīʿa. Further there is much detailed argumentation relating to *fiqh* and references to grammar and poetry that Nawawī does not reproduce, although he may well present the conclusions that al-Rāzī has argued.

In short, throughout the *Marāḥ Labīd* is a sense of the dimensions of al-Rāzī's thoughts and concerns, and of the wider context to which many of his citations from al-Rāzī belong. Sometime indeed it seems that he includes a phrase or idea from al-Rāzī to serve as a cue, to remind him to refer his circle to the more detailed treatment of a topic in the *Mafātīḥ*.

Nawawī then is basing his work on one of the greatest and most individual writers and thinkers in the history of Islam. Yet how did Nawawī become familiar with the work of al-Rāzī? Al-Rāzī does not seem to have been well-known in the Malay world, although admittedly the documentation is inadequate, and what there is has not been fully explored. It is unlikely that he would have devoted so much of his time and energy to the thought of al-Rāzī on his own initiative. It must have been largely through his teachers in Mecca where he lived between 1830–1897. As already mentioned, these included Aḥmad Nahrawī, Aḥmad Dimyātī and Aḥmad Zaynī Daḥlān, and from Medina Muḥammad Khaṭīb al-Ḥanbalī. That Nawawī should have been attracted to al-Rāzī, or at least to teachers who introduced him to al-Rāzī, indicates something of his exegetic and spiritual taste, and perhaps as well, of his earlier training in Java. Al-Rāzī being a fellow Shāfiʿite, there is a jurisprudential connection But the implications are more than jurisprudential. They include a rejection of the Ḥanbalī literalism espoused by the Wahhābīs.

Indeed, al-Rāzī has a thinly concealed contempt—in fact a totally unconcealed contempt for the literalists who rejected an allegorical interpretation of the Qur'ān in cases where the literal sense offered statements that contradicted an intellectual understanding of the nature of God, as for example in Qur'anic statements suggesting that God occupied place and extension.

How al-Rāzī, then? A probable answer lies in the fact that during the period between the defeat of the Wahhābīs by Muḥammad ʿAlī, i.e. between 1818, and the re-establishment of the Saʿūdi dynasty in 1902, there were present in Mecca *ʿulamāʾ* representing a variety of traditions, especially after the Indian Mutiny in 1857, among them teachers who introduced him to al-Rāzī. Al-Rāzī was well-known in India, and was one of the sources of inspiration of Sir Sayyid Ahmad Khan.[15] It is widely recognised that in the wake of the Indian Mutiny in 1857 and the dismantling of the Mughal Empire, many Muslims left India and British rule for the holy cities of Arabia and contributed a significant enrichment to the trends and tendencies of religious thought there.

It is against such a background that this essay is a preliminary investigation of Nawawī's *tafsīr* based on *sūra* 38 of the Qur'ān, *Ṣād*, to gain some idea of his approach, techniques and emphases, to explore what conclusions can be drawn concerning his principles of selection from al-Rāzī, and how this is complemented by the works of the other authors he cites. Nawawī indeed claimed that he was not interpreting the Qur'ān according to his own opinion, but as Wansbrough reminds us no writer merely transmits, and even a compilation reveals principles both of selection and arrangement.[16]

Thus Nawawī's work, for all its professedly derivative character, serves as an exemplary model of the transmission of *tafsīr*, and a study of it contributes to the understanding of *tafsīr* as a discipline, and the way in which exegetes learned from and related to each other, as well as enhancing our understanding of the Qur'anic text. In addition, it represents a significant contribution to the history of *tafsīr* in the Malay world, and to the tendencies in the Islamic tradition that found a home there, for inevitably the way in which the Qur'ān is understood is reflected in the lives and values of Muslim communities.

---

[15] Troll 1978:72–73, 82–85 and by index.
[16] Wansbrough 1977:20.

5. Sūra Ṣād

There are a number of reasons for choosing *Ṣād*. It is of manageable length; it probably dates from the late Mecca period, when the key themes of the Islamic revelation were clearly articulated and well-known among friend and foe of the prophet. It vividly presents the scorn shown for Muḥammad's teaching by his Meccan enemies; it sets out the main themes of Qur'anic teaching on the Divine Unity, Prophecy and Resurrection as the core both of Muḥammad's preaching and that of the prophets preceding him. It exemplifies a number of the rhetorical features characteristic of the Qur'ān, in particular a dramatic exchange in hell between the damned, and those who led them there. In a number of places the linguistic expression is so concentrated that help of the exegetical tradition is necessary if it is to be fully understood, thus the role of the exegete is crucial. In short it consists of a number of inter-related pericopes which make a distinctive contribution, or refer tangentially to similar themes developed elsewhere in the Qur'ān.

The *sūra* takes its name from the letter *Ṣād* with which it begins, although Nawawī points out that it is also known as *Sūra Dāwūd*,[17] information given by al-Shirbīnī, but not mentioned by al-Rāzī. The contents may be set out schematically as follows, although it should be stressed that the divisions are solely to facilitate discussion, not to make any definitive remarks about the internal organisation of the *sūra*.

I. Confrontation between Muḥammad and the leaders of Quraysh (Verses 1–16).

A warning to the Meccans of the fate awaiting them, for despite their knowledge of how their predecessors had been punished for their unbelief, they nevertheless reject Muḥammad and his message.

II. Stories of the Prophets (Verses 17–50).

Stories of eight Prophets preceding Muḥammad, arranged in order of decreasing length. Muḥammad is urged to follow their

---

[17] Nawawī *Marāḥ labīd*: 2, 225.

example, and be patient in face of insult and rejection. They include:

i. David (Verses 17–29).

a. David praying and praising God in concert with the hills and birds.
b. His confirmation as ruler.
c. A disputation scene, following on the entry of two intruders to his sanctuary.
d. David's appointment as Vicegerent
e. Creation for a purpose

ii. Solomon (Verses 30–40).

a. Solomon and the horses
b. Solomon set on the throne and put to the test
c. The gifts given to Solomon: the winds to carry him at his command, and the *jinn* to serve him.

iii. Job (Verses 41–44).

a. Job's crying out in distress,
b. the healing given to him,
c. the mitigation of the oath he swore to punish his wife.

iv. Abraham, Isaac and Jacob (Verses 45–47).

Their special role.

v. Ishmael, Elisha and Dhū 'l-Kifl (Verses 48–49).

A special group.

III. Heaven and Hell (Verses 49–64).

The delights of heaven (Verses 49–55).
The torment of hell (Verses 55–64).

IV. Counsel to Muḥammad (Verses 65–70).

V. The creation of Adam and disobedience of Iblīs (Verses 71–85).

VI. An exhortation to the Meccans (Verses 86–88).

Each section presents a theme characteristic of the Meccan *sūras*: Meccan hostility to Muḥammad's claim to be a prophet, and rejection of the doctrine of the resurrection; stories of the earlier prophets put to the test told both to comfort Muḥammad and convince the Meccans of the authenticity of his mission; the promise of heaven and the threat of hell; the creation of Adam, and Iblīs's refusal to bow to him, and an exhortation Muḥammad is to proclaim concerning the nature of his mission.

6. *On Tafsīr*

In coming to Nawawī's treatment of the *sūra*, it is important to have in mind the range of explicative procedures that an exegete may bring to bear to determine the meaning of Qur'anic logia. Wansbrough lists twelve such procedures. They include the use of *variae lectiones* (*qirā'āt*), poetic *loci probantes*, lexical, grammatical and rhetorical explanations, periphrasis, analogy, abrogation, circumstances of revelation, identification, prophetic tradition and anecdote. It is, he says, according to the frequency and distribution of the use of such techniques that a particular work may be classified as predominantly Haggadic, Halakhic, Masoretic, Rhetorical and Allegorical.[18] It is well, nevertheless to note Wansbrough's important qualification that such procedural devices are each potentially variable, but not beyond recognition, irrespective of the combination in which each one is employed, with the implicit warning that they should not be enumerated literally or mechanistically.

Alongside the types and formal techniques of Qur'anic exegesis however, it is important also to be aware of a further dimension. *Tafsīr* is not simply an academic pursuit. It has a religious and spiritual function. For Muslims, moreover, the Qur'ān is a book to be experienced, and experienced above all by hearing. It is this fact that has led to the development of the marvellous art of Qur'anic recitation.

Dominant among the motivations that lead a scholar to devote himself to *tafsīr* must surely in many cases be an inner urge on the part of the exegete to communicate his experience of the Qur'ān. For a great exegete, this is as multifaceted as the Qur'ān itself, for

[18] Wansbrough 1977:119–121.

the Book provides a focus for and so brings together his entire range of learning and spirituality. Hence the potential in works of exegesis for a richness and diversity in the movement of ideas, a shift from theme to theme, the occasional taking up of topics at an unexpected length, all expressive of the free ranging movement of the mind of a teacher addressing a circle of students. There is likewise scope for numerous asides, since the exegete is free to select from the tradition those elements best suited to his purpose.[19]

All this the exegete shares with his students, with the Book in its entirety present in his mind, and the sound of its surges and cadences in his ears, as he expounds. The quality of the end result ultimately depends on the richness of the mind of the exegete and the responsiveness of audience to whom he is giving his exposition. In this, the role of oral delivery in the presentation of *tafsīr* is central. It does not derive, in the first instance, from a man sitting at a desk with pen and paper. As Wansbrough remarks, the *sitz im leben* of exegesis is the oral sermon.[20] Thus the function of a gloss is never just the meaning of the words in an academic sense, but to ensure that the Qur'anic logia are fixed in the mind of the hearer, they are understood, and the religious lesson they contain is grasped and put into practice.

It follows that in studying *tafsīr*, one is not simply examining the way in which the exegete explains a word, a phrase or an image, but how he responds to the Qur'anic rhetoric and seeks to communicate this response. And when, for example, he treats a Qur'anic story, how he identifies with and understands the situation in which the characters in such stories play their roles.

Nawawī's work exemplifies a wide range of these features of exegesis and takes advantage of the scope the genre allows him to linger on topics that attract his attention, as indeed one would expect in any teacher responding to the mood and needs of a class and stirred by his own enthusiasms, which by the very nature of the case, may make for a certain arbitrariness in selection.

It is in the context of such general ideas that I present four segments of Nawawī's treatment of the *sūra*, to show his response to various aspects of the rhetoric of the Qur'ān, and draw attention both to his indebtedness to al-Rāzī at what might be called the micro-level,

---

[19] Ibid. 139.
[20] Ibid. 144–146.

and to the wider background of al-Rāzī's far more detailed treatment and numerous excursuses.

6.1 *On Section I, Sūra Ṣād*

The first is from section I (Confrontation between Muḥammad and the leaders of Quraysh). Verses 1–2 are as follows:

> 1. *Ṣād* By the Qur'ān embued with Warning [*dhī 'l-dhikr*]!
> 2. Rather those who disbelieve are arrogant and in contention [with you].

Nawawī's comments are taken from al-Rāzī, word for word.

> *Ṣād*—One view is that *Ṣād* is the key to those names of God of which it is the first letter, as when we say, "He is true to His promise", (*ṣādiq al-waʿd*), "Maker of created things" (*ṣāniʿ al-maṣnūʿāt*), or "One to whom all have recourse" (*ṣamad*). Another interpretation is "Muḥammad spoke the truth (*ṣadaqa*) in everything that he reported from God."[21]

Now *Ṣād* is one of the disconnected letters (*muqaṭṭaʿāt*) that preface about a quarter of the *sūra*s of the Qur'ān and the exegetes interpret them in a variety of ways. The significance of such letters is a matter al-Rāzī discusses at length in the various *sūra*s in which they occur, from *Baqara* on, and in his treatment of this *sūra* gives six meanings of *Ṣād*.[22] Of these Nawawī has taken the first two only.

Al-Rāzī's remaining four explanations may be summarised as follows: (iii) Ṣād is the first letter of the word *ṣuddu*, as it occurs in the Qur'anic verse *al-ladhīna kafarū wa-ṣuddū ʿan sabīli 'llāh*—those who disbelieve, and are impeded (*ṣuddū*) from following the path of God. Thus *Ṣād* refers to the unbelievers. (iv) *Ṣād*, being a letter of the Arabic alphabet, and the Qur'ān being composed of such letters, even those able to use these letters [i.e. those with literary skills] are not able to imitate the Qur'ān. Thus the letter *Ṣād* stands for a proof

---

[21] Nawawī *Marāḥ labīd*: 2, 225.

[22] Al-Rāzī *Mafātīḥ*: 26, 174. The description of such letters as keys is listed by al-Ṭabarī (*Jāmiʿ*: 1, 208) as an opinion concerning the meaning of the initial letters of *sūra* 2: *Alif Lām Mīm*. He attributes it to al-Rabīʿ b. Anas, who reports, "Each [of these letters] is a key to one of the divine names, and occurs in [the words designating] the blessings [He gives] and the tests [He imposes] . . . *alif* is the key to His name *Allāh*, *lām* is the key to His name *Laṭīf*, and *mim* the key to His name *Majīd*. *Alif*, then, is His blessings (*ālā'*), *lām* is His grace (*luṭf*), and *mīm* His glory." Early in his treatment of the *Sūra Ṣād*, al-Ṭabarī reports the view of Daḥḥāk that the letter *Ṣād* indicates *ṣadaqa 'l-lāh*. The confluence of authorities that come together in Nawawī, even if at second hand, is rich.

that the Qur'ān is miraculous. (v) Another possibility is that *Ṣād*, if pronounced with a *kasra* on the *dāl*, is derived from [the imperative of] *muṣāda*, which means "imitation", from which is derived *ṣadan*, meaning "echo", an echo being that which imitates your voice [being thrown back] from hard objects in empty spaces. The sense then is "imitate the Qur'ān in your deeds, doing what it commands, and desisting from what it prohibits". (vi) The implied sense is "This is *Ṣād*." *Ṣād*, then is simply the name of the *sūra*. For Nawawī's purposes however, the first two interpretations, one to do with God and the other with the Prophet are sufficient. Nor is this by chance. That God is true to His promise to reward and punish on Judgement Day, and that Muḥammad speaks truly in announcing this, are emphases central to the *sūra*.
Nawawī continues

> *By the Qur'ān embued with Warning* (*dhī 'l-dhikr*) i.e. embued with honour, or embued with an explanation, for in the Qur'ān are stories of those who are earlier and those who are later.

Both glosses of *dhī 'l-dhikr* are from al-Rāzī. Nawawī has simply taken the first, "i.e. embued with honour" (*ay dhī 'l-sharaf*) omitting the Qur'anic verses that al-Rāzī cites to justify this metaphorical sense of *dhikr*. In the case of the second, however, he has changed al-Rāzī's *dhī 'l-bayānayn*—embued with two explanations, to *dhī 'l-bayān*—embued with *an* explanation, giving only al-Rāzī's first, and omitting the second, "embued with an explanation of the basic and derivative disciplines."[23] That the omission is the result of a conscious decision is shown by Nawawī's change of al-Rāzī's dual, *bayānayn* to the singular *bayān*. Clearly, he is in control of his material.

This suggests, by way of comment, that if he has given two only of al-Rāzī's six significances of *Ṣād* for one reason, i.e. because in the conceptual structure of his *tafsīr* of this part of the *sūra* God and the prophet have a central position, and he does not want to introduce extraneous detail, this omission is due to another, more general reason: he is not expounding the Qur'ān as a source of *fiqh*, i.e. he is excluding a halakhic emphasis in his work.

Verse 2 he treats as follows:

> *Rather those who disbelieve*—among the leaders (*ru'asā'*) of Quraysh *are arrogant* (*fī 'izza*)—i.e. proud and resentful at [having to] follow

[23] Al-Rāzī *Mafātīḥ*: 26, 175.

> another—*and in contention [with you]*—i.e. Showing hostility [to Muḥammad] since they regard themselves as equal to the one they oppose.

An alternative recitation for *fī ʿizza* is *fī ghirra* i.e. heedless. The glosses are from al-Rāzī, but not the variant *qirāʾa* (*fī ghirra*), which occurs only in al-Shirbīnī and Abū ʾl-Suʿūd.

Al-Rāzī, however, draws attention to two further points that Nawawī passes over. One is the absence of an attestation, i.e. what is sworn to by the oath *By the Qurʾān embued with honour!*; the other, the absence of a propositional statement to which the words introduced by *bal* may be regarded as an exceptive alternate.

As for the missing attestation, al-Rāzī offers three possibilities. If *Ṣād* means "Muḥammad speaks the truth", this is the fact sworn to, i.e. "By the Qurʾān embued with honour, Muḥammad speaks the truth". If *Ṣād* is taken as the name of the *sūra*, then the fact sworn to is an implied phrase such as "is a miraculous statement", i.e. "The *Sūra Ṣād*—by the Qurʾān embued with honour—is a miraculous statement." Alternatively, *Ṣād* again being taken as the name of the *sūra*, the fact sworn to is, "This, by the Qurʾān embued with honour, is the *Sūra Ṣād*."

As for the exceptive alternate introduced by the particle *bal*, it is a rejoinder to a suppressed statement such as "Muḥammad is truthful in the delivery of his message", or "The Qurʾān (or this *sūra*) is miraculous" yet (*bal*) those who disbelieve are arrogant and in contention [with Muḥammad].[24]

Al-Rāzī's concern with these issues, and the suggestions he proposes for such phrases that are *muqaddar*, i.e. suppressed, derive from his *hearing* of the Qurʾanic logia. It is in the intonation detected by the ear of his mind that alerts him to what is understood. His bringing to the level of consciousness what is implied, not stated ensures a heightened, a more vivid experience of the dramatic tension implicit in these two verses, facilitating for his audience a hearing of the words as they might have been heard from the lips of Muḥammad in the situation in which they were revealed to him, thus intensifying the hearers' awareness of the obduracy of the unbelieving Meccans.

There are a number of reasons why Nawawī did not include these points. Perhaps these aspects of the rhetoric of the Qurʾān went beyond the parameters he had set himself. Possibly he believed they could be taken as understood, perhaps because students could be

---

[24] Ibid. 175.

referred to the *Mafātīḥ* itself, or perhaps because his exposition was oral, the teaching situation itself would make clear the relevant intonational signals, thus there was no need for such sophistications to be put in writing. Whatever the reason, it is certain that he knew them, and understood both the points at issue and the reasons behind al-Rāzī's elucidation of them: that the Qur'ān is the spoken word, and that when it is heard, the ellipses, whether indicated by morphological or lexical signals, or intonation, or a combination of all three are manifest. This sensitivity is shown throughout the *tafsīr*.

Verses 1 and 2 effectively set the scene for the succeeding verses of the *sūra*:

> 3. How many of [former] ages have We destroyed before them! They cried out [when destruction fell upon them] but then was no time for deliverance.
> 4. They are astounded that a warner from among themselves should come to them. The unbelievers say: "This is a sorcerer, a liar!
> 5. Does he make the gods into One God? This indeed is an astounding thing!"
> 6. The leaders among them then departed [saying]: "Go away [from those who believe in Muḥammad]. Remain true to your gods, this is what is required [of you].
> 7. We heard nothing of this in the last religion, this is something made up!
> 8. Is it to him from among us the Scripture is revealed?" Rather, it is they who are in doubt about My Warning;[25] rather, it is they who have not yet tasted My punishment.
> 9. Do they have [charge of] the treasure chests of the mercy of your Lord, the Mighty, the Bestower?
> 10. Is it they who have dominion over the heavens and the earth and what is between them? [If so,] then let them try to climb the stairways (*asbāb*) [to the stars].
> 11. Any army assembled there, would be defeated.
> 12. Before them, the people of Noah, [the peoples of] Ad, and of Pharaoh, he of the stakes, disbelieved,
> 13. [so too those of] Thamud, the people of Lot, and those of the thicket—they assembled together,
> 14. there were none of them but disbelieved the Messengers, so My punishment came to pass.
> 15. These [all of them] await a single cry, a cry that brooks no delay, yet [the Meccans] say:
> 16. "Lord of ours, give us our requital now, before the day of judgement."

---

[25] The Arabic word *dhikr* is protean in its significances, and the context here requires an English rendering other than "Scripture" to bring out the fact that former peoples may indeed have tasted God's punishment, but the Meccans not yet learnt from God's warning.

The following points of Nawawī's treatment of these verses may be singled out:

Ad verse 3: *How many of [former] ages have We destroyed before them.* He identifies *them* as "the Quraysh", and glosses *of [former] ages* as "of past peoples". *They cried out*—he sees implicit in this statement the questions: when did they cry out, and what did they cry out for, which he answers respectively: "when torment descended on them" and "for help and deliverance". But *then was no time for deliverance*—he is satisfied with a brief paraphrase to the effect that *then* was not a time when there could be deliverance [from this punishment].

Ad verse 4: in which God speaks scornfully to the Quraysh for their rejection of Muḥammad, he goes into greater length. *They are astounded that a messenger should come to them.* He comments:

> The Quraysh are astounded that a messenger of their own kind should come to them. They reject him violently, saying: Muḥammad is like us in outward appearance, inner disposition and lineage, so how is it conceivable that he be singled out from among us for this high office.

He turns his attention to the unbelievers, and the insults they directed at Muḥammad. *The unbelievers* he glosses "those in the depths of unbelief". *This* he identifies as Muḥammad, and then sets out the grounds why the epithets of *Sorcerer* and *Liar* are hurled at him: *Sorcerer* because of the wonderful event [of the resurrection] he claims will occur; and *Liar* in that he claims on God's authority that a messenger is sent with a revelation.

Ad verse 5: *Does he make the gods into One God*—here following al-Rāzī he uses a different technique. Instead of explaining the point of this question with a following gloss, he introduces it with an expanded *sabab al-nuzūl* that occurs in al-Rāzī verbatim, setting out the circumstances that led the Quraysh to utter these words:

> It is related that when ʿUmar accepted Islam the Muslims rejoiced greatly, and the news disturbed the Quraysh. Thus twenty five of their leaders assembled, and went to Abū Ṭālib and said to him: You are our Elder and the most senior of us. You know what these fools are doing, so we have come to you for you to adjudicate between us and your nephew. Abū Ṭālib then called the Messenger of God, and said to him: Son of my brother, these are your people, they wish to put a question to you; do not then turn away from them.
>
> The messenger of God said to them: What do you ask of me? They said: desist from troubling us, and desist from speaking [ill] of our gods, and we will let you be, you and your god. The messenger of

> God said: Will you consider? If I give you what you ask, will you give me in turn one sentence by means of which you will rule over the Arabs, and by means of which the foreigners will serve you. They replied: Yes! Then he said: Declare: there is no god but God. Thereupon they rose and said: *Does he make the gods into one God?*[26]

Nawawī expands: "How can one god suffice us for our needs as Muḥammad claims?" which prepares the way for the last part of the verse *This indeed is an astounding thing!*

For the Quraysh, what is astounding is that there is only one God, and Nawawī emphasises this by identifying the referent of *This* as *tawḥīd.* As far as clarification of the sense is concerned, it is not necessary, but the purpose is for rhetorical effect, as is his gloss on *is an astounding thing!*—deeply astonishing.

Ad verse 6: *The leaders among them then departed.* Nawawī identifies these leaders (*al-mala'* glossed as *al-ru'asā'*) as ʿUqbah b. Abī Muʿayṭ, and Abū Jahl, and al-ʿAṣī b. Wā'il, al-Aswad b. al-Muṭṭalib, and al-Aswad b. ʿAbd Yaghūth, who left the meeting Abū Ṭālib had arranged saying to the other Meccans *Go away [from those who believe in Muḥammad]* i.e. they said to one another, *Go away, Remain true to your gods* i.e. be constant in the service of your gods. *This is what is required [of you]* i.e. the denial of our gods is what Muḥammad requires of us so that he may assume authority over us, and dispose of our property and our sons for what purposes he wishes. Or: What is required of us is that we desist not from constancy in the worship of our gods.

Ad verse 8: *Is it to him from among us the Scripture (al-dhikr) is revealed?* In stressing that this is a continuation of the insults of the Quraysh to Muḥammad, Nawawī takes the opportunity to show why they reject him: "Is the Qur'ān to be revealed to Muḥammad, when we are nobles and leaders of the people. How is it conceivable that he be singled out for this exalted rank?"

This establishes the context of God's rejoinder to them, within which Nawawī enlarges the import of God's words, *Rather it is they who are in doubt about My Warning, rather it is they who have not yet tasted My punishment* i.e. the denial of the truth of the Qur'ān by the unbelievers of Mecca is not based on knowledge; rather they are not

---

[26] Al-Wāḥidī *Asbāb al-nuzūl*: 387. The editor identifies the commentators al-Wāḥidī refers to as the source of this passage as al-Baghawī and al-Qurṭubī.

convinced of it, and the reason for this is that they have not tasted My punishment. Had they tasted My punishment, then they would be certain of the truth of the Qur'ān and believe in it; yet their belief in it then, would be of no avail to them, for they would have made this profession under duress.

This leads to the Qur'ān's rhetorical question, *Do they have [charge of] the treasure chests of the mercy of your Lord?* which leads Nawawī to expand the biting sarcasm of God's words, "Is it they then who have charge of the treasure chests of the mercy of your Lord in regard to prophecy and the Book, so that they can dispense them both to whomever they will, in accordance with their own opinion," and to offer an excursus on the gift of prophecy—a meld of al-Rāzī and Abū 'l-Suʿūd:

> The meaning [of this] is that prophecy is a great office, a gift from God. Thus the One who has power to bestow the gift of it must necessarily be perfect in power, great in generosity, thus His bestowal of this favour does not depend on the one who receives it from Him being rich or poor, and this situation does not change by reason of his enemies liking or disliking it,[27] (al-Rāzī), for He is the Victor, one who is never vanquished, He is the Bestower, and it is His to give whatever He wishes to whomever He wishes (Abū 'l-Suʿūd).

There can be little doubt that foremost among Nawawī's goals is to bring out the drama of the conflict between Muḥammad and those who oppose him. No pronoun is left without an identification of the noun to which it refers. He is concerned to make clear the wickedness of those who reject Muḥammad, and draws on *sīra* material and *asbāb al-nuzūl* to present the Meccans' words *Does he make the gods into one God* as the climax of their challenge to Muḥammad's teaching, expanding the words of verse 6 into a dramatic verbal picture of the chiefs of Quraysh scoffing at Muḥammad's teaching, and urging their followers to leave him and remain true to their old gods. This is the occasion for this excursus on prophecy.

The *qirā'āt* Nawawī adduces in this section do not appear to be of major significance. He presents three, two with little difference as far as meaning is concerned: one unattributed, *ʿujjāb* for *ʿujāb* in verse 5; another attributed to Ibn Abī ʿUbla, in verse 6, who recites *wa'nṭalaqa 'l-mala'u minhum ani 'mshū* without *an.* Both are from al-Rāzī. It is

[27] Al-Rāzī *Mafātīḥ*: 26, 180. Disliking the bestowal of it, or disliking God? See below.

possible that Nawawī records them simply as a cue to remind himself to expound orally something from al-Rāzī, or to his listeners to refer to al-Rāzī for themselves. The third however, taken from Abū 'l-Suʿūd, is *ghirra* for *ʿizza*—in heedlessness. Al-Rāzī finds it necessary to explain *ʿizza*, and possibly Nawawī found *fī ghirra*—heedless, an acceptable and uncomplicated variant for al-Rāzī's glossing *fī ʿizza* as *fī taʿẓīm* which he explains as the sense of self-importance which prevents one person from following the leadership of another.

In his discussion of this passage Nawawī makes only one theological generalisation outside the acceptance or rejection of Muḥammad, but it is an important one: that faith professed under duress or out of fear is not accepted.

On the other hand he has shown how it is packed with dramatic tension. For the most part he has done so drawing on al-Rāzī, and in fact has done so successfully that the tension is palpable. He brings out the internal dialectic between past and present (verses 3–4) and between belief and unbelief within the pericope. Verse 2 he presents as a comment on the Meccans of Muḥammad's day—they are arrogant and in contention with Muḥammad. Verse 3 tells how the past ages cried out when destruction fell upon them—yet then was no time for deliverance. Verse 4 returns to the present of Muḥammad's day—his contemporaries are astounded that a warner from among themselves should come to them. This introduces a new arc of tension, created by the scorn of the Meccans' words as they parody the Qur'anic style, *Lord of ours, give us our requital now before the Day of Judgement!* intending by their ridicule both to cut Muḥammad to the quick and to encourage their followers to reject his message. Their blasphemy is confounded by God's reply, which reviews the destruction of "past peoples" who have done evil from the days of Noah onwards, and promises a destruction which will surely overtake them—as indeed it did at the battle of Badr. The result is that those listening to Nawawī experience vicariously the prophet's proclamation of the coming of a Day of Judgement, and the mockery this teaching provoked, and so share the sense of righteousness of being on the side of the prophet, and opposing those who reject him.

Nawawī contributes to this effect by identifying, from *sīra* material, the dramatis personae involved in the confrontation. For example he names Abū Jahl and al-ʿAṣī b. Wā'il and the others who walk away from the meeting Abū Ṭālib has called. Thus the student circle he is addressing is taken into the world in which the prophet lived, showing him delivering his message and the response it received. This naming of names, the repeating of the identities of the two sides involved, those who believe, and those who disbelieve, and the identification of pronouns by the nouns to which they refer is part of his technique. In particular, in verse 7 the pronoun *this*, which refers back to the Qur'anic reporting of the words of the unbelievers, *Does he make the gods into one God*, is identified as *tawḥīd*, a term for the declaration of the divine unity with resonantal power.

One should also draw attention to Nawawī's treatment of verse 16, which reports the Meccans scoffing at God, designed to rub salt into the wounds their insults have already inflicted on Muḥammad. His gloss for *requital* (*qiṭṭanā* taken from Abū 'l-Suʿūd) is "our portion of the torment that You are promising us". Such a presentation is expressive of the contempt the Meccans have for Muḥammad's message, and a natural occasion for God to comfort and strengthen him by saying *Iṣbir*—"Be steadfast, endure what they say, and reflect on our servant David", words which introduce the following section.

6.2 *On Section II, Sūra Ṣād*

The second passage is from II, stories of the Prophets. Of the nine prophets referred to this section, the most space is given to David. As already indicated, there are pericopes relating to four episodes in his career: his praising God in concert with the hills and birds, his confirmation as ruler, his confrontation with two disputants, and his appointment as vicegerent. Here, attention is to be given to episodes c, d, e.; i.e. verses 21–28. The first consists of verses 21–25, the "Disputation Scene." It may be rendered in English as follows:

> 21. Have you heard the story of the disputants, of when they mounted the wall of the sanctuary,
> 22. of when they intruded on David, and he was frightened by them? They said to him: "Do not be afraid, we are two disputants. One of us has wronged the other, so judge between us with justice. Do not act unjustly, but guide us to the right path.
> 23. This is my brother. He had ninety-nine sheep, and I had one sheep. Yet he said, 'Put it in my charge,' and was more powerful in speech than I."
> 24. David replied, "He wronged you by asking that your sheep be put with his sheep. Indeed, there are many dealers in livestock who wrong one another—except those who believe and do good deeds, and how few these are!" David thought that we had put him to the test, so he sought pardon of his Lord. He collapsed in prayer turning [to God],
> 25. So We pardoned him that [for which he sought pardon]. Indeed he is close beside Us and has a beautiful dwelling-place.

The rhetoric of this passage is of a different character to that of section I. While compact and vividly allusive, it is set in the past, and, not involving the direct confrontation between Muḥammad and the unbelievers, is pitched at a lower level of intensity.

In treating it, Nawawī, essentially, has made use of the same exegetic techniques of gloss, identification and periphrasis that he used earlier. There is little need to draw special attention to these features of his work other than to point out that in his use of them, his concern is not simply to clarify meaning or emphasise a lesson, but to bring out the essential coherence of the Qur'anic verses and ensure that every potential silence is filled with its implicit meaning. One example will suffice. On verse 22, when the two disputants say to David, *one of us has wronged the other*, Nawawī glosses *has wronged* as "has got the better [of me]", then inserts the words "We have come for you to judge between us" to bring out the force of the following Qur'anic words *so judge between us according to the truth*, which he explains by the paraphrase "by a decision that is in accord with truth". Of special significance, however, is his excursus on verse 21 and following:

> *Of when they mounted the wall of his sanctuary*, i.e. of the occasion when they came to the house David had entered, and in which he was devoting himself to the service of his Lord,—[they entered it] from the highest point, i.e. they climbed its lofty wall. *Of when they intruded on David, and he was frightened of them. They said: Do not be afraid, we are two disputants.* The story goes that a band of enemies were eager to kill David, the prophet of God. There was a day on which he used to withdraw alone to busy himself with devotion to his Lord, thus they took their opportunity on that day, and climbed into his sanctuary. When they had intruded on him, they discovered there was a crowd of people with him, who protected him from them. They became afraid, and made up a lie, saying *We are two disputants* i.e. we are two parties [to a dispute]—until the end of the story. David realised what their purpose was, and thought of taking vengeance on them.[28]

Nawawī's gloss on verse 24 *David thought that we had put him to the test* is consistent with this excursus:

> David thought we had put him to the test by this event, because it followed the course of a test. David realised this, *and so he sought pardon of his Lord* for the vengeance he had considered taking upon them.[29]

In this excursus, Nawawī has not drawn on the extensive *qiṣaṣ al-anbiyā'* material included in al-Ṭabarī and al-Thaʿlabī, deriving ultimately from Wahb b. Munabbih, which sees this pericope as an elliptic

[28] Nawawī *Marāḥ labīd*: 2, 227.
[29] Nawawī *Marāḥ labīd*: 2, 228.

presentation of the scene in 2 Samuel 11:15 in which the priest Nathan uses the parable of the sheep to reprove David for bringing about the death of Uriah in battle to marry his wife Bathsheba. The tradition they represent interprets the two intruders as angels in disguise who act out the parable, and after David realises his guilt, reveal their identity, then vanish.

Nawawī follows the scenario that al-Rāzī has constructed for the incident, presenting it not as a parable, but an actual event, with the intruders into David's sanctuary, not two angels but two individuals who had plotted to kill David, and made up the story of a dispute between them as an excuse for their presence there. The positioning of this *mise en scène* for the encounter so early in his treatment of the pericope indicates that it is his preferred understanding of it.

Al-Rāzī has constructed this scenario to interpret the pericope in a way consistent with his theory of the impeccability of the prophets, since he rejects the traditional understanding of the pericope that sees David as having been guilty of a grave sin and repenting after these angelic visitors had come to him. Since David had done nothing deserving of reproach, there was no need for angels to come to him in disguise to enact such a parable! David had not been put to the test by catching sight of Bathsheba bathing, he had been put to the test by the intrusion of two outsiders into his sanctuary. Their confrontation with him was the way in which God put him to the test.[30]

Al-Rāzī gives a number of possibilities as to how David responded to this test, and why he *sought pardon of his Lord* after it. Among them is that adopted by Nawawī: he concluded that they planned to kill him before he had proof that this was their intention. It was for this precipitate conclusion that he asked pardon. Al-Rāzī's preferred option however is that David *sought pardon of his Lord* not for any sin of which he was or might have been guilty, but on behalf of the intruders.[31] Nawawī has chosen a view that sees David as guilty of a *zalla*, a minor lapse which in the mainstream sunnī tradition is possible for a prophet. It is conceivable that his decision not to adopt al-Rāzī's preferred option, which sees David perfect and inerrant, is due to a distrust of Imāmī Shīʿite associations of the notion that a human being, even if a prophet, might possess such a measure of impecca-

---

[30] For an account of al-Rāzī's treatment of this pericope see Johns 1989.

[31] Al-Rāzī *Mafātīḥ*: 26, 198.

bility. Nevertheless, the significance of his acceptance of the scenario of al-Rāzī's devising is that it shows him selecting an interpretation of the Qur'anic text that excludes a haggadic expansion of it of Jewish provenance, in other words a story that belongs to the category of *Isrā'īliyyāt*. This was to be an issue of considerable importance for ʿAbduh. It is perhaps an (unconscious?) irony that the *tafsīr* of al-Wāḥidī printed on the *hāmish* of the printed text of Nawawī's book gives the traditional account.[32]

The next part of the David episode may be rendered as follows:

> 26. David, we have appointed you Vicegerent over the earth, so judge between mankind on the basis of what is true, and do not follow passion, for it will lead you astray from the way of God. Those who go astray from the way of God, theirs is a terrible punishment for their heedlessness of the Day of Reckoning.

Nawawī in treating this verse, shows the same concern in the application of his exegetical procedures to bring out the connecting ideas between syntactic units within the verse, and verses with each other that was referred to earlier. Here, he supports this aspect of his exposition by the insertion of excursuses devoted to theological and moral issues, sometimes in the manner of a mini-sermon.

Thus on verse 26 (*David, we have appointed you Vicegerent*) he glosses *khalīfa* as prophet and king, and explains that David's kingship is over the people of Israel, and his responsibility is to obey and implement the Law. This explanation both clarifies the meaning of these Qur'anic words, and demonstrates the close relationship between them and those that follow: *So judge between mankind on the basis of what is true.*

At this point Nawawī suspends the formal procedure of exegesis to introduce an excursus on the use of political power. It consists of al-Rāzī's expansion of God's words to David with one significant modification: it makes use of al-Shirbīnī's gloss of *bi'l-ʿadl*, with justice for the Qur'anic *bi'l-ḥaqq*, a phrase that al-Rāzī leaves unglossed:

> Judge with justice, because when judgements are in conformity with the true divine *sharīʿa*, the well-being of the realm is assured, and the gates of blessing are opened wide. However, if the decisions of the ruling authority are in accordance with his whim, and motivated by his worldly concerns, great is the harm he wreaks upon the populace, for he treats the people as creatures to be sacrificed for his own interests,

---

[32] Nawawī *Marāḥ labīd*: 2, 228.

> and this leads to loss of stability of the realm and the occurrence of lawlessness and chaos among the populace, and this leads in turn to the downfall of the kingdom.[33]

The opposite of ruling in accordance with justice is the use of personal authority to indulge one's passions. Thus this excursus leads directly to the next Qur'anic logia *Do not follow passion!* These words are glossed "the passion of the self in giving judgements and dealing with other matters to do with the world and religion," a periphrasis which is in harmony with and prepares the ground for the next Qur'anic words *for it will lead you astray from the path of God*, words which Nawawī expands into a passage of spiritual counsel: "The following of passion causes one to stray from the path of God, and deserves the worst of punishments, because passion leads to immersion in physical pleasures, and prevents the devotion of one's self to the quest for spiritual happiness,"[34] which leads directly to the Qur'anic warning that *those who stray from the path of God, theirs is a terrible punishment for their heedlessness of the Day of Reckoning.*

These words in turn Nawawī expands periphrastically, putting answers to the implicit question as to what constitutes heedlessness of the Day of Reckoning—not thinking about it, ceasing to believe in it, or failing to perform the works required for that Day. Indeed on such occasions, one might reasonably be in doubt as to whether to regard the passage as Nawawī preaching a sermon, the main points of which are emphasised by Qur'anic citations, or a sequence of Qur'anic logia which are the occasion for a sermon on this topic.

Part e. of this David pericope begins with verse 27:

> 27. We have not created heaven and the earth and what is between them to no purpose. That is the view of those who disbelieve [in Judgement Day]. Woe then to those who disbelieve because of the fire [that will afflict them].
> 28. Would We treat those who believe and do good deeds [as We treat] those who act wickedly upon the earth? Would We treat the devout [as We treat] those who do evil?

Nawawī glosses *to no purpose* (*bāṭilan*) as "in jest (*ʿabathan*), haphazardly (*juzāfan*), without Command or Prohibition". These glosses are followed directly by an excursus consisting of a nine line citation from al-Rāzī:

---

[33] Nawawī *Marāḥ labīd*: 2, 228; al-Rāzī *Mafātīḥ*: 26, 200.
[34] Nawawī *Marāḥ labīd*: 2, 228–229; al-Rāzī *Mafātīḥ*: 26, 200.

This verse proves that God is creator of [human] acts. Since they occur between heaven and earth, God must be creator of them. This verse is also a proof of the Resurrection, Assembly and Judgement, for this reason: God, having created mankind in this world, it may be said either that He created them for neither happiness (*intifāʿ*) nor misery (*iḍrār*) and this would be false, because this would be the case even when they were non-existent; or for misery, and this would be false, for such would not be appropriate to the Compassionate, the Gracious [God]; or for happiness, and this happiness would be either in the life of this world or that of the hereafter. Now were it to be said the happiness were for the life of this world, this would be false, because the causes of happiness in this world are few, and its miseries are many, and the imposition of much misery for little happiness would not be appropriate to Wisdom. Thus the doctrine [of the existence of another life after this worldly life is established, and this is] the doctrine of the Resurrection, Assembly and Judgement. Accordingly, what we have stated concerning God creating the heaven and the earth and what is between them not being to no purpose, is established. If the creation of them is not to no purpose, then the doctrine of the Resurrection, Assembly and Judgement is necessary, and whoever denies the doctrine of the Resurrection, Assembly and Judgement is in doubt as to the wisdom of God in creating the heavens and the earth. This is what the Almighty's words mean.[35]

The glosses, no less than this theological excursus, lead to and heighten the rhetorical climax in the succeeding Qur'anic logia *That is the view of those who disbelieve. Woe then to those who disbelieve because of the Fire [that will afflict them].* And Nawawī makes clear how heinous this disbelief is by his comments:

[Woe then to them] for the terrible punishment by the pains of Hell prepared for those who disbelieve in the resurrection after death, consequent upon their thinking there is no Resurrection and no Reckoning, this being a denial of the Wisdom of God in the creation of the heavens and the earth, and in His Command and His Prohibition.

The pericope concludes with two rhetorical questions:

28. Would We treat those who believe and do good deeds as those who act wickedly upon the earth? Would We treat the devout as those who do evil?

As to the first, Nawawī elaborates God's challenge:

Would We, anywhere in the world (*fī aqṭār al-arḍ*), treat virtuous believers as We treat evil-doing disbelievers, for this is what the absence of a Resurrection and Requital would entail, since both groups share equally in the enjoyment of life in this world—rather, unbelievers may

[35] Nawawī *Marāḥ labīd*: 2, 229; al-Rāzī *Mafātīḥ*: 26, 201.

> well have a more copious share of this enjoyment than believers! . . . But such an imputation is absurd! Thus the resurrection and requital are without any doubt specifically for the elevation of the former to the highest of places and the relegation of the latter to the lowest of the low.

As to the second question, *Would We treat the devout as those who do evil?* Nawawī draws on *sīra* material to present God as asking:

> Would We treat the most devout of the believers such as ʿAli b. Abī Ṭālib, and Ḥamza b. ʿAbd al-Muṭṭalib and ʿUbaydah b. al-Ḥarth (from ʿUjaylī) the heroes of Badr, in the same way as We treated the Qurayshites ʿAtaba and Shayba, the two sons of Rabīʿa and al-Walīd b. ʿAtaba, who came forward against them?

At this point Nawawī again suspends his exegesis to report an unattributed circumstance of revelation to the effect that this verse was revealed to counter a sarcastic claim by the Meccan unbelievers that "We will be given in the hereafter good such as you have been given."[36] He then continues:

> What establishes the truth of this verse is that we see those who obey God and refrain from doing evil, in poverty, sickness, and tribulations of various kinds, and we see the unbelievers and evil doers in comfort and bliss. Thus were there no Resurrection, Assembly and Judgement, the situation of the obedient would be worse than that of the disobedient, and this is not appropriate to the wisdom of the Wise, the Merciful. If this is indeed to the discredit of the wisdom of God, it is established that the denial of the Resurrection, Assembly and Judgement implies a denial of the Wisdom of God.

In so doing he brings out the rhetorical force implicit in the Qur'anic words *We have not created heaven and earth and what is between them to no purpose.*[37]

Nawawī's treatment of this pericope is in one way an expansion and in another a summary of al-Rāzī's views on why creation can not be to no purpose. Indeed he has a special concern with these Qur'anic words which are the occasion for this excursus. They lead him to argue that God's Wisdom demands a resurrection and judgement to redress the imbalance of the human situation in this world, in which the good may suffer, and the wicked enjoy a life of ease. Put differently, he is concerned with the question how is it possible that the good be treated in the same way as the wicked in the here-

---

[36] No such *sabab* occurs at this point either in al-Wāḥidī's *Asbāb al-nuzūl* or al-Suyūṭī's *Lubāb al-nuqūl fī asbāb al-nuzūl.*

[37] Nawawī *Marāḥ labīd*: 2, 229.

after—the evil who deny God's wisdom and mercy in their denial of Resurrection and Judgement. Thus while including al-Rāzī's use of the verse both as a proof text to establish that human acts are created as well as the basis of his argument that to deny the Resurrection is to deny God's wisdom, he chooses further to elaborate this aspect of the verse by drawing on Abū 'l-Suʿūd, and pointedly includes al-Shirbīnī's gloss of *bi'l-ḥaqq* in *fa'ḥkam bayna 'l-nāsi bi'l-ḥaqq* as *bi'l-ʿadl*; i.e. judge between mankind *with justice*, thus introducing a new dimension into the discussion.

It is this concern of Nawawī that has led him to draw on *sīra* material referred to above on *Would We treat the devout as those who do evil* and to put the rhetorical question: Would ʿAlī, Ḥamza and ʿUbaydah be treated in the same way as those who came out to challenge them at Badr? This reference to the heroes of Badr is also an effective teaching device, for by it he again gives his students a means of identification with the heroes and the villains in the story, by taking them into the world of the prophet's friends and foes. It is also the occasion for his reference to the unidentified *sabab al-nuzūl* mentioned above, to the effect that the verse was revealed to counter the boast of the Meccan unbelievers "We will have as much good in the hereafter as you"—words which, no doubt should be heard as uttered in scorn, meaning "After death neither of us will get anything, so *carpe diem*!"

Nawawī re-iterates in this passage the implications of God being Wise, as does al-Rāzī. The emphasis is of course thoroughly Qur'anic, for time and again God is spoken of in such terms as Wisest of the Wise, and Most Merciful of the Merciful. This, for al-Rāzī as for Nawawī following in his footsteps, is the core argument for the existence of the hereafter. This excursus is in fact a philosophical justification of God's wisdom, and stresses how great a sin it is to deny the wisdom of God in what He has created. The strong rationalist thread in the handling of this pericope, the concern it shows to establish a coherence of ideas, is nuanced by the gloss of *bi'l-ʿadl*[38] for *bi'l-ḥaqq—according to what is true*, which Nawawī has taken from al-Shirbīnī. As Nawawī develops his argument, *ʿadl* is presented as a quality of God, and David is urged to be just because God is just. Here we have an instance of Nawawī drawing on al-Shirbīnī to go beyond the parameters within which al-Rāzī is here working.

[38] Ibid. 228.

In this section then, alongside the traditional explicative procedures that are Nawawī's style—gloss, periphrasis, *sīra*, is Nawawī's use of excursuses to draw attention to what he regards as major issues. All have in common, alongside the clarification of meaning, the establishment of an inter-text for the Qur'anic logia. However, if the glosses and periphrases are usually constructed from a collage of the writings of his principal sources, and include contributions of his own, these excursuses, which provide an intellectual underpinning for his views, are from al-Rāzī.

Taken with the excursus in the previous section on the need for a ruler to rule justly, and the disorder and destruction wrought by unjust rule, it is not difficult to see a political subtext in such passages. That al-Rāzī felt moved to write this excursus in the context of David's appointment as vicegerent may be his response to the troubled times in which he lived, as has been mentioned earlier. Not every exegete responded to the verse in question in this way. Al-Bayḍāwī, for example, did not.

Nawawī's treatment of this final David pericope then has no less than four major excursuses at its core. They have to do with politics, with spirituality, with theology and with the justice of God. God, being wise and merciful, must be just, just as David is commanded to be just, for God, in telling David to be just, can Himself be no less. And it is God's justice that is the rational basis for belief in the Resurrection and Judgement.

In the excursus on the role of a sultan, and the way political authority should be exercised in general, there may at least be an allusion to the political situation in Nawawī's home-land, under infidel rule, giving it a particular significance. The length at which Nawawī argues the need for a resurrection and judgement to redress the wrongs endured in this life may perhaps suggest that he intended his *Jāwī* students to understand it in this way. This point is taken up again in the conclusion.

6.3 *On Section IV, Sūra Ṣād*

The next passage to be discussed is in section IV, the altercation in Hell. It is set in the eschaton. The Qur'ān presents the scene of a bitter exchange in hell between those led into hell, and those who led them there. It is introduced by a description of the pains of Hell in the vivid Qur'anic terms which may be rendered in English:

55. For the wicked, indeed is a terrible ending,
56. it is Hell, in it they burn. How terrible a place of repose!
57. This!—So let them taste it! In it is searing heat and scalding cold
58. and other pains such as this, many kinds!

Attention should be paid to verse 57 *This!—So let them taste it. In it is searing heat and scalding cold.* Nawawī treats it: *This* i.e. the torment of hell. He glosses *searing heat* (*ḥamīm*) as "boiling water which burns them with its heat" *and scalding cold* (*ghassāq*) he glosses "icy stinking fluid, which burns them with its intense cold". The language is graphic. The exclamatory use of the demonstrative pronoun *This* i.e. the taste of God's punishment is dramatic, and taken with Nawawī's glosses seems designed to hark back to verse 3 of the *sūra, they disbelieve because they have not yet tasted of My punishment. Now indeed they taste it!* In other words it suggests continuities in the thematic structure of the *sūra*. The reference to a *qirā'a* in relation to *madhūq*, the occasion of a lengthy excursus may be designed to contribute to this, since so much space is devoted to *experience* of the pain.[39]

The altercation proper may be rendered:

59. This is a throng about to plunge into hell with you! There'll be no comfort for them, they will burn in the fire!
60. They will say: Rather it is you for whom there is no comfort. It is you who prepared for us this. How terrible a place it is!
61. They will say: Lord of ours whoever made this for us add to his punishment in the fire two-fold.
62. They will say: Why is it that we do not see men we used to account as evil doers?
63. We took them as contemptible; is it that our eyes miss them?
64. This indeed is a fact, the altercation between those in hell.

The words, *This is a throng about to plunge into hell with you* Nawawī *hears* as spoken by the *khazana*, Keepers of Hell, addressed to the leaders (*ru'asā'*) of the damned, already in hell, at the sight of a band of their followers approaching to join them there in torment.

Their response to the Keepers of Hell is: "... *there'll be no comfort for them* i.e. there'll be no solace for them in their houses in hell, *they will burn in the fire*—i.e. they are about to enter it just as we entered it."

It is then the turn of the new arrivals, the followers, to speak. Having overheard what their leaders have said to the Keepers of Hell, they respond to them:

[39] Ibid. 232 and al-Rāzī *Mafātīḥ*: 26, 221.

> . . . *rather it is you for whom there will be no comfort*—i.e. God will not make spacious for you your houses in Hell i.e. what you called out in respect of us, you, leaders, who led us here, you are more deserving of it. *It is you who prepared this for us* i.e. it was you who perpetrated the wickedness for which this torment is the requital, and we followed you! *How terrible a place it is* i.e. how terrible a dwelling place is hell for us and for you!

The followers, having made this reply, turn away from their leaders and supplicantly address God,

> *They say*, i.e. the followers, turning away from their leaders, addressing God imploringly, *Lord of ours, whoever led us to this, increase his punishment in Hell two-fold*, i.e. Lord of ours, whoever of the leaders paved the way for us to this wickedness, increase his punishment in Hell two-fold.

Nawawī perhaps hears the next Qur'anic words as spoken in chorus by leaders and followers, by those already in Hell and new arrivals alike: *Why is it that we do not see men*—i.e. the poor among the believers *we used to account as evil doers*, and adds to the realism of his expansion of the verse by identifying one of the speakers as Abū Jahl whom he presents as saying: "Why is it that we don't see in Hell ʿAmmār, or Bilāl, and Ṣuhayb, and Khabbāb. We used to regard them as fools?", leading to the next Qur'anic logia *we took them as contemptible Is it that our eyes miss them?*

> *This indeed*—i.e. what We told of them as uttering, *is surely true*,—i.e. its occurrence is assured; for they are bound to talk about it; *the altercation between those in hell*—i.e. this is what those in hell say, due to their hostility one for the other.

Nawawī has heard these verses as a drama of contrasting voices, and his presentation of the scene is strikingly effective. It is as though he creates a verbal picture of the scene as he identifies the dramatis personae.

This reference to the *khazana* occurs in Abū 'l-Suʿūd though the Qur'ān does not here identify any speaking subject. In fact, in his comment on this passage, Abū 'l-Suʿūd is paraphrasing a similar scene describing Hell in 67:8, *Every time a throng is hurled into it, the Keepers (khazana) ask them "Did no warner come to you?"*

The words of verse 62 *Why is it that we do not see men we used to account as evil doers?* provide the occasion for an excursus based on two readings (*qirā'a*) of *attakhadhnāhum*, the first word of verse 63.

> . . . If there is a pause in the reading after the last word of verse 62, *al-ashrār*, and the *hamzah* of *attakhadhnāhum* is read as an interrogative

> marker, then there are two possible answers anticipated to the question as to why they are not to be seen in hell: Is it that we were mistaken in regarding them as contemptible in the world so they have not gone to Hell, and that is why we don't see them? Or, Is it that our eyes miss them, since we do not know where in Hell they are. . . .
> If on the other hand the *hamzah* of *attakhadnāhum* is elided, and there is no break between it and the preceding word *al-ashrār*, because *attakhadhnāhum* is a second phrase qualifying *men*, then the meaning is: Why is it that we don't see in Hell the men we despised and looked down on in the world, indeed, from whom we turned our eyes because we regarded them as of no account.

This excursus, based on a *qirāʾa*, is comparatively lengthy, given the scope of Nawawī's *tafsīr*. The point at issue is not a variant recitation, but the locating of a pause. It is thus a question as to how the text is heard at the level of discourse. The attention given to it suggests that the exegete is aware that he is dealing with the spoken word, and all that this implies. A teacher would no doubt dramatise the different recitations, using the different ways in which the exegetical tradition *hears* the words as a technique for communicating vividly this altercation in Hell, the space he devotes to it being an index of its importance.

Nawawī's treatment of this altercation then is important as an example of the way in which the exegetical tradition *hears* such Qur'anic pericopes, but is also of special interest in its own right. It exemplifies a didactic device which occurs elsewhere in the Qur'ān, and to which Leemhuis has drawn attention in *al-Ṣāffāt* (*Sūra* 37). He draws attention to the possibility that it is a counterpart to certain of the rhetorical devices used in Syriac Christian sermons, which give a graphic presentation of altercations between those in heaven and those in hell, and those in hell with each other.[40] It is, in fact, another aspect of the orality of the Qur'ān.

To make their impact, such passages need to be heard, recited with the intonation, inflection and dramatic pauses that are the skills of a master teacher. They are to be *heard*. The exegetical tradition is aware of this, and one of the concerns of an exegete is by all the resources available to him, to recreate a hearing of it, as has Nawawī, in this case by introducing the *khazana* among the dramatis personae in this altercation in Hell, although there is no explicit signal in the Qur'anic text to indicate their presence. It is a tradition of listening that seeks to hear the words uttered as they were heard by the Companions.

---

[40] Leemhuis 1991:176–177.

In presenting this scene, Nawawī has again drawn on *sīra* material to identify as one of the leaders of those in Hell Abū Jahl, and along with him his associates ʿUtba b. Abī Muʿayt, al-ʿAṣī b. Wāʾil who look around in vain in to see in Hell those they persecuted in this life, such as Bilāl, ʿAmmār and Khabbāb. This device heightens the realism of the presentation. But it is also important to be aware that Nawawī, in following al-Rāzī, by identifying Abū Jahl as one of the leaders of the Quraysh in Hell, establishes echoes of the events recounted in verse 6 of the *sūra* which tells of those leaders of the Quraysh including Abū Jahl, who walked away from Muḥammad saying to their fellow Meccans, *Go away [from him], and remain faithful to our gods.* Likewise the company of new arrivals approaching Hell in their wake, are to be identified with those of the Quraysh referred to in the earlier verse, who followed Abū Jahl and their other leaders, walking away from Muḥammad.

Nawawī by his use of the word *ruʾasāʾ* in his glosses in each section has brought out the coherence between them, a feature to which al-Rāzī constantly draws attention. He has thereby shown, rather than explained in so many words the coherence (*naẓm*) between the first section of the *sūra* (verses 4–6) telling of the leaders of Quraysh rejecting Muḥammad, drawing others too away from him, the appropriateness of the punishment in Hell for those who deny the Resurrection and Judgement in section II (verses 27–28), and the scene in hell in section III (verses 59–64) where those who rejected Muḥammad are in Hell, both leaders and followers, in a place of searing heat and scalding cold. Nawawī then, in explaining the pericope, has both provided the means to ensure that its drama may be experienced vicariously, and demonstrated its thematic integration in the *sūra* as a whole.

6.4 *On Section V, Sūra Ṣād*

The final passage to be discussed is Nawawī's treatment of V, the exhortation to the Meccans in last two verses of the *sūra*, which may be rendered:

> 85. Declare [Muḥammad]: I ask of you no reward [for delivering it]; I am not one of those who assumes a task [not proper to him].
> 86. [The Qurʾān] is none other than a warning to all creatures. You will surely understand its portent when the time has come.

It is a stirring peroration with as point of departure the last words of verse 85, *min al-mutakallifīn*, a peroration taken verbatim from al-Rāzī's concluding excursus. In treating these words, Nawawī follows a procedure he has used on similar occasions, of using his gloss of a key word or phrase to introduce an excursus. Thus he glosses *min al-mutakallifīn* as "one of those who impose difficulties on human kind by means of the Law (*min al-ḥāmilīna li'l-mashaqqa fī 'l-sharīʿa ʿalā 'l-nās*)". Strikingly, this interpretation neither occurs in any of his sources nor is supported by the classical commentators. He appears to have formulated it himself on the basis of the opening words of al-Rāzī's excursus: *lā yaḥtāju fī maʿrifati siḥḥatihi ilā 'l-takallufāti 'l-kathīra.* He then quotes al-Rāzī verbatim:

> This to which I am calling you is not a religion that has need for numerous legal obligations to testify to its authenticity, rather it is a religion, the authenticity of which is testified by reason. For I call on you first to profess belief in the existence of God; secondly I call on you to affirm His transcendence over all that is not appropriate to Him; thirdly I call on you to profess His being described by the attributes of perfect knowledge, power, wisdom and mercy; fourthly I call on you to profess His transcendence over any associates; fifthly I call on you to profess the inadmissibility of the worship of idols; sixthly, I call on you to profess the greatness of the angels and the prophets. Seventhly, I call on you to profess belief in the Resurrection and the Day of Judgement. Then, eighthly, I call on you to turn away from [the false delights] of this world, and [to look to] the world to come.[41]

The meaning given to *min al-mutakallifīn*, "one of those who imposes difficulties," which is how Nawawī, following al-Rāzī understands the phrase, is presented as the basis of these eight principles. This sense is not supported by the *Lisān al-ʿArab*[42] and in fact al-Bayḍāwī and other commentators explain the words as "one who takes on or lays claim to a responsibility not proper to him".

It is nevertheless this understanding of the word that for al-Rāzī (and Nawawī following in his wake) reveals the core of the thematic unity of the *sūra*, being a reprise of the topics that al-Rāzī (and Nawawī) have already highlighted: Judgement Day, the Unity of God, the role of the Prophets, the Mercy and Wisdom of God, the rewards for those who believe and accept Muḥammad and his message, the punishment for those who reject it, and the role of reason as guarantor

---

[41] Nawawī *Marāḥ labīd*: 2, 234.

[42] Cf. Ibn Manẓūr *Lisān al-ʿarab*: vol. 9, 307 (s.r. KLF). Nawawī appears to have read *mutakallifūn* as *mukallifūn*.

of the articles of Faith. Thus looking at the *sūra* through Nawawī's and al-Rāzī's eyes, we see reason establishing belief in an after-life, reason establishing that creation is for a purpose and reason establishing the importance of justice for the maintenance of order in the world.

There is a logical sequence in the arrangement of these eight principles: each depends on the one preceding: Belief in God is first, and for al-Rāzī the existence of God can be established by reason; God, given His nature must transcend any limitation; He must have certain qualities, His knowledge, power wisdom and mercy must be perfect; (it will be recalled how prominently God's Wisdom and Mercy featured in the second passage discussed ad verse 28 *Would We treat those who believe and do good deeds [as We treat] those who do wickedness upon the earth?*). He can have no partner (otherwise He would not be God). This being so, the worship of idols is inadmissible. Given the existence of God, one must revere the prophets He sends, each of whom has his own testatory miracle. Once a prophet has offered his testatory miracle, his mission and all that it implies must be recognised and the authority of the Book revealed to him accepted. Further the Book that has been revealed to the prophet speaks with authority. It is from the Prophets and the Books revealed to them that Man learns of the reality of the resurrection and Judgement—they are the proof of the resurrection. It is this special status of the prophet that leads al-Rāzī to argue that a prophet is inerrant and impeccable, for "God knows where he places his message" (6:124). The resurrection followed by reward and punishment proves that life is not to no purpose. Because the Book demonstrates that God is Just, Merciful and Wise, it is also the ultimate guarantee that injustices in this life, in which it often happens that the wicked live in ease, and the virtuous in misery, will be redressed; and because there is the Resurrection and Judgement to look forward to, man should turn away from the things of this world, and towards the world to come. This, as al-Rāzī often puts it, is not a circular but a sequential argument. Once the existence of God is established, everything else follows.

7. *Conclusion*

Nawawī's work can be seen in a number of ways. From one point of view, looking at it in his terms, it is a pastiche. He is not interpreting the Qur'ān according to his personal opinion, but presenting the understanding of it of scholars he regards as more learned than himself. A reading of his treatment of *Ṣād* alongside his five sources, reveals in fact that hardly a sentence in the *Marāḥ Labīd* is his own. And those sentences that do not occur in his sources are for the most part complementary glosses on glosses, or have to do with grammar, although there are a few exceptions. In general, he has woven his selections together with skill.

It is not practicable within the limitations of this essay to treat in detail this aspect of his work, thus one or two examples must suffice. One is ad verse 8 *Is it to him from among us the Scripture is revealed?* Nawawī's treatment of it has three components. An identification of the *ḍamīr* in *ʿalayhi* as Muḥammad, and a gloss on *al-dhikr* as al-Qur'ān, both from al-Shirbīnī; *min bayninā* is expanded to "We being leaders of and nobles among the people" from Abū 'l-Suʿūd, and a general comment "So how is it conceivable that he be singled out for this high rank?" from al-Rāzī.[43] Another is ad verse 27—*We have not created the heaven and the earth and what is between them to no purpose (bāṭilan). Bāṭilan* is glossed *ʿabathan* from Shirbīnī, with a second gloss *juzāfan, juzāfan* itself further explained as *bi-lā amrin wa-lā nahī* from al-Fīrūzābādī, followed by a lengthy excursus on God being the creator of human acts from al-Rāzī.[44] Finally, ad verse 59 *This is a throng about to plunge into hell with you,* he achieves a striking effect by drawing on a dramatic device identified only in one of his sources, Abū 'l-Suʿūd,—although in fact it has its authority in the *sūra* 67:8, being a paraphrase of the words, *Whenever a group is hurled into [Hell] its keepers (the khazana) ask them: Was no warner sent to you?* In short, without prior knowledge that the work is to such a degree composite, it would require an experienced student of *tafsīr* to distinguish its components.

Attention has already been drawn to Nawawī's control of his material and his introduction of appropriate changes in the Arabic grammar of his text as omissions from or changes in wording of his sources require. In this *sūra*, I noted only one instance of a possible grammatical error due to a change in wording he has introduced. At one point ad verse 9 *Do they have [charge of] the treasure chests of the mercy of your Lord, the Mighty, the Bestower,* explaining *al-Wahhāb* (The Bestower),

---

[43] Nawawī *Marāḥ labīd*: 2, 232.
[44] Ibid. 229.

Nawawī while quoting al-Rāzī, has rephrased al-Rāzī's *kawnuhu wāhiban*—"His being a giver", as *hibatuhu*—"His gift" or "His act of giving", then omits to change the gender of a later referring pronoun from masculine to feminine in accordance with this change, thus having it refer to God, instead of an act of God. While theoretically at least, there is an ambiguity in al-Rāzī's text, due to the principle that it is preferable for a pronoun to refer to its closest antecedent, in this context, logically it is more consistent that the Meccans should dislike what God chooses to do in exercising His will as to where He should bestow his gifts, than that they should dislike God. In choosing a feminine *maṣdar*, Nawawī has indeed removed an "ambiguity", but only at the cost of giving the sentence a less likely meaning.[45]

The word "pastiche" should not be misunderstood. The key as to how the book took shape in its present form is almost certainly to be found in its origins as an oral presentation. In the few instances where it might appear as a scissors and paste compilation, if presented orally, the various components may be heard as what they are, asides, clarifications and supplementary information and so come together naturally in the framework of his discourse. Wansbrough's remark that the sermon is the *sitz im leben* of *tafsīr* in this case cannot be overemphasised. Nawawī was a teacher, and many of the details and emphases occurring in his *tafsīr* arise from the flow of ideas and associations of a teacher in the *ḥalaqa*, the student circle situation. A corollary of this is that not everything that he says in the course of expounding the Qur'ān is necessarily recorded in the printed text of the work.

There is, however, a need to stress the qualitative difference between the material he takes from Abū 'l-Suʿūd, al-Shirbīnī, al-ʿUjaylī and the others, and what he takes from al-Rāzī. From all of them he takes glosses, periphrases, *qirā'āt, asbāb al-nuzūl* and the like—but it is from al-Rāzī that he takes what might be called his intellectual hardware, in that all his significant excursuses are from al-Rāzī, and from

[45] Al-Rāzī ad verse 9 (*Mafātīḥ*: 26, 180) *am ʿindahum khazā'inu raḥmati rabbika 'l-ʿazīzi 'l-wahhāb*. Part of al-Rāzī's gloss of *al-wahhāb* is *fa-lam yatawaqqaf kawnuhu wāhiban li-hādhihi 'l-niʿmati ʿalā kawni 'l-mawhūbi minhu ghaniyyan aw faqīran, wa-lam yakhtalif dhālika ayḍan bi-sababi anna aʿdā'ahu yuḥibbūnahu aw yakrahūnahu*. Nawawī in taking this passage into his own gloss of the verse substitutes *hibatuhu* for *kawnuhu wāhiban*, and in recognition of *hiba* being feminine, changes *yatawaqqaf* to *tatawaqqaf*. However, he omits to change *yuḥibbūnahu* to *yuḥibbūnahā* and *yakrahūnahu* to *yakrahūnahā* at the end of a long sentence. The difference in meaning is significant "whether they like Him or not" in place of "whether they like Him giving it or not".

time to time he makes tangential remarks that may serve as cues for him to make oral reference to al-Rāzī's writing. Indeed, his indebtedness to al-Rāzī is clear on every page of his work, although it is by no means total.

Al-Rāzī's treatment of the *sūra* is at least five times the length of that of Nawawī and is so various in content that it is difficult to give a full account of what Nawawī has omitted. Attention has been drawn to some examples of his omissions. In the discussion of his treatment of verses 1–3 in section I, for example, he focused attention on the faithfulness of God and the truthfulness of Muḥammad in the information he provided on the letter *Ṣād*, and consciously turned aside from the halakhic dimension of the Qur'ān. He does not take up al-Rāzī's excursuses on "difficulties" in the Qur'ān, his justification of *ta'wīl*, his concern to demonstrate *naẓm*, his attacks on the Mu'tazilites and the *ḥashwis* and the views of other exegetes. He does not reproduce or offer any counterpart to the range of arguments and prooftexts that al-Rāzī gives for and against the issues he takes up, or attempt to duplicate his battle array of *baḥth*, *faṣl*, *maqām* and *mas'ala*, or the repertoire of haggadic material on which he passes judgement. Thus he does not follow al-Rāzī down all the paths al-Rāzī chooses to explore in his response to the Qur'ān. Nevertheless, for all his selection and abridgement, Nawawī not only brings out, but appears to have absorbed salient features of al-Rāzī's thought. Clearly, he is sensitive to al-Rāzī's spirituality, his sense of the impossibility of understanding the riches of the Qur'ān without the active support of divine grace.[46] As does al-Rāzī, he constantly draws attention to the key doctrines of the Divine Unicity, Prophecy and Judgement, on each of which the unbelievers challenge Muḥammad.

Although he does not use the word *naẓm* to describe the interrelation between every part of the Qur'anic text, his understanding of the term and sensitivity to its implications is evident throughout his treatment of the *sūra*. At phrase, verse and pericope level, by his use of clarifications and periphrases that, as well as explaining the text, fill what might be regarded as pregnant silences between words, phrases and verses, he shows the inevitability of their sequentiality. And at the pericope level, he achieves the same effect by his emphases on themes—for example the emphasis on the resurrection, reward and punishment—and the repetition of key words in his glosses.

---

[46] Al-Rāzī *Mafātīḥ*: 26, 203.

Thus he brings out the continuities between the succeeding sections of the *sūra*, and, by way of example, ensures that those in hell, leaders and followers in section III, verses 59 to 64 are identified with the leaders of Quraysh who reject Muḥammad and those who follow them in section I verses 4 to 7.

He responds to al-Rāzī's filling out the line of Qur'anic narrative, of communicating the drama and tension implicit in much of the Qur'anic rhetoric—for example in verses 1–2—in such a way as to involve the hearers in the life and death struggle of Muḥammad, and the telling of those stories to which a Qur'anic word or phrase may simply allude. He clearly has a sensitivity to the intonation of the spoken word, in fact to the oral character of the Qur'ān to which, of course, the tradition of exegesis is no stranger.

He follows al-Rāzī's authority in the stories that he believes it proper to tell. If al-Rāzī disapproves of a story, Nawawī does not include it. Thus ad verse 34 *We put Solomon to the test* he relates only the haggadic narrative to which al-Rāzī gives his approval.[47]

But although he may accept this principle, and the stories and the scenarios of which al-Rāzī approves, he does not always accept al-Rāzī's interpretation of such stories. Reference has already been made to Nawawī's acceptance of al-Rāzī's understanding of the Disputation Scene in which David was confronted by two intruders. Nawawī does not mention al-Rāzī's preferred explanation as to why David should have asked God for pardon towards the end of this scene *so he sought pardon of his Lord* (v. 25): He sought pardon on behalf of those who had planned to kill him. Al-Rāzī chooses this explanation because, in a manner consistent with his concept of the sinlessness of the prophets, he is prepared to go to what might appear extreme lengths to interpret the Qur'ān in a way that will demonstrate the moral perfection of a prophet. Nawawī, however, in his treatment of this pericope, while accepting the scenario that al-Rāzī has constructed, that the intruders were human beings, not angels in disguise, but seeing David guilty of a *zalla* (in that he contemplated taking vengeance on them for planning to kill him) is following the mainstream sunnī view that a prophet may be guilty of a *zalla*. Nawawī indeed lists a number of the reasons suggested why David might have been regarded guilty of a *zalla*: one that Bathsheba was betrothed to Uriah, and David asked him to break off the betrothal in his favour, an-

[47] Nawawī *Marāḥ labīd*: 2, 230; al-Rāzī *Mafātīḥ*: 26, 207–209.

other that Uriah was already married to her, and David requested him to divorce her so that she be free to marry him.[48] However, he makes no reference to the grave sin of which some narratives hold David to have been guilty: the sending of Uriah to the forefront of the battle to be slain. In so doing he heeds al-Rāzī's warning that it is wrong even to mention such things, bearing in mind the *ḥadīth* quoted by al-Rāzī on the authority of Sa'īd b. al-Musayyib from 'Ali to the effect that anyone who repeats this story of David should be punished with 160 lashes.[49] That he saw David guilty of a *zalla* may well be regarded as a considered decision reached either on his own initiative, or, more likely, following a consensus of his teachers, who as sunnīs and Shāfi'ites were perhaps suspicious of conferring an imām-like status on the prophets, even on Muḥammad, who had stressed so often: I am a man like you.

There are further special concerns of al-Rāzī that Nawawī takes up. Among them is al-Rāzī's excursus on the divine adjuration to David when appointed vicegerent, to rule *according to what is true* (*bi'l-ḥaqq*, v. 26). Another is al-Rāzī's lengthy excursus to the effect that it is only those who disbelieve in the resurrection who say that creation is to no purpose, and that denial of Command and Prohibition, reward and punishment *is the opinion of those who disbelieve*. Hell is prepared for such, because they deny the wisdom of Almighty God in creating heaven and earth. A third is the stirring conclusion to his treatment of the *sūra*, quoting al-Rāzī *in extenso* summarising its themes, arguing that the religion Muḥammad brought rested its case for authenticity not on its imposition of numerous legal obligations, but on reason. In introducing this passage, he gives a definition of *mutakallifīn*, which is a paraphrase of al-Rāzī's understanding of the word. All in all, he shows his own perception and acceptance of the organic unity of the *sūra* and gives an endorsement not merely of al-Rāzī's synoptic understanding of the Qur'anic text, but demonstrates that he shares al-Rāzī's enthusiasm and passion for an essentially rationalistic understanding of the message of Islam.

Nevertheless, notwithstanding the many points at which he follows al-Rāzī, it is important again to draw attention to some of the points referred to earlier in this essay, at which he follows his own path: ad verse 1 in making al-Rāzī's *bayānayn, bayān*, ad verse 24, in making

[48] Nawawī *Marāḥ labīd*: 2, 228.
[49] Al-Rāzī *Mafātīḥ*: 26, 192.

his own choice as to the *zalla* for which David asked pardon; ad verse 26, in glossing *bi'l-ḥaqq* as *bi'l-ʿadl*; and ad verse 59, in introducing the *khazana* as speakers of its opening words, *This is a throng about to plunge into Hell with you.*

There is a further dimension to Nawawī's work that must not be overlooked: his awareness of the times in which he lived. The excursus from al-Rāzī relating to David's appointment as vicegerent and the importance of a ruling authority governing according to the *sharīʿa* is significant in this respect. I mentioned earlier that al-Rāzī lived in troubled times, and that he experienced at first hand the consequences of a break down of law and order. Thus as Nawawī brings out the drama implicit in the concentrated language of the Qur'ān in verses 2–3 in such a way as to involve his hearers in the confrontation between Muḥammad and the Quraysh to convince his hearers that they too are involved in the same struggle, so Nawawī's excursus taken from al-Rāzī on the need for a ruler to rule according to the *sharīʿa* may be an allusion to the plight of Muslim peoples under alien rule in, as he puts it "everywhere in the world (*aqṭār al-arḍ*)."

As already stated, there is no reason to doubt that Nawawī was aware of the fate of Muslims across the world under alien rule. If, indeed, his interest in al-Rāzī was fostered directly or indirectly under the guidance of Indian *ʿulamāʾ* making the holy land their *mahjar*, he would certainly have been aware of the consequences of the Indian Mutiny in 1857 for Muslims under British rule in the sub-continent, as well as what he learnt at first hand from his co-religionists, pilgrims and students from Banten and other areas of the then Dutch East Indies.

This needs to be considered in relation to the way in which Nawawī gives his audience a vicarious experience of Muḥammad's encounters with the unbelievers. In so doing, he instils in them a heightened awareness of Islam as a confrontation between one set of values and another, but in a frame-work much wider than the seminal event of Muḥammad's rejection by the Meccans: one that was world-wide, between believers and infidels, the oppressed and the oppressors. This confrontation is set in the context of a vision of a universalistic salvation history, one in which the evil reject the message of the good, up to the time of Muḥammad and are punished. It is into the continuation of this history that Nawawī, in handing on the exegetical tradition that he has drawn primarily from al-Rāzī, is taking his listeners, for the lesson to be learnt is still valid. It is not too far-fetched to discover in this emphasis on the need to *judge on the basis of what is true* i.e. with justice, an allusion to the fate of the Muslims in Nawawī's home land under unbeliever rule. It may indeed be his own concern with the injustice of Dutch rule that leads him to go beyond al-Rāzī in glossing *bi'l-ḥaqq* (v. 26) *on the basis of what is true* with *bi'l-ʿadl* "with justice".

Nawawī, as Snouck Hurgronje noted, was politically aware. He knew that many Muslims lived in subjection to unbelievers and the consequences of unjust infidel rule. It was evident to him that the Muslims lived in a state of inferiority to the unbelievers. His sub-text is surely that the balance will be redressed on the Day of Judgement (if not before), and that therefore denial of the Resurrection is a denial of God's justice, and is tantamount to a denial of the inevitability of an end to infidel rule. In his stressing this, the historical dimension of his response to the *sūra* should not be overlooked. The peoples before Muḥammad disbelieved, and were destroyed; Muḥammad's contemporaries who disbelieved in him were overwhelmed. Ad verse 11, he quotes Rāzī "They were to be overwhelmed in the very place in which they uttered those [insulting] words and that place was Mecca".[50] And those who oppress the Muslims in Nawawī's own time, will, sooner or later receive their deserts, as did the unbelieving Meccans. Indeed, is it going too far to see in Nawawī's highlighting those who follow Abū Jahl into Hell, referred to in verse 59, *This is a throng about to plunge [into Hell] with you* an allusion to those of his fellow countrymen ready to "serve the infidel government"?

Snouck Hurgronje's remarks on Nawawī's political attitudes would certainly apply to those of his associates and students, whether in Mecca, or after their return to Banten. The political sub-text of Nawawī's words would have been plain to them. Although expressing himself in a different idiom, Nawawī had then essentially the same motivations as al-Afghānī (who had personal experience of the Indian Mutiny) and Muḥammad ʿAbduh. Reading his work in this way we can in fact detect in it emphases shared with ʿAbduh. Shared, but set in a different frame of reference, and deriving from other lines of historical development. ʿAbduh's Reformism was a response to a direct experience of the West and association with Europeans at first hand both in Cairo and Paris. He was a great eclectic, and a

[50] Ibid. 181.

number of elements in his thought led the way to a rejection of the authority of the *madhāhib*.

Nawawī's intellectual development, it seems was totally within the Islamic tradition, and his commitment to the Shāfiʿite *madhhab* never wavered. It was nourished principally by the strand of that tradition represented by al-Rāzī. Nevertheless, each, in his approach to the Qurʾān had the perception of a realistic rationalism as an essential element in the Islamic revelation; each de-emphasised *fiqh*, and each in his own way represented stages in the abandonment in Qurʾanic exegesis of explanatory and background stories of ultimately Jewish provenance known as *Isrāʾīliyyāt*, a process that al-Rāzī's approach foreshadowed. It should be emphasised that Nawawī's teaching to succeeding cohorts of *Jāwī* students included these emphases years before the appearance of ʿAbduh's treatise *Risāla al-tawḥīd*, let alone publication of the *al-Manār* journal, or the *tafsīr* of the same name.

Nawawī's work, then can be seen as a chapter in the development of Qurʾanic exegesis in the Malay world, as an instrument in the spiritual and intellectual formation of generations of students and as a vehicle for the transmission of some of the central ideas of one of the great figures in the world of Islam. That he did this in Mecca highlights the importance of the holy land for the coming together and transmission of a variety of trends, tendencies and emphases in Islam, not as the centre of an established orthodoxy, but as a clearing house for a rich and diverse complex of spiritual and jurisprudential traditions.

It has often been remarked that ʿAbduh's Reformism established itself rapidly in the then Dutch East Indies. To the degree that this was the case, it could have been facilitated by Nawawī's work, although such a statement should not be understood simplistically. It is perhaps equally likely that he was also, and even more so, one of the sources for the continuing strength of the Shāfiʿite tradition in the area later to be known as Indonesia, exemplified by the vigour and adaptiveness of the *Nahḍat al-ʿulamāʾ* notwithstanding the rejection of this tradition by many of ʿAbduh's followers, and proof, if any were needed, that rationalism is not the monopoly of the Reformists in the line of Ibn Taymiyya and Ibn Qayyim al-Jawziyya.

This examination, admittedly selective, of Nawawī's treatment of *Ṣād* gives a general idea of his goals and his exegetic procedures. He has a concern for specific intellectual issues, both those arising from particular pericopes in the *sūra*, and those which comprehend the *sūra* as a whole. While following al-Rāzī in so much, he nevertheless is able to draw back from him, and take other paths. Although this, by its nature, is a preliminary study, it offers an insight into his importance in shaping the way in which many Southeast Asian Muslims understood the Qur'ān, and perceived their identity as Muslims. He was a great figure in the traditional mould. On the surface, he was a scholar's scholar, devoted exclusively to learning. Yet in his work of exegesis, concealed beneath a faithful application of the established procedures of his discipline, is a strong individuality, and a decisive commitment to political as well as religious ideals, and by his drawing on and transmission of al-Rāzī, he perhaps laid the groundwork for the resilience of the traditionalist understanding of Islam in what was to become Indonesia, represented by the *Nahḍat al-ʿulamāʾ*, against the best efforts of the Reformists who espoused the neo-Ḥanbalism of Rashīd Riḍā and his followers. There is still much to be learned from the work of this extraordinarily learned Bantenese scholar of the late 19th century of whom Snouck Hurgronje writes so vividly: "His bent body makes his little figure yet smaller, he goes along the street as if the whole earth were a gigantic book in which he reads."

ISLAMICIST AS INTERPRETER

David B. Burrell

While it would be redundant to remind anyone that the role of Islamicist in western society involves heavy doses of interpretation, it may be salutary to remind ourselves that Islamicists function *primarily* as interpreters of a religious culture quite foreign to the majority outlook of people in western society. That is, they ought to be doing so, and were they to have been more aware of this responsibility, some of the dimensions of "Orientalism" which gave its detractors such potent ammunition might have been avoided. If that sounds a bit paradoxical, think of the difference in self-conception between those who see themselves as interpreting to their own culture a society very different from the one with which they are familiar, and others who pretend to be offering to their readers an unvarnished description of how things really are in this quite different world. The second type offers a paradigm for "Orientalists", who must presume to "have gotten it straight", possessed as they are of "scientific" methods of description and of analysis. The first requires that any understanding be at least implicitly a comparative understanding, incorporating an awareness that one stands between two cultures and is speaking from and to one's own.

It might seem surprising that this difference, subtle as it appears to be, could be said to make so significant a difference, but I shall be arguing that it indeed does, and contending that the work of A.H. Johns offers us an exemplary model of Islamicist as interpreter. If the difference in approach between those who see themselves primarily as interpreting another culture to their own, and those who presume themselves to be offering a straightforward description of the other culture, seems a subtle one to us, that could be because we are used to being the interpreting culture, and used to having our interpretations taken to be the accurate account of the matter. But that is of course the quite unsubtle presumption which critics have uncovered in western writers on Islam, thereby generating the pejorative label of "orientalism". What that presumption clearly embodies is a bevy of premises long identified with the Enlightenment, which take *reason* to be a capacity for understanding which transcends cultural differences *and* which is exercised in its mature form in western "critical" inquiry. Given those parameters, *our* interpretation will indeed be presented as the accurate rendition of matters in other cultures, subject of course to criticism from other scholars who share our critical methods. And since something of that mindset will no doubt be shared by readers of these essays, trained as we are in such methods, they will immediately query: what do you propose as an alternative?

The answer is simple: use these critical methods quite consciously to assist one's attempt to understand the other culture in its differences, as *other*. This effort will require that we begin with an awareness of where it is that we stand, and incorporate in our writings something of what impelled us to attempt to understand this other culture, as well as some salient features of the journey which has carried us to the understanding which we now claim to possess. Yet since we do now claim some understanding, which we are intent on presenting to others, the difference between this approach and its enlightenment predecessor would be exceedingly difficult to explicate without the exemplars offered by Professor Johns' work. I refer principally to his work in presenting those Qur'anic figures who also appear in biblical narrative; others may verify whether his treatment of Indonesian literature displays similar features. His most recent rendition of the Joseph story begins, characteristically, "For Muslims of today, the Qur'ān is an event which entered history through the life of Muḥammad and the revelations given to him. It is experienced as a whole, beheld as a total revelation, complete in itself, and able on its own authority to confront any other book, any other religious tradition."[1] He then continues: "An awareness of the Qur'ān as exemplifying an inimitable language of ritual and liturgy is a key component of the authority it commands. The Arabic text is rarely, if ever, read with the eyes alone. . . . Whether the listener knows Arabic or not, the 'voice of the innermost heart' of the reciter projects the power and divine dimension of the words, and his dedication to and love of them. It is, to use William Graham's phrase, the Word as liturgy, and it is this presentation of the Word that communicates its power; it is a glorious celebration of the Qur'ān as event."[2]

---

[1] Johns 1993b:37.
[2] Ibid. 37–38.

Whether they are deliberately designed to do so or not, these expository comments incorporate resonances of recent work on scripture and liturgy in the Christian tradition which can help western Christians, at least, to appreciate the character of the Qur'ān in Muslim life and practice. What might loom central to a secular western commentator—questions of interpretation—comes second in Johns' treatment; what he rather invites us to focus on is "Qur'ān as event", indeed as liturgical event. In terms of my initial contrast in approaches, we have here a presentation of the Qur'ān in Muslim life which offers a description, certainly, and one which purports to be accurate, yet in terms which are best grasped by those familiar with the role which scripture plays in western liturgical practice. Similarly, recent work on narrative both sets the stage and poses difficulties for the approach he will invite us to take to understand the Qur'ān, and specifically the Joseph story.[3] For that story above all exemplifies the character of biblical narrative so dramatically portrayed by Robert Alter, in which the stage set by the divine agent in no way interferes with, but rather enhances, the dramatic quality of human interactions. Put in terms of the narrator, he avers that

> perhaps the most distinctive feature of the role played by the narrator in the biblical tales is the way in which omniscience and inobtrusiveness are combined. . . . The assurance of comprehensive knowledge is thus implicit in the narratives, but it is shared with the reader only intermittently and at that quite partially. In this way, the very mode of narration conveys a double sense of a total coherent knowledge available to God (and by implication, to His surrogate, the anonymous authoritative narrator) and the necessary incompleteness of human knowledge, for which much about character, motive, and moral status will remain shrouded in ambiguity.[4]

A significant implication for Alter is that narrative of this kind can succeed, where more conceptual schemes often fail, in sorting out the dilemmas inherent in expositions of divine and human agency. Yet one's artistry is pushed to the limit, for "it was no easy thing to make sense of human reality in the radically new light of the monotheistic revelation."[5]

What the Qur'ān tends to elide is precisely the ambiguity of human motivation, leaving all the initiative to God. Concerning the

[3] Cf. Alter 1981; more theologically, Frei 1974.
[4] Ibid. 183–184.
[5] Ibid. 176.

seduction scene, the Qur'anic narrator insists: "she made for him madly and he would have taken her had he not seen a clear sign from his Lord, that We might keep him clear of evil and lust. He proved a loyal servant of Ours" (12:24). So it is that "God was working out His purpose, unaware of the fact as most people are" (12:21).[6] This feature of the Qur'anic account of Joseph sets up most western readers, initially formed by the biblical story, for a decidedly negative appreciation. It is because he realises that fact that Johns takes pains to note the plethora of literary devices employed in the Qur'ān to give the story the dramatic effect it has in that medium. He will refer to the poetry of Gerard Manley Hopkins to alert us to features of Arabic which we would inevitably miss, and remind us more generally that the paranetic aim of the Qur'ān demands quick transitions and pithy incorporation of entire contexts by allusion. In short, it is not to be judged by the canons of narrative which Robert Alter laid out so perspicuously for biblical stories; in fact, the *Sūra Yusūf* in the Qur'ān is not intended to be a story so much as it is a warning and a guidance, in line with the overall aims of this revelation.

In summary, Johns employs the rich resources of western literary theory to explicate for us the *differences* in the Qur'anic text, so that we can appreciate it for what it is, and do so precisely by noting how it is *not* what we might have been led to expect a story to be. Yet those very devices, as we are led to see them operative in the text, allow us to discern a psychological subtlety as powerful *in its own way* as the "naturalistic narrative" of the Genesis story of Joseph. Allowing myself to generalise from Johns' practice, one can detect a logic at work which undergirds the theme of implicitly comparative presentation which I have been developing: the universality of religious revelations will emerge only by attending to their particularity.[7] And since that particularity extends to the traditions as well, one can detect in Johns' recourse to the commentators to alert us to the nuances hidden in the Qur'anic text a yet further respect for the particularity of Islam. We are invited to use all the tools of literary analysis available to us to step into another textual world, precisely to appreciate it in its *otherness*. And in the process we may have come to realise that our canonical notions of *narrative* in fact reflect those

[6] Qur'ān translations will be taken from Cragg 1988, unless otherwise noted.
[7] See DiNoia 1992:84–85.

traditions of revelation with which we are familiar, and so ought not simply be presumed to be generalizable.

Admittedly, reflections like this move at a certain level of abstraction, so I am relying on the reader's familiarity with Johns' careful critical work to provide the relevant examples. A bevy of questions begin to arise as soon as one seeks to move into an exposition of something different, and I have attempted to divert most of them by recalling us to the fact that work like this is inherently comparative, whether explicitly so or not, and that such a reminder should elicit the modesty appropriate to so daunting a task. The questions which immediately arise are similar to those which bedevil any account of translation: is there an overarching propositional field which allows one to proceed from one language to another? In fact, Johns begins the essay on the Qur'anic presentation of the Joseph story which we are considering with observations about the diversity of translations of the Qur'ān, and suggests at the end that his critical remarks "may have some relevance to the problem of Qur'anic translation."[8] And indeed they do, since the issue involved in translating is not so much the abstract conceptual conundrum of an "overarching propositional field" as it is the quality of judgements which one must make in selecting among alternative expressions which occur to one. Nor are these judgements the sort which one can adequately *explain*—to oneself or another, although one may indeed lay out the background for one's choice. Ludwig Wittgenstein's remarks are especially apropos here: "How do I find the 'right' word? How do I choose among words? . . . I do not always have to make judgements, give explanations; often I might only say: 'It simply isn't right yet'. I am dissatisfied, I go on looking. At last a word comes: '*That's* it!' *Sometimes* I can say why. This is simply what searching, this is what finding, is like here."[9]

That is what I take Johns to be doing as he introduces us to the Qur'anic presentation of biblical stories. He is helping us to learn how to *follow* their logic, without being constrained to move them into our narrative field, and so ask why they proceed so deficiently. As in translating, the tools of literary analysis can be extremely useful in alerting us to the different stage-setting for this dramatic narrative, yet the discernments will inevitably rely upon our enhanced

---

[8] An earlier essay is Johns 1981a.
[9] Wittgenstein 1953:218e (IIxi).

feeling for the movement of the text. That is the sense of "judgement" which I have been evoking. Again, Wittgenstein's remarks about whether "there is such a thing as 'expert judgement' in the genuineness of expressions of feeling" may be helpful here. With regard to feelings generally, he avers that

> correcter prognoses will generally issue from judgements of those with better knowledge of mankind. [But] can one learn this knowledge? Yes; some can. Not, however, by taking a course in it, but though "*experience*". Can someone else be a man's teacher in this? Certainly. From time to time he gives him the right *tip*. This is what "learning" and "teaching" are like here. What one acquires here is not a technique; one learns correct judgements. There are also rules, but they do not form a system, and only experienced people can apply them right.[10]

It is not surprising that someone as resistant to generalisation as Wittgenstein would be attuned to helping us understand the logic peculiar to revelational texts and traditions, where whatever can be generalised must emerge from close attention to what is particular to each tradition. We in the west have been taught to proceed in just the opposite direction: to find an overarching generalisation from which we can correctly classify and ideally even deduce particular instances. I have suggested that what plays that role in Johns' critical presentations are the skills of literary analysis, and precisely those skills which can alert us to how the Qur'anic text proceeds differently from our narrative expectations. So there are generalities at work, but they are embodied in skills of reading, allowing us to move into another tradition without needing to possessing overarching conceptual schemes. What we are invited rather to do is to proceed in a comparative fashion, using our modes of access to biblical texts as leverage into another textual world. If the comparative dimension is quite implicit in Johns' work, that is doubtless a useful strategy, since comparative textual studies are deemed to be fraught with difficulties. Yet to have seen that critical work purporting to introduce us to another tradition must be comparative in character, if it is to succeed in relating us to what is *other*, can serve to remind us that any other approach will unconsciously employ our standards as normative. And just as translating is something we must undertake even though we lack a satisfactory account of what we are doing when we do it, so studies of this sort, by offering us an utterly timely access to

---

[10] Ibid. 227e (IIxi).

another tradition, can serve to put us into better touch with our own. For the quality of judgement involved represents a skill which may assist us in moving into quite different corners of our own past as well. Indeed, such an awareness may alert us to the fact that every understanding is in some measure comparative, just as Wittgenstein wanted to remind us that every generalisation that would prove useful would be in an inescapable tension with its generating particulars. So attending to the logic of revelation may help us question whether the more conventional movement from general to particular is in fact as normative as we were taught. It just may be that the skills which teach us to respect the particularities of other traditions may also be the ones helping us illuminate our own.

THE TRANSMISSION OF NARRATIVE-BASED EXEGESIS IN ISLAM

al-Baghawī's Use of Stories in his Commentary on the Qur'ān, and a Malay Descendent

PETER G. RIDDELL

The literary form which most characterises our world view at the beginning and end of life is narrative. In early childhood, one is presented with narrative in the form of stories related by parents to children. In old age, one of the greatest contributions which an individual can make is in relating life's experiences and the lessons to be learned from these experiences to the young, either in the form of oral story-telling or literary memoirs. Indeed, between these two extreme points of an individual's existence, meaning to life is found within the broader context of that life. Lessons are learned from the past and applied to the present in order to prepare a path for the future. One draws on the narrative of one's own life; historical context is important in providing the individual with guideposts in life and points of reference in showing the way to others.

1. *Narrative and Theology*

Just as narrative underpins life in general, it is important not to underestimate the power of narrative in both reflecting and shaping theology. All of the great religious traditions allocate an important function to narrative in both serving to record the stories of the culture and heroes within those traditions as well as providing examples of ideal behaviour for the benefit of the followers of the religions in question. Thus, bas reliefs at the great Buddhist temples such as the Borobudur in Indonesia and the Angkor Wat in Cambodia relate the life of the Buddha in narrative form in order to provide his followers with a model path leading to enlightenment. Similarly, central to the formulation of Hindu worship and practice is the presentation of some of the great narrative epics, such as the *Rāmāyaṇa* and

Mahābhārata, which serve to provide examples for living to Hindus. The Jewish Bible is replete with rich narratives which are designed to illustrate a theological, doctrinal or moral lesson, such as the story depicting the conflict which developed between Moses and Pharoah. Such narratives from the Jewish tradition have been adopted by Christianity and supplemented by the parables of the New Testament, where Jesus couches his messages in narrative form; a clear example concerns the parable of the Good Samaritan. The third of the great monotheistic religious traditions, Islam, depends heavily upon narrative as a device for transmitting religious messages and morals. Exegetical works upon the Qur'ān often contain lengthy and colourful stories in order to expand, complement or make clear the Qur'anic text; the second great body of Islamic scripture, the *Ḥadīth* or Traditions of the prophet Muḥammad, are heavily narrative in form.

Some of the greatest theological expositions within the Jewish, Christian and Muslim traditions have been presented in narrative form. Within Judaism, for example, when the Prophet Nathan was faced with the task of pointing out to King David the latter's deceit in orchestrating the death of Uriah in order to marry Uriah's wife Bathsheba, Nathan chose to relate the story of the two men—one rich and one poor—in order to impress upon David the gravity of his sin. Nathan's story achieved its desired effect and the King responded in contrite and repentant terms.[1]

Within the Christian tradition one finds many similar cases where leading Christians employ narrative to outline theological doctrine. An example occurs in the interrogation of Stephen.[2] When confronted by the Jewish authorities who demand an exposition of Stephen's theological beliefs, Stephen responds with a recapitulation of Jewish history from the time of the patriarchs in order to demonstrate what he perceives to be the just claims of Jesus as the one anointed to deliver humanity from evil. Another example within the Christian tradition found outside the corpus of scripture is contained in *The Confessions* of Saint Augustine, where the early Christian saint provides a clear exposition of his theological and confessional commitment by relating in narrative form the historical development of his belief.[3]

---

[1] Refer to the Old Testament: II Samuel 11–12.

[2] Refer to the New Testament: Acts of the Apostles 6–7.

[3] In fact, the preaching of the early Christians was characteristically in narrative form, as it proved to be the most effective vehicle to enable new converts to reorient their lives to accommodate their new faith.

Within the Islamic tradition, from the earliest times the link is strong between story-telling and theological exposition. In pre-Islamic Arabia, the transmission of important information within and between tribes had been customarily via oral communication, and during the early Islamic period this was the means of transmission of the stories concerning the Prophet and his preaching which were taken up into the Islamic Traditions and the *Stories of the Prophets*. These traditions and stories in turn assumed an important function in providing material for the propagation of the faith. They were adopted in various Islamic locations, recounted in groups large and small, and in time grew in dimension, leading to the emergence of a series of accounts which had the dual purpose of proselytism and entertainment. With the spread of Islam beyond the Arab world, the use of narrative for preaching and spreading the faith was practised in the new regions. This was the case in the Malay world, where this approach appealed to the Malay penchant for rich narrative. Not only were Muslim stories recounted to emerging Malay Islamic congregations, but Hindu stories which had been popular among these communities for centuries were Islamized to aid in the spread of the new faith.[4]

With the development of the techniques of Qur'anic exegesis during the first centuries of the Islamic era, a narrative approach proved to be one of the most popular mediums for expressing this science. The great commentary by al-Ṭabarī (d. 923) represented a watershed in the history of Qur'anic exegesis, and in this monumental work the author drew upon virtually all exegetical studies which had preceded him in a most comprehensive manner. However, al-Ṭabarī was not only an exegete, but indeed was best known as a historian with his most famous surviving works being historical writings. The use al-Ṭabarī made of narrative as a device for theological exposition within his own commentary was to be developed further by subsequent exegetes.

1.1 *The Power of Narrative*

The important role played by narrative in the formulation of various theological traditions reflects the underlying power of this literary medium. Narrative serves to link an individual's past, present and

[4] Winstedt 1969:70.

future to form a continuum in which the individual can find his personal identity. The interlinking of past, present and future time as inter-related realities is stressed by St Augustine, who points to the common element of the present throughout time:

> But perhaps it might properly be said: there are three times, a present of things past, a present of things present, a present of things future.[5]

Stories serve to shape, interpret, and guide our response to existence, through addressing three basic aspects of our humanity: our intellectual life, our emotional life, and the struggle for our moral identity. Bettelheim[6] describes the appeal of stories to our primordial needs through their capacity to:

- Be world disclosing, where they assist us to find our way in a complex reality;
- Be self creating, where they assist us to find our personal identity;
- Be life directing, where they address moral dilemmas and present ways in which we can deal with such pervasive issues.

The unique quality of narrative is that it deals with all the above elements at the same time, and packages up a variety of responses to the basic dilemmas of the human condition. In contrast with explanatory modes of thought, such as rationalist criticism or abstract analysis, narrative provides the bridge to the world around—past, present and future—through our own experience, and provides us with the means to modify our world by identifying with others who have travelled this path before.

This seminal role of narrative in the individual's personal life story, and its incipient power, means that narrative, as the style which underlies the many facets of story telling, is a useful device in relating individual need to theological context. Crites' distinction of "sacred" and "mundane" stories[7] may be arguable in its application to various theological contexts, but one cannot escape the impression that it addresses a primordial distinction in the individual's world view. Sacred stories for followers of all faiths represent those unique stories which have the special resonance associated with the provision of an insight into God's knowledge and the individual's knowledge of

[5] Cited in Crites 1989:76.
[6] 1976:24–27.
[7] Crites 1989:69ff.

God. Such stories, typically anonymous, provide the essential element of belief across religious sectarian boundaries. Mundane stories, which could also be referred to as living stories, may not address the inner theological need or world view of the individual to the same degree as sacred stories, but nevertheless provide a living context through their function of representing everyday living circumstances, people and issues. Crites makes the important point that ". . . a religious symbol becomes fully alive to consciousness when sacred story dramatically intersects both an explicit narrative and the course of a man's personal experience."[8]

It is little wonder that narrative should be developed as a device for theological exposition by scholars of the various religious traditions. By the same token, it is understandable that narrative loses force as a theological device when individuals are unable to relate to particular stories adopted by a religious faith, whatever the reason may be. Elsewhere in this volume Burrell stresses the interconnectedness between canonical stories and our religious upbringing, pointing out that ". . . our canonical notions of narrative in fact reflect those traditions of revelation with which we are familiar." This has important ramifications for the role of narrative across religious traditions, especially where revelation plays a different role, such as in Christianity (where revelation serves primarily as a means for God to make himself known to his creation) and Islam (where revelation is a means for drawing attention to the coming of a Day of Judgement).

In the context of the preceding discussion, we proceed to examine narrative-based exegesis within Islam. The principal focus of this study is the commentary by al-Farrā' al-Baghawī, a prominent classical Islamic scholar who consciously chose narrative as his primary device for theological exposition. Attention is also devoted to two other Arab exegetes of the Qur'ān who together with al-Baghawī form a narrative triumvirate, as it were, and a work by one of their disciples in the Malay World.

2. *Al-Baghawī: Influences and Writings*

Some brief biographical information is necessary to provide a historical context for this study. Al-Ḥusayn b. Masʿūd b. Muḥammad

[8] Crites 1989:82.

al-ʿAllāma Abū Muḥammad al-Farrāʾ al-Baghawī originated from the vicinity of Herāt, in present day Afghanistan. The great medieval scholar al-Suyūṭī describes him as a Shāfiʿite authority in exegesis, traditions and jurisprudence. During his lifetime he had a reputation for temperance and piety, and it is reported that he renounced sumptuous foods, limiting himself to bread and olive oil.[9] This sparse diet does not appear to have affected his health; he died an octogenarian in Marw al-Rūdh sometime between 1117 and 1122,[10] and was buried beside his teacher Qāḍī Ḥusayn in the cemetery of al-Ṭālaqānī.

Al-Baghawī's great mentor in the field of Qurʾanic exegesis was al-Thaʿlabī (d. 1035), one of the first exegetes to work in the light of al-Ṭabarī. Al-Thaʿlabī is best known for two works:

- His Qurʾanic commentary, entitled *al-Kashf waʾl-bayān ʿan tafsīr al-Qurʾān*.
- A collection of stories of the prophets, entitled *ʿArāʾis al-majālis*.

Al-Thaʿlabī's approach to exegesis was narrative-based. He had key theological principles in which he drew upon a copious collection of traditions and stories to illustrate the particular theological issues or lessons which he wished to address. However, there is a degree of controversy which surrounds al-Thaʿlabī's commentary in Muslim circles, particularly regarding his use of traditions which were weak.

Al-Baghawī chose to develop his scholarly skills in a variety of areas, with the result that his literary output reflected a range of traditions: *Maṣābīḥ al-sunna* and *Sharḥ al-sunna* represent studies of the Traditions; *al-Tahdhīb* was a study of jurisprudence; *Maʿālim al-tanzīl*, which is the main focus of this present study, addressed exegesis of the Qurʾān. Despite this eclecticism in terms of focus, however, al-Baghawī's writings demonstrate an important common thread in an underlying commitment to the use of narrative as a major device for the illustration of doctrine and for interpretation of scripture. In this he was clearly influenced by his mentor, al-Thaʿlabī.

One of al-Baghawī's most famous works was *Maṣābīḥ al-sunna*, a comprehensive collection of Islamic traditions, which clearly demonstrates al-Baghawī's use of the Traditions as a tool of exegesis. This work presents traditions in a set order and hierarchy, according to authority:

---

[9] al-Dhahabī 1985: vol. 1, 227.

[10] Robson 1965:893.

1. Reliable traditions (*ṣaḥīḥ*, i.e. taken from Bukharī and Muslim).
2. Good traditions (*ḥasan*, e.g. from Abū Dā'ūd, al-Tirmidhī, et al.).
3. Traditions from a single authority considered unusual (*gharīb*).
4. Traditions considered weak (*ḍa'īf*); i.e. of questionable authenticity because of content or origin.

Note that al-Baghawī at times used the same methodology which had caused al-Tha'labī's commentary to become a cause of controversy; i.e. he included weak traditions. It is likely that he was influenced by al-Tha'labī in this. Nevertheless, al-Baghawī claims that he excluded all rejected traditions (*munkar*) and also all apocryphal traditions (*mawḍū'*) in this work. He did not indicate the various chains of authority (*isnād*) in this work, though the ordering of the traditions as described above somewhat offsets the lack of these chains.

2.1 Ma'ālim al-tanzīl

An examination of al-Baghawī's Qur'anic commentary *Ma'ālim al-tanzīl* ("The Signposts of the Revelation") quickly reveals his substantial dependence upon the commentary of al-Tha'labī, though he also drew on a range of supplementary sources which he identifies in the preface.

The compilation of al-Baghawī's commentary appears to have occurred in three stages.

- The first was probably the selection of what he intended to be the core of his commentary from that of al-Tha'labī. This practice was commonplace among classical exegetes;[11] rather than being seen as plagiarism, it was regarded more as an essential step in clarifying the author's own particular methodology or approach;
- The second was represented by al-Baghawī's references to the supplementary sources. Using a "cut and paste" approach, the author produced a work which was eclectic in terms of its source material;[12]
- The final stage is represented by that of editing or abridgement by

[11] Another example has been demonstrated by Tony Johns elsewhere in this volume, who showed that the *Marāḥ Labīd* of Muḥammad Nawawī al-Jāwī drew on the great commentary by Fakhr al-Dīn al-Rāzī for up to seventy-five percent of its exegetical discussion.

[12] Tony Johns also demonstrates that Nawawī did the same when compiling his commentary.

subsequent scholars. In classical exegesis, this might have occurred during the lifetime of the author, just after his death, or some considerable time after that. In the case of the commentary by al-Baghawī, it is recorded that it was abridged by Tāj al-Dīn Abū Naṣrī ʿAbd al-Wahhāb b. Muḥammad al-Ḥusaynī (d. 1471).

3. *Style and Content*

Al-Baghawī bases his work on a verse by verse treatment of the Qur'anic text, with a presentation of a range of opinions of the logia he is explaining, drawn from his source materials. The absence of lengthy chains of authority ensures that the text of his commentary is relatively uncluttered, and contains a fluid prose style which lends itself well to both skimming and detailed reading. However, not only does the relegation of source references to the preface prove beneficial to the style of the text, but it also points to the author's overriding concern with the text itself, rather than with a meticulous and scholarly listing of his sources. The author has chosen to focus on the text—and in most instances that means to focus on the stories within his text—rather than sacrificing some of the fluid narrative for philological detail.

The commentary not only concerns itself with theological exposition in narrative form, but addresses a range of other issues as well. There are regular discussions of variant readings on the Qur'anic text,[13] and occasional references to grammatical detail, though this is infrequent. But it is in presentation of story that al-Baghawī comes into his own. His commentary is memorable for its rich narrative content throughout. A cursory glance at the work quickly reveals the large proportion which is devoted to narrative commentary on Qur'anic verses, and a more detailed examination of the text reveals that al-Baghawī was eclectic not only in terms of the exegetical sources he drew upon, but also in terms of the religious traditions which he consulted in collecting the narratives contained in his commentary.

Al-Baghawī's work includes lengthy stories drawn from Jewish, Christian and Islamic traditions. At no stage does the commentator

---

[13] The great Malay exegete ʿAbd al-Ra'ūf of Singkel (d. 1693) continued the practice of taking discussion of the *qirā'āt* out of the narrative commentary and treating them separately, in writing *Tarjumān al-mustafīd*.

indicate that a story derives from non-Islamic sources, nor does he suggest that such stories are less worthy of attention than stories drawn from the Islamic tradition. An example is the account of David and Bathsheba presented in *Sūra Ṣād*, derived from Jewish traditions. A lengthy story drawn from Christian tradition which is included in his commentary is the account of the *Seven Sleepers of Ephesus* presented in al-Baghawī's treatment of the 18th Chapter of the Qur'ān, *Sūra al-Kahf*. Al-Baghawī's treatment of this story is examined in greater detail later in this study.

Though al-Baghawī's stories are lengthy, they are not the account of someone who merely wished to pad out his text. On the contrary, the style is that of someone who enjoyed story-telling and wished to address those who shared this pleasure. This is why al-Baghawī seems at times to be drawn into minute detail in his narratives, far more than is actually required for the purposes of his theological exposition. For it can quickly be seen in examining *Maʿālim al-tanzīl* that the length of the stories often seems to be out of proportion to the small theological point requiring amplification in individual Qur'anic verses. It is almost as if the commentator seemed to gain a measure of relief in leaving those sections of the Qur'anic text which are somewhat telescopic and entering the world of copious narrative where possible.

4. *Exegetical Descendents: Al-Khāzin*

Just as the commentary by al-Thaʿlabī provided the core of al-Baghawī's *Maʿālim al-tanzīl*, this latter work was itself to act as an exegetical ancestor for subsequent commentaries. The third generation in this triumvirate of narrative commentators is represented by the commentary by al-Khāzin (d. 1340) entitled *Lubāb al-ta'wīl fī maʿānī al-tanzīl*. Al-Khāzin was to enjoy significant popular acclaim beyond the Arab world because of the widespread appeal of the stories contained in his commentary. Ironically, al-Khāzin in a sense hijacked a significant part of al-Baghawī's popularity, for he reported the latter's stories generally verbatim,[14] but his popular appeal appears to have surpassed that of al-Baghawī.

[14] Though he did identify al-Baghawī as his primary source in his preface, as al-Baghawī had done with al-Thaʿlabī centuries before.

5. *The Popularity of the Narrative Commentaries in the Arab World*

It has been seen that the commentary by al-Thaʿlabī, the first of the narrative-based exegetical triumvirate, attracted criticism from certain Muslim circles. Some scholars, such as Ibn Ḥanbal, were opposed to the use of stories as a primary device for theological exposition per se. Nevertheless, al-Thaʿlabī's work appears to have had both its supporters and its detractors, and indeed some individual Muslim scholars were at once both supporter and critic. For example, ʿAbd al-Ghaffār b. Ismāʿīl al-Fārisī commends al-Thaʿlabī's reliability, but also refers to the controversy surrounding him, as follows:

> He is a true and reliable reporter. He reported from Abū Ṭāhir b. Khazīma and al-Imām Abī Bakr b. Mahzān the reader. Abū al-Ḥusn al-Wāḥidī based his commentary upon [al-Tha'labī's commentary] and commended it. It contained many traditions and many Sheikhs' names. But there are some scholars who consider that it could not be trusted and its reporting was not reliable.[15]

Though the criticism of al-Thaʿlabī was evidently somewhat counterbalanced by praise from various sources, such as Yāqūt (1179–1229),[16] the controversy surrounding al-Thaʿlabī's Qur'anic commentary may well be the reason that it is not widely used today.

The second work by the narrative triumvirate, al-Baghawī's *Maʿālim al-tanzīl*, attracted praise from a number of leading classical exegetes. Al-Khāzin described it as follows:

> . . . one of the greatest works in the field of exegesis, and one of [the field's] highest, most exalted and most brilliant; a collection of the most reliable of the Prophet's sayings, free from vagary, distortion, and alteration; adorned with stories of prophethood, embellished with legal judgements, decorated with strange stories and reports of the miraculous past, adorned with the best signs; clarifying by its analogies, and a model of eloquent language.[17]

It is noteworthy in this comment by al-Khāzin that he regarded al-Baghawī's inclusion of "strange stories and reports of the miraculous past" as representing a strength of the work.

---

[15] From *Siyāq Tārikh Nīsābūr*, reported in al-Dhahabī 1985: vol. 1, 221.

[16] Who writes in his *Muʿjam al-udabā'*, v. 5 p. 37: "Abū Isḥāq al-Tha'labī, reader, exegete, preacher, literateur, authority, memorizer, champion of significant writings: in [his] commentary are gathered various gems of meaning and signs, and words endowed with truth, and pointers for grammar and variant readings . . ." reported in al-Dhahabī 1985: vol. 1, 221.

[17] *Lubāb*: 3.

The great medieval scholar, Ibn Taymiyya, was also complimentary in referring to the *Maʿālim al-tanzīl*, but added an interesting comment with regard to its drawing upon al-Thaʿlabī:

> Baghawi's commentary is abridged from that of al-Thaʿlabī, but he safeguards his commentary from inferior traditions and heretical opinions.... It has been asked as to which of the commentaries is closer to the Book and the *Sunna*. Al-Zamakhsharī? Or al-Qurṭubī? Or al-Baghawī? Or others? As for these three commentaries and what is asked, [the one which] forsakes heresy and weak traditions is al-Baghawī; though his is an abridgement of al-Thaʿlabī's commentary, he deletes inferior traditions and heresies which are in [al-Thaʿlabī], and he deletes other things.[18]

Al-Baghawī attracts criticism from other quarters in terms which are reminiscent of the accusations levelled at the commentary of al-Thaʿlabī. Al-Katānī wrote in *al-Risāla al-mustaṭrafa*:

> There can be found in it—i.e. *Maʿālim al-tanzīl*—doctrines and anecdotes which can be judged by their weakness and shallowness....[19]

Nevertheless, al-Baghawī is forthright in defending the reliability of his work, and speaks as follows in the preface:

> That which is drawn from the Traditions of the Prophet of God within [my] book is either in conformity with a verse or is in clarification of a judgement; thus my book seeks its clarification from the *Sunna*... Moreover, I refrain from the mention of falsehoods and that which has no connection with the subject of exegesis....[20]

In this series of statements, al-Baghawī appears to be making an appeal to what he considers as orthodoxy in claiming that his writing is based on the *Sunna* and avoids including unreliable elements. This seems to be a formulaic response by the author which was of necessity presented in support of his writing, though the eclectic nature and style of his work suggests that his paramount concern was with presenting a readable and readily comprehensible text.

In spite of his declaration of reliability, however, the doubts cast on al-Baghawī's commentary not only relate to "weakness and shallowness" as suggested previously by al-Katānī, but challenge the veracity of the very stories which are so much a characteristic part of this commentary. Al-Baghawī has long been accused by some

---

[18] al-Dhahabī 1985: vol. 1, 229.
[19] Ibid.
[20] al-Baghawī *Maʿālim*: vol. 1, 31.

Muslim scholars of drawing on the *Isrā'īliyyāt*, stories brought into Islam by Jewish converts, without commenting on the reliability of these stories.[21] In other words, this is a double accusation: firstly, of drawing on potentially unreliable stories, and secondly of not commenting upon them with respect to their authenticity. Moreover, al-Baghawī's commentary copies contradictory reports from its exegetical predecessors, mentioning the sources in such cases, without weighing one report against another to determine comparative reliability.

The third of the narrative-based exegetical triumvirate, al-Khāzin, drew on his mentor al-Baghawī to provide the core of his work, and in the process adopted certain characteristic features which were to attract criticism from some quarters. As had been the case with its two narrative predecessors, the commentary by al-Khāzin was accused by some critics of reporting stories of dubious authenticity without employing appropriate critical tools. Again the basis of the criticism of al-Khāzin revolves around his recourse to the *Isrā'īliyyāt*, as is evident in the following critique:

> I read a great deal in this commentary and I found that it made mention in detail of the *Isrā'īliyyāt*: there was much which [al-Khāzin] copied from many commentaries which were concerned with this matter, such as the commentary by al-Thaʿlabī and others. But he mostly does not comment on that which is cited from the *Isrā'īliyyāt*, nor does he look at it with the eye of a discerning critic; on a number of subjects he passes on from the story without clarifying for us its weaknesses or falsehoods, except on rare occasions.[22]

In fact, the criticisms levelled at al-Khāzin's commentary serve to summarise the reservations felt by some Muslim scholars about all three members of the narrative triumvirate:

- Drawing on miraculous, strange stories, more akin to superstition,[23]
- Presenting stories which denigrate the good name of prophets,

---

[21] al-Dhahabī 1985: vol. 1, 230. The *Isrā'īliyyāt* were represented by a variety of narrative styles, ranging from essentially historical accounts of Biblical figures, especially prophets, to fables based in folklore derived from Jewish or Christian sources. It was especially the latter group, those stories clothed in folklore and fantasy, which resulted in the *Isrā'īliyyāt* being condemned per se by many leading Muslim scholars.

[22] al-Dhahabī 1985: vol. 1, 296.

[23] Note that al-Khāzin had described this as one of the strengths of al-Baghawī's commentary in a quotation cited earlier.

- Being unnecessarily verbose in presentation of minute detail,
- Presenting detailed stories without commenting upon their accuracy or reliability.[24]

Yet in spite of the various criticisms articulated so eloquently and clearly by various Muslim scholars over the centuries, the fact is that the stream of exegesis represented by Thaʿlabī-Baghawī-Khāzin gained a healthy measure of popularity in the Arab world. This is evident not only from the comments of certain scholars but also from an examination of various collections of Arabic manuscripts which date from the medieval and modern eras, where these commentaries, especially those by al-Baghawī and al-Khāzin, appear in significant numbers.

In this context, one must wonder why the narrative based commentaries by al-Baghawī and al-Khāzin which were considered by some scholars to be flawed could nevertheless continue to appeal to Muslim students and lay people. Before answering this question, it would be beneficial to address the final stage in our journey through the narrative exegetes: the Cambridge Malay commentary.

6. *The Influence of Narrative Exegesis in Southeast Asia*

The popularity of the narrative stream of exegesis in Southeast Asia has been considerable. The commentaries by both al-Baghawī and al-Khāzin have benefited from this; they acted as core sources for some of the earliest works of Qur'anic exegesis in Malay, while al-Khāzin's commentary served as a source for a number of other Malay language works and, indeed, has been translated in part into Malay.

6.1 *Content of the Cambridge Manuscript*

The library of the University of Cambridge holds in its manuscript collection the only extant copy of a commentary in Malay upon *Sūra al-Kahf*, the eighteenth chapter of the Qur'ān. This is one of the very oldest Malay language manuscripts extant, dating from around 1600.

This Malay language commentary drew heavily for its source

[24] For a detailed study of al-Khāzin's commentary and its reception throughout the Muslim world, refer Riddell 1993.

material on the narrative stream of Arabic commentaries.[25] In addition, other Arabic sources were used, including the authoritative classical work by al-Bayḍāwī. Unlike al-Baghawī and al-Khāzin before him, the anonymous author of this Malay commentary did not identify his principal sources in a preface, thus leaving us the task of dissecting his work in an attempt to reconstruct the research and writing technique employed by the author.

It appears that this work was written by the Malay author as he scanned the various sources which must have been laid out before him. He presents the text of the Qur'ān in Arabic in red letters, and follows each Qur'anic phrase with a section in Malay—sometimes long, sometimes short—which represents a literal translation of the particular source used.

His heavy dependence upon al-Baghawī and al-Khāzin meant that the Malay commentary is narrative based in exegetical approach. Indeed, it could be considered as a Malay descendent of the Arabic triumvirate examined earlier. It thus follows that, not only did the Malay author transfer to his work the rich and colourful stories contained in the works of his predecessors, but he also unconsciously transferred some of the characteristics of those earlier works which had attracted criticism from certain Muslim scholars. At no stage, however, does the Malay world of this period furnish us with conclusive evidence of a preoccupation with the debate which surrounded the Judeo-Islamic traditions and their use in exegetical works. We can find nothing which suggests that Muslim scholars in Southeast Asia were critical of this Malay commentary or other Malay commentaries which drew on any of the narrative exegetes examined earlier.

Though only one copy of the exegetical fragment in the Cambridge manuscript survives, its use of the narrative commentaries for source material was repeated in the compilation of *Tarjumān al-mustafīd* by ʿAbd al-Ra'ūf of Singkel (d. 1693), the first Malay language commentary on the whole Qur'ān, which used the *Jalālayn* commentary for its core, and which drew upon the work by al-Khāzin for supplementary narrative information. Thus the evidence for an interest on the part of Malay Muslim scholars during the early period of Islamisation in narrative based exegesis is considerable. Indeed, the interest shown in that region in the narrative exegetes has carried

[25] Riddell 1986:12; 1990:10–13.

through to the modern era, such that al-Khāzin's commentary is still one of the more popular exegetical works in Southeast Asia.

7. *A Sample Exegetical Narrative*

It would be useful to examine a sample of the narrative exegetical style under scrutiny in this paper. We will focus upon the Cambridge manuscript, in particular two stories—at least one and possibly both elaborated from sources ultimately of Christian origin—which are offered as exegetical comment upon several Qur'anic verses drawn from *Sūra al-Kahf*.[26]

The structure of the excerpt from the Cambridge Malay commentary reflects the structure of the commentaries of al-Baghawī and al-Khāzin from which it is largely drawn. A Qur'anic verse is presented; in the case of Qur'ān 18:9 the translation of the verse is contained in a twenty-five word rendering into English. This is then followed by a narrative commentary upon this short verse; the commentary occupies around 1700 words in the translated text, and only then does the work proceed to examining the next Qur'anic verse, Qur'ān 18:10.

An English rendering of the Cambridge Malay Commentary's treatment of Qur'ān 18:9 is as follows:

> (But do you consider), O Muḥammad, (that) concerning (all those) who entered into (the cave and) into (*al-raqīm*, they were one of our marvellous signs)?

It makes reference to two groups of people: the Companions of the Cave[27] and the Companions of *al-raqīm*. The commentary which follows the Qur'anic verse addresses the latter initially as that story is somewhat shorter than the story of the Companions of the Cave.

8. *The Companions of* al-raqīm

The Malay commentator has drawn the story of the Companions of *al-raqīm* from the classical commentary by al-Bayḍāwī (d. 1286). It should be noted that though al-Bayḍāwī's commentary includes

[26] The Malay text of part of this exegetical passage appears in Riddell 1989.
[27] Known in the Christian tradition as the *Seven Sleepers of Ephesus*.

extensive discussion of philological and linguistic issues, as well as matters pertaining to dogma and philosophy, the Malay commentator has chosen to select those sections which present rich narrative which can serve a didactic function. Moreover, although the meaning of *al-raqīm* itself is debated, the Malay commentator chooses to focus on that interpretation which tells a story.

The story commences with a graphic description of three young men walking down a road until they are forced to take refuge in a cave because of the rain. The entry to the cave is closed by a falling rock, thus preventing the young men from leaving. They then start recounting stories, ostensibly to find favour with God which will result in the cave door being unblocked, but also in a way which is easily imaginable for young people wishing to pass the time. The scenes which are portrayed by the young men are graphically simple but relevant, because they address real life issues. The first relates an experience which focuses upon worker dissatisfaction with employment conditions,[28] a circumstance which is as relevant today as it was at the time this story was written. The second young man speaks of real life problems concerned with hunger resulting from the high cost of rice. The third story relates to the devotion of a child to his parents in their old age, which again raises a series of issues of direct relevance to many readers.

These stories are appropriate candidates for fulfilling the role of narrative described in the first part of this article. They are useful as devices for providing a mirror of our everyday activity, serving to disclose the real world around us. They also succeed in providing guideposts to the reader who may well find himself in a similar situation of worker dissatisfaction or poverty or devotion to parents. The Malay exegete who compiled this commentary may well have chosen to include this story because of the real life situations depicted and their didactic potential.

9. *The Companions of the Cave*

The Malay commentator then turns his attention to the lengthy story concerning the Companions of the Cave. This story has its origins in

[28] This account is reminiscent of Jesus' Parable of the Workers in the Vineyard. Refer to the New Testament: Matthew 20:1–16.

the middle of the third century, when the Roman Emperor Decius[29] conducted a campaign of persecution throughout the Empire against adherents of the Christian faith. This particular story refers to a historical fact: the flight of seven young Christians from the city of Ephesus to a cave to escape the persecutions, where they were entombed when the soldiers of the Emperor blocked up the opening to the cave. In time, the story assumed legendary proportions, and it was related that the seven young men went to sleep and woke up after several centuries, by which time the Empire had adopted Christianity. The narrative contained in the Malay commentary records this story.

The earliest record of the legend in this form appears in Greek, and seems to have passed through several hands before being adopted by Islam. It is likely that Christian writers who wrote in Syriac learned the story and in turn transmitted it to Arab Christians, who probably represent the source of the tradition which is now found within Islam.[30] It is of interest to note that although the legend has Christian origins, it is now only generally known by specialists within Christianity, whereas it is widely known throughout the Muslim world because of its inclusion within the eighteenth chapter of the Qur'ān.[31]

The Qur'anic account of the story of the Seven Sleepers itself only provides the barest outline of the narrative and requires exegetical comment in order to fill out the details of the story; hence the copious narrative sections in exegetical works focusing upon the Qur'anic account. However, in order to obtain a clarification of the background and content of the story referred to in the Qur'ān, Islamic exegetes had to draw upon traditions deriving from Christian sources.

In the process, certain adaptions of these Christian stories evolved to account for the tastes and expectations of the Muslim readership. Such modifications were by no means unique; indeed, elsewhere in this present volume Frank has shown that Greek philosophy was likewise remoulded in part in the process of transmission to Muslim thought. The Islamic philosophers were the agents of such modifications, and responded to the requirements of their Islamic religious

[29] Ruled 249–251.
[30] Jourdan 1983:52.
[31] Indeed, the inclusion of this story in the Qur'ān has meant that Islam regards the events of the 309 year sleep as factual and historical, whereas within the Christian tradition this story is considered a legend.

audience. Moreover, Levtzion has similarly pointed to the assimilation of Sufi orders throughout the Islamic world into existing patterns of localised holy clans, leading to certain compromises with pre-Islamic regional customs. Rappoport[32] also provides crucial evidence for the methods of Islamic adoption of Jewish Haggadic tales, especially those relating to figures regarded as prophets by Islam: David, Solomon and Elijah. Thus it is not surprising that an originally Christian story such as that of the Seven Sleepers was partially recast to fit a Muslim mould in order to increase the likelihood of identification by Muslim readers with the story.

For this story, the Malay commentator draws his account from the detailed treatment in the narrative commentaries of al-Baghawī and al-Khāzin. The commentator does not risk criticism from Muslim scholars because of the Christian origins of this story for several reasons. Firstly, the core of the account was contained in the Qur'ān itself, thus assuring the enlarged version a considerable degree of authority. Secondly, the account of the legend had already been related by authoritative Muslim sources from the very earliest period of Islam. Ibn 'Abbās, one of the great forerunners of Qur'anic exegesis and a companion of the Prophet, recorded an early version of this legend sometime before his death in 687.[33] Thus the account already had a certain degree of royal lineage, as it were. Finally, the account was adapted to fit the expectations of the receiving milieu, as indicated above.

10. *Adaptation of the Account*

It is of interest to observe how this process of adaptation occurred. Close examination of the text reveals that, though the story relates to seven young Christians, Muslim terminology and concepts have been used to place the story within an appropriately Muslim context.

Certain formulaic expressions which are well established within Islam are used to create an Islamic environment for the story. These expressions serve to remind the reader that although the principal characters are Christians, the broad context of their faith is consistent with the basic tenets of Islam. For example, upon waking from their lengthy

[32] 1995.
[33] Jourdan 1983:15.

sleep, the young men are curious to know how long they have slept, but rather than discussing and reaching consensus on the amount of time, they acknowledge that "God alone knows how long we have slept"; this recalls the standard Islamic phrase of *wa'llāhu aʿlam* used to acknowledge God's omniscience in contrast to the limits of human knowledge.

Likewise, when faced with the danger of emerging from the cave, the young men place their fate in God's hands in saying "If we all die, let it be in [a state of] belief in the Unity of the One God *in shā'a 'llāh*". The inclusion of the Arabic phrase meaning "God willing" is in direct fulfilment of Qur'ān 18:23–24 which records how Muḥammad was rebuked by God for declaring he would do something without qualifying it with the words *in shā'a 'llāh.*[34]

Another example of the use of such formulaic phrases occurs with each reference to the name of Jesus, which is followed by the phrase "May peace be upon him", reflecting the standard Islamic formulaic pronouncement after each mention of prophets' names.

One of the most striking examples in the exegetical account presented in the Malay commentary which demonstrates the effort to assist the readers to identify with an Islamic story in spite of its Christian roots occurs when one of the seven young men, Yamlīkhā, approaches the city of Ephesus after waking from his centuries-long sleep. Expecting to find a pagan city ruled by an Emperor who persecutes followers of the One God, Yamlīkhā is astounded to see a sign over the main gate to the city which reads "There is no God but God, and Jesus is the spirit of God."[35] This is a direct adaptation of the first pillar of Islam.[36] As the story predates the Islamic era, it was not possible for the commentators to mention Muḥammad as does the first pillar of Islam; instead, they replace the reference to Muḥammad with the reference to Jesus, but the overall context of the declaration of witness is expressed in distinctly Islamic terms.[37]

A further example which demonstrates the exegete's desire to place

[34] The Cambridge Malay commentary includes a lengthy exegetical narrative upon these two verses, demonstrating the context for God's rebuke of the prophet. The narrative is again drawn from al-Baghawī's commentary.

[35] Arabic *lā ilāha illā allāh wa ʿĪsā rūḥ allāh.*

[36] "There is no God but God, and Muḥammad is the Messenger of God."

[37] It is interesting to note that while the Malay commentary expresses this declaration of witness in the above terms, al-Baghawī's account on which the Malay commentary was based does not specify what the sign said. Ibn ʿAbbās' account of the Companions of the Cave expresses the sign as follows: "There is no God but

the story within a strongly Islamic framework occurs when the Emperor Bandūsīs[38] and his followers arrive at the cave to marvel at the miracle that has been performed. The Cambridge manuscript, based on al-Baghawī, reports that ". . . they pronounced the *tasbīḥ* and the *taḥmīd*", referring to standard Islamic pronouncements in Arabic designed to glorify God.

Elsewhere, there are numerous ad hoc references placing the Seven Sleepers within an Islamic context. They are referred to as "followers of the Islamic faith"; they encounter indications ". . . of a Muslim city . . ." in entering Ephesus; they instruct Yamlīkhā to "buy . . . permissible food which has been sacrificed in the name of God. . . ."

At several points, the commentator indicates that some Christians averted religious infidelity by remaining "faithful to the religion of Jesus"; this statement is clarified immediately afterwards by the phrase "by way of asserting the Unity and worshipping God". The commentator further stresses the Islamic perception of the Qur'anic notion of what true Christianity was by having the young men declare before the Emperor that "we will not turn our back on the Unity".

Further on, the commentator refers to the young men performing their devotions in a way which is closely reminiscent of the five pillars of Islam; he states that "they occupied themselves in prayer, fasting, praising God, requesting prayer intercessions, giving alms and begging God's mercy." The only pillar which is not mentioned in this statement is the performance of the pilgrimage to Mecca, which would clearly have been out of place.

Finally, when the souls of the Sleepers are taken up to Heaven, the Emperor Bandūsīs instructs that a place of worship (called "mosque" in the text) be built on the site to commemorate the miracle.

All of these features are effective in acting as guideposts for the Muslim reader to negotiate the various contours of this story. They greatly assist the task of identification with the story by the reader, and enable the reader to seek and to find morals and examples for living within the story. The devices discussed above which were designed to cast the story within an Islamic mould achieved the desired effect of linking narrative with the personal experience and sacred story of the audience.

God, and Jesus is the Messenger of God", which is even more strongly reminiscent of the first pillar of Islam [Jourdan 1983:27].

[38] Theodosis II, who ruled 408–450.

11. *Narrative Style and Theological Perspectives*

The narrative style of the exegetical treatment of the Companions of the Cave story is replete with a variety of devices designed to add colour to the account and to captivate the reader. The narrative interpolations between the Qur'anic verses serve to add life to a somewhat compressed Qur'anic account, allowing the reader to journey off into the world of rich narrative but to come back from time to time to the Qur'anic essence.

The reader is elevated high above the tale; he knows throughout the story what is to become of the young men, although the young men themselves do not know. The reader is comfortable in the knowledge that the young men will not be captured and tortured by Emperor Daqyānūs, for the Qur'anic account identifies from the outset that the young men were "one of God's marvellous signs". In this sense, this story is at variance with the model presented by Alter[39] who in referring to biblical tales indicates that "the assurance of comprehensive knowledge is thus implicit in the narratives, but it is shared with the reader only intermittently and at that quite partially."

This story provides a window into the culture being depicted. The image of Yamlīkhā being surrounded and mocked as if he were insane when he returned to Ephesus gives us a poignant insight into the treatment of the socially marginalised at the time of the story. Human emotions are portrayed graphically; the story provides instances of suspense, violence, brutality, and fear, and these are counterbalanced by feelings of relief, friendship, loyalty and piety. This is a real life story with real life actors whose characterisation spans time and cultural differences. The spanning of time is reinforced by the interchange between the past and the present, with the former represented by the period of the flight of the young men, and the latter represented by their experiences after waking from their sleep.

The story neatly resolves the principal issues. The discovery of the box with the tablets recording the story of the Seven Sleepers by Emperor Bandūsīs answers all the lingering questions which any of the principal actors may have had.

The commentator's intention is not only to tell a good story, but even more so is it to provide a moral for his readership. The lengthy

---

[39] 1981:184.

story of the Companions of the Cave includes an overt moral, which is transmitted via narrative, as follows:

> God had put them to sleep for three hundred and nine years . . . to demonstrate the extent of His power to all his servants, [and to show] that He would resurrect the dead on the Day of Judgement, and so that they would know that the Day of Judgement would come, of which there is no doubt.

In other words, the miraculous event described briefly in the Qur'ān and retold in greater detail in the commentaries served several purposes:

- To point to the immense power of God;
- To demonstrate God's intention to resurrect all those who had ever lived on the Day of Judgement;
- To sound a warning to all people that the Judgement Day awaited them.

This portrayal of God is clearly one of transcendence, in line with Ashʿarite orthodoxy. God is all powerful and commands his creatures, who should obey his heavenly injunctions. There is no suggestion of God being immanent in this theology, as one would expect from reading Sufi mystical works by Malay scholars contemporaneous with the Cambridge manuscript, such as Hamzah Fansuri.

Moreover, these accounts also identify with the debate concerning determinism and free will. Al-Baghawī, as a product of the Shāfiʿite school, was not a supporter of those who argued that man had control over his own destiny. Rather al-Baghawī's belief in determinism as argued by the Ashʿarites is clearly demonstrated in the stories under examination. The commentary reiterates on many occasions that God is in control, and the young men recognise this.

Thus we have the example cited earlier of the young men acknowledging God as the one who knows how long they slept in the cave, rather than claiming the right of independent knowledge in this instance. Elsewhere, the entrance to the cave is sealed by the soldiers of Daqyānūs; in response the commentator writes:

> God in his wisdom ordered the cave to be sealed in order to bestow on them [His] blessing.

Further on, the cave entrance is unblocked by a shepherd seeking to establish an enclosure for his goats. Again, the commentator depicts this not as an action decided upon by the shepherd himself, but rather as an action carried out by the shepherd who is moved by God.

When entering Ephesus, Yamlīkhā is fearful of being recognised and arrested by the soldiers of Daqyānūs. However, ". . . through God's destiny, no-one recognised him. . . ." Again, the actions of men are merely the reflex actions determined by God's will for man and the world.

A certain symbolism surrounds the cave in both stories. It seems to be representative of the prison of human life, in which we are all enclosed. Only God is able to liberate us from entombment; this is demonstrated in both stories.

In the case of the Companions of *al-raqīm*, the commentator demonstrates that God provides humanity with an exit from all situations of entrapment; good works serve as good preparation for later finding favour with God, and if mankind is in times of trouble and if the way has been prepared through the performance of good works, then God will assist us. There is thus a clear theology of redemption underlying this story; the recounting of moral fortitude serves to win God's favour, leading to release.

Moreover, the story of the Companions of *al-raqīm* demonstrates that redemption comes from community. No single story recounted by the three young men is sufficient to provide them with an exit from their predicament; it is only when the various individual contributions are combined as a community effort that God's favour is forthcoming in full and the door is completely opened. This is consistent with the notion of *umma* (community), so central to Islamic thinking.

12. *Conclusions*

In this paper, we have examined the role of narrative within a theological context and established its significant contribution to theological exposition. We have seen that the success of narrative in theological writing depends very significantly on its ability to strike a chord in the reader in terms of personal experience, sacred story, and its ability to provide a sense of guidance and direction in interpreting the world around.

We have also seen that three important works of Qur'anic exegesis drew heavily on narrative as their principal device for theological exposition. The first of these three drew on certain weak traditions which led to criticism from certain scholarly sources, and the subsequent descendents of this work inherited the criticisms in adopting the stories which had been used.

It has also been shown that, in spite of the controversy surrounding the narrative commentaries because of their drawing on stories regarded as apocryphal in some quarters due to the lax use of source critical techniques, they achieved a measure of popularity, particularly in the non-Arab Muslim world, but also to a certain degree in the Arab world, because of their ability to meet the needs of narrative within a theological context. Once the stories were adapted and interpreted within a Muslim context, their acceptance by Muslim readers was more likely. Moreover, the comparative irrelevance of the Jewish-Muslim debate in Southeast Asia led to a greater degree of popularity in that area. But above all, the ability of these stories to address real life issues and to provide a point of relevant identification for readers meant that in spite of scholarly criticism, the works have survived within popular culture, especially on the geographical periphery of the Muslim world. In these locations, the narrative triumvirate, and their Malay descendent, appear to have achieved the essential intersection between narrative, sacred story, and personal experience.

TRANSLATION AS EXEGESIS

The Opening Sūra of the Qur'ān in Chinese

RAPHAEL ISRAELI

1. *The Problem of Translating the Qur'ān*

For Muslims the Qur'ān is not only a sacred book of divine inspiration revealed to the Prophet of Islam, but it is also the faithful reproduction of the Original Scripture in Heaven. Although the Holy Book was an Arabic Qur'ān intelligible to Muḥammad and his people, as the Scriptures of the *ahl al-kitāb* (People of the Book—Jews and Christians) had been revealed to them in their own languages, this distinction tended to fade in the religious consciousness of Muslims. The ideas of eternity and uncreatedness (*ghayr makhlūq*) of the Word of Allāh were applied by Muslim theologians to the Original Scripture in Heaven and then, by extension, to all Arabic copies of the Qur'ān. Following al-Ashʿarī, orthodox Islam held the view that the written or recited Qur'ān is identical in being and reality with the uncreated and eternal Word of God;[1] hence the traditional Muslim reluctance to translate the Holy Book into other languages. However, the Ḥanafī *madhhab* of which Chinese Islam is part, took a more liberal stand on this matter than the other *madhhab*s.

Another reason for this reluctance is that Islam, in theory, unlike Christianity for example, offers no facilities for those outside its pale to study its character before they embrace it. A man must become Muslim first by pronouncing the *shahāda* (there is no God but Allāh, and Muḥammad is His Prophet) before he can learn what his obligations are. Therefore, the Qur'ān may not be sold to Unbelievers and Muslim soldiers are advised not to take it with them into hostile territory for fear that the Infidel might get hold of it. Many copies of the Book bear upon them the warning to Unbelievers not to touch, and some pious Muslims refuse even to teach Arabic grammar to

[1] Buhl 1961:285.

non-Muslims, for fear that the rules might be illustrated by quotations from the Book.[2]

For a pious Muslim the inimitability of the Arabic Qur'ān (*i'jāz*) stated in the Book itself[3] and extolled by Muslim theologians and commentators throughout the ages makes any translation a vain and hopeless attempt.[4] The reality, however, is that for most Muslims Arabic is a dead language. So, while Muslim religious literature has, for many centuries, been written in languages other than Arabic (Persian, Turkish, Urdu, Bengali, Chinese etc.), the question about translating the Qur'ān itself has remained contested. On the other hand, the danger of alienating non-Arabic speaking Muslims from the Faith has always loomed more and more threateningly. It is significant, therefore, that some of the revivalist movements in the Muslim world which were concerned precisely with the preservation of Arabic as the Holy Language also encouraged the translation of the Qur'ān into other languages,[5] something like the tense intermixture of radical fundamentalism and determined modernism which characterised some Muslim reformers. Thus we find such a revivalist as Shāh Walī Allāh in India simultaneously initiating a movement of intellectual appreciation of the Qur'ān by laymen, by founding a school (in 1743) where Qur'ān and *ḥadīth* were taught under his personal direction, while at the same time writing a treatise on the problems of translating the Qur'ān.[6]

According to many an author, any translation of the Qur'ān not only betrays the meaning of the original, but also loses much of its poetic and emotional effectiveness:

> Anyone who has read it in the original is forced to admit that this caution seems justified; no translation, however faithful to the meaning, has ever been fully successful. Arabic, when expertly used, is a

---

[2] Cf. Margoliouth 1938.

[3] "Truly, if Man and Jinn agree to produce the like of the Qur'ān they will not produce the like of it" (17:90).

[4] For example, al-Ṭabarī wrote: "Among the miracles of the Prophet is the Qur'ān ... I have never met a book written by an Arab, or Persian, or Greek, which contained, like the Qur'ān, unity and glorification of the Most High God ... Who has ever written, since the creation of the world, a book with such prerogatives and qualities ... while the man to whom it was revealed was unlettered, not even knowing how to write ...", cited in von Grunebaum 1953:97–98.

[5] Note the similarity with Reform Judaism in America which maintains schools to teach Hebrew to the young, but recites the ritual in English during services (not prayers) in temples (not synagogues).

[6] Ahmad 1966:205–206. See also Zwemer 1915.

> remarkably terse, rich and forceful language, and the Arabic of the Qur'ān is by turns striking, soaring, vivid, terrible, tender and breath-taking . . . It is meaningless to apply adjectives such as "beautiful" or "persuasive" to the Qur'ān; its flashing images and inexorable measures go directly to the brain and intoxicate it . . . It is not surprising, then, that a skilled reciter of the Qur'ān can reduce an Arabic-speaking audience to helpless tears, that for thirteen centuries it has been ceaselessly meditated upon or that for great portions of the human race, the "High Speech" of Seventh-century Arabia has become the true accent of the Eternal.[7]

Three verses of the Qur'ān explain the intrinsic value of the Book as specifically Arabic: "This is the miracle manifested in the Book's revelation, that we have sent it down as an Arabic Qur'ān" (12:1–2), and: "Had we made it a Qur'ān in a foreign tongue, they would have said: why is the miracle of its revelations not performed in plain view? Why a foreign speech and an Arab listener?" (41:44). True, Jews and Christians had their own books in their own languages (Hebrew and Aramaic), but the fact that the latest divine message was dispensed to humanity in Arabic, displaces and replaces, as it were, not only the validity of the previous messages but also their linguistic manifestation. The Arabic version remains, then, supreme and any attempt to render it into other languages by definition depreciates its significance.[8]

2. *Chinese Translations of the Qur'ān*

All the problems inherent in any translation of the Qur'ān acquire an added complexity in Chinese, due to the peculiar structure of the Han language, which gives rise, among others, to the following challenges:

- How to render phonetically Islamic names and other terms in Arabic;
- How to make the original meanings of the Holy Text relevant and intelligible to the Chinese world of discourse;

---

[7] Williams 1961:2. See also Gibb 1953:37, "no man in fifteen hundred years has ever played on that deep-toned instrument with such power, such boldness, and such range of emotional effect."

[8] For this discussion, see also Pedersen 1984:12–19.

- While the Book had one Arabic canonical version, which was universally recognised, like the canons in other faiths, different translations of the Qur'ān into Chinese necessarily produce various meanings thereof, with all attending difficulties of interpretation and relevance.

It is therefore no coincidence that very early on, two different opinions were voiced among Chinese-Muslim scholars regarding the advisability of translating the Qur'ān into the Han language; some were loathe to risk the alteration of meaning via interpretation, especially as most Chinese Muslims were ignorant of the context of the revelations of the text and of its original significance; others, understandably argued that if the text were not translated, it would be difficult to diffuse it and to make it dominant in the lives of Chinese Muslims.[9] This argument had started under the Ming Dynasty (1368–1644) and lasted until the Qing (1644–1911), before consensus was achieved to the effect that the Qur'ān must be translated into Chinese so that those who are unable to comprehend the original could at least come in touch with the Chinese version.[10] All that long while, since the introduction of Islam in China as early as the Tang period (618–906), the Qur'ān had never been mentioned by its proper name, although it had been alluded to in written phrases or in epigraphs in mosques as "The Scripture is all in a foreign language", or the "Muslims are absorbed in reciting the Scripture."[11]

During the Qing period, the word Qur'ān in various transliterations began taking root in Chinese writings (*Kuruan* and the like), while Muslim scholars earlier on leaned towards *Gulan* (a "Scholar Flower"). However, the little Arabic the Muslims in China learned at the mosque with their *Akhund* with the advent of the Qing was hardly enough for them to read the Qur'ān, and most of them were only able to commit to memory the most familiar passages thereof, without understanding much, or anything, of its meaning. Often, even the *Akhund* had no better than a general idea of the significance of the text. Thus, until the Qing, the Islamic Scripture and its meaning

[9] Ma 1982:2–3.
[10] Ibid.
[11] Jin 1981:128–132. Interestingly enough, in some Chinese sources which knew little or nothing of Arabs and Arabia, the Qur'ān is called the "Buddhist Scripture" (ibid.).

were principally expounded only orally throughout the Muslim community. The oral transmission of the Qur'ān produced errors in the recited text, so much so that ultimately it became unintelligible.[12]

According to Jin Yijiu, the history of translating the Qur'ān can be divided into three periods:

- Extract translations occurred when the translators combined their own writings and commentaries about the Qur'ān with selected translations of certain passages of the Qur'anic text. These were the great 17th and 18th century masters such as Wang Daiyu, Ma Zhu and Liu Zhi.[13]
- While the above category of "translations" was of not much practical use to Chinese Muslims, inasmuch as they could not lean on those occasionally translated passages of the Book for their rituals, the end of the 18th century marked the beginning of selective translations from the Qur'ān into Chinese, for practical use. These first attempts of systematic translations were of two kinds: transliteration of the selections into Chinese characters, so that Chinese believers could recite the text in "Arabic" on their own.[14] Another kind was a real translation into Chinese that was added to the transliteration, with a commentary.[15]
- Finally, entire translations of the Qur'ān were attempted from the 1920s,[16] on several occasions. While Jin Yijiu has identified five complete translations done to date,[17] Ma Song-ting speaks of eight

---

[12] This author can attest from first-hand experience in the 1970s with Muslim *Akhunds* in Taiwan that the scope of their knowledge of the Qur'ān and its significance was very flimsy indeed.

[13] Wang Daiyu, in his *Zhengjiao Zhenquan* ("Explanation of the Correct Religion"), published non-systematic translations and commentaries of some forty chapters of the Book; Ma Zhu, in his *Jinjing Shu* ("A Memorial to the Throne for Presenting the Scripture"), compiled some of the main passages of the Book for the perusal of the Emperor (Kang-Xi) without affording him the reality of holding the Book itself. Liu Zhi, similarly, made many quotes from the Qur'ān followed by an approximate translation into Chinese. See Jin 1981:98–99.

[14] Under this category see *Hanli Heting* ("Qur'ān into Chinese characters", 1882); and *Heting Zhengjin* ("Selection from the True Qur'ān"). Ibid. 99.

[15] E.g. *Jing Han Zhujie Heting* ("Selections from the Qur'ān in Arabic and Chinese", 1866), Ma Kuilin and Yang Deyuan's *Baoming Zhenjing* ("Selections from the Precious Qur'ān", 1919), and Li Ting Xiang's *Tianjing Yijie* ("A Paraphrase of the Qur'ān", 1924). Ibid. 99–100.

[16] According to Jin Yijiu, even earlier attempts were made in the 19th century, e.g. by Ma Fuchu which were never brought to completion. Ibid. 100.

[17] Ibid. 100.

such translations,[18] some of which overlap with the former. Only after these complete translations of the Qur'ān had been achieved, did research begin in China about the substance of the Book, and teaching of the Holy text became part of religious studies curricula throughout China.

2.1 *Missionaries Interpret the Word of Allāh*

One word should be said about the role of the missionaries in interpreting the Chinese Qur'ān for the Believers. Ironically, the Christian missionaries in China, as in other countries, had shown great interest in the translations of the Arabic Qur'ān into local languages in their places of service. Part of the reason for this curiosity regarding their rival religion was certainly apologetic in import, emerging as it did in the context of showing in the well-understood local tongue that "much similarity between the Qur'ān and the Bible could be utilised"[19] in the missionary presentations to the native populations toward their evangelization. Missionaries in China, for example, had noted that when they entered into conversation with their prospective proselytes, one of the first remarks made by Muslims was that "our faith and theirs are very similar and that they also know about the Ehr-sa ('Īsā = Jesus) that we preach."[20] However, translating the Qur'ān into the local language, in order to make it available, acceptable and understandable to the Muslims, exposed the vast theological gap between Jesus as the Son of God, as the Christians would have it, and His Prophetic image as the Muslims grasped it. Furthermore, by positing Muḥammad, the human Messenger of God, as the Seal of the Prophets and their greatest, this would have necessarily dwarfed Jesus as the Saviour and elevated Muḥammad in his place. The Missionaries realised full well that if they had no other Christ to present than the Muslim one, then they no longer had a mission. Faced with this impasse, Christian missionaries in China determined first to study the local versions of the Qur'anic translation[21] in order

[18] Ma 1982:1–2.
[19] Syrdal 1937:72.
[20] Ibid. The Chinese Muslims also remarked, according to the author, that they considered Jesus as a Prophet and not the Son of God. The Missionaries who worked among Chinese Muslims thought that the Qur'anic concept of Jesus "breathes of the earth and carnality" and that He was thereby "robbed of His divinity and His glory".
[21] See above.

to gauge the natives' cast of mind. They soon discovered that "where a passage became dangerously similar to Christian teachings, it was sapped of its direct meaning by the explanation given by zealous [Muslim] commentators."[22] Sometimes, the problem was resolved by a joint translation of the Qur'ān into Chinese made by a local Muslim and foreign non-Muslim experts.[23] This sort of translation made serious searches to find the bridges that could span the deep abyss between the two theological approaches.[24]

3. *The* Fātiḥa *in Chinese*

At the turn of the century, a "Chinese Commentary on the Qur'ān" was diffused in China, which carried neither the name of the author nor the exact date of publication. Chinese phonetic rendering is indicated after the Arabic text, all followed by a Chinese explanation (not commentary). The Arabic text itself was not translated into Chinese, perhaps under the assumption that the Chinese Muslims still understood the original meaning, and the explanation in colloquial Chinese amounted to no more than a general annotation of the key terms.[25] This text, the original of which I have not so far tracked down, is however indicative of the cast of mind of the Muslims at the end of Imperial China and of the way the Qur'ān was interpreted and understood by them, in comparison with the most recent versions published in the People's Republic of China, which are entirely in Chinese without annotation or explanation, and are written, as one would expect, in simplified characters. This modern Chinese, as it is used in contemporary intellectual circles, might shed some light on the way the Qur'anic text is understood and interpreted today. In Taiwan too there has been, since the forced transfer of the "Republic of China" to that island, a surprisingly high Muslim scholarly activity in the Qur'anic field. Surprising, because unlike the Muslim community in Mainland China, which could be

[22] Ibid. 73.
[23] Ma 1982.
[24] Rev. William Goldsack, a missionary of the Australian Baptist Society, was a great master in the field. He undertook to translate the Qur'ān into Bengali in 1908. It was printed with Christian comment and the explanation of difficult passages. This method was believed to allow a "schoolmaster to lead Moslems to Christ". See Zwemer 1915:258.
[25] See Farjenel and Bouvat 1908:540–547. See also Zwemer 1915:256–257.

counted by the tens of millions, Muslim supporters of Chiang Kai-shek, who moved to Taiwan in 1949, hardly accounted for more than a few tens of thousands. A translation, done in Chinese classical characters (unlike the Communist simplified characters in the People's Republic), was published by the Islamic Research Institute of the Chinese Academy of Science, during the 1950s, and was authored by Bai Jianmin. The full title advertised a "Translation and Explanation in Mandarin of the Qur'ān". Bai wrote in his version, that he found no translation of the Qur'ān that was "adequate". He set out specifically to correct the early translation by Wang Jing-Jai, but after many attempts he had to admit that it "was easier to start afresh with a new translation rather than correct an existing one". The fruit of his seven years work was first published in 1958 in Taipei, and then again in 1968, one year after his death.

One of the latest and authoritative translations published in the Mainland was authored by Ma Jian and saw the light of day in 1981, under the auspices of the Social Science Publication House in Beijing.

In the following pages, an attempt will be made to compare the earliest text of the anonymous beginning-of-the-century version with the 1981 version of Ma Jian. When necessary, Bai Jianmin's version of 1958, published in Taiwan, will be invoked to clarify points of controversy. Bai's version has the advantage of adding at the end of each *sūra* his own commentary in modern literary Chinese, to supplement the quasi-classical text of his translation. In this article these three versions will be referred to as:

1. The "early text", i.e. that of the early 20th century
2. The "Taiwan text", i.e. Bai's version of 1958; and
3. The "Mainland text", in Ma's version of 1981.

Let us delve into the *Fātiḥa*, the opening *sūra* of the Qur'ān, as an example.

3.1 *The Title*

The early text simply carries the title *Fātiḥa*, transliterated into Chinese. Since all believers repeated this text in their prayers, they all supposedly knew what the term meant.

In the Mainland text, the term *Kai Duan* (a beginning, a start) is preceded by "Chapter Number One" and followed by the transliteration *Fa-ti-hai* between parentheses to signify the original vocal rendering of the text. A sub-title explains that "This chapter is of Mecca—i.e. Meccan" (not "revealed in Mecca"), and that the entire chapter (*zhan*) consists of seven verses (*jie*). However, while the *basmala* (*bi'smi 'l-lāhi 'l-raḥmāni 'l-raḥīm*) is only an introduction in the original Arabic text and not considered to be the first verse, the Chinese translations take the title as an introduction and the introduction as Verse One. It is interesting to note that in subsequent chapters, the *basmala* is not numbered, and only serves as an introduction to the verses thereafter enumerated. Bai's Taiwan version, which of all three versions is the only one to carry both a translated text and a commentary in Chinese, adds an explanation based on the classical commentaries regarding the revelation of the *Fātiḥa*. He specifies that the *Fātiḥa* "descended" or was "revealed" twice from heaven, once to Mecca and then again to Medina. This probably refers to the Muslim classification of the entire Qur'ān into "Meccan" or "Medinan" *sūras*, corresponding to the successive periods of prophecy of Muḥammad in those two cities. As Islamic tradition has it, the entire Qur'ān "descended" in the "Night of Destiny" (*layla al-qadr*) into the soul of the Prophet.

The author/commentator further explains that the whole *Fātiḥa* has descended in a style of prayer to teach the believers how to address God. This opening chapter, comments the author, is also called the "seven verses which are to be often read", based on the command of 15:87, which reads: "We have given you the seven oft-repeated verses of the great Qur'ān." Bai also mentions in his commentary that before people recite any passage of the Qur'ān out loud, they "must make it clear that what they recite is in the language of Allāh." Presumably, Arabic being the original Word of God, anyone who recites it in another language might either be led to forget that it had been originally transmitted in Arabic by God to the Prophet, or to believe that Chinese is or was the language of God. Hence the emphasis of the commentator on the need to repeat the *basmala* before every chapter, as it is indeed written in the Arabic text itself, where a *basmala* precedes every *sūra* of the Holy Book, except for the ninth *sūra*, which is considered a continuation of the eighth *sūra*, and therefore is exempted from the *basmala*. The commentator stresses that the *basmala* itself was not sent down from Heaven, and that it only has become a matter of custom for

Muslims to cite it aloud before they do or say something, including reciting text from the Qur'ān.

3.2 *Verse 1—In the Name of Allāh, the Beneficent, the Merciful*

The early transliterated text explains the *basmala* sentence as "May the adored name of God be exalted, who spreads his compassion over everyone in this world, and will remain the only compassionate in the hereafter."

The Mainland text is much more complex and telling.

3.2.1 *Allāh*

Allāh is rendered *Zhen Zhu* = "True Lord". Since the Rite controversy under the Emperor Kang Xi (1660–1720) when the Jesuits and their opponents struggled to find the Chinese equivalent of their Christian God,[26] there has hardly been a conclusively and universally accepted rendering of the monotheistic God. *Zhen* was frequently used in Buddhism and Daoism in China, meaning "true" or "real", as in *Zhen Ren* = a True Man, the person who has perfected himself before attaining the Dao (Daoism) or *Zhen Zi* = the "True Son" of Buddhism.[27] In the Muslim context in China, the term acquires an added significance of specificity, because Islam dubs itself *Ching Zhen Jiao* (pure and true teaching), and in this context Allāh would mean the true Lord of the true faith, "true" being, of course, Muslim. Moreover, one of the Buddhist connotations of *Zhen Ren* is the "one who bears testimony to orthodox principles", a strikingly similar

[26] This debate in which various Christian denominations have been in disagreement centres around the question whether existing Chinese words should be borrowed, with all the attendant problems of inter-cultural exchange of idioms, or a new term be coined. The existing terms: *Shang Di* (The Supreme Ruler), *Tian* (Heaven) and others, had profoundly different connotations in the Chinese mind and would easily be misapprehended by new Chinese converts. Schereschevsky, the first translator of the Bible into Chinese, preferred the term *Tienzhu* (Lord of Heaven). I am grateful for this illumination of the terms and the relevant bibliography to my colleague Irene Eber, who has been working on Schereschevsky's translation of the Bible. See also Barnett and Fairbank 1985; Legge 1832; and Bloget 1893.

[27] In Daoism the term *Zhen ren* also means the "person who has attained the Dao", and is no longer under the grip of what he sees, hears or feels. In Buddhism this same term has a striking similarity to the Muslim who recites a *shahāda*, as explained in the article. Further Buddhist meanings which may have inspired the translators: *Zhen Xin* (true hearted); *Zhen Ru* (substantial, unchanging); *Zhen Kong* (a situation of unalterable truth). Note also that Daoism *Zhen Jing* (true scripture) may be applied to the Qur'ān.

concept to the Muslim who recites the *shahāda*, the first of the Five Pillars of Islam (*arkān*), in which the believer bears witness to the unity of God and to the verity of the mission of his Prophet.

The list of Buddhist translatable connotations into Islam is very fertile, if one should extend its letter and spirit to the limit. For example, *Zhen Yan* (true word) in Buddhism can be paralleled to the Word of God that is the Qur'ān, and both are "true" in the sense of sacred and eternal. *Zhen li* (true principles) can be easily equated to the Pillars of Islam or to the *uṣūl al-dīn* (the sacred foundations of the *sharīʿa*). *Zhen Zhi* (true wisdom) may be likened to the *sharīʿa* (the true path of God), and the *Zhen Kong*, the Buddhist situation where confusion is ended and the unalterable truth reigns, is naturally mirrored in the Islamic clarity that the Prophet brought to the confused and sinful Arabia to put an end to the *Jāhiliyya*.

Zhu (Master or Lord), the second component of the Allāh construct, suggests a differentiation from the Chinese religious terms (Buddhist and Daoist) lest the Believers, or the uninformed non-believers, might find too much of a terminological rapprochement between them and Islam. *Zhu* is not frequently used in Chinese religion, but rather in Christianity and Islam (see note 27 above). However, unlike the Christian usage of *Tian Zhu* (the Master of Heavens) for the Judeo-Christian God, the Muslims have their "True Master" perhaps to indicate that he is Allāh who leads to the Path of those he has favoured, not the Path of Those who earned his Anger (the Jews) or those who go astray (the Christians), as will be explained below.

In fact, Chinese Muslims sought not only to distance themselves from the Christians who appropriated to themselves the Lord of Heaven (*Tian Zhu*) but also from the Chinese who currently used the same appellation for Catholic Christianity: *Tian Zhu Jiao* (the Teaching of the Lord of Heaven). Similarly, Chinese Buddhism used *Tian Zhu* for the Lord of Heaven, and Emperor Song of the Southern Dynasty (420–589) also took on the title of *Tian Zhu*. Moreover, not only was the *Tian Zhu* construct too crowded with meaning and overly loaded in the world of China's religions, but it was sullied by the *Tian* (Heaven) component which in the Chinese context was also heavy with Chinese significance which was potentially anti-Islamic. To wit, acceptance of *Tian* may also drag in its wake recognition of *Tian Zi* (the Son of Heaven), that is the Chinese Emperor. While Christianity had perhaps nothing to fear from this deduction, due to its own concept of the Son of God (God being defined as *Tian Zhu*), the Muslims were aghast to associate anyone with God and to drift into the irreparable sin of *shirk*.

Interestingly enough, the Taiwan version simply uses the *An-lah* transliteration for Allāh, apparently in order to steer clear of all these controversies. However the *An-lah* transliteration in itself may carry other connotations, whether or not it was intended by the author (Bai Jian-min). *An* basically signifies: quiet, stable, benevolent, with derivatives which may find a strong appeal among Chinese Muslims. For example:

1. *An-Min* = "to make people stable"; or
2. *An-Quan* = "safe"; or
3. *An-shen* = "settle"; or
4. *An-yang*, a Buddhist term, describing the Paradise of the Amida Buddha; or, in more mundane and literal terms, to "keep one's mind in good order or health"; or
5. *An-le* (*Guo*) = "a peaceful and happy (state)".

La carries the meaning of "to destroy", "to pull". An *An-lah*, who can both impose peace and wreck havoc, would be quite in accordance with a Muslim conception of Allāh the Omnipotent whose compassion and wrath can be manifested in this world.

3.2.2 *The Beneficent* (al-raḥmān)

The Chinese texts, both mainland and Taiwan versions, found no other equivalent to this loaded and heavily contested term, than the Confucian *Ren*, in spite of the other possible dictionary translations in Chinese, such as *Xing Shan De* and *Ci Shan De* (to perform good deeds). The Confucian *Ren* means a perfect virtue which frees the being from selfishness. The *Jün-Zi*, the ideal Confucian virtuous man, of whom there are only few,[28] personifies and expresses that virtue, usually translated as "humane-ness". But *Ren* also connotes the exercise of love between father and son,[29] the family metaphor being often used in Confucian tradition to depict the relations between ruler and ruled, superior and subordinate. This view, which sustains the superiority of the benevolent man who cannot be opposed by any-

[28] The Confucian sentence is *Ren Bu Ke Yi Wei Zhong ye.*
[29] *Ren Zhi Yu Fu Zi Ye.*

one under him,[30] fits perfectly in the Muslim mind with the supremacy of Allāh to whom are imputed the anthropomorphic qualities of being benevolent or beneficent.

The quality of *Ren*, as attributed to Allāh, also made sense in the context of the Five Constant Virtues of the Confucian tradition where it leads the list: *Ren* (humaneness), *Yi* (righteousness, justice) *Li* (propriety), *Zhi* (wisdom) and *Xin* (sincerity). For a Muslim minority, which had always sought accommodation with its environment, by apologetically showing the similarities between Confucian and Islamic wisdom,[31] to find a parallel between the Five virtues and Islamic values, and especially to attribute to Allāh the leading Confucian virtue of *Ren*, must have been deemed not only acceptable, but even desirable to the Muslim scholars who undertook their translation of the Qur'ān.

3.2.3 *Merciful* (al-raḥīm)

The term *Ci*, used in both modern texts, is of Buddhist origin, and it connotes, very interestingly, the "Barge of Compassion" which ferries departed spirits from this world to the bliss of the hereafter. That Chinese Muslims, who are obsessed like others of their co-religionists by questions of Hell and Paradise, and have cultivated a rich literature which describes both in concrete and plastic terms, should take a ride on the Buddhist Barge seems quite natural. Their idea of bliss under the wings of the angels was not diminished in the least by the fact that their vehicle was Buddhist. After all the bliss was the goal and the vehicle only the means.

In other Buddhist contexts, *Ci Yun* means the "merciful cloud" which shaded the Buddha, and, more significantly, *Ci Yan*, is usually explained as "kind and stern", i.e. "kind as a mother and stern as a father". Allāh, who can be compassionate in his attitude towards man, can also show his stern face when angered by man's behaviour. This is an image perfectly acceptable to Muslims seeking Chinese equivalents to their idea of Allāh, and it concords perfectly with an important Muslim commentary on the Qur'ān which says that *raḥmān* and *raḥīm* signify the "one who has mercy, i.e. wishes well to his family" (or to his people).[32]

---

[30] The Confucian phrase says *Ren ren Wu Di Yu Tian Xia* (the benevolent man has no one under Heaven who can oppose him).

[31] See Israeli 1980:33–35.

[32] See al-Suyūṭī *Tafsīr al-Jalālayn*: ad this verse.

3.3 *Verse 2 (in Mainland text = verse 1 of the Taiwan and original Arabic texts) "Praise to Allāh, Lord of the Worlds"* (al-ḥamdu li'l-lāhi rabbi 'l-ʿālamīn)

The early Chinese untranslated text simply explained that *al-ḥamd* (praise) consisted of five characters corresponding to the five celestial orders that Allāh decreed and that were identical with the Five Pillars of the faith.[33] *Li'l-lāh* (to Allāh) consisted of three characters (in Chinese *Lin-lia-hi*), which together with the former five amounted to the eight dwellings in Paradise. Any Muslim who recited all the eight syllables with devotion and intent can be sure that Allāh will open for him all these dwellings to choose from his permanent place in the hereafter.[34] And so it goes for the next ten characters of *rabbi 'l-ʿālamīn* (Lord of the Worlds) which, when added to the previous eight, constitute the foundations upon which Allāh constructed eighteen magnificent palaces. God will open the gates of these palaces to all devout believers and will also thereby permanently lock before them the eighteen heavy doors of Hell.[35]

3.3.1 Rabbi 'l-ʿālamīn *(in the New Translated Texts)*

The Mainland version says: *Quan Shi-Jie De Zhu*, which literally means: "The Lord of the entire world". Instead of "worlds" in the plural in the original, the Chinese translation specifies "the entire world" in the singular which means "everything on the ground" and by extension "all the countries on earth". In this sense, it is much closer to the Chinese concept of *Tian Xia* (everything under Heaven), that is the physical universe that is given to the rule of the Chinese Emperor, the Son of Heaven. This contrasts strongly with the traditional Islamic exegesis which encompassed under the "worlds" (*al-ʿālamīn*) everything relating to man and to the Devil, as well as to the angels in Heavens.[36] This three-dimensional world of Islam (the Devil under the ground, man on the ground and angels in Heavens) was not related in the modern Chinese translation, although in the earlier text, as we have seen, vent was given to the mystical meaning of the words in Islamic exegesis and to the link between the earthly world and the heavenly one.

---

33 See Farjenel and Bouvat 1908:541.
34 Ibid. 542.
35 Ibid.
36 See al-Suyūṭī *Tafsīr al-Jalālayn*: ad this verse.

It should be pointed out, incidentally, that "Lord" (of the worlds) was exactly translated into Chinese as *Zhu*, the same character that, when modified by *Zhen* (true = true Lord) amounts to Allāh, as explained above. The consistency in the usage of the same Chinese characters in spite of the varying significance of "Allāh" and *rabb* (Lord), points to the care of the translators not to deviate from a terminology that they had painstakingly arrived at.

In the Taiwan translation there is a slight variance from the Mainland one, in that, *Quan shi-jie* (the whole world) is replaced by *Yangyu jung shih-jie* which signifies the Lord "who rears the entire world". Here the original Arabic *rabb* is translated as meaning of "bring-up", or "foster". The translator/commentator Bai deduces from his *Yangyu* designation of *rabb* that the Lord not only created the world and is its Master, but is also bent on perfecting its character. According to Bai, readers might not limit their understanding to the literal significance *Yangyu* as "bringing up" or "rearing". He quotes verses *Sūra* 43:84–85 to emphasise that Allāh had created "Heaven and Earth and everything between them", which probably includes human beings, thus referring back to the traditional Islamic exegesis of *al-ʿālamīn* as including man.

3.4 *Verse 3 (= Verse 2 in the Taiwan and Original Arabic)* al-raḥmān al-raḥīm *(the Beneficent, the Merciful)*

The turn-of-the-century commentated text continues the mystical numerical equivalents explained above and determines that *al-raḥmān* is constituted by six characters which, added to the previous 18, amount to the 24 parts of the year created by the Lord. Thus, any believer who recites these words with intent and devotion, will be pardoned by Allāh for all the sins he has perpetrated during the 24 parts of the year, and will be accorded divine mercy. Similarly, *al-raḥīm* (The Merciful), again made up of six characters, when added to the previous 24, amount to the 30 days that Allāh has created for each month. Likewise, any devout Muslim who performs his prayer as required will benefit from divine mercy during the entire 30 days of each month.[37]

The modern texts simply repeat the terms already used and commented upon in verse 1 above.

[37] Farjenel and Bouvat 1908:542–543.

3.5 *Verse 4 (= Verse 3 in the Taiwan and Original Arabic)* māliki yawmi 'l-dīn *(Owner of the Day of Judgement)*

The older untranslated text again offers a numerical explanation to wit: "This expression has twelve Arabic characters which, with the thirty preceding ones, make forty-two, on the basis of which Allāh has created the forty-two kinds of diseases of the human heart. Thus, any believer who recites those words with devotion will be granted cure by Allāh of all these forty-two illnesses."[38]

3.5.1 *Owner (in the Modern Texts)*

In the Mainland text, "Owner", like "Lord" (respectively *mālik* and *rabb*) used in the previous verses are both translated into Chinese as *Zhu*, the same word which, as part of the *Zhen Zhu* construct, had been used for Allāh. Consistency would have overruled variety in the minds of the translators, in spite of the repetition and the apparent deviation from the linguistic plurality of the Qur'anic text. However, Bai's Taiwan version adds the words *Zhi Zhang* meaning "in charge of", "in control of" at the head of the verse, in order to differentiate between *Zhu* as Lord and *Zhu* as owner, which were combined in Ma Jian's Mainland translation. In his commentary to this verse, Bai specifies that *mālik* has two pronunciations: a) *Ma-li-ke*, in the sense of "master", "owner" (*Zhu-zen*), and *Mai-li-ke*, which means "monarch", in this context preferring the first pronunciation.[39] To strengthen his case, the author produces *sūra* 43, verse 77, where the word *mālik* also carries the meaning of "owner", rather than "king".

3.5.2 *Day of Judgement*

The Mainland translation here resorted to one half of a popular four-character Buddhist idiom: *Yin Guo Bao Ying*, i.e. "cause and effect retribution", meaning that if one performs good deeds, he will have good retribution, and if he does bad deeds he will suffer bad retribution. Three points are interesting in this translation:

---

[38] Ibid. 543. See also Zwemer 1915:257.

[39] This "difference", of course, only exists in the two various ways of transliterating the same Arabic word (*mālik*) into Chinese; by establishing this artificial bifurcation of the same word into two "different" meanings, the author obviously hopes to carry to his readers the two variants of the Arabic original.

1. Since there is no exact equivalent to the monotheistic concept of the Day of Judgement, the Qur'anic idea of Allāh the Merciful who is also the owner of that awesome Day, had to be rendered in terms of retribution for good or bad deeds.
2. The early Muslim commentary cited above, which connects retribution with the forty-two illnesses as a matter of fact, addresses positively the believers, trying to encourage them to pray devoutly in order to avoid incurring the sicknesses that are there as part of creation. There is no direct threat to discourage them from acting adversely, as if the believer had been locked into an Allāh ordained do-well situation where he had no freedom of choice. The Buddhist text explicitly stresses the two alternatives with their resulting consequences.
3. *Bao Ying Ri* (*the* Day of "Retribution") a specific day in Islam, that is, "The Day of Judgement", which is loaded with the eschatological meanings absent in Buddhism.

The Taiwan version, *Huan Bao Ri*, does not carry the heavy Buddhist connotation, and probably means "Retribution", "Recompense".[40] The author/commentator explains that *yawm* in Arabic does not necessarily mean "one day" nor "daylight"[41] but any extent of time determined by Allāh for the "Day of Judgement". This conforms, of course, with the various Muslim commentaries in the multi-millennial length of that awesome Day (see Verse 5 below). For that reason, he comments, that the Day ought to be dubbed the "Time of Judgement" (*Huan Bao Shi*) rather than *Han-Bao Ri.* He says that the "Day of Judgement", making no specific reference to a particular Day, not even the Day of the Revival of the Dead, has to be understood, contrary to popular wont, as the continuing process of judgement and retribution by Allāh at any time. *Huan Bao,* the term he uses for "retribution" is also problematic. Probably to avoid the Buddhist connotation of *Bao Ying,* the translator resorted to a more modern rendition of "retribution": *Huan Bao,* even though it is in reverse order of the usual construct of *Bao-huan.*

[40] This is the meaning in all standard dictionaries.

[41] In Chinese, *Ri,* the equivalent for "day", is represented by the ideograph of "sun", which originally signified daylight, and by extension grew to express the entire day.

It is noteworthy that in the introduction to his translation of the Qur'ān, Bai emphasises that he is intent on making the contents of the Book understood to Chinese in general, not only to Muslims; therefore, he purposely avoids terms loaded with religious connotations, and more often than not uses plain modern Chinese. That is also the reason why religiously loaded terms like Allāh and *mu'min* (believer) are transliterated into Chinese rather than translated; and so it goes even for the names of the *sūras*: *Fa-ti-ha*, or *Bai-ge-lai* (*Baqara*) etc.

3.6 *Verse 5 (= 4 in the Taiwan and Arabic Original)* iyyāka naʿbudu wa-iyyāka nastaʿīn *(Thee we worship; Thee we ask for help)*

The transliterated text once again pursues its enumeration of the characters. *Iyyāka naʿbudu* comes to eight syllables, which together with the forty-two preceding ones amount to fifty, which served as a base for Allāh in his creation of the Day of Judgement due to last 50,000 years, but would only be counted as one day. To any person who recites his prayers with full sincerity and devotion, the Lord will accord not only deliverance from the flames of hell but also peace and tranquillity and will even give him a resting spot at the front of the celestial *ʿarsh* (throne). The second part of the verse (thee we ask for help) is transliterated into eleven syllables, which together with the preceding fifty, comes to sixty-one, equivalent to the sixty-one profound seas that Allāh has created. Thus, any person who prays with sincerity, even though his sins may look to him as numerous as the waters of those oceans, will be pardoned by the Lord.[42]

The only differences between the two modern versions of this verse are in their usages of different equivalents for "worship" and "help". The Mainland text resorts to *Chong Bai*, with a connotation of "worship" or adoration in general,[43] while *Shi feng* in Bai's translation means more like "believe in" and "serve" the Emperor, or a master. Thus, the latter seems to have a more worldly connotation than the former.

Ma Jian uses *You zhu* for "[God's] help"; it usually refers to divine assistance or help that derives from transcendental sources, while Bai's *Yuan zhu* simply means assistance in modern human terms.

---

[42] Farjenel and Bouvat 1908:543–544.

[43] For example, during the Cultural Revolution in China (1966–1976), popular adoration of Mao was expressed in terms of *Chong Bai*.

3.7 *Verse 6 (= 5 in the Taiwan and Arabic)* ihdinā 'l-ṣirāṭi 'l-mustaqīm *(Show us the Straight Path)*

According to the transliterated text of the turn of the Century, the nineteen characters of this verse, added to the preceding sixty-one, amount to eighty. In the Day of Judgement, those who have committed adultery will be punished by eighty lashes of a fire whip. But those who recite faithfully this prayer will be exonerated even if they had sinned.

In both modern texts there is a straightforward translation of "lead" or "guide" us through the straight "Way" or "Path". However, while Ma uses the word "lu", the mundane term for "way", or "road", Bai resorts to the more formal and philosophically/religiously loaded term of *Dao* (as in the Dao religion, or the Confucian *Dao*).

3.8 *Verse 7 (= 6–7 in the Taiwan Text, and 6–7 in the Arabic) Ṣirāṭa* 'l-ladhīna anʿamta ʿalayhim ghayri 'l-maghḍūbi ʿalayhim wa-lā 'l-ḍāllīn *(The Path of those whom you have favoured; not of those who earn Thine Anger; or those who go astray)*

According to the earlier text, the first part of this verse (6 in the Arabic) has a total of nineteen syllables, which together with the previous eighty amount to ninety-nine, corresponding to the ninety-nine corporeal maladies Allāh created on the fringes of Heaven, against which all pious believers shall be protected. The second part, consisting of fifteen characters, makes up a total of 114, which are the *sūras* of the Holy Book. Any devout Muslim who recites the prayer with sincerity will be rewarded as if he had recited all 114 *sūras*; in addition, he will be awarded 114 benefits, exempted from 114 evils and at the end of the world, Allāh will listen to 114 of his prayers. The last part, which includes ten characters, making up a total of 124, corresponds to the 124 saints that Allāh has created. Allāh will reward all pious believers who pray with devotion, with the rewards he has accorded the 124 saints.

3.8.1 *"The path of those you have favoured"*

"Favoured" is translated by Ma Jian as *You*, which means "help", "assistance", interestingly the same word he used in the previous verse of "Thy help we seek". This can of course signify that those who are meritorious enough to seek Allāh's help, and also receive it, are the

Muslims, just as is understood from the verse in traditional Islamic exegesis.

Bai's version translates: "those to whom you have accorded your grace (or kindness)." Again, "to accord" (*Shi*) is part of a Buddhist construct *Shi Zhu*, i.e. the person who accords grace, or a benefactor. Bai explains that, as in verse 69 of *sūra* 4, these are the people to whom Allāh has shown favour, i.e. the prophets, the saints, the martyrs, and the righteous.[44]

3.8.2 *Not Those Who Earn Thine Anger*

"Anger" according to Ma Jian is divided into *Qian* (blame, condemnation, denunciation) and *Nu* (anger). This signifies, of course, that Allāh's anger was generated by their blameful deeds. Bai is closer to the literal version of the Qur'ān, and only talks about Allāh's anger (*Nu*). Bai also comments that "those who have earned thine anger" are the Jews who have killed the saints,[45] and the pagans.

He explains that Protestants (*Ye-su-Jiao*), polytheists (*Duo-shen Jiao*) who regard the saint as their God, have "missed the right Path", implying that this is the reason why they earned God's anger. The first (Jews and pagans) are still short of arriving to the right Path; the latter (Protestants and polytheists) have overshot the Path, and gone too far. Therefore none of them has adopted the right Path, and anyone who truly believes in the Lord ought to know the difference between the two. He quotes *sūra* 2, verse 61: "Humiliation and wretchedness were stamped upon them and they were visited with wrath", and 5:77, "O people of the Scripture! Stress not in your religion other than the truth, and follow not the vain desires of the folk who erred of old and led many astray."

3.9 *Āmīn*

The early text, which transliterated the *Fātiḥa* for purposes of prayer, also ended with *āmīn* (amen), for which the same numerological value is provided: four characters: *alif*, the letter A, corresponding to Adam, the saint; *mīm*, the letter M, corresponding to Muḥammad, the saint and the messenger of God; *yā'*, the letter Y, for Saint Yehaye (probably yaḥyā = Isaiah); and finally *nūn*, the letter N, for Saint Youha

---

[44] See Bai 1958:2.
[45] Reference to the killing of Jesus Christ.

(= probably John).[46] Any person who recites this word with devotion as part of the prayer, will receive the honour reserved to those four saints. Furthermore, the recipient of this honour will also be awarded four precious assets at the end of days.

4. *Conclusion*

In both traditional China, and the People's Republic, the Muslim Hui minority has been imparting Qur'anic education to their youth, in Arabic (or Persian). The more education spread, the more it has been felt necessary to base Qur'anic teaching upon Chinese translations of the Qur'ān, the knowledge of Arabic having become the domain of the learned *A-hong*, or *Man-la*.[47] In fact, in some areas, Muslim children pursue the study of the Qur'ān at home privately, if for any reason they cannot attend the *madrasas*.[48] This, of course, poses the serious question of the nature and essence of the messages Chinese-Muslim educators are dedicated to transmit to their offspring. For, even when the Qur'ān is taught in the original Arabic, it has to be explained/commentated upon in Chinese in the process, in order to make it understood both literally and in terms of the symbols and notions that Chinese Muslim youth are expected to internalise.

Any translation of canons presupposes a world in which the word of God can be transmitted to humanity in various languages to fit in with different casts of mind. However, while the Bible, for example, was often translated from English into Chinese, and not always directly from its Hebrew original, making room for a pluralistic approach, the Qur'ān was translated into various languages directly from the Arabic, for the most part by bi-lingual and bi-cultural Muslims who could easily pour the Arabic content which they had well absorbed and internalised into a Chinese mould which they understood and which reflected their worldview. Even so, as we have seen in the Qur'anic versions in Chinese, the translators had much difficulty in transposing their translated text into another cultural environment. Hence the multiplicity of translation attempts, and the

[46] According to Farjenel and Bouvat 1908:545, note 4, this may be a misspelling of Nouha, Nūḥ in Arabic, that is Noah.

[47] Imams and students in preparation to become imams, respectively.

[48] See Gladney 1991:125–127.

inability of any one of them to achieve a "canon" or "semi-canon" status, the way some biblical translations into English have, as if to conform to the old Jewish adage that "Every generation has its own commentators."

Relativization of a "canon", perhaps a contradiction in terms in Western civilisation, is the final product(s) that we obtain in the Chinese translations of the Qur'ān. The Islamic notions of Allāh and his attributes, the hereafter, and the like, when cast into Buddhist or Daoist moulds, are at quite a variance with what a devout Muslim has in mind when he pronounces the same words or thinks about the same concepts. We have also seen that as a yardstick to "respectability", the Qur'ān, translated into Chinese, could be made more or less close to the vernacular. There has decidedly been a wide gap between the Mainland translations which are more formal, tight and "canon-like" in their solemnity and thriftiness of words, and the Taiwan more "open" version, which makes for a "looser" and more "relaxed" narrative. This may seem paradoxical, because we would have expected contemporary Mainland Chinese translations to embrace a less mystic, less "religious" and less "superstitious" way, while we expect Taiwanese versions to lean more towards the "conservative" and "traditional" line of translation. But it seems that this differentiation is not always kept. The explanation may lie in the historical context of translation development in China. While the early attempts to provide Chinese renderings of the Qur'ān were conscious of the need of the Muslim minority to demonstrate its "Chineseness", an inevitable sinification of the Islamic vocabulary and worldview became the only way for Muslims to "prove" their loyalty. Out of this initially apologetic attitude of Islam, which is detectable since the 18th century,[49] there grew an "accepted" (not "canonised") vocabulary that subsequent translations under the Communist regime had to "preserve", lest the translators might be accused of tampering with the Holy Text.

Thus, we are facing here a rather interesting phenomenon, whereby the translation of the Qur'ān into Chinese was meant not only to carry its message to the believers in a language they could comprehend, but also to placate the Chinese learned elite that Islam, couched in Chinese religious terms, was not so different, after all, from the

[49] See Israeli 1980.

Chinese classics. This attitude had also tinged Chinese renderings of the Qur'ān with a specific character which distinguished them from their biblical parallels. The Chinese Qur'āns were irreversibly seen as a "Chinese product", as it were, addressed to the Chinese (Muslims or not), as they were translated by native Chinese of the Muslim faith, unlike the biblical Chinese translations which almost always entirely rested on foreign missionary initiatives, albeit often with native assistance. This is also the reason why Chinese Qur'āns were often the fruit of one scholar's work, while the missionaries toiled in teams, or committees, to achieve an acceptable Chinese version of the Scripture.

A lot more research would be needed to draw more sweeping conclusions regarding Qur'anic translations into Chinese. We are as yet only at the beginning of this long path, and if the present questions raised with regard to the *Fātiḥa*, the opening *sūra* of the Qur'ān, are further pursued, this study will ultimately turn out to be only an opening step.

ANALOGICAL AND SYLLOGISTIC REASONING IN GRAMMAR AND LAW*

M.G. Carter

It is well known that grammatical and legal reasoning are virtually identical, in that both involve the systematisation of irrational data predominantly by means of analogical reasoning. This identity has been cogently expounded by Ibn al-Anbārī (d. 1181), whose *Lumaʿ al-adilla* represents the culmination of a long process of methodological symbiosis between law and grammar.

In looking again at those two disciplines, this paper, which is here dedicated with pleasure to my respected colleague Tony Johns, will concentrate on the two types of reasoning employed, analogical and syllogistic, with special attention to the terms *ʿilla* and *qiyās*, proceeding from the assumption that not only are analogy and syllogism historically and qualitatively different, but that they also have different applications. Briefly, analogy is a technique for infinitely extending a finite corpus of data to meet new circumstances, while syllogism authenticates the rationality of that technique without itself creating new law or linguistic usage (or indeed anything). The two systems are thus complementary and therefore mutually exclusive, that is, not only does syllogistic reasoning not create new law or language, but analogical reasoning cannot prove its own rationality. These ideas will easily be recognised as derived from the Aristotelian use of logic as the organising principle of all the sciences, which is precisely what we find in the first classifications of the sciences in Islam, notably those of al-Fārābī and Ibn Sīnā.

Although this has been already noted in studies of the legal *uṣūl*, the position now being taken here requires a far more radical distinction than is suggested by Hallaq's observation that "deduction and analogy were used side by side in one logical operation."[1] Again it must be emphasised that the two kinds of reasoning performed wholly different functions. The analogical system may best be thought

---

* Adapted from a paper given at the 203rd conference of the American Oriental Society, Chapel Hill, NC, April 1993.

[1] Hallaq 1987:42.

of as "operational" (producing law, as *furūʿ*) and the syllogistical system by contrast as "methodological" (justifying the procedure, as *uṣūl*). As it happens the same objection can be made against an otherwise very perceptive study of grammatical reasoning by Suleiman (1991), which has contributed a number of important ideas to this paper; he makes no mention of analogical and syllogistic reasoning or the contrast between operational and methodological reasoning, still less their inherent incompatibility.

There is some support in legal writings for this clear differentiation between analogy and syllogism, firstly in the *uṣūlī's* own strict separation of juridical *qiyās* and syllogism, e.g. in al-Āmidī (d. 1233), who leaves little doubt that the latter is not a productive source of *furūʿ*.[2] Then there is al-Ghazālī's reduction of juridical *qiyās* patterns to syllogistic figures,[3] surely a mere *post facto* exercise with no implications for the ability of syllogisms to generate new law, and lastly there is the general consent that legal *qiyās* was neither apodeictic nor absolute,[4] a fact which the lawyers very properly never tried to hide and indeed considered an essential quality of legal reasoning.

As far as the history of legal thought is concerned, the interplay of analogy and syllogism is already well documented. The jurists made an early start in "creating a legal theory grounded in a well-structured logical system of proof for justifying the positive conclusions of the Sharīʿa",[5] in response to the obvious need for a *logical* connection between the positive law and the revealed texts, and eventually reached the position described by Ibn Qudāma (d. 1233) where, in Hallaq's paraphrase, "syllogistics . . . stands as the methodological foundation of any science, be it rational or legal".[6] Since legal reasoning is abundantly illustrated in the secondary literature, only a couple of representative grammatical specimens need be given here for the purpose of comparison.

A straightforward case of analogical reasoning is seen in the theory of the so-called *muḍāriʿ* form of the verb (approximately our "imperfect" verb). As early as Sībawayhi (died late 8th century) the functional

---

[2] *Iḥkām*: IV, 104–111. Note that al-Āmidī admits that others may use *istidlāl* loosely to refer to all kinds of legal reasoning but his own discussion of the term explicitly limits it to the meaning of non-legal syllogism. For a detailed treatment see Weiss 1992: esp. Part I, Postulates, and Part II, chs. 12–15.

[3] Cf. Hallaq 1989:299.

[4] Cf. Brunschvig 1971:359.

[5] Hallaq 1987:42.

[6] Hallaq 1990:323.

similarity between nouns and this class of verb, namely their distributional overlap as predicates and their ability to be made more definite by prefixing *alif-lām* and *sawfa* respectively, was used to explain their partial formal identity in inflection (both take *-u* and *-a*, nouns only take *-i*, verbs *-Ø* only), which is, of course, what the term *muḍāriʿ* "resembling" actually means. By another analogy in the other direction the incomplete inflection of nouns of the form *afʿal* is ascribed to the fact that *afʿal* is basically a verbal pattern. The grammatical literature provides many such instances of analogical classifications and explanations.

By the 10th century, however, Greek reasoning enters grammar in the shape of *taqsīm*, diaeresis (a taxonomic device which has much similarity, still unexplored, with *al-sabr waʾl-taqsīm*), in which the criteria are no longer purely formal but rather logical. Thus there are two *taqsīms* for classifying speech into three parts: in one, words are divided into those with an intrinsic meaning and those without it, which isolates the particle (*ḥarf*), then the meaningful words are divided into those connected with time and those not, identifying verbs and nouns respectively. In the other scheme predictability is the criterion: words that can be both subjects and predicates are nouns, words that can only be predicates are verbs and words that can be neither subjects nor predicates are particles.[7] In both cases the *taqsīm* confirms the empirical facts by proving logically that there can only be three parts of speech.

If we add now the *a fortiori* arguments used from the earliest times in grammatical reasoning, as described by Gwynne,[8] we can safely assert that grammatical and legal reasoning have always exactly paralleled each other. The historical similarity is profound: from the 10th century lawyers and grammarians were both exploring the theoretical aspects of their discipline under the same rubric, namely *uṣūl*.

Suleiman's[9] study of the "methodological rules of Arabic grammar" shows that these *uṣūl* reached a highly developed level. The fully elaborated system was founded on generally acknowledged theorems, e.g. that no linguistic event could have more than one cause (*ʿilla*!), and was controlled by principles of labelling, equilibrium, symmetry, priority and consistency, with hierarchies of linguistic elements,

---

[7] E.g. Ibn al-Sarrāj (d. 928), in *al-Uṣūl*: I, 37.
[8] 1990.
[9] 1991.

e.g. nouns over verbs over particles, the *-u* (independent/*raf*ʿ) case over the *-i* (oblique/*jarr*) and *-a* (dependent/*naṣb*) respectively, masculine and singular over feminine and dual/plural etc.[10] The distribution of the case endings is thus rationalised by claiming that the phonologically "heaviest" vowel, "u", is given to the most important case, the *raf*ʿ, while the phonologically "lightest" vowel, "a", is given to the syntactically least well-defined case, the *naṣb*. These explanations have little to do with the actual behaviour of speech elements but are simply interpretations of the data prompted by the urge to systematise, to elicit what in the 10th century was called the *ḥikma*, the rationality of language.

All these arguments rely on the axiom that for every phenomenon there is a reason, *ʿilla*, and that the linguistic implications, both practical and theoretical, can be deduced by *qiyās*; it will not need to be emphasised that the grammarians are here performing essentially the same manoeuvres as their colleagues in law. In a famous passage al-Zajjājī (d. 923) distinguishes three kinds of *ʿilla*, (1) *ʿilla taʿlīmiyya*, the pedagogical *ʿilla* which merely asserts the fact (e.g. the noun after *inna* takes dependent/*naṣb* form), (2) the *ʿilla qiyāsiyya*, the analogical *ʿilla* which justifies the fact on the grounds that *inna* resembles a verb, and (3) the *ʿilla jadaliyya wa-naẓariyya*, the speculative-dialectical *ʿilla* which asks why, in what way and under what conditions etc. etc. *inna* resembles a verb.[11] In time the system became so complex that al-Suyūṭī reports the existence of no less than twenty-four kinds of *ʿilla*![12]

The term *ʿilla* is ultimately from Syriac, meaning defect, fault, i.e. grounds for the return of merchandise,[13] and had already entered

---

[10] Although most of these hierarchies may have existed in Sībawayhi's time they play little or no role in his descriptive grammar, and the assumption must be that they form part of an earlier tradition which was of no great importance to him (but see Baalbaki 1979).

[11] *Al-Īḍāḥ*: 64–66; see now Versteegh 1995:87ff., and Fleisch 1979:1128, who points out that this level of reasoning was recognised very early as unreal (*mustanbaṭ*).

[12] Al-Suyūṭī *al-Iqtirāḥ*: 115, quoting from the *Thimār al-ṣināʿa* by Abū ʿAbdullāh al-Ḥusayn ibn Mūsā al-Dīnawarī al-Jalīs. The editor's footnote states that this grammarian is frequently quoted by Abū Hayyān al-Gharnāṭī in his *Tadhkira* and refers also to al-Suyūṭī's *Bughya*: I, 541 (where also *Thimār al-ṣināʿa fī l-naḥw* is mentioned). He wrote before 1187 (see Fleisch 1979, referring to *GAL*: SI, 114). Note however that elsewhere al-Suyūṭī argues that lexical and legal *qiyās* are quite different, according to Petit 1982:123.

[13] See Köbert 1945:280. Note also that *ʿilla* meaning "defect" is still current in Arabic phonology, though never confused with *ʿilla* in the sense of "cause".

the Syriac logical vocabulary before the Arabs became acquainted with Aristotle. It is a mystery why *ʿilla* replaced *maʿnā* for *ratio legis* as early as the 9th century,[14] unless *maʿnā* was forced out by the new logical terminology, and more precision on this change would definitely shed light on the evolution of the *uṣūl*. While on the subject of precision, it is surely regrettable that *ʿilla* is so often translated as "middle term" in contexts where it is still the reflex of the abandoned *ratio legis*. In the history of science it is dangerous to impose one's own categories on the technical vocabulary, all the more so in a culture like Islam where the same word can be a technical term in several disciplines, sometimes with vastly different meanings, e.g. *khafḍ*, in grammar "oblique case" but in another context "female circumcision".[15]

Qiyās is ultimately from Hebrew,[16] but so ancient as to have become a fully assimilated Arabic root. The danger here is of misapprehending analogical reasoning as somehow "Semitic" (i.e. primitive), which Brunschvig only partially counters in his Levi della Vida paper (1971: 18). Moreover we find the same inconsistency in translating this term as we do with *ʿilla*, since *qiyās* can refer both to the pure Aristotelian syllogism and to the legal analogy. This has of course long been realised: "*Qiyās* . . . should be regarded as a relative term whose definition and structure vary from one jurist to another",[17] but we should never lose sight of the fact that the Muslims themselves always knew whether *qiyās* referred to analogy or syllogism, and by the same token this often implicit distinction should always be made carefully explicit in any western treatment.

The notions of *ʿilla* and *qiyās* inevitably have profound reverberations within a theology which took a specific view of causality and its implications for human responsibility. The systematisation of law and grammar (and theology) in Islam is in part the history of the acclimatisation of logic, eventually reaching a position not so much of faith *and* reason, as it used to be polarised, but of faith *in* reason.[18]

---

[14] Brunschvig 1971:16–17. *ʿIlla* in the meaning of "cause" seems to have been available in Arabic from a very early period, to judge by its occurrence in the epitome of the Hermeneutics by Abū Muḥammad ʿAbdullāh b. al-Muqaffaʿ, who died in 757; cf. Troupeau 1981:242–250 (esp. p. 250).

[15] Cf. van Donzel 1978, (article on *khafḍ*) where there is no mention of its grammatical sense. This certainly provides a new perspective on the term "genitive".

[16] Cf. Bernand 1986. See also Versteegh 1980 for a lengthy survey of the background of this term.

[17] Hallaq 1990:305.

[18] Ironically al-Ghazālī's achievement seems to have been to incorporate logic

The result is the familiar incongruity of processing irrational data by rational means, and neither grammarians nor lawyers had any illusions about the arbitrariness of the data or the fallibility of the reasoning.[19] The lawyer's *naṣṣ* is the grammarian's *samāʿ*, and the grammarians were not only healthily sceptical about their Bedouin informants but were also aware that even their own colleagues could be caught with forged data in their notebooks!

The mere existence of the terms *ʿilla* and *qiyās* is evidence for the belief in the basic rationality of the grammatical and legal systems and their *uṣūl*. The grammarians were deep into their *uṣūl* debates throughout the 10th century, with long discussions of linguistic causality which concluded that language is no more rational than man himself is, though the Muʿtazilite grammarians, notably Ibn Jinnī and al-Rummānī, obviously wanted to believe that it was (and were predictably opposed by the Ẓāhirī Ibn Maḍāʾ al-Qurṭubī). There are also references to linguistic responsibility phrased in the theological terminology of the source of man's acts which, as is well known, was finally rationalised through the Ashʿarite metaphor of *kasb*, acquisition. Grammarians and lawyers moved side by side in the erection of an abstract system of reasoning, with the *Uṣūl* of Ibn al-Sarrāj (d. 928) having first place in the grammatical tradition. By contrast, the appearance of the first *uṣūl* work in *fiqh* by Abū ʾl-Ḥasan ʿAlī ibn ʿUmar (d. 909)[20] seems—not to mince words—incredibly early, and one wonders why there are apparently no more *uṣūl* books for well over a century, until Abū ʾl-Ḥusayn al-Baṣrī, d. 1044. This is an enigmatic lacuna, which has yet to be accounted for, though once the genre became established the parallels with grammatical *uṣūl* are strikingly obvious.

It is worth recalling at this point that the *uṣūl* were never conceived as instruments for determining actual behaviour, whether legal or grammatical. As Ibn Khaldūn summarised it, religious data cannot be developed rationally but only by analogy,[21] i.e. analogy alone

---

into the sciences in a way which can only have compromised its metaphysical independence (in any case the normal price for obtaining religious acceptance).

[19] We might say that a philosopher is thus the opposite of a Muslim, for whereas the latter finds certainty in the data and uncertainty in the reasoning, the former finds certainty in the reasoning and uncertainty in the data!

[20] *Muqaddima fī uṣūl al-fiqh*. The MS is extant, see Jackson 1993: esp. 86, n. 3.

[21] Ibn Khaldūn *Muqaddima*: 779f.; in the Beirut edition: Book VI, Section 4, but in Rosenthal's translation: II, 436 (following Quatremère), the Section is no. 9.

is the appropriate technique for perpetuating and extending a pattern of behaviour based on a single and unrepeatable precedent, the Prophet, who is literally a "model" *qudwa* to be imitated. Brunschvig's well-intentioned attempt to de-emphasise the alleged contrast between "Semitic" and "Indo-European" thinking is thus a red herring:[22] the Imitatio Christi of medieval Europe implies exactly the same preference for analogical reasoning to deduce right behaviour, that is to say it is the demands of the religion itself, not the (ethnic) mentality of its followers, which impose analogy as the dominant mode of ethical reasoning. Recent work of Jackson seems relevant here: al-Qarāfī (wrote in 1262) saw the prophet as a *qudwa* in four different ways, as *rasūl, muftī, qāḍī* and *imām*,[23] which may be interpreted as a deliberate extension of the prophetic role-model into areas where this had not previously been so clear or unanimously accepted.

Such factors may also explain the Islamic resistance to philosophical ethics, which arrives syllogistically at ethical conclusions,[24] a procedure which was in principle unacceptable to believing Muslims. There is a deep systematic incompatibility with syllogistic ethics in Islam: as Hallaq has remarked,[25] legal *qiyās* reasons from one particular to another, and this is inconsistent with the deductive principles of syllogistic ethics. The lawyers, we may assume, intuitively grasped that the ethical content of the revelation dispensed with any inductively derived ethical system. Deductive ethics was likewise superfluous because all individual ethical acts had been set before the community in the detailed model of the Prophet. This goes double (*a fortiori*!) for linguistic behaviour, which can only be based on a model, in this case the fiction of the perfect language spoken by the perfect tribe.

A short passage from Ibn Rushd conveniently illustrates how an argument can be constructed with a mixture of different kinds of reasoning, beginning with syllogism and ending with analogy. It is taken from the opening pages of his *Faṣl al-maqāl*,[26] where he aims to prove that the philosophical approach to God's creation through apodeictic reasoning is not only logically obligatory but also a religious duty. The argument falls into four well defined sections, beginning

---

[22] Brunschvig 1971:18.
[23] Jackson 1993:74.
[24] Cf. Butterworth 1987.
[25] Hallaq 1989:300.
[26] Ibn Rushd *Faṣl al-maqāl*: 28–31.

dialectically by stating the first thesis and its consequences, viz. that since philosophy is nothing but the study of beings in terms of their creator, and since knowledge of their creator is gained only through knowledge of how they are created, the more we know about the way they are created the more we will know about their creator.

There follows an appeal to authority. Divine law has recommended and indeed urged the contemplation of beings, hence philosophy is either recommended or compulsory: various Qur'anic verses support this claim. The third phase demonstrates that syllogistic reasoning must be studied from its beginnings in order to reach the highest levels of reasoning. The fourth and final section switches again, now to purely legal reasoning, drawing an analogy between a lawyer's need for sound knowledge of legal *qiyās* and a philosopher's need for a sound knowledge of syllogism. It ends with the *a fortiori* argument that if the lawyer arrives at his conclusions by legal arguments how much more so must the philosopher reach his through logic.

The purpose of citing this example here is to show how a good dialectician draws upon the whole range of methods of argument. This short passage displays all four principal weapons of debate: syllogism, textual authority, legal analogy, and *a fortiori* argument (a fifth, *ad hominem*, is not used, but we can be sure that Ibn Rushd was capable of doing so as the occasion required!). The modern reader perhaps needs to be reminded that neither Ibn Rushd nor his audience would at any time have failed to recognise the different methods being used.

Although the theme of this enquiry has been restricted to grammar and law, it also has a wider relevance. In the history of general philosophy, for example, it would appear from the above that Islam may represent a particularly successful case of the complete and conscious synthesis of two fundamentally different, even incompatible modes of thought. As Suleiman remarks,[27] the methods evolved by the grammarians "seem to relate to views in Islamic/Arabic culture concerning the nature of man and the universe [whose] elucidation would . . . have to bring together the effort and expertise of grammarians, theologians and philosophers". This is tantamount to saying that Islamic culture is an organic intellectual unity with many complex interrelationships, in which methods of reasoning are selected

[27] Suleiman 1991:263–264.

according to the nature of their object, the whole blending into a harmonious system of complementary sciences. And this brings us back to the dedicatee of this paper, who has devoted much scholarly effort to the study of Islamic exegesis: he is thus in the best position to appreciate that *Tafsīr* is beyond question the most comprehensively eclectic of all the Islamic disciplines!

CURRENTS AND COUNTERCURRENTS

R.M. Frank

Philosophical and theological traditions, systems and subsystems, are generated within particular cultural and social milieux and their histories are necessarily bound to the histories of these broader contexts. Certain fundamental givens of the historically common world are inevitably taken for granted and incorporated at some level. In some cases this takes place on the explicit basis of tradition or of religious belief while in others it occurs simply because of the way the world presents itself "naturally" and so manifestly is. "Language is Being's house and in its dwelling man resides."

For the ancient Greeks, the Gods (θεοί, δαίμονες) had always been features or elements of the world, beings whose activity lies just below the manifest surface of things, of natural events and some human actions, and are the source of our amazement and fascination with the natural world. The philosophers, rejecting the testimony of traditional report (μῦθος) for that of rational discourse (λόγος), found "god" (or the gods), s.c., the divine (τὸ θεῖον) in the most proper sense, to be ungenerated and eternal, that which is "first and most dominant"[1] in ordering the universe and on which therefore in some sense "the heavens and nature depend".[2] The stable and well ordered universe (κόσμος) is simply there—taken for granted as being eternal and the divine, whether conceived as a nature or principle (φύσις or ἀρχή) that is "separate and immovable" (χωριστὴ καὶ ἀκίνητος) as with Aristotle or as permeating all things as with the Stoa, is seen as an impersonal element or an aspect of the Whole which may be discovered through speculative reasoning. There may be a kind of "providence" (πρόνοια), but it is altogether impersonal. It is a principle of philosophy that one must follow the path of critical reasoning wherever it leads—ταύτῃ ἰτέον ὡς τὰ ἴχνη τῶν λόγων φέρει—but however firm one's resolve to submit all judgements and beliefs to critical and rigorously logical scrutiny, there is and can be

[1] Aristotle *Metaphysics*: 1064a.
[2] Ibid. 1072b.

no absolute intellectual space wholly uncontoured by the historically present matter of his world into which he can withdraw in order to take the measure of things exactly as they are without bias or preconception. The determinant criteria of plausibility and of "elegance" are not freely chosen. The Gods of Greek religion were elements or aspects of the natural order of the world and this understanding of the divine was carried over into Greek philosophy. For this reason the assimilation of Greek philosophical thought posed a serious problem for early Christian thinkers.[3]

Islam was founded in a prophetic message and its sense of the world developed and was articulated largely along with and in terms of readings and interpretations of that message. The theologians of the predominant sunnī schools found the world to be radically contingent: from not-being (*ʿadam*) it came into being (*wujūd*) at a time finitely removed from the present through an act of the creator. The creator exists altogether apart from and independently of the world. God acts freely by choosing; he makes himself known through particular individuals to particular peoples at particular times as he chooses.

Greek philosophy, the Neo-Platonized Aristotelianism of late antiquity, was partially remoulded in the contexts of its transmission to Muslim thinkers and modified again in the milieux which took it up. It was embraced, however, as received tradition. Over a millennium had elapsed since Plato and Aristotle had founded the tradition and the Muslims who found the tradition appealing were not historically prepared to make a radically new beginning. According to al-Fārābī, philosophy had attained a level of perfection in the time of Aristotle such that, as there remained no subject for further investigation, it could be transmitted and taught as "demonstrative science."[4] In its own peculiar way, thus, philosophy had become a kind of μῦθος in those intellectual circles for whom it furnished an authoritative paradigm by which to interpret present reality, the natural world and the human world and the divine. The transmitted tradition, by virtue of its comprehensiveness and its claim to be independent of, and therefore superior to, particular historical cultures and religious traditions, gave its adherents a sense of high intellectual power and control. Their boundless confidence in the certitude available through the

[3] See Pannenberg 1967:296–346.
[4] Al-Fārābī *Kitāb al-Ḥurūf*: 151f.

Aristotelian logic is reminiscent of Xenophon's naïve enthusiasm for the dialectic of Socrates; inherited premises and the world they presupposed were not called seriously into question. Avicenna alone explicitly criticised the orthodox tradition of the "peripatetics" and claimed personally to have improved upon it.[5] Most seem to have assumed—and some assert—each that his own peculiar views are nothing less than the consistent elaboration of the true sense and intention of the original tradition.

In appropriating Greek philosophy to their own use the *falāsifa* introduced a number of significant and interesting modifications into the basic tradition they had received, some specifically as adjustments to the Islamic religious milieu. The most important of these, at least for the context of our present considerations, is that the divine was no longer seen simply as responsible for the consistently ordered progression of phenomena, but rather the "First Cause" was conceived as the transcendent cause of the very existence of the world.[6] Thus, whereas according to the emanationism of Plotinus the One underlies (grounds) the presence of form and intelligibility and thereby too the principle of ordered movement and activity, and so ultimately the coming to be and the passing away of things, in the emanationism of al-Fārābī and Avicenna "the First cause" is the originating, efficient cause of the existence of the universe, of the form of what has form and of the matter of what has matter, wherefore the existence of the whole, of the world as such and in its entirety, is wholly contingent with respect to the one being whose existence is necessary in itself. The world is not itself the Whole (τὸ πᾶν) of what is and simply there as it was for the Greeks; it has to be explained, to have a cause beyond itself.[7] The First Cause, however, produces the world necessarily, "by its essence" (*bi-dhātihī*), and therefore eternally; the perfection of God's being entails the emanation of the world. God thus needs the world insofar as his being would not be complete did it not exist. Carrying through the theory of the determinant necessity of the sequential emanation of the hierarchy of celestial beings

[5] See generally Gutas 1988.

[6] E.g. al-Kindī *Rasā'il*: 62 and 182f.

[7] Cf., e.g., al-Fārābī *al-Siyāsa al-madaniyya*: 31f., *Mabādi'*: 88f., and Avicenna *al-Ilāhiyyāt*: 402ff. One inside the closed system of the universe can truly know the nature of a cause which exists outside the system and is unconditioned by anything within the system because such knowledge is given through the action of one of the necessarily emanated intelligences (*al-ʿaql al-faʿʿāl*) which has a mediated intuition of the first emanated being and through it a knowledge of its cause.

one from another together with their essential natures and order, Avicenna teaches a radical determinism which embraces every event in the sublunary world, human voluntary actions included. So too, the consistently held doctrine of a separated "active intellect" furnished not only an explanation for prophetic dreams and visions—things the "fact" of which was universally taken for granted—but also for the origin of religious prophecy. Significantly, however, as al-Fārābī and Avicenna take the agent intellect to be a celestial being, the mind is not conceived as the autonomous agent of its own intuitions. Avicenna's concentrated focus on necessary and contingent being and on essences as possibles whose instantiations are necessary *ab alio* stands in conspicuous contrast with the traditional Aristotelian focus on the substantial being of entities.[8]

What I wish to do, then, is to call attention to the fundamental differences that underlie several views that were widely held in sunnī Islam concerning the relation of God to the world and to man, viz., those originally Muslim systems of the Basrian Muʿtazila and of the Ashʿarites on the one side, and on the other that of al-Ghazālī, who was heavily influenced by the philosophy of Avicenna. Though very broad in that a number of diverse elements have necessarily to be taken into account for each system considered, our present remarks are nonetheless quite narrowly focused on the most basic theological differences that characterise and distinguish the three schools of thought. Textual citations have been restricted to a few basic texts and there to but one or two passages as seemed appropriate for illustration.[9]

1. *The Muʿtazila*

God's existence is necessary in itself;[10] eternally he knows everything, what shall come to exist and what shall not come to exist and has the infinite power to create any thing whose existence is not impossible.[11] The power to act is the power to act or not to act freely and

---

[8] Compared to οὐσία in the philosophy of Aristotle, *jawhar* stands as a relatively secondary concept in Avicenna's. The sublunary world with its "substances" is merely contingent, having of and in itself no being (Avicenna *al-Ilāhiyyāt*: 356).

[9] Additional references regarding several of the Ashʿarite theses here discussed may be sought in Gimaret 1990.

[10] ʿAbd al-Jabbār *al-Mughnī*: 11, 432f.

[11] ʿAbd al-Jabbār *Uṣūl*: 80 and *al-Mughnī*: 8, 68, and 11, 94.

autonomously and, since God's being is such that it is impossible that its perfection be increased by the existence of any contingent entity or diminished by its non-existence, it is possible both abstractly and concretely that he have created nothing at all.[12] The real possibility of the existence of any contingent entity is grounded in the power of the agent that can cause it to come to be and God's power is unlimited, embracing an infinity of classes of beings[13] and an infinite number of individuals in each class.[14] The primary classes of created entities, real and possible, are two: (1) the spatially extended atoms, which are essentially identical one to another and are independent entities in that each "subsists in itself" (*qā'imun bi-nafsihī*) and not in another, and (2) the various classes, subclasses, and varieties of entitative "accidents," instances of which exist in individual atoms. Corporeal beings are basically composites of atoms and accidents. Living beings have a proper ontological unity as such since their characteristic states and activities require the structured, organic composite,[15] and accordingly, predicates that are particular to living bodies—of men and of animals—are properly said of the structured, organic whole.[16] Even under the restriction of the limited number of kinds of essential entities (*dhawāt*), sc., atoms and accidents, that make up the present world God could have created a world radically different from that which presently exists; he could, for example, have created other kinds of living creatures and need not have created any or all of the kinds he did create;[17] the forms and constitutions of corporeal beings, living and inanimate, that actually exist were chosen freely by God. There are, however, absolute ethical principles of what is good and bad to which all knowing agents are subject.[18] Because God's being transcends benefit and harm it is concretely impossible that he be moved to do wrong or injustice and for this reason there are certain factual limitations on what God can create:[19] he could not create a universe in which there were no living beings, for this would be a pointless act and to do what is pointless (*al-ʿabath*) is wrong; similarly it is factually impossible that he have

[12] Ibid. 11, 98f. and 14, 205f.
[13] ʿAbd al-Jabbār *Mutashābih al-Qur'ān*: 1, 50 and *al-Mughnī*: 6/1, 162.
[14] Ibid. 6/1, 63.
[15] Ibid. 7, 33f.
[16] Ibid. 6/2, 22f. and 11, 352ff.
[17] Ibid. 11, 154.
[18] Cf. generally Hourani 1971 and 1960, and Frank 1983.
[19] See Frank 1985a.

created living beings without creating also the things they need for their sustenance.[20] It is, however, ethically legitimate that God do or not do whatever he does gratuitously[21] and consequently the fact that he does not create all the good that lies within his power to create does not entail his being miserly, for miserliness (*al-bukhl*) is to withhold what is obligated.[22]

In the school of Abū Hāshim, man is conceived essentially as a living being that has the power of voluntary action (*ḥayyun qādir*),[23] though more completely, "the being that is alive and has the power of voluntary action is this individual body (*shakhṣ*) that has a particular structure (*binya*) by which it is distinguished from all other animals and to which are directed command and prohibition, blame and praise".[24] God could have chosen to create man immediately in the state of paradise[25] or to have created him with intelligence but without the power of autonomous choice,[26] but chose instead to create him "having autonomous power of action, cognition, perception, life and volition" and so *mukallaf*, i.e., a free and autonomous subject that as such merits reward and punishment for his actions.[27] Having

---

[20] ʿAbd al-Jabbār *al-Mughnī*: 11, 154.

[21] Ibid.

[22] Ibid. 127. According to al-Naẓẓām and some masters of the Mutʿazilite school of Baghdad, God has to do what is best (*al-aṣlaḥ*) for his creatures. This thesis is not, however, intended to assert (and was not understood by its opponents as implying) that there is a unique best possible universe or order of the universe that God must create, if he chooses to create man; it says, rather, that knowing what choices each free human agent will make under what circumstances, God is ethically obligated to make the world and the human condition to be such that a maximum number of individuals freely act so as to achieve each his ultimate well being (*al-ṣalāḥ*); cf., e.g., al-Ashʿarī *Maqālāt al-islāmiyyīn*: 576 and ʿAbd al-Jabbār *al-Mughnī*: 14, 140ff. Note that the Muʿtazila and the Ashʿarites alike tend to avoid saying that God acts or creates "for a reason" (*li-ʿilla*) because the expression is ambivalent and may be taken to imply the necessity of creation, even though there is in God's wisdom that which makes creation (and the creation of man) good (*ḥasan*); cf., e.g., ibid. 11, 92f. (where note that the first line on p. 93 belongs at the bottom of the page).

[23] Ibid. 11, 311f. and 345.

[24] Ibid. 11 and 311.

[25] Ibid. 11, 71f. and 14, 137f.

[26] Ibid. 11, 137.

[27] Ibid. 11 and 309. God's imposition of moral obligation (*al-taklīf*) consists, most strictly speaking, in his "either making known directly through intuition or by presenting adequate evidence for inferring that those acts that are obligatory are in fact obligatory" (Ibid. 11 and 150). That the freedom to act is necessarily the freedom to do wrong as well as right (to obey God and to disobey), cf., e.g. ibid. 128 and 168. That the voluntary acts of men are truly free, see generally Frank 1982. Knowledge of the basic rules of good and bad in action are given by God in immediate

freely chosen to create man so, God is not altogether free with respect to his living creatures, but bound by the rule of justice and right action. Because human life inevitably involves some degree of hardship and pain and to live according to the fundamental principles of right action is often difficult, God owes his servants some proportionate compensation for the difficulties and pains they endure and has, moreover, willed to grant a reward that greatly exceeds any thing that could strictly speaking be merited.

Because man's acts are not causally determined by antecedent states and events, but are performed freely for some intended good, the being of the individual, as he consciously anticipates his own future as or through action to be done, transcends the immediate state of the atoms and accidents that constitute the individual whole or body that is he. Beings that lack the power of autonomous action have no intrinsic activity of their own. There is no "nature" (φύσις) in the classical sense; most "natural events"—all events that do not take place directly or indirectly as actions of living creatures—are directly or indirectly created by God.

There was no intrinsic need or necessity for God that he create man *mukallaf*.[28] He did so gratuitously[29] simply for the ultimate benefit and good of his creature.[30] Having created man thus as an autonomous agent responsible for his own actions, however, God is obligated to give him some basic kind of assistance (*luṭf*) towards the fulfillment of his duties,[31] i.e., that he furnish some incentives or motivations (*dāʿiya*) given which the individual will or is more likely to choose to do what is good and to avoid what is bad.[32] Prophetic

---

intuition; cf. Hourani, *op. cit.* Note that volition, according to the Basrian school is itself an act. The formulations of the proposition that what is an object of human agents' power of voluntary action cannot be an object of God's power may sometimes give the impression that what is meant is that there are possibles with respect to the power of human action that are excluded from God's power, but what is intended is that no act of a human agent can occur through God's power. Those who hold that God must do "what is best" assert that the *taklīf* is ethically necessary; cf. ʿAbd al-Jabbār *al-Mughnī*: 14, 100f. and 140ff. and also 13, 7.

[28] Ibid. 11, 71f. and 15, 115ff.

[29] Ibid. 11, 134f. and 154.

[30] Ibid. 11, 238.

[31] Ibid. 11, 222 and 224f.

[32] Ibid. 11, 258 and 13, 39, and ʿAbd al-Jabbār *Mutashābih al-Qur'ān*: 1, 24f. It is a central teaching of the Muʿtazila that God cannot be the cause (agent) of man's actions, that no action can occur through the power of two agents. Because of the disputes with the Ashʿarites, discussions of this are frequent and lengthy, involving much tedious detail; similarly with the thesis that God cannot constrain (*aljaʾa*, *iḍṭarra*)

revelation is a special form of this obligatory assistance.[33] Whereas, however, the primary rules of ethics are rationally given and as such (as *al-taklīf al-ʿaqlī*) are incumbent on all men of sound mind, those peculiar to the prophetic laws (*al-taklīf al-sharʿī*) are not,[34] but are rather particular enactments whose aim is to foster adherence to the universal principles of moral action.[35] The action of God with respect to man is essentially personal; whether in creating intuitive cognitions directly or in causing spontaneous thoughts and motivations (*khawāṭir*) that are conducive to right action.[36] God acts individually towards particular individuals whose natures he has determined in creating them and in prophetic revelation he makes knowledge of himself and his will for men expressly available to selected communities through chosen individuals. The human agent interacts with God as he responds to or rejects the revelation or any of the other kinds of assistance (*alṭāf*) that God offers him. The basic recognition that there is a creator, since it is achieved through logical inference, is the result of a voluntary action. God's action in creation, both in the basic ordering of the world[37] and in his various levels of gracious assistance, calls for a response on man's part—for obedience to the moral law, for recognition of God's goodness and for gratitude. The human intellect is ordered to action, the doing of what is obligatory and right, and thereby is oriented towards God, the ultimate judge and giver of reward and punishment. Accordingly, the world has consistency and meaning as the manifestation of God's power, will, and

---

the individual to act, since this would vitiate the agent's freedom and render the resultant act valueless. That to know God is a universal obligation, cf., e.g. *al-Mughnī* 12, 352ff. and that it must be achieved as voluntary act through rational reflection (ibid. 11, 150 and 15, 59).

[33] Ibid. 15, 9ff. and 23ff.

[34] Ibid. 13 and 187.

[35] On this see Gimaret 1974:16ff., Hourani 1971:126ff. and 132ff., and Frank 1978a:124ff.

[36] ʿAbd al-Jabbār *al-Mughnī*: 15, 509.

[37] The question of the order of the world as conceived by the Muʿtazila has received no systematic study. The Basrians, generally speaking, hold that sequences of events which, under known conditions, occur invariantly are due to the lawful operation of secondary causes (*asbāb*) related to the essential characteristics of particular accidents or structured composites (e.g. ʿAbd al-Jabbār *al-Mughnī*: 4, 42 and 124; 8, 186; 9, 53, 96, and 109; 11 and 79; and Abū Rashīd *al-Masāʾil*: 56 and 122f.), while those that vary consistently within a given range but for which the exact causes or conditions are not known are created directly by God according to his consistent custom or habit (*ʿāda*) (e.g. ʿAbd al-Jabbār *al-Mughnī*: 11, 79 and 115; 12, 52 and 86; 16, 307, 310, and 311 and Abū Rashīd *al-Masāʾil*: 37f.).

justice and the structured locus and context of man's interaction with his fellows and with his creator under a single set of moral rules to which all are obligated.

The theology of the Muʿtazila was fundamentally at variance with the basic religious sense of more conservative religious scholars and it was the teaching of that of the Ashʿarites that came to form the school theology for the Shāfiʿites and the Mālikites.

2. *The Ashʿarites*

God with his essential attributes exists eternally and necessarily.[38] To be God (*al-ilāhiyya*) is to possess unique and all-encompassing knowledge, power, and will;[39] what he wills comes to be, what he does not does not.[40] Where for the Muʿtazilites the non-existent possible is in some sense a being as a known or posited instance of a given class,[41] for the Ashʿarites, the possible as such is pure non-existence, a mere nothing (*ʿadam maḥḍ*); it has being only as God creates it[42] and creating it makes it to be what it is.[43] The primary classes of created entities are atoms, and accidents.[44] The Ashʿarite view differs significantly, however, from that of the Muʿtazila. Life and the phenomena associated with it do not require any specially structured substrate,[45] wherefore no primary predicates are properly said of any composite as such, whether animate or inanimate, but only of the individual atoms as they are qualified each as a separate locus of

---

[38] Al-Bāqillānī *al-Tamhīd*: §53, al-Juwaynī *al-Irshād*: 84, and al-Anṣārī *al-Ghunya*: fol. 25r.

[39] Al-Anṣārī *al-Ghunya*: fol. 33r, al-Isfarāʾīnī *al-ʿAqīda*: §II, 10 [= 134], and al-Qushayrī *Lumaʿ*: 59.

[40] Al-Juwaynī *al-Shāmil* [1969]:271.

[41] See Frank 1979:54f. and 65f.

[42] Al-Juwaynī *al-Shāmil* [1981]:22.

[43] Ibn Fūrak *Mujarrad*: 253f. and al-Juwaynī *al-Shāmil* [1981]:22. God makes the different kinds of things to be different (see the references in Frank 1992:52, nn. 95–97). There are possible kinds of contingent beings of which God has not created actual instances (Ibn Fūrak *Mujarrad*: 246); whether, however, the subclasses of certain classes are limited or not, was debated; v. Frank 1992: *loc. cit.*

[44] Al-Bāqillānī *al-Tamhīd*: §37 and al-Juwaynī *al-Irshād*: 17. Note that even though they do not occupy space and so are not "independent beings" (*qāʾimun biʾl-nafs*), accidents, for the Ashʿarites, as also for the Muʿtazila of the same period, are nonetheless conceived as being entities in the full and proper sense.

[45] Al-Juwaynī *al-Shāmil* [1969]:410 and 415ff.

particular instances of one or more accidents;[46] "knows" is properly said and is true only of particles (*ajzā'*) in which resides the accident, cognition, and "acts" only of the particle in which the event occurs. While atoms, once created, may continue to exist,[47] no accident endures beyond the instant (*waqt*) of its creation.[48] Bodies are conglomerates of two or more atoms, whose conjunction, each with its neighbour, is an accident. No created entity or event can be the cause of any other; whatever is or occurs God creates immediately, either according to the known and generally foreseeable pattern of his consistent "custom" and "habit"[49] or in unusual events as wonders on behalf of saints and magic for sinners,[50] or in uniquely peculiar events as miracles for prophets.[51] Since God is conceived as altogether transcendent and altogether separate in the necessity of his eternal being from all contingent beings, it would seem that the world as created and distinct ought to have some proper ontological density that belongs to it as such. Plainly, however, this is not the case, for it has no intrinsic or natural order, no substantiality, form, content or act of its own, but consists simply of the featureless atoms that are the passive recipients of God's ongoing activity as they receive the transient accidents that qualify their actuality from moment to moment, "signs" that are the manifestations—the correlates and referents—of his "action attributes" (*ṣifātu afʿālihī*). The existence of any created entity in being what it is God's act of creating it.[52] The texts evidence some interest in the regular and sometimes invariant association between certain kinds of phenomena as antecedents and consequents, but the discussion is most often focused, directly or indirectly, on the determination of the criteria by which genuine miracles

[46] Ibn Fūrak *Mujarrad*: 146, al-Juwaynī *al-Shāmil* [1969]:665ff., and al-Anṣārī *al-Ghunya*: foll. 155r ff.

[47] Opinions as to how this is so differ; some early authorities (e.g. al-Ashʿarī and al-Isfarā'īnī) hold that since "continues exist" is not equivalent to "exists" or "is an atom", there must exist an accident, "perdurance" (*al-baqā'*), which God creates in each atom in each successive instant; most later authorities deny such an accident and hold that perdurance is simply that the atom go on existing. The details of this we need not go into here. Only intrinsic or essential property of the atom is that it occupies a minimal volume of space. Atoms, therefore, cannot exist without one or more of the set of accidents that determine and define location and position.

[48] Ibn Fūrak *Mujarrad*: 13 and al-Anṣārī *al-Ghunya*: fol. 92r.

[49] Ibn Fūrak *Mujarrad*: 131 and 283.

[50] Al-Mutawallī *al-Mughnī*: 52 and al-Anṣārī *al-Ghunya*: foll. 183v ff.

[51] Ibn Fūrak *Mujarrad*: 134, al-Bāqillānī *al-Tamhīd*: §§12 and 639 and al-Juwaynī *al-Shāmil* [1969]:284, 501, 529, and 590.

[52] Al-Bāqillānī *al-Tamhīd*: §556 and al-Juwaynī *al-Shāmil* [1981]:47f.

may be distinguished from other unusual events within the overall framework of an occasionalistic universe. God's action, moreover, is bound by no principle or rule of right or of justice; his power and authority are absolute and any action of his is good as such. Whatever he might do and whatever its relation to or effect on any creature is good (*ḥasan*) and is just (*ʿadl*), simply and exclusively by virtue of its being his act.[53]

Man has no essential nature as such, but is simply a conglomerate body having a particular configuration.[54] The individual is an accidental whole that is one and centred only in the accidental continuity of the sense or impression of unity and wholeness that God creates in a part of it from one instant to the next. Volitions are accidents that God creates in particular parts of the whole which at the moment are said to will and similarly the power of voluntary action (*al-qudrah*) is an accident created simultaneously with the event which is its correlate or object (*mutaʿalliquhā*) in the particular substrates in which the event takes place and by virtue of which the event is described as the individual's "performance" (*kasb, iktisāb*) rather than as something he merely undergoes. Whatever may follow a basic or primary act as an apparent consequent is a distinct and separate act of God's—a whole set of acts, in fact, simultaneous and sequential. The consequent may be related juridically to the primary act or performance (e.g. drinking to inebriation), but they are not causally related. Nothing can be willed but what God wills. Within the context of Ashʿarite theocentrism it is unthinkable that God not be the efficient agent of every event that takes place in the created universe and so therefore that he have created man as an autonomous agent of his own voluntary acts, for the occurrence within God's realm of anything that he does not will and do would indicate that his knowledge and power were not absolute.[55] There can be but one autonomous cause of any existence or occurrence.

For the human agent, good is what God commands and bad is what he forbids; there is no moral obligation (*taklīf*)—no ethical right

---

[53] See generally Frank 1983:207ff. "Good" is predicated of God's acts and of human acts that conform to God's commands and prohibitions. That "good" is not predicated of God is highly significant for the conceptual development of both the Ashʿarite and the Muʿtazilite theologies. In origin this has to do with the semantics of Arabic "*ḥasan*", which originally is employed of the aesthetically beautiful and from this of the ethically good.

[54] Al-Bāqillānī *al-Tamhīd*: 194, 2f.

[55] Al-Ashʿarī *al-Lumaʿ*: §§51ff. and Ibn Fūrak *Mujarrad*: 69f. and 72f.

or wrong—prior to or apart from the promulgation of the revealed law.[56] God commands belief and creates belief in some individuals, in others unbelief; his doing the former is termed "gracious assistance" (*luṭf*) and his doing the latter "abandonment" (*khidhlān*).[57] The human individual is nothing more than the passive locus of some of God's acts, as he may choose to create or not to create knowledge of himself and belief in some of the body's elemental particles and obedience or disobedience in others. Beatitude and damnation are meted out in accord with belief and unbelief, obedience and disobedience, but not because of them,[58] for God can owe nothing to a creature.[59] God speaks to men through his emissaries, the prophets, calling them to acknowledge his being and to obey his commands; some respond, some do not, as God chooses and does. In those who cannot recognise the truth of the revelation, their rejection (*kufr*), is an event willed and created by God and is, accordingly, the manifestation of his concealing himself from them. Similarly, the knowledge of God's being on the part of those who recognise the truth of the revelation is also willed and created by him so that, in effect, their recognition of God's signs (*āyāt*) as such—the verses of the revealed text as his self-revelation—is itself one of his signs. Here God discloses himself, as it were, on two levels. The believer's basic knowledge of God and his attributes normally follows reflection on evidence presented in the world and argued as such in the text of revelation; God's eternal being remains remote. What the believer hears and understands through the articulated words (*al-ʿibārāt*) of the revealed text, on the other hand, is God's own, eternal speaking (*kalāmuhu l-qadīm*),[60] one of his essential attributes. In creating this understanding of the prophetic text, therefore, God communicates something of his eternal being. The sacred text, thus, does not merely impart information about God and his commands, but presents *kalām al-ḥaqq*: the true, eternal speaking of God himself. The believer, however, remains always the passive recipient of God's action; there is, strictly speaking—and can be—no interaction between them.[61]

---

[56] See Frank 1983:210ff. and 1985b:42ff.

[57] Al-Mutawallī *al-Mughnī*: 43 and al-Anṣārī *al-Ghunya*: fol. 161v.

[58] Al-Mutawallī *al-Mughnī*: 38 and al-Anṣārī *al-Ghunya*: fol. 155r.

[59] Ibn Fūrak *Mujarrad*: 163 and al-Anṣārī *al-Ghunya*: fol. 173r.

[60] Ibn Fūrak *Mujarrad*: 59ff. and al-Qushayrī *al-Fuṣūl*: §§35ff., pp. 63f.

[61] The Ashʿarite masters draw very precise logical distinctions regarding how an event can be ascribed to God under one description and to the human agent or

Whatever one may think of it, the Ashʿarite account of the world and human existence does preserve the appearances. Often, in the discourse of the jurists (*al-fuqahāʾ*) and in that of the orthodox sufis especially, one talks in terms of reasons or causes and, in the analysis of human acts, speaks with considerable insight of motivation, purpose and intention, of actions as produced or occasioned by prior events and present circumstances, and of the formation of character and habit, but the final ontological analysis here finds only God's action. Thus al-Kiyāʾ al-Harāsī,[62] a student of al-Juwaynī, says that people commonly talk of "reasons" or "causes"—for example, that eating is the cause of satiety—and that such popular usage is acceptable enough in legal reasoning, though in fact "there is no cause (*ʿilla*) in the strict and formal sense", but only the occasionalistic occurrences of God's customary action. Whatever consistency the world has and whatever meaning that is not illusory, is that it is the material manifestation or expression—the Äußerung—of God's power and will. What belongs to man as strictly his own is (whether he understand it so or not) his experience of God's immediate and personal action. All experience is the experience of God's activity and consciousness itself, together with its contents, is God's act.

The teaching of the Ashʿarite school is the formal articulation of a common sunnī sense of the being of God, man and the world and as such presents one aspect and level of the religious vision of a particular segment or region of Muslim society at a given historical period. It is, however, a narrowly focused vision, one in which the world is almost excluded from view save as a kind of background or stage for the believer's contemplation of God's all-powerful presence. Though it is akin to and was long associated with the theology of some of the orthodox sufis, it was not conceived and elaborated on the foundation of that more intimate level and modality of religious experience, but on the basis of a religious sense that was widely shared amongst religious scholars.

---

subject under another (see Frank 1983:212), but it remains that any state of being or event (in their terminology, any accident or performance) that qualifies the human subject is, in its existence and in its being essentially what it is, the act of God's creating it, even though it may be predicated of the subject and not of God under one or another description (e.g. "movement" or "performance" [*iktisāb*] or "obedience").

[62] *Uṣūl*: fol. 201r.

3. *Al-Ghazālī*

As the transmitted heritage of Hellenistic science and philosophy came to be more widely known and cultivated in Muslim intellectual circles, a number of religious scholars came to have an increasing sense that traditional *kalām* was fundamentally incapable of serving as the foundation for an adequate and sufficiently comprehensive account of the basic truths of religion. It is within this context that al-Ghazālī undertook the construction of a new synthesis of Muslim theology and the acclaim with which his *Iḥyā᾽ ʿulūm al-dīn* was received is witness to the extent of the dissatisfaction with traditional *kalām*, at least in some circles.

As with the Ashʿarites, and the Muʿtazila too, al-Ghazālī holds that God is the one being whose non-existence is impossible and whose knowledge and power are infinite and that the existence of the world is contingent on his will, whose act is neither entailed by his essence nor moved by any need or expectation of return. In its general conception as also in its detail, however, the theology of al-Ghazālī departs significantly from the common Ashʿarite doctrine of the Shāfiʿite colleges in which he was trained and in which subsequently he taught, in his adopting and adapting basic elements of the teaching of the *falāsifa* and, with regard to the principal matters of our present considerations, of Avicenna in particular, which he amalgamated with elements of various sufi currents.[63] The actual beings that make up the universe are conceived as instantiating essences or essential natures (*ḥaqā᾽iq*). They are divided into a number of basic

[63] There are significant elements of his thought which closely resemble and may likely be derived from matters derived from the school of al-Kindī; this, however, has yet to be studied. Some of the material al-Ghazālī took from sufi sources, moreover, may prove to be closely related to elements of the ethical teaching of al-Kindī. Other elements may derive from Ismāʿīlī sources (cf. Leibholt 1991). It should be noted that while al-Ghazālī in a number of places expresses himself plainly in quite formal terms, especially in *al-Maqṣad al-asnā* and *Mishkāt al-anwār*, major elements of his theology often remain unstated or are implied only obliquely in other works and are largely obscured, e.g., in *al-Iqtiṣād*. Though he insists on the value and importance of logic and talks earnestly about rational proof and justification, he seldom offers seriously elaborated arguments for his own most important theological positions and his presentations of logic are, for all his earnestness, conspicuously superficial. There is, in fact, some reason to suspect that he never really thought through the detail and the implications of a goodly number of the theses and propositions that he states or that seem to be implied by theses he does clearly assert. Concerning the questions discussed here see generally Frank 1992; and concerning al-Ghazālī's relation to the Ashʿarite school, see Frank 1994.

classes, the material and the immaterial on the one hand and on the other into those, celestial and sublunary, which make up the "universal, fundamental, permanent, and stable causes",[64] and those sublunary beings, which come to be and pass away.[65] Accordingly, al-Ghazālī enthusiastically discards the propositional analytic of the Ashʿarites in favour of the Aristotelian logic.[66]

The essences of contingent beings are unoriginated and are finite in number, already there as possibles instances of which God has the power to create.[67] God's being, moreover, is "necessary in its every aspect"[68] whence, albeit the world has existed for only a finite period of time, from eternity he wills necessarily what he wills.[69] Al-Ghazālī rejects the emanationism of al-Fārābī and Avicenna;[70] God creates, rather, the universal, permanent components of the universe, according to his wisdom, justice, and liberality, ordering them in precisely that order which is necessary and right (*al-tartīb al-wājib al-ḥaqq*) in order that everything in the world should be "as it ought to be"[71] so as to produce the one best possible universe.[72] What is good, right, and best here is not determined arbitrarily and gratuitously merely by being what God wills as in traditional Ashʿarite teaching, for his choice, according to al-Ghazālī, is effectively limited and determined by what is good and best in terms of the essential natures of the finite set of contingent possibles.[73] God's action is purely voluntary (*ikhtiyār maḥḍ*), but it is not totally free, since he could not have chosen otherwise.

---

[64] Al-Ghazālī *al-Maqṣad*: 100.

[65] Though his general conception of material being is "Aristotelian" (essential forms are transmitted from a celestial agent; some accidents are "concomitant" and endure so long as the subject they qualify continues to exist, while others are transitory, of shorter or longer duration), he seems nonetheless to have held an atomistic conception of bodies as such; cf. Frank 1994:48ff.

[66] Cf. al-Ghazālī *Miḥakk* generally and also *Mustaṣfā*: 1, 11ff. and *al-Maqṣad*: 17ff.

[67] Though, curiously enough, al-Ghazālī does not discuss the origin of the possibles and whether their classes or "forms" are infinite in number, that they are finite and in number and unoriginated is the only view that is consistent with what he does say; cf. Frank 1992:52–63. It seems likely that he may have failed to see the theological importance of the question.

[68] *Miʿyār*: 195 and *al-Maqṣad*: 43.

[69] *Iljām*: 68f.

[70] *Tahāfut*: 110ff.

[71] *Iḥyā'*: 4, 252 and *al-Maqṣad*: 109.

[72] Ibid. 68 and 81.

[73] On this see Frank 1992:63ff. Al-Ghazālī's conception of God's will would appear to have been worked out chiefly against Avicenna's thesis that creation emanates from God because of his very nature (*bi-dhātihī*) and therefore must exist coeternally with God; v. ibid. 77ff.

The universe functions as a complexly integrated machine in which every event is determined by the nature of its major operating components given the way in which they are ordered to one another[74] under the governance of the outermost sphere (God's "Throne") which, with its attendant "angel" (a "separated intelligence" in the lexicon of the *falāsifa*, to which al-Ghazālī occasionally refers as "the Well guarded Tablet"), contains, as it were, the program for the entire history of the world.[75] Albeit with the passage of time an increasing, though ultimately finite, number of immortal souls are produced, it remains that one can—at least from one perspective—hardly speak of history in the proper sense, for if one could know, as God does, the precise state of the entire system in all its detail at any given moment he could foresee every detail of all future states in succession and, even though the operation of the machine may not be reversible (the water cannot, consistently with al-Ghazālī's image of the water-clock,[76] run back up into the aperture from which it escaped), one could in principle calculate from the present all past states as well. In any case, it is God who is ultimately, through his creation of the system, "the one who makes the causes to function as causes"[77] so as to bring to existence everything whose being is in fact possible. He "is the existent whose existence is necessary in itself and from which exists everything whose existence is in possibility."[78] God's power is, in effect, limited to what must be, given the natures of the contingent possibles and the constraining necessity that there be the best possible world. Accordingly, "everything which lies in God's power is willed"[79] and "what lies in God's power [eventually] comes to be".[80] God, moreover, cannot intervene in the operation of the system.[81]

---

[74] *Al-Maqṣad*: 99f.

[75] E.g. *Iḥyā'*: 3, 18. Cf. Frank 1992:42ff. and refs.

[76] Al-Ghazālī *al-Maqṣad*: 99. It might be well to note that, howbeit al-Ghazālī conceives the universe as a kind of automaton, what is required in order to know all future states and events within it is not simply the knowledge of an initial state and of a limited set of universal laws, but rather the knowledge of an initial state together with an exhaustive knowledge of all the properties of each of the entire panoply of essential natures, material and immaterial whose instances make up the universe.

[77] E.g. *Iḥyā'*: 1, 74 and *al-Maqṣad*: 116.

[78] *Al-Maqṣad*: 47.

[79] *Al-Iqtiṣād*: 107.

[80] *Al-Maqṣad*: 103.

[81] Al-Ghazālī occasionally speaks of the secondary causes as the "conditions" of the existence of their effects (see Frank 1992:25ff.) and insists that within the universe God can create only those things the "conditions" of whose coming to be are

There can, thus, be two accounts of the occurrence of any event in the universe; the one as it is "created," i.e., as out of the mere possibility of its coming to be, its existence is ultimately determined and caused by God's original "determination" and subsequent creation and ordering of the universe and the other as it is the necessary result of more proximate secondary causes.

The being of the human individual—his essential reality—is, most properly understood, the soul (most often referred to by "spirit" or "heart"), an immaterial entity which, though not strictly speaking "located in" the body, governs it through the mediation of the brain.[82] The individual is not created directly by God, but rather through the intermediate agency of "angels", as a product of the operation of the universal system. Though similar in their elemental human constitution (*al-fiṭra*), individuals differ in accord with the differences of the particular mixture (*al-mazāj*) of the humours and elemental properties that make up their bodies and as they are endowed with greater or lesser intellectual potential; whatever his native endowments, however, each one through the course of his life develops his state of being with its peculiar level of perfection or imperfection as is determined by various events, physical, sensory, or intellectual, that occur in the successive stages of his ongoing interaction with the material world, with others, and, directly and indirectly, with causal agencies of the celestial world.

Every human action occurs as the inevitable product of the physical and psychological state of the individual and the immediately effective occurrence of particular, antecedent sensations and impressions or cognitions which determine motivation and thereby volition and action or forbearance. Man, in short, is endowed as such with the faculties of cognition, deliberation, and will and with the power to act, but the act of the will and the consequent action or forbearance are caused deterministically (*jabran, iḍṭirāran*) by antecedent states and events which are not chosen and whose existence derives ultimately from the operation of external causes, sublunary and celestial.[83] In

fulfilled (e.g. *Iḥyā'*: 4, 249f. and *al-Maqṣad*: 125). The structure and operation of the universe and all its parts is necessary (*Iljām*: 68f.); if God were to alter the universe in any way in order that some particular evil be avoided, the result would be that even more evil occur (al-Ghazālī *al-Maqṣad*: 68).

[82] That al-Ghazālī holds the rational soul to be immaterial and immortal has been disputed, but a more thorough examination of the texts shows clearly that he did; cf. Frank 1994:55ff.

[83] E.g. *Iḥyā'*: 4, 248ff.

effect, thus, the human individual is in no way autonomous or free. Volitions are simply moments in causally determined sequences of events and the power of voluntary action is therefore not the originating efficient cause of his acts. The being of the living individual, in short, is never anything more than the essentially passive subject of the complex of forces and stimuli, physical and psychological, which converge upon him through the operation of cosmic forces ordained and created by God. However much al-Ghazālī's teaching may differ from that of his Ashʿarite predecessors with regard to how God acts in creation, it remains that he can, no more than they, entertain the thought that God does not ultimately will everything that is willed and do everything that is done; no more than they can he imagine the possibility that human volitions and actions are free.

Prophetic revelations are given through the agency of the celestial intelligences and operate as a stimulus and guide for souls to seek and attain their proper perfection. Against the Muʿtazila al-Ghazālī insists[84] that it was not necessary for God either that he create man or that, having created them, he send prophets; but "necessary" is used here as an ethical term describing what an agent must do for his own interest and advantage, wherefore the thesis in no way conflicts with al-Ghazālī's assertion that from eternity God necessarily wills to create this uniquely best universe.[85] The occurrence of prophetic revelation through particular individuals at particular times and to particular social groups has thus also to be one of the phenomena that are determined by the requirements of the universal system, an infrequent, but nonetheless "programmed" moment or output of the operation of the system. The "prophetic light" is automatically transmitted by the angelic agent to a given individual when the conditions of its reception are fulfilled and its specific content, as it becomes (again according to a predetermined necessity) a functioning element within the cultural tradition (as an operative factor in the interaction of various individuals and groups within the society), has diverse, though in each case, inevitable, causal effects on the lives of various individuals.[86]

The soul is brought to one or another degree of imperfection or perfection according to the amount of true "light" which, originating

---

[84] *Al-Iqtiṣād*: 174.
[85] See Frank 1992:66ff.
[86] E.g. al-Ghazālī *Iḥyāʾ*: 4, 86f.

in God, is received by its various faculties, sensory, imaginative, intellectual, or prophetic[87] from the highest angelic "light"[88] through the intermediate activity of various angelic agencies[89] according to the particular conditions that obtain in each individual case. Attaining its true perfection, the intellectual faculty sees the true natures of things and their causes and so achieves the vision of God's wisdom in creation[90] and at the highest level perceives only unity in God:[91] "they see in existence only the True One".[92] The "light" of created intellects is, like their existence, given ultimately from God; it is "borrowed" from God who "is light in and of himself"[93] and "apart from whom there is no light".[94] In a sense, then, the fully enlightened soul may be taken to participate in the divine light, but the creature remains fully distinct from the creator. Moreover, this light is not, as in traditional Ashʿarite teaching, held to be given directly and, as it were, personally by God, for it is given by the highest "angel" as a function of its general governance of the universe. Only a few are destined to attain the highest levels of enlightenment.

Between al-Ghazālī's conception of the universe and man and of God's relation to them and that of traditional Ashʿarite doctrine the contrast is thus considerable. Although he insists (following Avicenna) that for all created beings existence is an accident[95] so that they are, in and of themselves, nullities or non-beings,[96] al-Ghazālī's universe has nonetheless a proper ontological substantiality of its own. Essential natures (*al-ḥaqāʾiq*), howbeit their particular instantiations may be purely contingent, are unoriginated and as such are given—in themselves already there—for God's creating the only universe he can create. The universe, moreover, is conceived as a sort of machine that once built and set in motion runs itself as inevitably it must (the image is twice set forth quite explicitly). One does not contemplate the beauty of nature as that of an organism suffused by the One as in the doctrine of Plotinus, but rather the wisdom and liberality of

---

[87] Al-Ghazālī *Mishkāt*: 76ff.
[88] Ibid. 52f.
[89] Ibid. 60.
[90] Ibid. 45.
[91] Ibid. 63ff.
[92] Ibid. 57.
[93] Ibid. 54.
[94] Ibid. 59f.
[95] *Miʿyār*: 57.
[96] *Al-Maqṣad*: 137 and *Mishkāt*: 55f.

the creator in his ordering and construction of the whole. Like the Ashʿarites, al-Ghazālī says that "there are in existence only God and his actions",[97] but what he means and asserts is altogether different. For al-Ghazālī the being of every contingent entity and its being essentially what it is is not God's immediate act of creating it. Nor does one contemplate single entities and events of the sublunary world as things—as signs—each of which is willed individually and created by God immediately. On the contrary, God's relation to the world and men is essentially impersonal. He willed necessarily to create the best possible universe—knew and therefore chose amongst possibles the one that "ought to be". By implication, thus, he created man, not particularly and as such, but because the human is one of the given essential natures each of which must be instantiated in the best possible world.[98] Though God knows particulars and therefore each individual as such and the details of his life as a given focal point of numerous determinate series of causes in the operation of the universal system, he does not, strictly speaking, choose the destiny of each individually and for himself; rather, each one comes to be and prospers or suffers and is brought to a predetermined level of perfection or imperfection (and ultimately, since the soul is immortal, to eternal bliss or perdition) as is demanded by the good of the whole and of the species as one of its constituents.

It is within this overall framework—this conception of God, the universe, and the rational soul—that the significance and nature of al-Ghazālī's sufism is to be understood, for this is the context in which he explains it. That he appeals to the witness of non-rational states of mind for the ultimate confirmation of his theories does not diminish the rational assumptions and the structure that govern the conception and elaboration of the whole.

4. *Concluding Remarks*

Summarising the salient characteristics of the three systems, then, we see that for the Muʿtazila God exists necessarily and is altogether self-sufficient; he need not have created anything at all and creating could have created an altogether different universe. The universal

[97] E.g. *al-Maqṣad*: 57.
[98] Cf. Frank 1992:63f.

principles of right and wrong action, however, impose certain limitations on the kinds of universe that he might have chosen to create.

God, a free moral agent, chose freely and gratuitously to create man an autonomous moral agent and so with the opportunity of gaining a reward for doing good and avoiding evil that is great beyond any possible merit. The revelation was given as an aid and incentive to this end. Nature is not simply given nor is the universal moral code merely conventional.

Sentient creatures have a claim of justice and right on each other and on God. The basic principles of good and bad in action are absolute for all intelligent agents. God knows them and imparts them to human intuition as a part of the *taklīf.* God's action in relation to man and the world is essentially personal. In being naturally oriented to his own highest good, man is oriented towards God as creator, benefactor and judge. God's being and actions, the world and the revelation are rationally intelligible to human reason.

With the Ashʿarites, God is totally self-sufficient and totally free; he might have created any kind of universe or nothing at all. Even with creation, however, the primary sense of "being" (*mawjūd*)—all that can properly be said to be—is God, his attributes, and his actions (*Allāh wa-ṣifātuhū wa-afʿāluhū*). Human beings, whatever they are or do or undergo, whether in this life or in the next, are most strictly speaking God's acts, immediate and direct. His being and his acts are essentially personal.

God commands his creatures but is not himself subject to any rule; his acts, like his commands and prohibitions, are altogether autocratic and arbitrary. They can be described both as such (in themselves and as God's) and, occurring as human performances, juridically, but can be rationalised under neither description; their occurrence is occasionalistic and their juridical classification in the case of human performances is arbitrary. The fate of individuals in the next life is not intrinsically related to the juridical status of their actions in this life. No contingent being or event can be rationally accounted for.

Al-Ghazālī is bound to a neo-Platonic paradigm. God is not totally free; creating, he must create the uniquely best possible universe. Moreover, if the assertions that God being is necessary in its every aspect and that his will is both eternal and necessary (*azalīyatun wājiba*) mean what apparently they must mean, then God, as conceived by al-Ghazālī, is not absolutely self-sufficient either, since it is impossible that he not have willed to create the world. The world, then, will be a kind of complement to God's being—not in so radical a way as it is in the philosophy of Avicenna, perhaps, but a complement nevertheless—something without which his being would be in some way incomplete.

God creates all sublunary events, human choices and actions included, through the determinate operation of unalterable sequences of secondary causes according to a program eternally determined (*muqaddar*) in his knowledge and wisdom and fixed in the outermost sphere at the first moment of creation. The revelation itself is a necessary output of the system. God's relationship to the world and to his creatures is fundamentally impersonal.

The good of man is determined by the nature of the rational soul and the good of action accordingly is subordinate and ordered to that of the intellect. God is just and generous, but nothing he does is, strictly speaking, gratuitous; nothing is arbitrary. Every contingent being and event, including the nature and order of the universe, the principles of ethics, the entire content of the revelation, and the ultimate status of each individual in the next life, is as it must be in the best possible universe and can therefore in principle be rationally explained.

CONCERNING THE LIFE AND WORKS OF FAKHR AL-DĪN AL-RĀZĪ

Tony Street

I was introduced to the writings of Fakhr al-Dīn al-Rāzī through the good offices of Professor Tony Johns, and I have always been grateful for that introduction. Al-Rāzī was born about 1148, lived in Persia and Transoxiana, and died in 1210; during his life, he wrote a great many works on theology and philosophy, including a massive commentary on the Qur'ān.[1] At a time when people studying the later Ashʿarites tended to be dismissive of al-Rāzī, Tony Johns was attracted by the narrative flair and literary acumen of the *Tafsīr al-kabīr*.[2] I think that al-Rāzī's importance is more widely appreciated these days, a reassessment which owes a great deal to Tony Johns and his work on the *Tafsīr*. For all that, there remain some common assessments of al-Rāzī's life and works which invite reconsideration. The assessments with which I am concerned are based on his last will and testament and on his autobiographical account of a series of controversies he held in Transoxiana. I take up each document in turn.

1. *The Last Will and Testament*

Al-Rāzī was very ill in Muḥarram, 1209, and from his sick-bed dictated his last will and testament[3] to his pupil Ibrāhīm b. Abī Bakr ʿAlī al-Iṣfahānī. The document taken down comprises two parts, the first of which is concerned to state al-Rāzī's religious beliefs and the claims he makes for his own theological and philosophical works; the second part deals with the transaction of household affairs, and

[1] Jomier 1980 gives what is probably the best overview of the important dates, journeys, and works of al-Rāzī's life. Also valuable in this regard is Jomier 1977.

[2] Also known as *Mafātīḥ al-ghayb*.

[3] I translate *waṣiyya* as "last will and testament," or just "testament." "*Waṣiyya*" and "testament" are both terms of art, one from Islamic, the other from English, law; the fit, while not precise, is sufficient for present purposes.

need not concern us at all. Some months after dictating his testament, al-Rāzī died, and was buried secretly to forestall the desecration of his tomb by his enemies. The testament came to be characterised as "a death-bed repentance for having used *kalām*,"[4] a view that has not been challenged in modern scholarship. A careful reading of the relevant parts of the document, however, shows this assessment to be wrong. I present the first part of the testament in translation below, excluding its opening.[5]

A few words are in order regarding the provenance of the text of the testament and the format of the translation. The full text is given in two of al-Rāzī's biographers: Ibn Abī Uṣaybiʿa (d. 1270) and al-Subkī (d. 1370).[6] A short passage from the document is also quoted by al-Ṣafadī (d. 1363) in his biography of al-Rāzī.[7] The two full versions differ in many places,[8] but not on any points of substance. Since the fragment in al-Ṣafadī supports Ibn Abī Uṣaybiʿa's version, that is what I have followed in the translation given below. I have divided the testament into paragraphs. The division is not completely arbitrary. §1 contains all of the text that has been translated up to now, though not even the whole of that paragraph has been translated; I set off in square brackets those fragments that have been translated.[9] Further, §4 contains that fragment of the text which is given in al-Ṣafadī's biography.

> §1. [Know that I was a lover of knowledge, and I wrote something about every question, that I might come to know about its quantity and quality, regardless of whether it was true or false,] meagre or gross. I exempted from this process that which I saw in the books I held in esteem, that this sensible world is under the direction of a Director who transcends any likeness to space-occupying entities and accidents, who is to be described as omnipotent, omniscient, and merciful. [I tried the methods of the *kalām* and philosophy, and I did not find in them the profit which I found in the great Qurʾān, for the Qurʾān ascribes all greatness and glory to God, and prevents preoccupation with objections and contradictions. These serve only to teach us that the human intellect comes to nothing and fades away in these treacherous defiles and hidden ways.]

---

[4] Makdisi 1962/63: vol. 18, 31.
[5] Ibn Abī Uṣaybiʿa *ʿUyūn*: 2, 27.12–28.8.
[6] Ibid. 27.2–28.18; and al-Subkī *Ṭabaqāt*: 5, 37.7–38.17.
[7] Al-Ṣafadī *al-Wāfī*: 4, 250.14–251.11.
[8] Note that al-Ṣafadī and al-Subkī also differ in their versions even though they were talking to each other about the problem of assessing al-Rāzī and his works; see al-Ṣafadī *al-Wāfī*: 4, 254.15–18. From ibid. 254.4, we know that al-Ṣafadī was also looking at Ibn Abī Uṣaybiʿa's biography of al-Rāzī.
[9] In Kholeif 1966:21–22.

§2. So I hold all that is confirmed by obvious indications concerning the necessity of His existence, His oneness, and His having no partner, either in all eternity, or in control or effective agency. This is what I hold, and shall take before God. As for those things which culminate in minute discussions and obscurity: everything which is found in the Qur'ān and in sound Traditions which are agreed upon by trustworthy leaders of the faith as having one meaning, these things are as they are.

§3. As for that which is not so clear, I say: O God of the worlds! I see that everyone holds you to be the most generous and merciful of all. You know everything I have written, and everything I have thought. I call your knowledge to witness, and say: If you know that I intended to make the false true or the true false, then do to me that for which I am worthy. But if you know that I only tried to establish what I believed to be the truth and conceived to be right, then let your mercy be according to my intentions, not according to my achievements. These were the efforts of a destitute man, and you are too generous to bear down heavily on a weak person who falls into error. Be merciful to me, hide my error, and forgive my sin, O you whose dominion is neither increased by the knowledge of savants, nor decreased by the wrongs of evil-doers.

§4. I say that my religion is following Muḥammad, the best of the messengers, my book is the great Qur'ān, and my refuge is the seeking after faith through these two things. O God, you listen to pleas and answer prayers, you do away with stumbling blocks, you are merciful to tears, you support temporally created and contingent entities: my hopes have always been in you, I implore your mercy. You have said: I am with my servant, so let him have hope in Me,[10] and you have said: "Who is it who answers the sore pressed when he calls?" (27:60), and you have said: "If my servants ask about me, I am close" (2:186). Even given that I have produced nothing, you are self-sufficient and generous, while I am lowly and needy. I know that I have none other than you, and I can find none beneficent other than you. I confess my errors, shortcomings, faults and lassitude. Do not disappoint my hope, nor turn away my prayer. Keep me safe from your punishment, before death and during death and after death. Make easy for me the agonies of death, and lighten for me the descent to death, and do not beset me with pains and illness, for you are the most merciful of the merciful.

§5. As for the academic works I wrote, in which I multiplied the posing of questions on those matters considered by the ancients, if someone looks at them and finds something pleasing, let him remember me in his pious prayers and ask blessings for me. If he does not find anything pleasing in my books, let him forgo wicked words about me. I only intended to increase research and sharpen the mind, relying in all things on God.

---

[10] Reading *fa'l-yaẓunna bī khayran* from al-Ṣafadī *al-Wāfī*: 4, 250.18, omitted in Ibn Abī Uṣaybiʿa *ʿUyūn*: 2, 27.pu.

This document is hardly a repentance for having used *kalām*. The reference to God transcending "any likeness to space-occupying things and accidents" (§1) is at least reminiscent of *kalām* terminology. Moreover, even the most unrepentant Ashʿarite would agree that the Qur'ān is nobler than *kalām* and philosophy (§1), and that a Muslim is obliged to accept unambiguous statements of doctrine in the Qur'ān and sound Traditions (§2). In fact, it is a common Ashʿarite doctrine that proofs for the basic dogmas are to be found in the Qur'ān and the Sunna and, though in non-technical language, these proofs are at once probative and immediately obvious.[11] But the crux of the testament, for present purposes, is §3: "I only tried to establish what I believed to be the truth and conceived to be right." Al-Rāzī is not disowning his works, but simply recognising his own scholarly limitations. And, in §5, he clearly hopes that people will continue to read his works after he dies. As al-Ṣafadī says, the testament serves "to show the soundness of his belief... and what he hoped for regarding his writings."[12]

2. *Assessments of the Testament*

How did the testament come to be taken as a death-bed repentance? The answer lies in the paraphrase of it put about by the Ḥanbalite, Ibn Taymiyya (d. 1328).

> He acknowledged at the end of his life that the method of the [philosophers] and the [theologians] neither cured illness or quenched thirst. He said: "I have contemplated the methods of the *kalām* and philosophy, but I found them neither to cure illness nor quench thirst; I found the closest path that of the Qur'ān."[13]

This is in fact quite close to the wording of parts of the original testament, but the spirit of the paraphrase is quite unlike that of the original. Especially the words, "he acknowledged at the end of his life," imply that there was a time in al-Rāzī's life when he denied the Qur'ān's superiority over *kalām*. But if he did deny this in his

[11] Frank 1991/92:223 n. 31. See also Frank 1989a:50.
[12] Al-Ṣafadī *al-Wāfī*: 4, 250.13.
[13] Ibn Taymiyya *Risāla al-furqān*: 97.6–9. This epistle is a pathology of heresy, and the comments on al-Rāzī are part of a larger and deeply coherent attack on non-fideist articulations of Islam; the whole epistle is worthy of careful study. (Mis)quoted and wrongly referenced in Maʿṣūmī 1967:366.

works on *kalām*, he would hardly commend their being read in the midst of repenting for having written them.

Why would it serve Ibn Taymiyya's interests to misrepresent al-Rāzī's testament? Al-Rāzī was a great and respected rationalist theologian and jurist, working toward an articulation of Islam which differs markedly from that of the fideist Ḥanbalites. A direct attack on al-Rāzī might fail to convince someone who revered him that his rationalism was a bad thing. But if al-Rāzī could be represented as resiling from the rationalist project at the end of his life, that representation might succeed where a direct attack would fail. This is the perfect conspiracy of approval: "God bless this good man, who was the first to realise how bad his works on theology and philosophy were."

Two Ashʿarites, al-Subkī and al-Ṣafadī, fought against the interpretation the Ḥanbalites compelled upon al-Rāzī's testament. The strategy al-Subkī and al-Ṣafadī followed in writing their biographies of al-Rāzī was, first and foremost, to restate the testament, and let people see for themselves how unfair the paraphrase was. The second strategy was to take issue with general bias in the Ḥanbalite writing of theological history.[14] Al-Ṣafadī mentions the famous attack on al-Rāzī and the *Tafsīr al-kabīr* made by Ibn Taymiyya ("it contains everything *but* commentary"), and al-Subkī's response ("it contains everything alongside commentary").[15] Al-Subkī, rather than traverse the same ground as his colleague, turns to deal with the attacks on al-Rāzī made by another fideist, al-Dhahabī.[16]

But the third strategy is the most subtle. Most of the biographers agree that al-Rāzī had trouble with the Karrāmites through his life, and some even say that he was poisoned by them.[17] But in the earliest biography of al-Rāzī that records the testament, that of Ibn Abī Uṣaybiʿa, no real account is given of al-Rāzī's troubles with anthropomorphists; the biography records (roughly) al-Rāzī's education, his relations with his brother, his fame amongst the Mongols, then gives the testament, and concludes with extracts of his poetry and a list of his books. Al-Subkī and al-Ṣafadī, on the other hand, write

[14] Makdisi has argued in his careful study (1962/63: vol. 17, 59) that the *Ṭabaqāt* is a piece of propaganda designed to endear the Ashʿarites to the Shāfiʿites, and that "the Ḥanbalite-traditionalists come in for a lot of old name-calling."

[15] Al-Ṣafadī *al-Wāfī*: 4, 254.16–18.

[16] Al-Subkī *Ṭabaqāt*: 5, 36.

[17] E.g. Ibn al-ʿImād *Shadharāt*: 5, 21.13; al-Subkī *Ṭabaqāt*: 5, 35.14; al-Ṣafadī *al-Wāfī*: 4, 258.6.

their biographies after Ibn Taymiyya's paraphrase had got about, and the context in which they present the testament differs significantly from Ibn Abī Uṣaybiʿa. Al-Ṣafadī, after speaking of the attacks the Karrāmites and al-Rāzī made on each other,[18] turns immediately to the story of how the Ḥanbalites fabricated defamatory stories about al-Rāzī's wife and son.[19] Then the testament is given, in a context which makes it seem that the people likely to desecrate al-Rāzī's tomb are the same Ḥanbalites who fabricated the defamatory stories. In other words, the fideists are seen as motivating the composition of the testament. Similarly, in al-Subkī, the testament comes straight after recounting the defamations, which this time are attributed to the Ḥashwites.[20] What al-Subkī and al-Ṣafadī seem to be saying is that these literalist Muslims, Karrāmites, Ḥanbalites, and Ḥashwites, have always gathered against al-Rāzī, and the testament should be read as an answer to their attacks.

Despite the efforts of al-Subkī and al-Ṣafadī, however, the fideist paraphrase continued, as in Ibn al-ʿImād (d. 1678):

> Al-Quṭb al-Ṭūʿānī said . . . that he heard Fakhr al-Dīn al-Rāzī say: "Would that I had not busied myself with the *kalām*"; and he wept. And it is recorded of al-Rāzī that he said: "I have tried the methods of *kalām* and philosophy and I did not find they quenched my thirst or cured my illness; I decided that the most correct path is that of the Qur'ān."[21]

This has remained the dominant interpretation of the testament in modern scholarship. Al-Rāzī is widely taken to prove that "some of the profoundest spokesmen of Islam turned away from *kalām* with contempt and disgust; they heard only idle talk, *kalām*, not theology."[22] But we have seen that in fact he did not turn away from *kalām* in his testament; nor, as we shall see below, did he turn away from it in the works of his maturity and old age.

---

[18] Al-Ṣafadī *al-Wāfī*: 4, 249.u.
[19] Al-Ṣafadī *al-Wāfī*: 4, 250.1f.
[20] Al-Subkī *Ṭabaqāt*: 5, 36.23f.
[21] Ibn al-ʿImād *Shadharāt*: 5, 21.apu–22.2.
[22] Van Ess 1970a:42. See also van Ess 1966:32; Kholeif 1966:21 (note that for the parts of the testament Kholeif translates, Ibn al-ʿImād is given as a source alongside al-Subkī and al-Ṣafadī, 22 n. 1!); Kraus 1938:137; Makdisi 1962/63: vol. 18, 31; Maʿṣūmī 1967:366.

3. *The* Munāẓarāt

Al-Rāzī wrote the *Munāẓarāt* to record sixteen debates he held in Transoxiana on questions of *kalām* and *fiqh*. It is fascinating that the *Munāẓarāt* has been most valued by modern scholars for the light it sheds on al-Rāzī's personality, not for its exemplification of the process of dialectic, nor for its testimony on disputed points in twelfth century Islamic thought. The sixteenth debate in particular has been taken to show al-Rāzī's "crookedness in argument,"[23] "how he gratuitously insulted his host,"[24] and what a "craving for intellectual superiority and a momentary ill-humour" could drive him to do.[25] The *Munāẓarāt* is generally held to be the work of an aggressive young man who becomes more agreeable later on in life.[26]

But are these views of the *Munāẓarāt* right? Consider the sixteenth debate, in which al-Rāzī argues about the eternity of the world. He forces the debate on his host, al-Ghaylānī, as condign punishment for his failure to observe certain duties of hospitality. Whatever al-Rāzī's ulterior motive, it has nothing to do with the formal or material content of the ensuing debate. Al-Rāzī allows al-Ghaylānī to choose the topic, and al-Ghaylānī decides to defend the Muslim doctrine of the temporal creation of the world against the Philosophers' doctrine of its eternity. Having heard al-Ghaylānī's arguments, al-Rāzī first shows that they only deal with an eternally existing dynamic world (an Avicennian model), but fail against a doctrine of a world existing from all eternity statically which subsequently begins to move (the model of Rhazes). Al-Ghaylānī then reduces his claim, and says that his argument is meant only to deal with models like those of Aristotle and Avicenna. Al-Rāzī goes on to show that even then his argument is incoherent, failing as it does to define the term "infinite" properly.[27]

The point of the debate has been achieved: al-Ghaylānī does not have an argument which can adequately defend the Muslim position against the arguments of unbelievers. It is important to understand that this is the motive for dialectic; it is not an occasion for instruction, but is rather a testing ground for arguments, which is conducted in

[23] Kholeif 1966:143.
[24] Frank 1968:229.
[25] Van Ess 1970a:25 footnote 20.
[26] A view most clearly expressed in Kraus 1938:137.
[27] Kholeif 1966: Question 16.

a style designed to search out weaknesses in a given formulation. To find a straightforward exposition of the doctrine, we may turn to al-Rāzī's systematic works on theology.[28] Throughout the *Munāẓarāt*, however, we have to expect the "closed fist" of dialectic, testing the durability of arguments. These considerations of genre must figure in any assessment of either the *Munāẓarāt* or the personality of its author.

There is, therefore, some reason to doubt that the *Munāẓarāt* reveals al-Rāzī to be gratuitously insulting, craving intellectual superiority, and crooked in argument. It is rather the case that the *Munāẓarāt* records dialectical debates, and the dialectician will always appear harsh. There are also good reasons to question whether the *Munāẓarāt* was among al-Rāzī's early compositions. Internally, we find one *terminus a quo* in the *Munāẓarāt* (1186).[29] Externally, we find that some of the biographers say that al-Rāzī went to Transoxiana when he was a young man, or at least before he had become wealthy, and only got back to Persia after a series of controversies.[30] But a *terminus a quo* is just that; and there is no good reason to think that al-Rāzī wrote the *Munāẓarāt* straight after his return from Transoxiana. Quite the contrary, some of the controversies recorded seem separated from the others by considerable stretches of time; the fourth controversy takes place "long years" after the event described in the third controversy.[31] There is a statement at the beginning of the fifteenth controversy that al-Rāzī came back to Ghazna after some years in Samarqand.[32] Further, in the last controversy, al-Rāzī obviously has a retinue,[33] from which it seems reasonable to suppose that he has become wealthy by this time. From what little has been reconstructed of al-Rāzī's travels by Jomier, it would be consistent if he were in Ghazna late in life.[34]

Stylistically, some of the last works of al-Rāzī are written in a clenched and dialectical prose, especially the *Maṭālib al-ʿāliya*, in which we find evidence for a composition date after 1203.[35] This shows

[28] E.g. al-Rāzī *Maʿālim*: 35f.

[29] Kholeif 1966: §78. There are also references to the *Mulakhkhaṣ*, *Sharḥ al-ishārāt*, and the *Mabāḥith al-mashriqiyya* §162, which help set the ordinal interrelation of al-Rāzī's works.

[30] See e.g. al-Subkī *Ṭabaqāt*: 5, 35.8f. and al-Ṣafadī *al-Wāfī*: 4, 249.10f.

[31] Kholeif 1966: §41.

[32] Ibid. §143.

[33] Ibid. §161.

[34] See Jomier 1977:256–259.

[35] See al-Rāzī *al-Nubuwwāt*: 213.16 (*ka-mā fī hādhā ʾl-zamāni ʾl-ladhī naḥnu fīhi*

us that al-Rāzī continued to use dialectic till the end of his life and, indeed, continued to suffer the setbacks of the controversialist recorded in the *Munāẓarāt.*

> Some people, when their opponent raises an argument, and they are left without any reply, say: He beat me because of his knowledge of the method of dialectic, and my own inability in that [craft], yet he knows in his heart that I hold the truth. Then the theologian can only . . . say: By God, the matter is as I say.[36]

Style does not lead us to conclude that the *Munāẓarāt* was written early in al-Rāzī's career. Nor does the evidence, be it internal or external.

4. *The Aims of the* Munāẓarāt

Why did al-Rāzī compose the *Munāẓarāt?* The book has been taken to exemplify the methods a typical *mutakallim* follows in debate.[37] To an extent, I think this was one of the uses al-Rāzī had in mind for the *Munāẓarāt.* At the very least, he certainly did want to stress the sort of argument techniques that should not be employed.[38]

Another possible reason for the composition of the *Munāẓarāt* has been put forward by Kraus. Kraus compares the *Munāẓarāt* with three autobiographies of great medieval scholars (Ḥunayn b. Isḥāq, Abū Bakr Muḥammad Zakariyyā al-Rāzī, and al-Mu'ayyad fī 'l-Dīn Hibatallāh al-Shīrāzī), all of which were written to justify certain intellectual positions adopted. Kraus ventures:

> I am inclined to think that an analogous want induced Fakhr al-Dīn to compose this treatise. The necessity to leave Transoxiana, because of the trouble which the propagation of his ideas gave rise to, could have been one of the reasons which led him to write his "Controversies" with the purpose of justifying himself both in the eyes of his contemporaries and in his own eyes for the positions he had taken in his different discussions and which finally led to his expulsion.[39]

---

wa-hwa awā'ilu 'l-sittimiya mina 'l-hijra); this is a commercial printing of an extract from the *Maṭālib* (reviewed in *MIDEO* 18 (1988) 303–304), and the reference I have given is to the 2nd *faṣl* of the third *qism.* The whole first section of the book is written in a dialectical style. External evidence for the date of composition of the *Maṭālib* is in Ibn Abī Uṣaybiʿa *'Uyūn*: 2, 29.apu.

[36] Al-Rāzī *al-Tafsīr al-kabīr*: 28, 193.12f. ad *sūra* 51. There are, however, problems in the dating and authorship of this section of the commentary; see Jomier 1977:276.

[37] E.g. van Ess 1970a:31; van Ess 1970b:375.

[38] Kholeif 1966: §§38, 88.

[39] Kraus 1938:141.

Comparing the *Munāẓarāt* with other autobiographical works is a good strategy for finding out what might have been the reasons for its composition. But other autobiographies might be used for the comparison, highlighting different possible reasons for composition.

Al-Ghazālī's autobiography, *al-Munqidh min al-ḍalāl*, provides another point of comparison for the *Munāẓarāt*. Some doctrinal background is necessary to understand the importance of this autobiography. For al-Ghazālī, and for other Ashʿarites, it was a significant Tradition that God sends a renovator of the faith at the turn of each Islamic century. This renovation of the faith is connected to Ashʿarite doctrines of knowledge and *taqlīd*. Roughly, *taqlīd* is total adherence to someone else's teaching; the beliefs of the *muqallid* are based on the assertions of another scholar, and the *muqallid* does not have true control over the justifications for his beliefs. According to al-Juwaynī, even highly trained specialists in *kalām* are not necessarily in control of the doctrine they teach and defend. Though they have plausible justifications for what they believe, they are unable to extend their doctrine in new ways to meet unexpected objections. Their belief remains in "the arena where opinions clash" (*fī multaṭami 'l-ẓunūn*).[40] Al-Ghazālī held that the sort of scholar who can rise above these limitations is very rare, this level "being reached perhaps by one or two individuals a century."[41] One way that al-Ghazālī stakes his claim to be that renovator of the faith is in the *Munqidh*, where he charts his intellectual training, shows his competence to be comprehensive, and claims as a result to be able to refute all kinds of specious, wrong arguments.[42] With some reluctance, overcome by reference to the Tradition on the centennial renovation of the faith, the needs of the age, and his own abilities, al-Ghazālī returns to public life.[43]

In the light of al-Ghazālī's autobiography, a possible interpretation for al-Rāzī's *Munāẓarāt* may be sketched out. Though no study has been consecrated to al-Rāzī's doctrine on *taqlīd*,[44] it seems reasonable to assume that he shared many points with earlier Ashʿarites on the

---

[40] Frank 1989:57.

[41] Frank 1991/92:218.

[42] Jabre 1959:48.14f. (Arabic text).

[43] Ibid. 49.15f.

[44] I get the impression that al-Rāzī would be closer to al-Juwaynī than al-Ghazālī on the issue of *taqlīd*; he certainly did not feel that *taqlīd* could lead to inherently stable belief (cf. Frank 1991/92:208), nor did he ever seem ambiguous toward the *kalām* (cf. ibid. 218 note 22).

subject. The fact that it was the turn of the century was in al-Rāzī's mind.[45] Further, the stagecraft of the *Munāẓarāt* portrays a series of interlocutors lost in confusions and shifting suppositions (*iḍṭirābāt, intiqālāt*) when confronted by al-Rāzī's objections; they are grateful to al-Rāzī for his solutions.[46] Al-Rāzī emerges from the *Munāẓarāt* as someone who is not *muqallid*, and who is able to answer new and unexpected objections to the faith. Like al-Ghazālī, al-Rāzī may be making claims to be the renovator of religion for the age. In fact, al-Rāzī came to be counted as the sixth renovator of *kalām*, and the *Munāẓarāt* may have been one of the documents that helped establish his claim to the title.[47]

5. *Concluding Remarks*

I conclude this study by indicating two related, and unfortunate, consequences of holding the views of the testament and the *Munāẓarāt* which I have been concerned to challenge.

The first consequence has been to see al-Rāzī's intellectual career as following a trajectory, moving from a young, brash dialectician to an old, pious man, sceptical of the theological enterprise. Paul Kraus, in his study on the *Munāẓarāt*, describes al-Rāzī's life as a triptych.

> [Al-Rāzī in the *Munāẓarāt*] shows himself to be a dialectician who knows how to prove a point, and possesses convincing arguments against every possible position.
>
> On the other hand, he is not yet the great preacher who touches the deepest feelings of his auditors. Neither is he yet the sage who will finally reject futile theological argumentation of *kalām*.[48]

But the *Munāẓarāt* is not necessarily early, and the testament is not a rejection of theological argumentation. The triptych needs to be

---

[45] Al-Rāzī *al-Nubuwwāt*: 213.16.

[46] Kholeif 1966: examples of confusion, §§13, 27, 37, 139; examples of gratitude (and comparison with previous great scholars) §§51, 97, 160. Note that the whole of the 16th question is designed to show that existing scholarship cannot answer an important non-Muslim challenge to the doctrine of the temporal creation of the world.

[47] He was so counted by al-Subkī *Ṭabaqāt*: 1, 104–106. This volume of al-Subkī is not available to me, so I have to rely on Kholeif 1966:12; note that the reference to the tradition that every hundred years a renovator of the faith will arise in the community in Kholeif 1966:9, footnote 1, should read: Wensinck 1932: vol. 1, 324.

[48] Kraus 1938:137.

reconsidered. Al-Rāzī's life and works should not be measured against a calculus which assumes he developed from a dialectician who is interested only in scoring debating points to a sage preferring a spiritual path to an intellectual one. It is rather the case that considerations of audience and subject matter determine the tone of al-Rāzī's works.

The second consequence follows on the first. There seems to be the feeling that since the al-Rāzī of the testament rejects the young al-Rāzī's work, that work cannot be very good. Whenever we are confronted by al-Rāzī the dialectician, we assume he has adopted a given intellectual position for the eristic fortunes of the moment. For example, when in the tenth and eleventh controversies of the *Munāẓarāt*, al-Rāzī takes issue with al-Ghazālī's methods, his objections have been dismissed as mere jealousy and arrogance.[49] But if the arguments put forward by al-Rāzī are actually examined, they will be seen to deal with important matters.[50] The fact is that the al-Rāzī of the testament did not disparage the work of al-Rāzī the dialectician; nor should we.

---

[49] E.g. Kraus 1938:150; van Ess 1970b:375; Frank 1968:229.

[50] Al-Rāzī is particularly concerned to challenge al-Ghazālī's methods of exposition. This is so even in works known to have been written in al-Rāzī's maturity: see, e.g. *al-Tafsīr al-kabīr*: 1, 85. For problems of dating the early sections of the work, see Jomier 1977:254.

EIGHTEENTH CENTURY SUFI BROTHERHOODS

Structural, Organisational and Ritual Changes

Nehemia Levtzion

Papers presented at a conference held in Jerusalem on Eighteenth Century Renewal and Reform in Islam were published in 1987 in a volume that carries the same title. In the introduction to that volume the following points were emphasised:[1]

In the eighteenth century individuals and groups sought to bring a revived sense of adherence to Islam, and by the end of the century there were activist movements of renewal and reform in all parts of the Muslim world; in China, Indonesia, Bengal, India, the Caucasus, the Arabian Peninsula, Egypt, Algeria, Morocco and West Africa.

These movements could not have been ramifications of the anti-sufi Wahhābiyya, because they developed within reformed sufi *ṭuruq*.

Leaders of these movements, including Muḥammad ibn ʿAbd al-Wahhāb, were linked together through networks made up of numerous scholastic and Sufi chains (*salāsil*, sing. *silsila*) of masters and disciples.

Circulation of peoples and ideas within these networks was aided by the growing number of pilgrims to the Haramayn. Mecca and Medina were the hub of this dynamic network, that brought together centre and periphery to create a global Muslim intellectual community.[2]

Networks that cut across regions brought together scholars from different schools of law (*madhāhib*), who studied under the same teachers because of the emphasis on *ḥadīth* and *taṣawwuf* (mysticism), which are not confined to one *madhhab*.

At the Jerusalem conference the term "Neo-Sufism", coined by Fazlur Rahman for the eighteenth century reformed Sufi *ṭuruq*, has been adopted.[3] Shortly after the publication of our volume the term

[1] Levtzion and Voll 1987:3–20.
[2] See also Levtzion and Weigert: 1996.
[3] Fazlur Rahman 1960: chapter 12.

"Neo-Sufism" came under criticism. Thus, O'Fahey and Radtke concluded an article entitled "Neo-Sufism Reconsidered" as follows: "If the use of the term 'Neo-Sufism' is to be retained, it should be restricted to the organisational innovations of certain Sufi brotherhood in specific regions of the Muslim world."[4]

Because we believe that organisational innovations are at least as important, often even more important, than changes in ideology or teachings of religious institutions, O'Fahey and Radtke's concluding remark will be the starting point for the present essay. We seek to prove that changes in the structure and organisation of Sufi brotherhoods in the eighteenth century were far reaching, and that they occurred not in "certain Sufi brotherhoods", but in many of them, and not "in specific regions of the Muslim world", but all over the Muslim world.

1. *The Organisation of Sufi Brotherhoods Before the Eighteenth Century*

The organisation of the Sufi orders and their relations with the population at large raise important questions for which the sources fail to provide satisfactory answers.[5] But the accumulated evidence suggests that before the seventeenth century the great majority of the brotherhoods were rather diffused, without a central organisation, and without strong links among their members or among their dispersed branches.

The Shādhiliyya and the Qādiriyya had no central organisation, and there was no control over the nomination of *shaykh*s in individual *zawāyā*. Even the descendants of ʿAbd al-Qādir al-Jīlānī in Baghdad, guardians of his tomb, were not recognised as their superiors by other Qādiri *shaykh*s. The Shādhiliyya and the Qādiriyya brotherhoods did not encourage popular forms of devotion. Their members wore no common habit, and there were no regulations or practices through which affiliates to the brotherhoods could be recognised. They all shared only the respect for the founders of their respective *ṭuruq*.[6] Similarly, the Suhrawardiyya and the Kubrāwiyya

[4] O'Fahey and Radtke 1993:87.

[5] Lapidus 1967:105–106; Winter 1982:126.

[6] Trimingham 1971:50 and 179; Winter 1982:89 and 10; Clayer 1994:341; Zarcone 1993:76.

in India were not unified brotherhoods, but only lines of ascription. Their branches were localised independent convents.[7] The absence of a strong central authority in the Khalwatiyya, and the autonomy of its wide spreading *zawāyā*, are considered among the reasons for a perpetual process of fragmentation, so typical of this brotherhood.[8]

Only for two brotherhoods, both Ottoman, is there evidence of greater cohesiveness. The Mawlawiyya was a centralised organisation, and all its members acknowledged the authority of the supreme *shaykh* of Konya, who also maintained his right to confirm the accession of heads of local lodges. Similarly, the Bektāshiyya developed into a highly organised and centralised brotherhood. Its supreme *shaykh*, who resided in the chief *tekke* at Ḥajji Bektāsh, claimed the right to present candidates for the positions of heads of all the Bektāshi *tekke*s to the central Ottoman government.[9] It is likely that the power of the supreme *shaykh*s of these brotherhoods resulted from the policy of the Ottoman government. In order to control the dervishes of these brotherhoods, who exercised considerable influence over the common people, the government sought to integrate the brotherhoods into the centralised bureaucratic state.

It follows that before the eighteenth century most brotherhoods had not been self-supporting social organisations in their own right. In the absence of centralised structures, Sufi brotherhoods were socially allied with other organisations. In the countryside they became embedded in social (family and clans) and regional units, which *shaykh*s were able to manipulate through their charismatic power. In urban societies the brotherhoods were linked to the *futuwwa*, the *akhī*, and *aṣnāf* (trade guilds). Sufis also allied themselves with military formations, such as the *ghāzī*s and the Janissaries.

2. *From Diffusive Affiliations to Large-Scale Organisations*

The direction of the change that took place in the eighteenth century was from old patterns of decentralised diffusive affiliations to larger scale organisations, more coherent and centralised.

In the Nilotic Sudan the Qādiriyya and Shādhiliyya had been

---

[7] Trimingham 1971:55–56, 65 and 179.
[8] Trimingham 1971:74–75; Clayer 1994:34–35.
[9] Trimingham 1971:61–62 and 179; Faroqhi 1976:76.

assimilated into localised holy clans before the eighteenth century, each with its independent *shaykh*. The relationship between the *shaykh* and his followers was direct, face to face and personal, without any hierarchical organisation. But since the last quarter of the eighteenth century new Sufi brotherhoods entered the Sudan—the Sammāniyya, Khatmiyya and Rashīdiyya—that incorporated local holy families into large scale organisations.[10]

Even in Morocco, a country of Sufism *par excellence*, there had been no structured hierarchical brotherhoods before the seventeenth century, only independent *zawāyā*, seats of holy men or *marabouts*. They all followed the Shādhili Sufi tradition, which at that time lacked any meaningful organisation. Only since the late seventeenth century did new brotherhoods evolve out of the local *zawāyā*, on a wider geographical and societal scale.

Before the eighteenth century the Khalwatiyya in Egypt had been "marginal and of little significance".[11] It had adherents mostly among the Turks and members of the upper classes. But within a few years after 1737, the Khalwatiyya spread like a brush fire, winning adherents among the common people in Cairo, as well as in the provincial towns and in the villages of Egypt. For the first time the Khalwatiyya became a truly Egyptian order.[12] In terms of orthodoxy, al-Jabartī described the Khalwatiyya as "the best of the orders (*khayr al-ṭuruq*)".[13]

In 1769 Muḥammad b. ʿAbd al-Raḥmān al-Azharī returned to the Kabiliya from Cairo, where he had been initiated into the Khalwatiyya. In the Kabiliya he propagated the Khalwatiyya so successfully that by the time of his death in 1793 the Raḥmāniyya (as it became known after him) was the most popular *ṭarīqa* in Algeria. Its rapid expansion may be explained by al-Azharī's strategy of incorporating local saintly lineages into the expanding network that he created, making local *marabouts*, who had controlled the spiritual life of the Berbers of Kabiliya, *muqaddams* or local representatives of the Raḥmāniyya.[14]

It is clear from the evidence that hierarchical centralisation of the *ṭarīqa* organisation was a novelty. The Kurdish Shaykh Khālid of the

---

[10] Karrar 1992:x, 20.
[11] de Jong 1987:123.
[12] Weigert 1989.
[13] Al-Jabartī 1390 AH: I, 295.
[14] Clancey-Smith 1986.

Naqshabandiyya, who died in Damascus in 1826, created a network of over one hundred *khalīfa*s, each with a delineated geographical area of responsibility.[15] In the Sudan, al-Mirghānī, founder of the Khatmiyya, appointed and deposed *khalīfa*s as mere administrative officials, who were completely dependent on the central leadership of the *ṭarīqa*. He also repeatedly reminded his representatives that they were not independent *shaykh*s, and that they owed their *baraka* to him.[16]

Before the eighteenth century, according to Kissling, brotherhoods had not created dynasties, and only rarely did a son succeed his father as *shaykh.*[17] Succession passed from the *shaykh* to a disciple, elected for his spiritual merits. The change to hereditary succession signified the shift from the transmission of spiritual mystical qualities through teaching to the transmission of the *baraka* through descent. This change occurred with the growing importance of the founder's tomb. In Sind it was in the middle of the seventeenth century, when the *daragh*, the tomb, became administered by the saint's descendants.[18] Hereditary succession was also related to the enhanced authority of the *shaykh* over his disciples, the growing numbers of lay affiliates, and the accumulation of material assets.

3. *Ritual Changes*

We shall now argue that these changes in the structure and organisation of brotherhoods might also explain changes in rituals. The *rābiṭa* was practised by the Naqshabandiyya and other *ṭuruq* to bind the heart of the *murīd* with the perfect *shaykh.* The *murīd* was instructed to keep the image of the *shaykh* in his imagination even when the latter was absent. Shaykh Khālid, who created his own branch of the Naqshabandiyya, instructed his deputies that their own *murīd*s should link directly with him, and concentrate on his image only. He did so against the general trend of the Naqshabandiyya that the *rābiṭa* was between the *murīd* and his immediate spiritual guide. Khālid introduced this innovation in order to enhance the Khālidī-Naqshabandiyya as a centralised disciplined organisation.[19]

15 Algar 1990:138; Abu Manneh 1990:295.
16 Hofheinz 1990:28–29; Grandin 1990:645; Karrar 1992:126 and 130–131.
17 Kissling 1954:29; see also Winter 1982:138; Eaton 1978:204.
18 Eaton 1978:207.
19 Abu Manneh 1990:302.

The *dhikr*, which is the central ritual in all the *ṭuruq*, is performed by the repetition of the name of Allah either in silence (*dhikr khafī*) or aloud (*dhikr jahrī* or *jalī*). The silent *dhikr* had the aura of orthodoxy, whereas the vocal *dhikr*, which may also be accompanied by music and dancing, was often criticised by the purists.

Joseph Fletcher suggested that the cause for the eighteenth century split within the Naqshabandiyya in China, between the so-called "Old Teaching" and "New Teaching", occurred when Ma Ming hsin introduced the vocal *dhikr*, and thus alienated the older Naqshabandis that insisted on the silent *dhikr*.[20]

The "New Teaching" of Ma Ming hsin was not the only case of an eighteenth century revivalist movement that changed from the silent to the vocal *dhikr*, namely from the more to the less orthodox. Muṣṭafā al-Bakrī, who inspired the revival of the Khalwatiyya in Egypt, also made that change. Al-Bakrī presided over *dhikr* ceremonies in Jerusalem, where participants fainted because of excitement and exhaustion. His disciple al-Ḥifnī adopted the vocal *dhikr* enthusiastically, and the ceremonies he conducted in Cairo became so popular that he had to repeat the *dhikr* days and nights to admit the many thousands who wanted to attend it.[21]

By changing to the vocal *dhikr* Muṣṭafā al-Bakrī offered a larger scope for the participation of common people in the rituals of the Khalwatiyya, which helped to make it more popular. At the same time al-Bakrī applied stricter discipline in the performance of the litanies by the *murīd*s of the *ṭarīqa*, and emphasised adherence to the *sharīʿa*. This would explain the success of the Khalwatiyya in Egypt, which as a cohesive, *sharīʿa*-oriented *ṭarīqa*, accommodated leading scholars, but also reached out the common people.

There are other examples to demonstrate that the change to a vocal *dhikr* was associated with a trend to popularise the *ṭarīqa* and to recruit adherents. According to the sixteenth century Naqshabandi *shaykh* Khwaja Makhdūm-i Aʿzam: "the Lords of the Naqshabandiyya preferred the silent *dhikr*, but some of them, if necessary, also performed the vocal *dhikr*. When Khwaja Aḥmad al-Yasawi set out to Turkestan he saw that the people did not take to the silent *dhikr*, and he immediately took up the way of the vocal *dhikr*".[22] At a much

[20] Fletcher 1986:19–21.
[21] al-Jabarti 1390 AH: 302; Weigert 1989:109–111.
[22] Fletcher 1977:116.

later date, in the nineteenth century, the most prominent of the disciples of Shaykh Khālid in the Volga region, the Bashkir *shaykh* Zaynullah Rasulev, went about recruiting *murīd*s with a speed that alarmed other *shaykh*s. Hostile rumours began to circulate that Zaynullah practised the vocal *dhikr*.[23]

Another innovation, also connected with more intensive recruitment, was introduced by Shaykh Khālid. In the Naqshabandi tradition the initiation of a *murīd* began through *ṣuḥba*, the association and companionship with a *shaykh*. This period extended from a few months to a few years. But Khālid felt a strong urge for a quick expansion, and he therefore replaced the longer *ṣuḥba* procedure with an intensive spiritual training of forty days only. His *murīd*s entered into seclusion in a *khalwa*, a sort of a cell, under the close supervision of Khālid or one of his deputies.[24]

4. *Ṭuruq Affiliation and Exclusivity*

Before the eighteenth century Sufi *shaykh*s obtained initiation into several *ṭuruq*. The sixteenth century Egyptian *shaykh* al-Shaʿrānī was initiated into twenty six *ṭuruq*.[25] A *shaykh* in Bijapur gave the *bayʿa* to eleven brotherhoods.[26] Because medieval Sufi brotherhoods were only chains of mystical saints (*salāsil*), that represented alternative devotional mystical ways (*ṭuruq*) to approach Allah, Sufis even saw an advantage in experiencing more than one way. Hence, meaningful distinctions between brotherhoods were blurred. Belonging to a brotherhood signified little more than an additional title to one's name. When the *shaykh* himself belonged to two brotherhoods simultaneously, his followers identified with neither one in particular, but rather with the person of the *shaykh*.[27]

It was not only that some Sufis belonged to two or more brotherhoods simultaneously, but in Bijapur there were Sufis who belonged to no brotherhood at all.[28] In Ottoman Egypt, the more orthodox and educated Sufis did not incline to pronounce their affiliation with

---

23 Algar 1992:118–119.
24 Abu Manneh 1990:292–293.
25 Winter 1982:92 and 97.
26 Eaton 1978:xxxi–xxxii, 207.
27 Eaton 1978:207; Ansari 1992:23.
28 Eaton 1978:xxxi–xxxii.

a brotherhood, but expressed their loyalty to the Islamic community at large, to the *sharīʿa*, and to Sufism generally (*ṭarīq al-qawm*). Al-Shaʿrānī sympathised with the Shādhili way, but did not adhere to this brotherhood.[29]

Al-Shaʿrānī continued a tradition of Egyptian Sufis who were not affiliated to Sufi brotherhoods. These Sufis—like al-Matbūlī, his disciples al-Dashtūtī and ʿAlī al-Khawwās, al-Shaʿrānī's mentor—were venerated because of their *baraka*. The Bakrī *shaykhs* of Cairo of the sixteenth century constituted a *bayt* (house) not a *ṭarīqa*.[30] These Bakrī *shaykhs* were spiritual mentors of the scholars of Timbuktu, who were themselves practising Sufis without an affiliation to a brotherhood.[31]

Like other Sufi *shaykhs* Muṣṭafā al-Bakrī was affiliated to several *ṭuruq*; to the Khalwatiyya, the Naqshabandiyya, the Qādiriyya and perhaps also to the Shādhiliyya. But later he insisted that his own disciples would be affiliated exclusively to the Khalwatiyya, and ordered them to break their former allegiance to other *ṭuruq* and *shaykhs*. This was not a minor innovation in the world of medieval Sufism, and it was not easily implemented. Al-Bakrī had long arguments over this issue with two of his senior disciples.[32]

Exclusivity gave greater cohesion to a *ṭarīqa*, and added to the commitment of its adherents. The concept of exclusive affiliation to a *ṭarīqa* was adopted from the Khalwatiyya, even with greater zeal, by Aḥmad al-Tijānī. The exclusivity of the Tijāniyya, in its turn, affected rival *ṭuruq* in the Maghrib and in West Africa, in particular the Qādiriyya, that also became more assertive and cohesive.[33]

5. *The Reformed Ṭuruq: Positive Attitude to This World*

Sufism oscillated between individualist renunciation of this world and community-oriented legalist world-affirmation.[34] Even the most pragmatic Sufi could not completely separate himself from the other-worldly aspects of mysticism. The *sharīʿa*-oriented brotherhoods were on the side of This World. This was the attitude of the Naqshabandiyya in Central Asia, the Suhrawardiyya in India, and the Shādhiliyya in

[29] Winter 1982:26 and 92–93.
[30] Weigert 1985.
[31] Levtzion 1977:419–420.
[32] al-Jabarti, 1390 AH: vol. 1, p. 295; vol. 2, pp. 61–62; Weigert 1989.
[33] Harazm 1929; Abun-Nasr 1965:15–57; Martin 1969; Brenner 1988.
[34] Karamustafa 1994:29–30, 96 and 98.

Egypt. The Shādhilis shunned mendicancy and renunciation of the world, and insisted that their adherents and sympathisers should lead socially active and economically productive life.[35] But many other Sufi brotherhoods had an otherworldly orientation, practised asceticism and adopted a negative attitude towards material possessions.

In China the older Qādiriyya, introduced in the late sixteenth century, had emphasised poverty and ascetic withdrawal from society, whereas the Naqshabandi *shaykh*s, who came in the late seventeenth and in the eighteenth centuries, had families and enjoyed material wealth accrued from the donations of their followers.[36]

In Sumatra, the old Sufi *ṭuruq* blended peacefully into the agrarian landscape, and issued no challenge to the wider society. Their teaching was concerned with esoteric knowledge and in pursuing the path to God. This other-worldly orientation was challenged by Sufi *shaykh*s who responded to the rapid growth of commercial agriculture late in the seventeenth century. Sufi *shaykh*s became involved in trade, and had a venerated *shaykh*, Tuanku Nan Tua, who became known as "patron of the traders".[37]

In Fez, Aḥmad al-Tijānī lived in comfort without any manifestations of asceticism. He opposed withdrawal from this world, and promised his adherents access to paradise without forsaking their possessions. This positive attitude to worldly affairs attracted rich merchants and senior officials who joined the brotherhood.[38]

In the Sahara, Sīdī al-Mukhtār al-Kuntī advocated a positive attitude towards the accumulation of wealth, and emphasised the direct link between religious piety and economic prosperity. For him wealth was a clear sign of dignity and status.[39]

This change in attitude towards this world prepared reformed Sufi brotherhoods to be more actively involved in social and political life.

6. *Mystical Verse in Vernacular Languages*

Our final argument is that the drive of the reformed Sufi brotherhoods to reach out to the common people and to recruit adherents

---

35 Winter 1982:90.
36 Gladney 1991:44–47.
37 Dobbin 1983:125–127.
38 Levtzion and Weigert 1995:193–194.
39 Brenner 1988:39.

explains the simultaneous emergence of Islamic literatures in the vernacular languages, written in the Arabic or Persian script, all over the Muslim world in the seventeenth and eighteenth centuries. It is even more significant in this context that the predominant genre in all the vernacular literatures was the mystical verse.

Oral mystical poetry in folk idioms had been composed as early as the fourteenth century, mainly for *samāʿ* assemblies. In order to facilitate the spread of mystical teaching among the masses, poets resorted to imageries taken from daily life and from the landscape that surrounded them. It was meant to be recited or sung and was not written down until a much later period.[40]

It is likely that the writing down of folk mystical poetry was encouraged by the emergence of centralised brotherhoods, whose leaders sought to communicate with affiliates who lived not only in their immediate vicinity, but also in remote communities. Poems in the vernaculars, that had been sung and recited orally, were written down in Arabic script, and were disseminated in written copies among the literati, who gave them a wider circulation through public recitation.

The oldest known texts in the Muslim African languages—Fulfulde, Hausa and Swahili—date from the eighteenth century.[41] Before that Islam had been the concern of a literate minority, and all those who took part in the scholarly discourse were literate in Arabic. But with the progressive diffusion of Islam, when scholars sought to disseminate Islamic knowledge to the common people, poetry became a major vehicle for teaching and preaching. Poems were readily committed to memory and were therefore an excellent pedagogical device.[42]

The oldest documents from Northern Nigeria were poems written by the leaders of the reformist movement. The reformists were active preachers and composed poems in Fulfulde that could be recited in public. Written versions of the poems were made to help the memory of the singers, and to facilitate the diffusion of the texts.[43]

ʿAbdallāh dan Fodio described the preaching of his brother, the Shaykh ʿUthmān dan Fodio, in the vernacular verse:

---

40 Schimmel 1982:135–136, 141–142, 148 and 150.

41 Sow 1966:13 and 15; Hiskett 1975:18; Knappert 1979:102–103.

42 Seydou 1973:184; Brenner & Last 1985:434.

43 Sow 1966:12; Haafkens 1983:25.

> Then we rose up with the Shaykh, helping him in his mission work for religion. He travelled for that purpose to the east and west, calling people to the religion of God by his preaching and his *qaṣīdas* in *ʿajamī*.[44]

ʿAbdallāh dan Fodio also described how the vernacular mystical verse was used to mobilise support. When the Shaykh ʿUthmān dan Fodio saw that his community was ready for the *jihād*, "he began to incite them to arms... and he set this in verse in his non-Arabic Qādiri poem (*qaṣīda ʿajamiyya qādiriyya*)." This mystical verse had a hypnotic effect upon devotees on the eve of the *jihād*.[45]

It is significant that on the East African coast too, the oldest surviving Islamic text in Swahili, the *Ḥamziyya* by ʿAidarūsī, a poem in praise of the Prophet (*madīḥ*), was written in the second half of the seventeenth century.[46]

Malay was the *lingua franca* of the Muslims in Southeast Asia, and an essential vehicle for the spread of religious ideas throughout the region. The oldest Malay manuscripts in the Arabic script date from the end of the sixteenth and the beginning of the seventeenth centuries. Malay literature developed mainly through translations from Persian and Arabic.[47] A.H. Johns described these literary activities as "enriching the language of the tribe".[48]

Some of the most profound writings on metaphysics and *taṣawwuf* were by two Sufi poets, Ḥamza Fansuri (end of the sixteenth century) and Shams al-Dīn of Pasai (d. 1630). Ibn ʿArabī's doctrine of the *wujūdiyya* was widely articulated in their poetry, as well as in the writings of an anonymous author of the first half of the seventeenth century. The *wujūdiyya* was challenged by the Shaykh Nūr al-Dīn b. ʿAlī al-Rānīrī, a Gujarati who came from India to Acheh about 1637. During the seven years of his residence in Acheh, al-Rānīrī wrote strenuously, in Malay and in Arabic, against the pantheism of Ḥamza and Shams al-Dīn.[49]

The next important event in the literary history of Islam in South-East Asia was the translation of the Qur'ān to Malay by ʿAbd al-Ra'ūf of Singkel (c. 1620–1693). He returned in 1661 after a residence

---

[44] ʿAbdallāh ibn Fūdī 1963:85.
[45] ʿAbdallāh ibn Fūdī 1963:51.
[46] Knappert 1979:102–103.
[47] Andaya 1987:235; Ronkel 1987:240.
[48] Unpublished paper by A.H. Johns presented to the conference on Eighteenth century Renewal and Reform in Islam, Jerusalem 1985.
[49] Johns 1957:10, 33 and 35; al-Attas 1971:1220; Roolvink 1971:1233.

of nineteen years in Medina, where he had been initiated to the Shaṭṭāriyya brotherhood by al-Qushāshī (d. 1660) and Ibrāhīm al-Kurānī (d. 1690). ʿAbd al-Raʾūf propagated the Shaṭṭāriyya, which later played an important role in the Padri movement. He also composed a Malay textbook of practical mysticism giving detailed information about the methods of *dhikr* and containing litanies (*rawāṭib*). ʿAbd al-Raʾūf rejected the pantheist mysticism of Ḥamza and Shams al-Dīn, though he did not associate himself with the violent polemics of al-Rānīrī.[50]

Towards the end of the eighteenth century Malay scholars seem to have moved away from the teachings of Ibn ʿArabī towards the more sober mysticism of al-Ghazālī, as evidenced by the translation of some of al-Ghazālī's works to Malay. Between the years 1779 and 1788, a shortened version of al-Ghazālī's *Iḥyāʾ ʿulūm al-dīn*, was translated into Malay by ʿAbd al-Ṣamad of Palembang. ʿAbd al-Ṣamad had been resident in Medina for many years and was also responsible for the introduction of the Sammāniyya brotherhood to Indonesia.[51]

In India, not only Muslim Sufis but also Hindu mystics, turned to the regional idioms for their preaching, because the sacred liturgical languages—Sanskrit, Arabic and Persian—were inaccessible to the masses. Mystical poetry in the regional idioms had been recited for *samāʿ* assemblies since the thirteenth century, but it was not committed to writing before the seventeenth century.[52]

There is hardly any text in the north-western regional languages of India dated before the end of the sixteenth century. Sufis, especially those of the Chishti order, who sought to reach people that had no access to Arabic and Persian, led the way in breaking the literary taboo against the use of the Indian vernaculars.[53] The flowering of literature in the regional languages—Sindhi, Muslim Panjabi, and Urdu—early in the eighteenth century, followed the decline of Mughal authority and the emergence of local states. It seems that the breakdown of the Mughal empire, which had cultivated Persian culture, opened the way for new experiments with languages that had not been previously considered a medium fitting the expression of lofty ideas.[54]

---

[50] Johns 1957:10; Voorhoeve 1960:88; al-Attas 1971:1220; Roolvink 1971:1233.
[51] Voorhoeve 1960:92; Andaya 1987:235.
[52] Schimmel 1975:132–133 and 171; Schimmel 1976:12; Schimmel 1982:138, 141–142 and 148–150.
[53] Shackle 1993: 265 and 285; Roy 1985:58.
[54] Schimmel 1975:163; Shackle 1993:287–288.

Indeed, far from the centre of the Mughal court, where the influence of the Persian culture was weaker, literature in the regional languages had developed earlier. The consolidation of the independent principalities of Bijapur and Golkonda in the fifteenth century helped the growth of literature in Dakhni, the language of the Deccan, two centuries before the appearance of Urdu literature.[55]

In Delhi Sufi literature in Urdu developed only at the beginning of the eighteenth century. But even later, theologians and mystics continued to write also in Arabic and Persian, the classical Islamic languages. Even Mir Dard (1721–1785), who wrote the most perfect Urdu mystical verse, composed the largest part of his mystical poetry and prose in Persian. Hence, the discourse of the elite continued in the classical languages of Islam, whereas the vernacular literature was important in building bridges to the common people.[56]

Bengali Muslim literature is unique among the Indian regional vernaculars in that it was written mostly in the Bengali script, and not in the Arabic-Persian script. But, like the other vernacular literatures it was mainly the product of *pir*s, who in the sixteenth and seventeenth centuries developed mystical verse.[57]

Muslim literature in Chinese was also written mostly in Chinese characters. It developed since the middle of the seventeenth century, and as elsewhere mystical works were important. It was composed in an easy style, with tendency towards the spoken language, which suggests that it was addressed to the common people, with a limited literary culture, and not to the highly literate.[58]

There is additional evidence that Sufi texts were in a simple language addressed to the common people. In the sixteenth and seventeenth century, a period of literary decline in Egypt, when works of theology and law were written in bombastic style, Sufis wrote in precise, down-to-earth language.[59] Also, the preaching of Imam Mansur in 1785 in the Caucasus, is said to have been simple and directed to the peasants.[60]

[55] Schimmel 1975:131 and 135; Eaton 1978.
[56] Schimmel 1973:48–50; Schimmel 1976:xi, 11.
[57] Haq 1985:39–40; Roy 1985:58 and 71–73.
[58] Aubin 1990:496–497.
[59] Winter 1982:27.
[60] Bennigsen 1964:195.

7. *Conclusions*

Sufi brotherhoods played important roles in Muslim societies since the twelfth and thirteenth century. They provided moral guidance to voluntary associations, opened opportunities for release from the hardships of everyday existence, gave confidence to individuals, and helped sustain social stability. They also maintained lines of communications between the common people and the authorities. But pre-eighteenth Sufi brotherhoods had been localised and loosely organised.

The restructured brotherhoods of the eighteenth century mobilised popular following, a process that was closely associated with the expansion of Islam from towns to the countryside, and deeper into all strata of the population. The elitist discourse in the classical Islamic languages, Arabic and Persian, was supplemented by Islamic writings, mainly in mystical verse, in vernacular languages.

Structural, organisational and ritual changes prepared the reformed Sufi *ṭuruq* to play more active political and social roles. Under charismatic leadership some of these Sufi brotherhoods turned militant and developed into *jihād* movements. The Tijāniyya provided the framework for the *jihād* of *al-ḥājj* ʿUmar in West Africa. The Mahdī of the Sudan was a member of the Sammāniyya, which like the Tijāniyya was an offshoot of the Khalwatiyya. The Naqshabandiyya-Khālidiyya found expression in the *jihād* of Imam Shamīl in the Caucasus, where, according to Hamid Algar, the teaching of Shaykh Khālid survived in its purest and most integral form.[61]

When their countries were invaded by colonial powers, these three movements redirected their major efforts from internal reform to defending *Dār al-Islām*, but they were crushed by the military superiority of the Europeans. Thus the inroads of colonialism put an end to a process of revivalism of Muslim societies under the leadership of reformed restructured Sufi brotherhoods.

[61] Algar 1990:145.

MASS PRODUCING HOURI'S MOLES

or Aesthetics and Choice of Technology in Early Muslim Book Printing

Ian Proudfoot

Transmissions of Islam have been radically affected by the use of print. Print has been as significant for Islam over the last two centuries as it has for Christianity over the past five centuries. In both cases the fires of reform and fundamentalism have been stoked by the new technology of communication. Muslims adopted his powerful technology from the West by processes that are still little understood. If the initiation of this change were better understood, we might also gain a better appreciation of why Muslims spurned print for three centuries while it flourished in Christian Europe.

My argument is that Muslims took up printing by two paths.

1. *The First Book Printing in the Middle East*

The Ottoman Government was consistently wary of printing. Early decrees in 1485 and 1515 forbade the printing of Arabic, though importation of books was allowed. Turkey's Christian and Jewish communities printed in Hebrew, Latin and Armenian from the sixteenth century, and Syrian Christians began sporadic printing in Arabic in the eighteenth century.[1] In 1728, the Ottoman court initiated Muslim printing under government sponsorship, but no independent Muslim presses were permitted until well into the nineteenth century. The press law of 1888 kept book printers and importers under tight administrative control.

The initiative of 1728 was part of the Ottoman court's project to emulate aspects of the France of Louis XV. A press was operated from 1728 to 1745 under the management of Ibrāhīm Müteferriḳa. It used imported French printing equipment with type cut and cast in Istanbul to produce rather costly books for well-placed Ottoman

[1] Oman 1989.

literati. Specifically excluded from the press were works on religion, namely the Qur'ān, *tafsīr, ḥadīth, fiqh* and *kalām*. Later, as part of a renewed military and fiscal modernisation program, semi-official printing was revived at Istanbul in 1780. With a similar purpose, a government press at Cairo was established at Būlāq in 1821–22 by Muḥammad ʿAlī, who had watched Napoleon use imported printing equipment disseminate administrative orders and proclamations in Arabic and believed that the Būlāq press would serve as an efficient means of improving the army and agriculture.[2]

The repertoire of these government-controlled presses in Cairo and Istanbul was rather restricted. The Ottoman ban on printing works of religion had been waived in 1803 for the publication of the Turkish catechism *Risāla-i Birgewī*, but the early diet of printed books overwhelmingly comprised technical manuals, dictionaries and grammars, with a few collections of *fatāwā* and works on dogma. Books on religious topics, which enjoyed longer print runs, began to be advertised for sale in the Ottoman Government gazette after 1831.[3] By 1850, about 650 editions of all kinds had appeared at Istanbul, while Būlāq under Muḥammad ʿAlī issued about 350 titles, of which about half were technical and scientific manuals, many translated from French.[4]

Marketing was primitive in this early period. There was but one book depository for Egypt, at Būlāq, with "pyramids of unsold stock". In 1831, an uncharitable French observer commented:

> ... Books on tactics and medicine may have their uses, but address themselves to only a tiny number of readers. None of the others, with few exceptions, have any market or any circulation. They are multiplied by the press only to be stacked up in warehouses where it seems they are condemned to an eternal oblivion. No-one buys them, no-one reads them, because they do not accord with the needs of the present, nor with the spirit of the populace who require instruction and

---

[2] Berkes 1969, Duverdier 1987, Albin 1988.

[3] Baysal (1981:122) says a *firman* (not a *fatwa*) authorised this; Berkes (1964:127) says "the change seems to have come about gradually without fuss or a new authorisation."

[4] See Hammer 1831:7.583–595, Baysal 1981, Bianchi 1843, 1859–63, Verdery 1971, Heyworth-Dunne 1940, Albin 1988. The later fame of the Būlāq press may lead to an overestimate of its early scope and impact. Only after its disbandment and relaunching in 1861 did it take up large scale printing of books on history, language, literature and religion, in addition to technical works. Most of the Būlāq editions of Arabic classics date from the last thirty years of the nineteenth century (Crabbs 1984:201).

> enlightenment. Even at first glance it is easy to see how it stands with this printery, set up at such great cost, like so many other industries imported from Europe with insufficient care taken to adapt them to the country.[5]

The most saleable works were apparently put through the Būlāq press by private editors on their own account.

2. *Muslim Printing in India*

The picture in India is quite different.

The presence of the European press in India is very old, reaching back to the Jesuit press in Goa in 1556. However, not much printing of significance took place, beyond some Christian mission printing in Madras, until about 1780, when a fair number of presses began operating in the Presidency capitals of Calcutta, Bombay and Madras. In contrast to the Ottoman government, the English Company had an ideological preference for independent presses, whether run by Europeans or Indians. Yet Muslim involvement in this typographic printing remained marginal. The printing of literary and historical works in Persian in Calcutta (after 1781) and Bombay (after 1818) was undertaken on presses run by Europeans or Parsees respectively, with only editorial participation by Muslims. The first Muslim-sponsored printing came with the inauguration 1819 of a Royal Press by the Nawwāb Ghāzī al-Dīn Ḥaydar of Oudh. From this press over the next decade there issued several Persian works in praise of the Nawwāb, and two publications in Arabic: a *Panjsūrah* (five *sūra*s of the Qur'ān) and the first three volumes of an Arabic dictionary, *Tāj al-lughāt*.[6]

Then, suddenly, everything changed. In 1824 the Indian Company equipped each of its Presidencies with several of the recently invented lithographic presses, which it judged would provide a versatile and cheap means of printing administrative documents. Four of these presses were handed over to the Bombay School Book and School Society, and immediately applied to the printing of textbooks in Maratha, Gujarati and Hindustani (Urdu). In the first year, Indian operators were trained and 17,000 books were produced.

[5] Geiss 1907/08:212.
[6] Storey 1933, from Sprenger 1844.

Simultaneously, a history of Bengal, in Persian, was lithographed at Benares.[7] Over the next decade and a half, lithographic presses mushroomed all across northern India. The great majority of the new presses were Muslim owned and operated. They were private presses, independent of government subsidy or control—which was formally held at bay by the 1835 Press Act.[8] Major centres of Muslim publishing emerged at Lucknow-Cawnpore, Agra, Delhi, Lahore and Hyderabad (Deccan). Lucknow alone had more than a dozen lithographic presses in 1848, all in Muslim hands. By that time the presses of Lucknow-Cawnpore alone had published about 700 titles, some in up to ten editions, mainly comprising student's books, polemics, and religious tracts.[9] And the pace continued to quicken. By mid-century, Urdu was printed all over India, and practically all the important towns in northern India had their own lithographic printing presses. A contemporary observer estimated that there were about 112 such presses in different parts of the country. Lithography had become a very lucrative trade.[10] Indeed, so attractive was lithography that the Royal Press of Oudh switched to the new technique mid-way through the publication of its multi-volume Arabic dictionary.

While the marketing of books was disorganised, the conjunction of commercial drive and popular repertoire ensured strong demand. A sales agent for Ḥājj Ḥar[a]main Sharīfain, the first Muslim printer of Lucknow,

> would venture off with thousands of books in a bullock cart, going as far afield as Rawalpindi. In those days books were very rare, and a great novelty. He would be received with pomp, and could sell at any price he chose: usually Karima ma Muqiman for a few annas, Gulistan or Bostan for 3 or 4 rupee per volume. Even so, supply could not meet demand. After books had run out, it would be months before another consignment could be arranged.[11]

This sketch of Indian private enterprise in the market place is a far cry from the contemporary account of the Egyptian official press at Būlāq that was quoted earlier.

---

[7] Caresajee 1958.
[8] Govi 1977, Davis 1983.
[9] Diehl 1973.
[10] Haider 1981, Mohl 1853.
[11] Sharar 1975:107.

3. *The Influence of the Indian Model*

By mid-century, printing in Cairo and Istanbul was still a trickle beside this Indian torrent. The Indian model, with its commitment to lithography, proved influential. In Persia, after a brief flirtation with government-sponsored typography in Tabriz in 1819 and in Tehran in 1824, lithographic printing began in Tabriz 1835 and in Tehran 1844, and soon after in Isfahan and other cities. As in India, lithography spread quickly. By about 1860, any Persian town of consequence had at least one, and often several, lithographic presses.[12] As Browne remarked,

> One of the strangest things connected with the history of the art of printing in Persia from the time of its introduction until the present day is that notwithstanding the chronological priority of the introduction of typography into Persia, it entirely went out of fashion in a short while, and that for a long time (more than fifty years) the presses of Persia confined themselves exclusively to lithography . . .[13]

In Southeast Asia, where Muslim printing began in 1848, the following half-century of Muslim printing was similarly almost wholly lithographic. In both cases, Indian-style lithographic printing was focused from the outset on religious texts.

The government presses of Turkey and Egypt also employed lithography, but in the European manner. It was used for maps, illustrations, diagrams, formulae etc., a substitute for etching as an adjunct to typography; it was also used to reproduce administrative circulars, like the *Jurnāl al-Khidīw*. When we do find books printed by lithography, the presses belong to technical agencies. So when the *Dalā'il al-Khairat* was lithographed in the hand of the celebrated calligrapher Raḳīm Efendī in 1857, it was printed on the lithographic press of an Ottoman Engineers Regiment. By the 1850s lithographic book printing had begun to gain ground in Istanbul particularly, but it remained the poor cousin of typographic printing.[14]

This began to change in the 1860s. The turmoil surrounding the disbandment of the Būlāq press in 1861 made space for vigorous commercial printing for a popular religious and literary audience. A

---

[12] Polak 1865:279, Walther 1990:230. Avery 1991:817–819, Farmayan 1968:145. For Iraq, see Albin 1981, 1985:15.

[13] Browne 1914:9.

[14] Peron 1843, Geiss 1907/08, Hsu 1985, Walther 1990, Schlechta-Wssehrd 1853–55, Baysal 1981.

handful of private presses had been operating in Egypt in the previous decade, but private printing became significant as skilled personnel who had previously worked at the Būlāq press found their way into private printing. Private printeries using both typography and lithography proliferated, and publishers-cum-bookshops began printing works in popular demand, or commissioning them from jobbing printers. These were "private enterprise establishments, whose sole motive was profit and which published fast turn-over, dubious quality books, mostly on religion, popular reading and fiction."[15] These speculatively printed books were supplied to the book merchants who operated in the shadow of al-Azhar Mosque. They had previously specialised in providing cheaply copied manuscripts, and now saw a profitable alternative.

Muslim printing in the various centres of the Maghrib followed in the wake of these Egyptian developments, and similarly employed a combination of typography and lithography, usually under government supervision.[16]

In short, the history of early Muslim book printing reveals two separate initiations of printing, one in the Middle East, the other in India. The government-sponsored typographic printing in the Middle East is earlier, but had no influence on the rapid adoption of lithographic printing by Muslims in India. The two initiatives are further distinguished by different initial repertoires, one in which religious works are absent or marginal, and the other in which religious works are central. The power of lithography in this first era of book printing is evident. Lithography held sway from the beginning in India, Iraq, and Southeast Asia, displaced typography in Persia, and stimulated a great upsurge in the bulk and variety of printing in Turkey, Egypt, and the Maghrib.

4. *Preconditions for Printing*

This unexpectedly complex history of printing initiatives has implications for our understanding of the circumstances in which printing was adopted by Muslims. The notion that Islam was resistant to print is generally extrapolated from the Ottoman experience. The con-

[15] Rizk 1978:555.
[16] Safadi 1981, Albin 1988, Roper 1982, Demeerseman 1953:363, 1954:2.

trasting experience of Indian Muslims, however, provokes the question of how generalisable this Ottoman experience was.

Explanations that rely upon the exercise of state power need to be reconsidered. It is wholly credible that an authoritarian government whose writ ran sufficiently wide for a prohibition to have effect might well wish to avoid the immensely disruptive consequences of print that could be observed on its doorstep in Europe. No Christian government in Europe's print era ever enjoyed this option, so fragmented was political authority in Christendom.[17] Nor, significantly, did any government achieve more than fleeting control across the Indian sub-continent before 1857. It is also wholly credible that the Ottoman application of state power was shaped by its alliance with a clerical magistracy. Watt[18] reflects a general opinion when he characterises the higher grades of the Ottoman religious hierarchy as a privileged aristocracy "more interested in maintaining their own power than in promoting the welfare of the empire as a whole." He adds: "This is exemplified by their opposition to the introduction of printing." In fact the Ottoman evidence here is a little ambiguous: the high religious authorities approved, supported and administered Müteferriḳa's printing experiment.[19] The Ottoman integration of state and clerical interests, though normative in its day, was far from universally achieved in other societies in which Muslims pursued their fates, as British India and the Dutch East Indies remind us.

Or was conservatism intrinsic to the organisation of Islamic tradition itself, independent of state power?[20] Robinson takes up this question in his "Technology and Religious Change".[21] He adapts Graham's ideas of concurrent oral and written transmission,[22] in which Qur'anic recitation set the pattern for other dogmatic transmission, and "writing and literacy have always danced attention on a superior oral tradition." For Robinson the important dimension of this

[17] Realpolitik is in play here: the Christian Dutch East India Company enforced Ottoman-like restrictions on printing in Muslim Southeast Asia, where its writ ran wide, while in Europe the Dutch enjoyed perhaps Europe's freest and most diverse press. Europe's disunity undermines Duverdier's (1987:354) position on European reluctance to provide printing technology to Muslims.

[18] 1988:34.

[19] See Káldy-Nagy 1974, Mardin 1962:217, Duverdier 1987:336. Alleged protests by the scribes' guilds of Istanbul against the first experiments with printing are not well attested. Káldy-Nagy 1974:204–205.

[20] Bulliet 1987, Safadi 1981 etc.

[21] 1993.

[22] Graham 1987.

dualism is that "person to person transmission was at the heart of the transmission of Islamic knowledge. Muslim scholars travelled the world to receive in person the reliable transmission of knowledge." The written word, unexpounded, is a veil that separates the student from discovery of meaning. The principally valid transmission is from teacher to pupil, recorded in the *ijāza* awarded on completion of the study. (The same path to knowledge prevailed in the mystical orders, and among calligraphers.) Printing, by striking at person-to-person transmission, "struck right at the heart of Islamic authority". Therein, for Robinson, lies the explanation for Islam's conservatism toward print. "No Muslim was likely to adopt it until he saw a good in printing greater than the evil it might cause." This extreme situation arose, Robinson argues, under Christian colonial rule, when "Islam itself was at stake and print was a necessary weapon in defence of the faith."[23] In Robinson's view, this is why the first active involvement in religious printing is evident among Muslims in India (and in Russia).

However it is not clear that Islamic transmission was always so conservative as Robinson's sketch suggests, nor that Muslim printing is best understood as a response to any external threat. In the early nineteenth century there were Hindu revival movements, like that of Rammohan Roy, which responded to the Western challenge. They were led by English-educated Hindus, a class that had no Muslim counterpart until the later rise of Sayyid Aḥmad Khān and the Aligarh College group. Muslim printing was therefore not innovated by a déraciné élite, but—as Robinson concedes—exploited by active mainstream leaders concerned to reform and intensify Muslim belief. The notion that it was the European challenge which broke a conservative Islamic mould in India may underrate the dynamics of the Indian Muslim cultural environment.

Indeed, Levtzion and Voll identify vernacularisation as a major theme in their survey of Islamic renewal and reform in the eighteenth century in those societies with significant non-Muslim populations or residues, including India.[24] The push for vernacularisation involved experimenting with new paths of transmission. Reformist *ʿulamāʾ* and sufis who had long been challenging the old Perso-Islamic ways had begun to transmit knowledge in regional languages.

---

[23] Robinson 1993:237.
[24] Levtzion and Voll 1987.

In the eighteenth century, sufi ideas were spread through rural areas by means of mystical poems in the vernacular. "Urdu . . . became the recipient not just of many translations of the Quran and the Ḥadiths but also of dozens of classics of Islamic scholarship from al-Ghazali to Ibn Khaldun. Sufis followed suit, translating more and more of their *malfuẓāt* and *maktubāt* from Persian into Urdu so that the example of the saints could reach fresh generations. . . . This shift away from the old imperial language coincided with the introduction of the lithographic printing press."[25] The nineteenth-century rise of the press in India parallels the transformation of Hindustani into the new written vernaculars Urdu and Hindi.[26] The adoption of printing thus coincides with a great upsurge in vernacularisation, internal reform, and revival. Indeed, it is exceedingly difficult to disaggregate these concurrent developments. An example used by Robinson illustrates the point. Sayyid Aḥmad Barelvī's followers were active users of the press to promote their reformist ideas, notably through lithographic editions of *Sirāṭ al-Mustaqīm*, complied by Sayyid Aḥmad first in Persian, but soon translated and published in both Persian and Urdu, and *Taqwiyyat al-Imān* composed and printed directly in Urdu. Undoubtedly the press was critical in the momentum of this group, but the fact remains that Sayyid Aḥmad had compiled *Sirāṭ al-Mustaqīm* in 1819[27]—at a time when the only Muslim printing in India was undertaken on the Royal Press at Oudh—and so could hardly have written it for the press.

So, at the time when print was adopted there were already long-standing forces for vernacularisation, and active reformist and revivalist groups who had shown an interest in cultivating new modes of transmission, and who indeed took enthusiastically to print . . . but only in the early nineteenth century. The precise timing of the adoption of printing by Indian Muslims seems not to be wholly explained by the ideological climate. A more mundane fact cannot be overlooked: that is, that a new printing technology had just become available. It can be shown, I believe, that lithography has qualities that could explain its attractiveness to Indian Muslims who had not previously taken up typographic printing.

[25] Robinson 1991:124.
[26] Brass 1974:186.
[27] Metcalf 1982:56.

5. *Qualities of Two Printing Technologies*

Typographic printing and lithography are quite different technical processes. Both are means of achieving multiple reproduction of text, and carry the immense cultural and social implications which flow from that. However, the two processes have significantly different implications on the aesthetic and commercial level.

Moveable type printing has been invented twice, probably independently, once in China in the eleventh century, and again in Germany in the fifteenth. The idea is a simple extension of wood block printing which profits from the fact that the script to be reproduced is made up of independent items arranged in a line of uniform height or width. These were characteristics of both Chinese and European writing systems. Moveable type did not flourish in China but did so in Europe for reasons of economy. The major capital investment in printing using moveable type is the stock of interchangeable character types. Moveable type printing proved uneconomic for the morphemic Chinese writing system which required thousands of types. The European languages, which have alphabetic writing systems operating on the phonemic level, require about the number of characters provided on a standard typewriter.

In the Middle East early wood-block printing of Qur'anic verses and other religious formulae several centuries before Gutenberg,[28] did not develop into typography. An easy transition to moveable type was barred by the nature of the Arabic script. The Arabic writing system, though operating on the phonemic level, is neither alphabetic nor based on the linear arrangement of independent items. Its letter forms vary according to position, and in the scribal hand it abounds with non-linear ligatures and kerning. A reasonable approximation of the scribal hand might be achieved in moveable type, but only with ingenuity and at considerable cost. At the time of Turkey's script reform in 1928, a single-font printer's case for printing Turkish in upper and lower case Roman script required 99 types. For printing Turkish in Arabic script, 645 types were needed, and that after ignoring many ligatures.[29] A modest press would require at least

[28] Oman 1989:795, Bulliet 1987.

[29] Duda 1935:241–242, with illustration. Hammam (1951:158) records that in about 1950 the standard Būlāq press font had 465 letters, while private presses got by with 365, though with reduced aesthetic effect. Hourani 1982:38, cf. Ellis 1955:11–12.

a couple of type sizes, if not a couple of styles—each requiring a font of similar size. Thus the same economic barrier that crippled early Chinese typography was also a hurdle, set not quite so high, to Arabic typography.

In fact the initial demands confronting Arabic typography were more stringent than this suggests. They can be understood, perhaps, by recalling the transitional forms of early printing in Europe. In reality, European manuscript writing was not a purely linear arrangement of independent items. The prevalent Gothic manuscript hand was semi-cursive, and included a number of conventional abbreviations marked by diacritics, a few alternative medial and final letter forms, and many ligatures. Gutenberg and other early printers took as their brief the closest possible reproduction of manuscript forms. To achieve this, they cast many additional types, making the technology considerably more costly and expensive. Gutenberg's font comprised about twice as many types as became the standard later.[30] The cost was, in the beginning, a price that had to be paid if print was to satisfy the book reading and buying public. Over the first hundred years moveable type printing became increasingly alphabetised, and thereby more efficiently adapted to typography. In Gothic print, scribal abbreviations fell into disuse and ligatures were reduced in number. More radically, the Roman and Italic types (whose discrete letter forms better suited typography) began to displace the scribes' Gothic script. But it took about a hundred years until it was no longer necessary to disguise a book as a manuscript.[31] From this time, an increasing divergence between Europe's printed and handwritten scripts occurred.

No such initial concessions were made in Arabic typography. This is not surprising, since all the early typographic presses, in Europe, the Middle East and India, depended upon European technicians already accustomed to a strongly alphabetised type script, who no longer appreciated the need to make the same concessions to Arabic readers that Gutenberg had made to his European customers. In India and Southeast Asia the Christian missions were serious offenders. Early Muslim experiments, like that of Müteferriḳa or the early Būlāq press were more sympathetic, but still depended upon European

---

[30] Hirsch 1978.
[31] Chappell 1970:101.

technicians and faced constraints inherent in the technology.[32] A serious accommodation of manuscript reading would require a huge number of types. The capital costs would be prohibitive and the task of the type composers extremely complex. As practised, typography did not have the capacity to match the copyist's hand. The results appeared consistently ugly to readers used to manuscript styles. European-printed Arabic texts were poorly regarded. In the early eighteenth century, for instance, a Jesuit-printed copy of Ibn Sīnā's *al-Qānūn fī 'l-ṭibb* languished in an Istanbul bookshop, priced well below comparable manuscripts.[33] The problem was often conceived as one of poor type design. Undoubtedly there was enough of this. In the seventeenth century, Ibrāhīm Efendī identified this as the reason for Muslim rejection of books printed in Europe. Their many errors and poor choice of characters were no better than the writing of African Muslims![34] But whether the type fonts were cast in Europe, India or the Middle East they evoked negative reactions. The problem lay deeper. Typographic print was less dense than readers were accustomed to, while the lines of print themselves comprised dark, stilted, uniform imprints, not the subtly varied strokes and styles of the manuscript.[35] When eventually in 1906 the Būlāq press commissioned new fonts designed by a committee of calligraphers,[36] satisfaction with the outcome reflected not only improvements in letter forms and typesetting techniques, but also nearly a century of habituation to a new style of representing text.

Lithography altogether lacked the mechanical rigidities of type. Its complete flexibility in reproducing graphic forms made it an illustrator's medium in the West. This was critically important for its success in the Islamic world, for it meant lithography was capable of reproducing calligraphy, and achieved immense popularity for that reason. A book printed by lithography was essentially a manuscript reproduced. Lithography could accurately convey the grace and fluidity of

[32] The missionaries, always prescriptive, kept their fonts small by imposing alphabetic principles on to Arabic writing, equating one letter with one type element and allowing only for the canonical initial, medial and final forms. For reproductions of mission printing, see Gallop 1990. Müteferriḳa's type was aesthetically ahead of its contemporaries (Duda 1935). On Būlāq, Albin 1988:342.

[33] Roper 1988:51.

[34] Demeerseman 1954:41.

[35] Medhurst 1829, Roper 1988:43, 125 and 264, Oman 1989:803, Weil 1907:52, Baysal 1981:122.

[36] Hammam 1951.

a good manuscript, in all respects except the use of colour—and that too was achieved sometimes by overprinting, by hand rubrication, or by gilt stamping. Lithography could reproduce the nine scripts, as required.[37] By contrast, typeset printing offered a travesty of scribal form.

In case this argument seems too squeamish about aesthetic preferences, or is thought to imply an innate conservatism in Islamic attitudes, consider the uses of lithography in the West. When Senefelder discovered lithography, his first thought was that it could be used to reproduce musical notation.[38] Interestingly, musical notation, though linear in principle, is rather like Arabic script in requiring complex ligatures. Musical notation had never been reproduced successfully by moveable type, and at the end of the eighteenth century was most commonly etched. Lithography provided a practical alternative, and in the later form of photolithography became the technique of choice for printing music.[39] By contrast, lithography was never used in Europe for extensive reproduction of written text. After three and a half centuries of typography, the European eye had become habituated to the typographic style of public text, which had become markedly different from the handwriting used for private text. Lithography would reproduce handwriting, and was therefore deemed unsuitable for printing books. The results looked amateurish and untidy.[40] This conviction blinded European missionaries to the potential of lithography as a cheap and adaptable means of spreading their message. Lithography was considered for Arabic printing by the Malta mission in 1827, but rejected because the perfect standard of calligraphy required was unobtainable, "and less than perfect will not do".[41] The alternative of neat and tidy but clumsy type was considered more perfect. In Batavia, the missionary-printer Medhurst acknowledged the advantages of lithography—its flexibility, its ease of operation, its cheapness—and yet was concerned over the "irregular appearance of a book thus printed" and the fact [!]

[37] See Diehl 1973:123, Demeerseman 1953:354 and 378, Dewall 1857:194, Bianchi 1859–63:§103, Walther 1990:231.

[38] Senefelder 1819:13.

[39] Satisfactory results with typography became possible only during the nineteenth century with the development of "mosaic" type which abandoned the linear principle, required very large fonts, and involved very complex typesetting; see Poole & Krummel 1980; Humphries & Smith 1970:26–29 and 34–36.

[40] Cf. Twyman 1990:119–125.

[41] Roper 1988:125.

that lithography could not readily be combined with European letters. Knowing however that his native audience rejected the only Arabic type font available to him, Medhurst used lithography to reproduce an extremely regular stiff Arabic script that imitated an Arabic type font of his own design.[42] A comparable sensitivity to graphic conventions is at work on both sides, with opposite results: Muslim objections to an alphabetised Arabic typography because it did not resemble the handwritten manuscript, and Christian rejection of lithography for book printing precisely because it did resemble handwritten script.

6. *The Special Place of Calligraphy*

Typography's shortcomings become more marked when the wider literate landscape is considered. Books and other written materials demand varying degrees of aesthetic attention. At the lower end, on a utilitarian level, were the staples of the book trade, the products of professional scribes. Where there was an established market for books scholarly works and literature in Arabic and local languages might be copied by a professional scribe, the *warrāq* or *kātib*. A steady, clear hand was adequate. In such cases the demands placed upon print reproduction were not so onerous. Indeed, it was here that typographic print was allowed to make its first inroads, under Müteferriḳa, and the later government-run presses of Istanbul and Cairo. Nevertheless, even here, the graphic flexibility of lithography better suited the tastes of the early market place. The preface to a Lucknow literary lithograph of 1843 made this telling comparison with its typographic predecessor:

> The story was published in Calcutta and in other places more than once. But it was never brought out with such beauty and elegance as in this print which simply charms the readers . . . The print is lovely beyond praise: the title page is in white letters, so different from earlier editions. The popular stories are printed in bold letters looking like a garden with beds of flowers here and there.[43]

Lithography, not typography, could rival the scribal product—at, of course, a fraction of the price.

---

[42] Medhurst 1829, 1838:573. Similarly, the Singapore missionary, Keasberry, who experimented with lithography to produce multi-coloured books and magazines in the Arabic script, never used it for Roman script.

[43] Diehl 1973:123–124.

Also in this utilitarian domain lay scholarly texts. Such texts might be copied professionally or compiled by disciples of a teacher under whom the text was read and verified.[44] Again clarity rather than stylishness was uppermost. However the typical mode of instruction proceeded by commentary on an earlier master's text, and this is given form in the scribal conventions of the scholarly manuscript. The result could be a tangled skein of text on the scholar's page: text, commentary, supercommentary, or marginal or interlinear glosses, or charts and diagrams, in script of different sizes and emphasis. Lithography could reproduce all this as readily as plain text. For typography it was a struggle. It could manage to convey these functionally critical hierarchies and interconnections only rather clumsily through parentheses and marginalia. In time, typographic printing would offer compensating advantages by adopting new organising conventions, including paragraphing and punctuation, but its initial deficiencies were certainly a handicap.

Moving up the scale of social prestige and religious potency, we find the higher realms of writing in the hands of the calligrapher (*khaṭṭāṭ*). The calligrapher was as much an artist as a scribe. Few books were actually copied by calligraphers. In fact, the Qur'ān was the only full manuscript usually calligraphed, and even then usually only the first few pages would be fully decorated and illuminated. Indeed a good calligrapher might regard it as beneath his dignity to copy a whole manuscript, other than the Qur'ān, for high standards could not be maintained throughout.[45] Calligraphers generally displayed their skills, and earned a living, by writing prayers, selections of poetry, and religious icons: the *basmalah*, the names of Allah, invocations, and above all Qur'anic verses and extracts believed to have special potency. A fine piece of this kind could serve as an amulet or, put on display, fill the house of its owner with blessing.[46] Such items of calligraphic art were not only the main sources of the calligraphers' income, but also—and this must be stressed—the most

[44] Pedersen 1984: ch. 3.

[45] Sharar 1975:103–105. Sharar is amusing on this point. He relates (106) the following story, with rather fetching snobbery: "When Haji Harmain Sharifain inaugurated a printing press [probably the first private press in Lucknow], after much exhortation he got Mir Bandey Ali to agree to write out *Panj Sura*, five subsections of the Qur'ān. Mir Bandey Ali put in an immense amount of work and took many days to accomplish the task. When he took it the Haji and had a last look at it in his presence, something about it displeased him and instead of handing it over to him, he tore it up and said, 'I can't do it.'"

[46] Benjamin 1887:290, Schimmel 1984:35.

popular uses of the written word. This terrain lay well beyond the reach of typography, for no mechanical technique could emulate its subtle strokes and the intricate interlacing of graphic forms. Lithography, as an illustrator's medium, could do so.

Resistance to any typographic perversion of calligraphy was reinforced by a sense of calligraphy's contribution to Islamic cultural self-identity. The high standing of calligraphy, and its elaborate development, is peculiar to Islam. This is not just an argument that the calligrapher's writing has an aesthetic and spiritual dimension. As in Europe or China, so in Islam, skill in calligraphy was a fitting attribute of the scholar, calligraphy and medicine being the two vocational studies worthy of *'ulamā'*. But in Islam the position of calligraphy was extraordinarily elevated, surpassing even the scholarly cult of calligraphic brushwork in China. In Hitti's words, "The art of calligraphy, which drew its prestige from its object to perpetuate the word of God, and enjoyed the approval of the Koran (68:1, 96:4) . . . became the most highly praised art."[47] The strictures placed upon representations of the human form, and a preference for avoiding naturalistic depictions of any kind, promoted calligraphy to the supreme visual art. As a seventeenth century Indian Muslim noted, "If someone, whether he can read or not, sees good writing, he likes to enjoy the sight of it."[48] As a hallmark of high culture, and an aristocratic recreation, calligraphy has played a role analogous to painting in the post-Renaissance West. For Ibn Khaldūn, calligraphy was "a noble craft, since it is one of the special qualities of man by which he distinguishes himself from the animals . . . The quality of writing in a town corresponds to the social organisation, civilisation, and competition for luxuries (among its inhabitants)."[49] The very authenticating symbol of authority, the equivalent of a European coat of arms, was the *ṭughrā*, an elaborately wrought monogram of a ruler's name. The practice and collection of fine calligraphy became an indulgence of the aristocratic aesthete. In such circles, a page of fine calligraphy might be worth an Arab horse.

As the deep rationale for calligraphy was embellishment of the Qur'ān, so the Qur'ān was calligraphy's most fit subject. For the people of the Book, the Qur'ān was honoured above all through

---

[47] Hitti 1960:423.
[48] Schimmel 1984:33.
[49] Rosenthal 1967^2: §5.29.

embellishment and ornamentation of its vocal performance according to the canons of *tajwīd*. But as Graham has pointed out, the Muslim tradition has been both the most oral and the most elaborately chirographic. "Muslim veneration of the written Qur'ān exemplar, or *muṣḥaf*, and delight in the elaborately calligraphed qur'anic word have been prominent parts of the highly oral Islamic milieu."[50]

This intimate association of calligraphy with the revealed Word and its role as the supreme visual art have inspired poetic and mystical imagery. Islamic poets could interpret everything as a book, and see writing everywhere. As Schimmel (1984) reminds us, a poetic trope was to compare the face of the beloved to a flawlessly written copy of the Qur'ān, mirroring the calligraphic conceits that made images of animals and men from prayers or verses of the Qur'ān. The dots of a famous calligrapher were transformed into moles on the cheeks of the houris in Paradise. The same intimacies excited sufi thinkers, who drew analogies from the creative processes of calligraphy; for instance, the relation of the Hand and the pen. Deep meditations in this vein, which allude to an abstraction of calligraphic theory to express the undifferentiated eternity, have been brought to our attention by Johns in his study of the *Daqā'iq al-Ḥurūf* of 'Abd al-Ra'ūf of Singkel.[51]

Calligraphy was thus, at once, the most popular and the most prestigious mode of formal writing in Islamic culture, the embodiment of high culture, and the physical vehicle of the text of the Holy Book. This aesthetic citadel resisted typography, but opened its gates to lithography.

7. *A Muslim Technology*

Lithography not only met the aesthetic demands of calligraphy, but also seemed to preserve its cultural and ritual functions. When Müteferriḳa raised his ten points in favour of printing, the ninth was that "the making of books in Arabic or in non-Arabic languages is blessed when it is done by hands of Islam. When printing is done by infidels there will be no blessing in it." This was repeated by the

[50] Graham 1987:89 and 158.
[51] Johns 1955b:68–69 and 72.

great sufi Muḥammad Ḥaqqī's tract in praise of printing 1839.[52] The desire to keep religious literature within the fold is partly explained by the belief that merit accrued from the copying of the Qur'ān, ḥadīth and poems on the Prophet.[53] Conversely, the Qur'ān can only be touched or recited by those in a state of ritual purity. The text of *Sūra* 56:79, to this effect, is commonly displayed on the front page of manuscript and printed copies of the Qur'ān alike. The copying of the Qur'anic text therefore requires the calligrapher to renew his *wuḍū'* time and time again. Herein lies a source of concern with printing: the fear that the process of printing will defile the name of God or the word of God by exposing it to some source of impurity. In Egypt in the 1830s the belief prevailed that it was forbidden to print the Qur'ān or let it pass into the hands of a Christian.[54] The notions of printing and falling under Christian control are closely linked. Typography was after all a Western invention, and had been actively used by European and Syrian Christians to print in Arabic. The complexity of the processes and the specialised skills they required ensured that when government-sponsored printing began in the Middle East, the press equipment was imported from Europe, and European supervisors or operators were employed. Müteferriḳa was himself a Hungarian seminarian who converted to Islam after being enslaved as a prisoner of war. His press was acquired in Paris. To operate it, he hired the Jewish foreman of a Hebrew printing shop in Istanbul, and brought several French compositors from Paris. The Būlāq press was the successor of Napoleon's official press, re-equipped with Italian presses, advice and training, employing Italian printers, and run by a Lebanese Christian.[55]

As if to reinforce the impression that typography was intrinsically a Christian technology, it was actively promoted by Protestant missionaries not only as the supremely effective tool of Christian proselytising, but also as an emblem of Western scientific progress.[56] The

[52] Abdulrazak 1990:92.

[53] The benefits of copying the text of the Qur'ān are naturally the greatest: calligraphers are destined for paradise because of this work, and the pious among them would retain the wood of the pens they had used to copy the Qur'ān to use as kindling to heat the water used for their funeral ablutions. Ink washed off written fragments of Qur'anic text has healing powers (Schimmel 1984:86, 58 and 84).

[54] Lane 1836:283, Demeerseman 1954:59.

[55] Abdulrazak 1990.

[56] Once, amusingly, by the Singapore missionary Keasberry in a lithographed edition (1843). Again the complexity of the process is relevant, for typographic printing

association of government presses in Istanbul and Cairo with programs of military, administrative, and fiscal modernisation along Western lines hardly dispelled this perception. That is why, perhaps, after the Būlāq press had already been in operation for a decade, Lane could record that he was "acquainted with a bookseller here who has long been desirous of printing some books which he feels sure would bring him considerable profit, but cannot overcome his scruples as to the lawfulness of doing so."[57]

Lithography suffered from none of these associations. This cheap, accessible, and simple technology could be transparently under Muslim control.

Its simplicity was stunning. In 1806 its inventor, Senefelder, launched lithography by reproducing a note written by the crown prince of Bavaria in court before his very eyes.[58] Not fifty years later, when the first lithographic press was set up in Sumatra, its owner, Muḥammad Azharī, repeated the novelty for the visiting Dutch Assistant Resident, extemporising a poem of welcome and printing it on the spot.[59] This new technique required only the simplest of materials: grease, lampblack, water, paper, and fine limestone. Within a year or so of the first arrival of lithography in India, all requirements except paper were readily available locally. Lithographic ink was locally made, stones finer than those of Bavaria were found near Madras, and later in Sindh. Only European printing paper had to be relied upon until 1862.[60] Later in Cairo a distinctive locally-produced yellow paper gained popularity for printing copies of the Qur'ān and other religious works, perhaps as an indication that European paper was not involved.[61] Nor did skilled operators have to be imported for lithographic presses. The prime skill needed to produce good lithography is precisely the skill of the copyist or calligrapher. Indeed, the transfer of skills was so direct that in India local scribal mannerisms were carried across into lithographic imprints.[62]

---

was the first mass-production technology involving a high degree of craft specialisation, and thus an outstanding instance of the division of labour, which since Adam Smith's day had been recognised in the West as the foundation of European economic strength.

[57] Lane 1836:283.

[58] Senefelder 1819:65.

[59] Dewall 1857:194.

[60] Caresajee 1958:98, Butt 1988:156.

[61] Cf. the remark of the Turkish calligrapher-historian Mustaḳīmzāde that neither the Qur'ān nor a *ḥadīth* should be written on *firangī* paper (Schimmel 1984:81).

[62] Diehl 1973:120 and 126; Ahmad 1985:142 and 146.

Lithography thus acted as a direct extension of the manuscript tradition. This was important for those who scrupled over the need to reproduce the Qur'ān in writing by the pen, given the Qur'ān's own references to the pen as an instrument conveying divine instruction to mankind (68:1, 96:4). Indeed, the care lavished upon lithographed Qur'ān texts tended to blur further the boundary between manual copying and lithographic printing when the customary embellishments of coloured frames and gilt verse markers were added by hand.

The simplicity and flexibility of lithography made possible printing that was patently Muslim in style and process. It resolved aesthetic and ritual concerns over the reproduction of calligraphy, and specifically of the text of the Qur'ān. It provided a credible means of reproducing the written form of the Holy Book, and all the associated items of popular calligraphy—the *basmalah*, the names of Allah, invocations, verses and extracts of special potency.

And it was just such material that had a ready-made mass market. Lithography flourished supplying it. Popular calligraphy, along with illustrations of the Ka'ba and Shī'ite portraits of 'Alī, Ḥusain, and Fāṭimah were being printed in Istanbul at least as early as 1851. (The printing of such ephemera, unfortunately, goes largely unrecorded.) They became a popular purchase for pilgrims, being sold in great numbers at Mecca.[63] Better attested are early printings of the Qur'ān. The Qur'ān or excerpts from it were regularly among the first books to be printed by private Muslim lithographers. The first Arabic language printing in Persia 1828 was a Qur'ān, lithographed in the hand of a famous calligrapher. As we have seen, the first private press in Lucknow, too, commissioned a Qur'ān selection again from an esteemed calligrapher. And in Southeast Asia, the second item of Muslim printing after a *mawlid* text recited to honour the birth of the Prophet, was again a Qur'ān.[64]

The reason, besides piety, was profit. There was a vast unmet demand for copies of the Qur'ān. Learning to recite the Qur'ān was the first stage in any Muslim child's education, and traditionally students were unlikely to have a copy of the Qur'ān to read from. They learned lines written by their teacher across the top of their slates, or worked from written fragments of the text made by the

[63] Demeerseman 1953:360.
[64] Browne 1914:8, Sharar 1975:106, Kaptein 1993, Dewall 1857.

teacher or senior pupils. Supply of printed copies of the Qur'ān for personal and educational use became a staple of the Muslim printing industry, with Bombay and Cairo eventually emerging as the major suppliers. In the early days of printing, profits could be substantial. Though lithographed copies of the Qur'ān had to be carefully prepared high-quality editions, they could command good prices because a hand-copied Qur'ān was very costly for the same reason. The Agra Qur'ān of 1850, in Arabic and Urdu, made its publisher a fortune at Rs 5 per copy.[65]

Where Muslims lived under colonial rule alongside significant non-Muslim populations, lithography took on a distinctly Muslim hue. As European printing was typographic, and most non-Muslim vernacular printing followed the European model, consistent use of lithography was a mark of Muslim culture. This pattern is strongly evident in both India and Southeast Asia.[66]

With this understanding of the printing technologies available and how they were applied, it seems less useful than ever to generalise about Islamic conservatism. The inadequacy of the technology of typography, especially in the alphabetised form in which it was accessible to Muslims, must be accepted as a significant factor in the long delay in the Muslim adoption of printing. When typographic printing was taken up by the Ottoman government in the face of growing European power, its ineptness and complexity, its Christian odour, and government direction of its uses all restricted its currency and scope. Consequently typographic printing remained marginal to the Muslim tradition and was making only slow headway when lithography burst upon the scene. However, once an appropriate technology for reproducing Arabic script became available, it was adopted rapidly. Lithography was launched in Europe only during the years 1806–1817, and reached India—as we have seen—in 1824. In that very year the first Muslim lithographic press was established. Twenty-five years later, the new technology was widely used in India and Persia, making headway in Turkey, Egypt, and the Maghrib, and about to arrive in Southeast Asia. Let us not forget either, that this new technology was not only speedily adopted, but was also raised to unprecedented levels of technical excellence in its application to book printing.[67]

---

65 Ahmad 1976:137.
66 Proudfoot 1986:108.
67 E.g. Sharar 1975:108.

Thus for most of the Muslim world, lithography provided the whole answer to printed book production. Only in the Middle East and the Maghrib did it flourish alongside a continuing use of typography, mainly by government presses, and here, Demeerseman argues,[68] lithography facilitated the wider acceptance of the principle of printing, and hence typographic printing as well. Thus, in different contexts across the Muslim world, lithography ushered in the print revolution.

8. *Why has Lithography been Neglected?*

If lithography was as important in early Muslim book printing as this survey suggests, then why has it continued to be overlooked? The reasons for this continuing blind spot lie both in the subsequent history of Muslim printing and in certain scholarly attitudes.

In South Asia, lithography has fully held its ground. To this day in India and Pakistan, lithography, or comparable means of reproducing handwritten script, remain the common technique for printing not only Muslim books of all kinds, but newspapers and magazines as well. Outside the sub-continent there has been a rationalisation of printing techniques: typography has largely captured the old field of the copyist and the new applications of print that have no precedent in the manuscript culture; lithography continues to serve in the field of calligrapher.

By the end of the nineteenth century periodicals and newspapers had become the leading print medium. The economics of this new genre required speedy production of large print runs, and this favoured typography. Commercial newspaper reading and government-printed school texts began to create a new literacy in typography free from manuscript antecedents. Also in the latter part of the nineteenth century, the Ottoman government's typographic presses became major printers of religious treatises in Arabic and the vernaculars. The prestige of books printed in Istanbul and above all in Mecca (after 1883) gave credibility to typography.[69] Meanwhile, in a development paralleling the early European experience of print, the graphic poverty of typography, which had at first made it a poor substitute for the manuscript style, was coming to be seen as having the virtue of

[68] Demeerseman 1954:45.
[69] Proudfoot 1993:41.

greater clarity. The advance of typography was noticed by Browne in Persia. In the passage quoted earlier he remarked upon the displacement of early typography by lithography. He then went on to point out that after fifty years of lithography, "typography again became current and popular" at the turn of the century. An analogous change took place in Southeast Asia, at about the same time, with lithography claiming a slowly dwindling audience.[70]

On the other hand, in the realm of the calligrapher, and especially in the printing of the Qur'ān, lithography gained ground and held it. When the Ottoman government allowed the printing of the Qur'ān with Turkish commentary for the first time in 1865, it was done with typography. But the same text was re-issued lithographically in 1879 and thereafter. Analogously in Cairo, early typographic editions of the Qur'ān from 1864 were succeeded in 1889 by lithographed editions. With few exceptions, the Qur'ān has ever since been printed using lithography or allied techniques.

These later developments have overshadowed the early days of printing. The familiarity of the periodical press, and the obvious importance of its impacts, make it too easy to overlook the ways and needs of earlier days, and forget that print was not at first used in this way at all.

Until very recently scholarship has done little to remove this blind spot.[71] Antiquarian bibliography, with its technical interests, and communications history, with its sociological interests, have found little to say to one another. This mismatch has not been mitigated by some prevalent perceptions of Muslim societies.

One is the tendency to base generalisations about Islam on a rather abstract and idealised version of Middle East realities. This may lead to misrepresentations. As we have seen, the history of early printing in the Middle East is not common to the societies in which a majority of Muslims lived. An antidote is to take a view closer to the ground in one place or another away from Istanbul, Mecca and Cairo. This is what makes Demeerseman's contribution to the history of Muslim printing so enriching. By using his local knowledge of Tunis, he was able to avoid some Orientalist ideal-types.

---

[70] Farmayan 1968:145, Walther 1990:236, Proudfoot 1993:57.

[71] Recent doctoral studies have begun to mend the rift. Roper (1988) and Abdulrazak (1990) should be mentioned.

Running deeper is another generalisation. It is the attitude described in the opening paragraph of this essay: namely, a rather too-ready willingness to characterise Islamic societies as intrinsically conservative, or at best reactive. One can avoid the need to explain a great deal by relying on this conviction. The history of lithography in Muslim hands suggests that there may often be more to be said.

* * * * *

Although I have been a student of Professor Johns and later his junior colleague, regretfully I have never had the opportunity to study Islam under him. Nevertheless, in the field of printing history—which must be tangential even to his wide-ranging interests—I have found my way lit by beacons which he has tended. These are his convictions that there are insights to be gained by "observing Islam" away from Mecca and Cairo; that a powerful source of understanding lies in the sensitive juxtaposition of Christian and Muslim experiences; and that at the heart of Muslim consciousness is the multi-faceted beauty of the Qur'ān. For these lights, I am grateful.

PART II

SUNAN KALIJAGA AND THE RISE OF MATARAM

A Reading of the Babad Tanah Jawi *as a Genealogical Narrative*

JAMES J. FOX

1. *Dedication*

In the course of his academic career, Professor Johns has consistently focused attention on the historical foundations of Islam in Southeast Asia and on the literary works that reflect the ideas of various early Muslim communities. A brilliant example of this scholarship is Professor Johns' paper, "Islam in Southeast Asia: Problems of Perspective" which he contributed to the collection of essays dedicated to Professor D.G.E. Hall. For this present collection of essays dedicated to Professor Johns, I would like to follow Professor Johns' example and examine the initial sections of a major source of Javanese literary history, the *Babad Tanah Jawi*, and to consider the fundamental role assigned to important Islamic advisers within this work's overall genealogical structure.

2. *The* Babad Tanah Jawi *as a Genealogical Narrative*[1]

There is no more elaborate genealogical narrative in the whole of the Austronesian-speaking world than that of the *Babad Tanah Jawi*. Only the *Tantara ny Andriana* of the Merina rulers of Madagascar may approach it in length but not in complexity. The "*Major Babad*" is a massive composition of nearly 33,000 lines of verse that narrate the remarkable actions of the rulers of Java, their close court circle of kin and councillors, and their Muslim teachers and spiritual advisers.[2]

[1] I would like to express my appreciation and thanks to my colleagues, Professor Merle C. Ricklefs and Dr S. Supomo, who carefully read an early draft of this paper and provided me with invaluable comment, which I have endeavoured to utilise.

[2] Europeans also figure prominently in the latter half of the *Babad* as do other

Beginning with Wisnu's realm on Java and Watu Gunung's mythic kingdom of Giling-Wesi, the *Babad* proceeds to give an account of the succession of kingdoms on Java from Pajajaran to Majapahit, and then to Demak, to Pajang, and finally to the kingdom of Mataram. With the founding of Mataram, the *Babad* describes in detail the history of this kingdom in its various phases to the second half of the eighteenth century.

Composed in times of extended dynastic conflict, the *Babad Tanah Jawi*, for all its detail and complexity, acts as a genealogical charter for the kingdom of Mataram and its rulers. The opening stanzas of the Great *Babad* make this notion explicit, identifying the work as "a recounting of the ancestors, intended from early times always as a religious declaration, a sacred heirloom in the form of a book: *pamilanging luluhur, pan inguni kalimosadi, pusaka pinustaka*".[3]

Early in the narrative, the *Babad* further announces its genealogical intent: "This is a history of the rulers of Java beginning with the Prophet Adam. . . ." The *Babad* thus begins with an initial genealogy that proceeds from Adam through Sis, Nurcahya, Sanghyang Wening, Sanghyang Tunggal to Batara Guru. At this point, there occurs a narrative convention that is repeated at various junctures in the *Babad*: the genealogy introduces the names of several descendants and alludes to lines of origin created by these separate persons. The creation of these separate lines of origin becomes critically important, later in the *Babad*, in the struggle for the rightful rulership in Java.

At the outset, however, the *Babad* is principally concerned to define the principal line of the rulers of Java. Although it designates other lines of origin, it quickly reverts to its chief narrative concern with the principal ruling line. It is this line that leads to Brawijaya, the ruler of Majapahit, and from Brawijaya eventually to the rulers of Mataram.[4]

non-Javanese protagonists in the dynastic struggles of the kingdom of Mataram. This paper is, however, specifically concerned with the rise of Mataram to the reign of Senapati.

[3] See Ras 1986:255; 1987a:ix.

[4] Of the many commentators who have discussed the *Babad Tanah Jawi*, C.C. Berg seems to have been the first to recognise its significance as a genealogical narrative and to have directed attention to this aspect of its narrative structure (Berg 1938). J.J. Ras, in various publications (1986, 1987a), has since examined other genealogical aspects of the *Babad*.

3. *The Genealogy from Batara Guru to Brawijaya*

The genealogy from Adam to Batara Guru constitutes the first segment of the genealogy. At this stage, the first divergent lines are designated with the naming of Batara Guru's five children: Sambo, Batara Brama, Batara Mahadewa, Batara Wisnu and Dewi Sri. Batara Wisnu is initially named as the first ruler of Java. He takes for his wife a princess of Mendang intended for his father, Batara Guru, and because of his father's anger, he must leave the court to do penance.

Immediately thereafter the *Babad* recounts another genealogy, that of Watu Gunung of the kingdom of Giling Wesi, his two wives, and his twenty-seven children. After narrating the encounter of Watu Gunung and Batara Wisnu that gives rise to the creation of the Javanese Pawukon calendar whose months bear the names of Watu Gunung and his family, the *Babad* reverts to its principal concern by tracing the continuation of the line from Adam through Batara Brama, his daughter Bramani and her son, Tritrusta.

Tritrusta gives rise to a line of succession that is recognisable as a recitation of the names of the heroes of the *Mahābhārata* as performed in Javanese *wayang*. This section of the genealogy proceeds from Tritrusta through five generations to Abiasa and then on to Pandu Dewanata with his court at Astina, and from Pandu on to Arjuna, Abimanyu, and Parikesit.

From Parikesit, the genealogy continues for several more generations to Jayabaya of Kediri and from Jayabaya seven more generations to Sawelacala who is described as ruler of all of Java with his court at Purwa Carita. The genealogy continues for two more generations to Kandiawan whose youngest son, Resi Gatayu, becomes Lord of Koripan.[5] The sons of Resi Gatayu become the rulers of Jenggala, Kediri, and Gegelang and his daughter marries the ruler of Singasari. His son, Lembu Amiluhur, the ruler of Jenggala, has a son, Panji, who marries a princess of Kediri. They, in turn, have a son, Kuda Laleyan, who becomes the ruler of Pajajaran.

It is at this point that the *Babad* takes up the narrative of the kingdom of Pajajaran. The genealogy proceeds from Kuda Laleyan

[5] Kandiawan has five children who are assigned rule over the different occupational groups: 1) Panuhun at Pagelan, lord over farmers; 2) Sandhang Garba at Japara, lord over traders; 3) Karung Kala at Prambanan, lord of the hunters of the forest; 4) Tunggul Metung, lord of the craftsmen including palmtappers; and over them all, 5) the youngest son, Resi Gatayu, who becomes Lord of Koripan.

through three generations to Pamekas and his sons, Arya Banyak Wide, Arya Bangah, the ruler of Galuh, and Raden Susuruh who is driven from Pajajaran and becomes the founder of the kingdom of Majapahit. Raden Susuruh's genealogy leads in five generations to Brawijaya.

The initial segments of the *Babad*, however peculiar in their combination of Hindu, Javanese and Arabic derived genealogies, reveal, in clear and unmistakable fashion, the organisational structure of the narrative and how it will unfold as a succession of episodes introduced by a genealogy of persons. This succession of episodes recounts a succession of kingdoms on Java. The *Babad*, especially in the narrative to the founding of Mataram, purports to relate significant events that have given rise to the principal dynasties of Java. This organisation strives for coherence by attempting to meld disparate traditions in a single narrative.

Numerous family genealogies are interspersed throughout the text. The connections in these genealogies, however, are not limited to relations of direct lineal descent. Women endowed with special powers transmit their heritage to the lines into which they marry. Affinal relations are thus critical and succession may often pass from father-in-law to son-in-law. Equally important at crucial junctures are relations established by adoption. Personal relationships can also be based on more than kinship. Throughout the *Babad*, the idea of spiritual genealogy derived from becoming the pupil of a particular teacher is of critical importance.

The *Babad* in its written form as a book was regarded as a sacred heirloom (*pustaka*) and therefore formed part of the royal regalia. Its narrative also traces the genealogies—and particularly, the origins—of other important pieces of the royal regalia. Such key objects are identified by specific names and their transmission over generations establishes the legitimacy and authority of the dynasty.

4. *The Genealogy of Brawijaya as Narrative Focus*

The organising genealogy of the entire *Babad Tanah Jawi* is indeed the genealogy that leads to Brawijaya, the ruler of Majapahit, and, with the fall of Majapahit, from Brawijaya to the destined rulers of Mataram. There are three genealogical lines that emanate from Brawijaya. Each gives rise to a ruling dynasty and to a successive

Javanese kingdom: first, Demak, then Pajang and finally Mataram. The relations among these related dynasties and their rivalries are the major focus of the narrative. Intermarriage and adoptions among these dynasties interweave separate strands into a grand genealogy. As it proceeds, the narrative of the early portions of the *Babad* recounts individual segments of the separate strands of this grand genealogy, each as an introduction to the next sequence in the progression it is intent on revealing. This narrative of separate episodes with what seem to be curious stops and starts has, in fact, an almost relentless coherence that leads to the founding of Mataram.

As it leads toward the founding of Mataram, the *Babad* also recounts the origin of practices that were to be enshrined as part of the identity of the rulers of Mataram. Thus the narrative must include episodes that relate a prohibition on the wearing of a particular kind of cloth, or the creation of a specifically named *kris* or spear, or the appearance of a staff or cloak, as well as the transmission and use of these objects by precursors. What may seem as oddly irrelevant episodes about peculiar practices or particular objects are all part of the same relentless coherence.

Table 1

The Principal Genealogy of the Babad Tanah Jawi from Adam to Brawijaya
Adam
Sis
Nurcahya
Nurrasa
Wening
Tunggal
Batara Guru
Brama
Bramani
Tritrusta
Parikenan
Manumanasa
Sakutrem
Sakri
Palasara
Abiasa
Pandu Dewanata
Arjuna
Abimanyu
Parikesit

(cont. Table 1)

The Principal Genealogy of the Babad Tanah Jawi from Adam to Brawijaya
Yudayana
Gendrayana
Jayabaya
Jayamijaya
Jayamisena
Kusuma Wicitra
Citrasoma
Pancadriya
Anglingdriya
Sawelacala
Mahapunggung
Kandiawan
Resi Gatayu
Lembu Amiluhur
Panji
Kuda Laleyan
Banjararan Sari
Munding Sari
Munding Wangi
Pemekas
Susuruh
Prabu Anom
Adiningkung
Ayam Wuruk
Lembu Amisani
Bratanjung
Brawijaya

An important feature of the *Babad* is its concern with the spread of Islamic teaching. After the fall of Majapahit, all dynastic rivalries are played out in a predominantly Islamic context. Different figures in the narrative align themselves with particular spiritual mentors. The genealogies of these spiritual mentors and their inter-relations are also of critical importance. Moreover, men who have shared the same teacher and learned his secret wisdom become like brothers to one another and they entrust their children to each other. Thus the alignment by allegiance to a particular Muslim saint is as important as the alignment by genealogy.

5. *Kalijaga and the Rise of Mataram*

Among the various Muslim saints in the *Babad Tanah Jawi*, there is one figure who stands out as the spiritual patron of the kingdom of Mataram. This is the Muslim saint or *Wali*, Sunan Kalijaga. In the *Babad*, Sunan Kalijaga is a figure of considerable mystery who spans the generations from Majapahit to Mataram. Born during Brawijaya's rule in Majapahit, Sunan Kalijaga fashions the central pillar of the great mosque of the kingdom of Demak; he is teacher to the ruler of Pajang; and he makes his last appearance to advise Senapati who stands on the verge of the founding of Mataram. Throughout the *Babad*, by word and deed, he foretells the rise of Mataram and intervenes, at critical moments, to see that ancestors of Mataram succeed to their destiny. He also transmits across generations pieces of regalia that will be the pride of Mataram.

In this paper, my principal concern is with genealogies and relationships but my focus throughout is on the figure of Kalijaga. My discussion traces the role of Kalijaga from his first to his final appearance. In the face of such a complexity of episodes, my task is to concentrate on the main lines of the genealogy that organises the narrative and to examine the way in which Sunan Kalijaga interacts with the main figures of this genealogy. From this perspective, various episodes in the narrative that may appear as either peculiar or trivial can be seen to have specific significance.

Since my interests are neither those of a historian nor of a philologist, I offer no comment on the reliability of the *Babad* in recounting events of the past nor am I concerned with the various versions of these events recounted in other *Babad* or in different recensions of the *Babad Tanah Jawi*.[6] For my reading, I have relied on the prose version of the *Babad* by R.Ng. Kertapradja, edited by J.J. Meinsma and translated into Dutch by W.L. Olthof. This version offers the great advantage of accessibility, especially to someone with only a limited ability to read Javanese. More importantly, it offers a Javanese-selected synopsis of the "Major *Babad*" and thus provides a core text for analysis.

Since my focus is on Sunan Kalijaga, it is worth noting that there

[6] There is a substantial scholarly literature that examines the evolution, composition and reliability of the *Babad Tanah Jawi*. The best recent sources on these issues are Ricklefs 1979 and Ras 1986 and 1987b.

is a tradition first reported by Winter[7] that a descendant of Sunan Kalijaga was responsible for fashioning part of the *Babad Tanah Jawi.* Evidence would suggest that the *Babad* was composed in stages over a period of more than a hundred years, with the possibility that its earliest sections took shape sometime after 1640 during the reign of Sultan Agung. Scholars have speculated that a succession of Kalijaga's descendants, Pangeran Adilangu I and Pangeran Adilangu II, may have been responsible for the first two stages in the composition of the *Babad* in the seventeenth and in the early eighteenth century.[8]

One of the tasks of this paper is to present the narrative as a systematic progression. This presentation inevitably requires a succinct retelling of important episodes in the *Babad.* It also involves drawing together episodes that are recounted separately—at times seemingly without relation to one another—identifying connections between them, and noting their more general significance. Much of the narrative of the *Babad* consists of prophetic foreshadowings. Incidents of little apparent consequence take on significance as the narrative unfolds and the prophetic nature of these incidents is implicitly revealed.

6. *The Genealogies of the Muslim Saints*

With the coming of Islam, the genealogies of the Muslim saints become part of the narrative structure and these genealogies become intertwined with the different lines of origin that derive from Brawijaya. Having considered the genealogy that leads to Brawijaya, it is necessary to consider the genealogies of the various Muslim saints and how they relate among themselves and to the line of Brawijaya.

The narrative of the Muslim saints, or *Wali,* begins with the figure of Makdum Brahim-Asmara who is credited with the conversion of the ruler of Cempa who had already sent his first daughter to marry Brawijaya in Majapahit. After his conversion, the ruler of Cempa gives his second daughter to Makdum Brahim-Asmara who has two sons, Raden Rahmat and Raden Santri.

With the permission of the ruler of Cempa, Raden Rahmat and his brother, Raden Santri, together with the son of the ruler of Cempa, Raden Burèrèh, journey to the court of Majapahit. There Raden

---

[7] 1848, I 354.

[8] See de Graaf 1965:125 and 129; Ras 1986:260–261; 1987b.

Rahmat marries the daughter of Ki Gede Manila who holds the court position of Tumenggung of Wila-Tikta (Majapahit). Ki Gede Manila's son is Jaka Said who is destined to become Sunan Kalijaga.

That Raden Rahmat marries the daughter of Ki Gede Manila and that Jaka Said is identified from the beginning by a Muslim name would imply that Ki Gede Manila's position was that of a Muslim adviser at the Majapahit court.

Raden Rahmat and his wife move to Ampel-Denta and settle there. Raden Rahmat thus becomes the first in the line of Muslim saints who bear the title, Sunan Ampel-Denta. Raden Santri and Raden Burèrèh marry the two daughters of Arya Teja and they take up residence in Gresik which eventually becomes the site of the Muslim saint known as Sunan Giri. In the developing narrative, Ampel-Denta, Giri and Arya Teja's realm in Tuban stand as Islamic centres that eventually come to oppose Majapahit.

The next important Muslim saint to make his appearance in the *Babad* is the mysterious Shaykh Wali Lanang from Juldah who arrives in Java and settles in Ampel-Denta and imparts his knowledge to Sunan Ngampel. Shaykh Wali Lanang then moves to Blambangan where he marries the daughter of the ruler, fathers a son, and then departs for Malaka when the ruler refuses to keep his promise to convert to Islam.

When Shaykh Wali Lanang's child is born, he is laid in a chest and cast upon the sea. A pious widow at Gresik, the wife of a former court official in Blambangan, finds the chest, raises the child and sends him to study Islam with Sunan Ngampel. The child, known as Santri Giri, undertakes his studies with Sunan Ngampel's own son, Santri Bonang. In time, the two decide to go to Mecca but, on their way, they encounter Shaykh Wali Lanang with whom they study for a year. In the end, Shaykh Wali Lanang gives them new names: Giri is named Prabu Set Mata, and Bonang Prabu Nyakra Kusuma. Both are then sent back to Java. Santri Giri becomes Sunan Giri and Santri Bonang becomes Sunan Bonang.

Thus in the initial stages of the narrative, during the time of Majapahit, there are three learned saints—Sunan Ngampel, Sunan Bonang, and Sunan Giri—all of whom have had the same religious teacher, Shaykh Wali Lanang. The fourth Sunan to join this group is Sunan Kalijaga who is in fact led to his commitment to Islam by Sunan Bonang, his father's sister's son.

7. *The "Conversion" of Sunan Kalijaga*

In the *Babad*, Jaka Said is described as someone who is extremely fond of gambling. He wanders to Japara and there, when he has lost his money, he becomes a robber who preys upon travellers who make their way through the forest of Jati Sekar to the northeast of Lasem. Sunan Bonang happens to be passing through this forest and Jaka Said attempts to rob him. Sunan Bonang tells him that there will soon be someone passing through the forest dressed in dark blue and wearing a *wora-wari* flower behind his ear. It would be better to rob him. Jaka Said agrees and Sunan Bonang continues on his way. Three days later the stranger in dark blue with a *wora-wari* flower appears and Jaka Said attempts to stop him. It turns out to be Sunan Bonang again and Sunan Bonang transforms himself into four persons.

Jaka Said is terrified. He repents and decides to give up his evil ways and to practise asceticism. On the instructions of Sunan Bonang, he fasts and meditates for two years. He then goes on to Cirebon where he continues his fasting and meditation beside the river Jaga. It is from this river that he takes on his new name and identity as Sunan Kalijaga. There he marries the younger sister of Sunan Gunung Jati who rules in Cirebon (see Figure 1).

8. *Dynastic Lines Emanating from Brawijaya*

In the *Babad*, Brawijaya gives rise to three distinct genealogical lines, each of which produces, in succession, a ruling dynasty. Each line derives from a separate marriage. Recounting the complicated background to Brawijaya's various marriages occupies a crucial segment of the *Babad.*

The first of these marriages is with a princess of Cempa. Brawijaya dreams that he is to marry this princess and sends his *patih* (chief administrator), Gajah Mada, to request her. Gajah Mada returns not only with Brawijaya's bride but also with three important pieces of regalia, the gong kyai Sekar Delima, the coach kyai Bale Lumur, and the cart kyai Jebat Betri.

Brawijaya's next marriage is with a forest ogre who assumes the form of a beautiful woman, Sasmita Pura, when she arrives in Majapahit. When Brawijaya discovers his mistake, he tries to kill her but succeeds only in driving her into the forest where she gives birth to

Figure 1

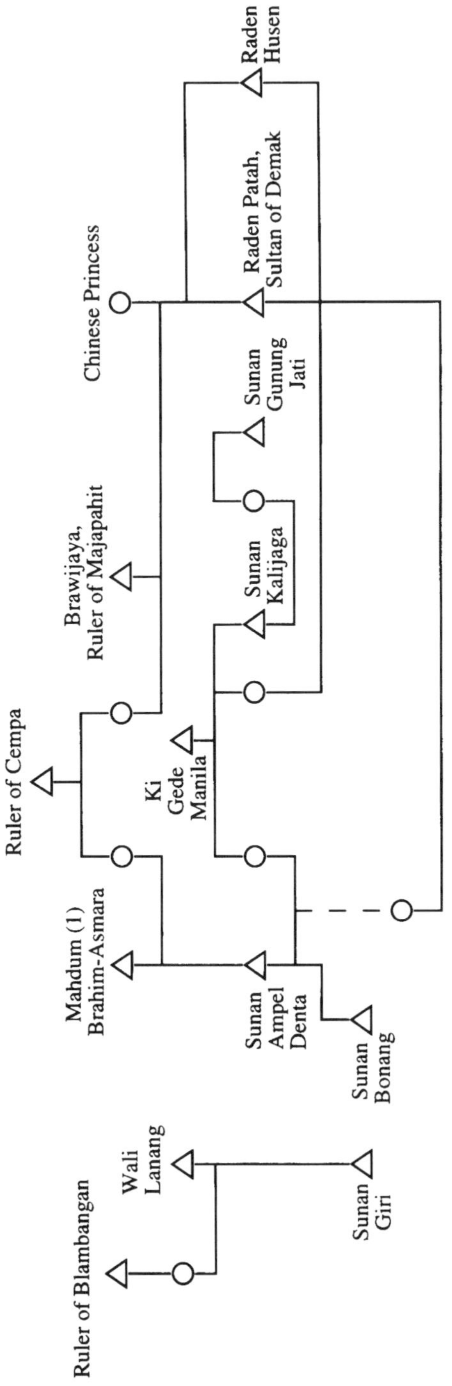

GENEALOGIES OF THE MUSLIM SAINTS

a son called Dilah. Dilah becomes a court jester but when he succeeds, with the help of his mother, in driving wild animals to the palace for Brawijaya's hunt, Dilah is made Lord of Palembang and is given the name, Arya Damar.

Brawijaya marries yet again, this time a Chinese princess. But when his first wife, the Cempa princess objects, Brawijaya gives the Chinese princess to Arya Damar but forbids him to take her as his wife until she has given birth to Brawijaya's child. When Brawijaya's son is born, he is given the name, Raden Patah; Arya Damar has a son by the same princess who is named Raden Husen. Both boys grow up together in Palembang and then decide to return to Java. They take up residence in Ampel-Denta where they study Islam under Sunan Ngampel and become Muslims. Raden Patah marries a granddaughter of Sunan Ngampel and is sent by Sunan Ngampel to the forest of Bintara where he builds a mosque and begins his teaching of Islam.

Brawijaya's next union is even more curious. He asks his court diviners whether, after his demise, there will come a successor whose power will be as great as his own. His diviners tell him that there will indeed be such a successor from among his descendants but that successor will move his court to Mataram and from there rule over all the inhabitants of Java. Soon thereafter Brawijaya is afflicted with venereal disease and no cure can be found. In his sleep a voice tells him that he can only be cured by sleeping with a Wandhan woman whose skin is yellow. His wife from Cempa has brought such a woman with her and so Brawijaya sleeps with her and is cured.[9] The woman becomes pregnant and bears a beautiful child. Because of the diviners' claim that this child will put an end to Brawijaya's rule, Brawijaya orders that the child be given to Kyai Buyut Masahar, who is the superintendent of the king's rice fields, to be killed when he is one *windu* (or eight years) old.

The child is given the name, Raden Bondhan Kejawan. The wife of Kyai Buyut Masahar loves the child too much to allow her husband to kill him and so Kyai Buyut simply reports his death to Brawijaya, who is delighted. Later when Raden Bondhan Kejawan is older, he follows Kyai Buyut Masahar to the palace and in the *Sitinggil* he plays the *gamelan*, kyai Sekar Delima. Brawijaya is startled

[9] de Josselin de Jong (1986:228–230) discusses this incident of the "sick king" in the *Babad* from different comparative perspectives, and it is worth noting that in a footnote he draws attention to the three lines that derive from Brawijaya.

but when he sees that it is the son of Kyai Buyut Masahar, he gives Raden Bondhan Kejawan two *kris*es, kyai Maesa Nular and kyai Maléla, and a pike called kyai Plèrèd. Brawijaya also orders Kyai Buyut Masahar to entrust the boy to Kyai Ageng Tarub.[10]

On his way to Kyai Ageng Tarub, Raden Bondhan Kejawan is attacked by robbers and forced to defend himself using kyai Maléla. The tip of the *kris* is broken and Raden Bondhan Kejawan declares that none of his descendants may again use this *kris*. Eventually these weapons become part of Mataram's regalia; kyai Plèrèd is particularly important in the transfer of power to Mataram.

Kyai Ageng Tarub receives Raden Bondhan Kejawan and, as Brawijaya wishes, he treats him as his own child. He changes his name to Lembu Peteng. Lembu Peteng marries the Kyai Ageng Tarub's beautiful daughter, Retna Nawang Sih. As the daughter of a heavenly nymph, Retna Nawang Sih is one of the women of special power who contribute to the spiritual aura of the Mataram dynasty.[11]

In addition to the line of Raden Patah and the line of Raden Bondhan Kejawan, there is a third dynastic line of importance that emanates from Brawijaya. This line derives from Brawijaya's daughter who is given in marriage to Dipati Jayaningrat. Dipati Jayaningrat has two sons, Ki Kebo Kenanga who converts to Islam and Ki Kebo Kanigara who remains unconverted. Ki Kebo Kenanga establishes himself in Pengging and becomes known as Ki Ageng Pengging. In

---

[10] The *Babad* is at pains to relate the history of Kyai Ageng Tarub, who is in fact a foundling adopted by the hermit, the earlier Kyai Ageng Tarub. The child is the offspring of an improper union between the son of Kyai Ageng Kudus and the daughter of Kyai Ageng Kembang Lampir.

[11] The tales involving Retna Nawang Sih's mother are variants of folk tales that have a wide distribution that extends well beyond the Javanese world. According to the *Babad*, as a young man, Kyai Ageng Tarub came upon a group of heavenly nymphs bathing at a waterhole in the forest. By stealing the robe of one of the nymphs, Nawang Wulan, he forces her to marry him. The beautiful Retna Nawang Sih is the child of this union. Each day Nawang Wulan cooks rice for Kyai Ageng Tarub but warns her husband never to look inside the cooking pot. Although she always cooks rice, the rice stores never diminish. Kyai Ageng Tarub cannot restrain himself; and so one day, he looks inside the cooking pot and discovers that his wife provides him all his rice by cooking one grain of rice. When her secret is discovered, Nawang Wulan loses her powers and is forced to pound rice each day but in doing so, she discovers her robe hidden under the rice in the rice barn. She is able to put on her robe and return to heaven, promising always to come to the aid of her daughter when someone casts burnt glutinous rice (for her) on the *pepanggungan*. Her daughter, Retna Nawang Sih, grows up to resemble her mother.

the development of the narrative, Ki Ageng Pengging invites the Muslim saint, Pangeran Siti Jenar, to be his teacher. Siti Jenar forms a group of pupils who introduce yet another dimension to the rivalry among competing dynastic lines.

The struggles of these dynastic lines occupy the next critical stage in the *Babad.*

Table 2

The Three Dynastic Lines from Brawijaya

The Dynastic Line of Demak	
Brawijaya	= Chinese Princess
Raden Patah (Bintara)	= Granddaughter of Sunan Ampel-Denta
Raden Sabrang-Ler (e) Raden Trenggana (y)	
(Raden Prawata)	
The Dynastic Line of Pajang	
Brawijaya	
Daughter of Brawijaya	= Jayaningrat
Ki Ageng Pengging (Kebo Kenanga)	
Sultan Adi Wijaya (Jaka Tingkir)	= Daughter of Sultan Trenggana
Pangeran Benawa	
The Dynastic Line of Mataram	
Brawijaya	= Wandhan Woman
Raden Bondhan Kejawan (Lembu Peteng)	= Retna Nawang Sih
Ki Getas Pandhawa	
Ki Ageng Sela	
Ki Ageng Ngenis	
Ki Ageng Pamanahan	= Daughter of Nyai Ageng Saba
Senapati-ing-Alaga (Raden Ngabehi Lor-ing-Pasar)	

9. *Events Leading to the Fall of Majapahit*

When Raden Patah goes to Bintara, his younger brother, Raden Husen, who as the son of Arya Damar is a grandson of Brawijaya, goes to Majapahit. He is well received at court and is made the regent of Terung. He marries the daughter of Ki Gede Manila, and thus becomes the brother-in-law of Sunan Kalijaga.

As regent of Terung, he acts as an intermediary between Raden Patah and Brawijaya. When Brawijaya learns who the lord of Bintara is, he accepts him as his son and sends Terung to convey to him his new title, Adipati of Bintara, and a company of ten thousand soldiers.

It is not the rise of Bintara that disturbs Brawijaya but the influence of Giri. When Brawijaya's troops first attack Giri, they are driven back by Sunan Giri's pen which turns into a *kris*, kyai Kalam Munyeng. When the first Sunan Giri dies and is replaced by his grandson, Parapen, the forces of Majapahit are victorious and burn Giri to ashes. Yet when these forces attempt to disturb the grave of Sunan Giri, Brawijaya's entire army is attacked by swarms of bees that drive them back to Majapahit.

When after some time the Adipati of Bintara fails to come to the court of Majapahit, Brawijaya sends the regent of Terung with another contingent of ten thousand troops. When Bintara explains that he can not pay homage to a ruler who is not a Muslim, his brother, the Regent of Terung, is too afraid to return to Majapahit having failed in his mission. Instead the Muslim rulers—the Regent of Madura, Arya Teja of Tuban, the Regent of Surabaya and Sunan Giri—unite under Raden Patah of Bintara to attack Majapahit.

When Brawijaya sees that his son is in the *pagelaran* and about to enter the palace, he chooses to disappear and take his loyal troops with him to heaven. Raden Patah conquers an empty palace. Sunan Ampel-Denta declares that Raden Patah is to become the new ruler of Majapahit but first Sunan Giri must reign for forty days to eliminate the infidel traces of Brawijaya's rule. After these forty days, Raden Patah becomes the ruler of all of Java. He assumes the title, Senapati Jimbun Ngabd'ur Rahman Panembahan Palembang Saidin Panatagama and establishes his court at Demak where all the Muslim saints gather to build a great mosque.

10. *The Emergence of Sunan Kalijaga as Patron of Mataram*

It is only with the fall of Majapahit that Sunan Kalijaga emerges as a key figure in the narrative and the first hint is given that his role is to insure the rise of Mataram. Thus when the decision is taken to build a great mosque in Demak, all the saints except Sunan Kalijaga gather in Demak and divide the work among themselves. Sunan Kalijaga is absent because he has undertaken a spiritual visit (*tirakat*) to Pamantingan. This mention of Sunan Kalijaga's visit to Pamantingan is a critical allusion. By this act, which occurs just prior to the building of the mosque, Sunan Kalijaga provides a link between different periods of Javanese rule in a way that foreshadows the rise of Mataram.

Early in the *Babad*, Pamantingan is named as one of the eight abodes over which Batara Guru sends Batara Wisnu to rule. Later when Raden Susuruh flees from the kingdom of Pajajaran, he meets the mystic teacher, Cemara Tunggal, who directs him to the site of the *maja* tree where he is to found the kingdom of Majapahit. Cemara Tunggal reveals that she is a princess of Pajajaran who fled the kingdom because she refused to marry. She shows herself as an extraordinarily beautiful woman and she foretells that Raden Susuruh and his descendants will rule over all of Java. When she has moved to the sea and taken up her residence at Pamantingan, she will rule over all the spirits. In time, Raden Susuruh's descendants will take up residence to the north of Pamantingan and to the south of Merapi. Whoever is to be the ruler of Java will marry her and when he is in difficulty, he can call upon her to bring her entire spirit army to his assistance. The prophecy is that of the Nyai Rara Kidul, who will marry with Senapati, thus linking the kingdoms of Pajajaran, Majapahit and Mataram. Sunan Kalijaga's task is to prepare the way for these events to come to pass.

When Sunan Kalijaga finally arrives in Demak from Pamantingan, all of the other saints have finished their tasks in building the great mosque. Sunan Kalijaga hastily assembles some pieces of wood and binds them together. In the night these pieces miraculously become the great pillar of the mosque.

As a result, on the first of the month of Dulkangidah, the mosque is completed. Sunan Kudus becomes the head (*pengulu*) of the mosque. Henceforth Sunan Kudus will be the patron of Demak and protagonist in its struggle for power. A tacit rivalry thus develops between Sunan Kudus and Sunan Kalijaga.

A week after the completion of the mosque, the saints gather as a group to perform chants in God's praise (*dikir*). Sunan Kalijaga, however, sits apart from the other saints near the great drum of the mosque. Suddenly a packet wrapped in a goat's skin drops from on high. Wrapped in the goat's skin is a prayer mat and a shawl from the Prophet. The saints propose to divide this heavenly gift among themselves but Sunan Bonang urges that they throw the packet into the air. He on whom the packet lands will be its owner. They throw the packet into the air and it lands on Sunan Kalijaga's lap. He is overwhelmed by this rare gift and immediately begins a fast in a deep hole for forty days. During this time, he sews the goat's skin and it becomes the Anta-Kusuma or kyai Gundil which is to be worn by the rulers of Java on their accession to power and when they wage war. The narrative concludes with the statement that neither the Sultan of Demak nor the Sultan of Pajang would wear the Anta-Kusuma. The Anta-Kusuma is destined to become part of the royal regalia of the kingdom of Mataram.

Important in this episode is the role of Sunan Bonang who intervenes to the benefit of Sunan Kalijaga. After this account of the creation of the Anta-Kusuma, there follows an episode about the creation of two special *kris* from Sunan Bonang's iron staff. When the work is completed, the smith becomes blind and can make no more *kris*. The two *kris* are also destined to become part of the royal regalia of the rulers of Java.

11. *The Rivalry Between Demak and Pengging*

With the establishment of the rule of Demak by Raden Patah, a son of Brawijaya, the *Babad* begins to differentiate among the different genealogical lines and among the different saints associated with them. As Sultan of Demak, Raden Patah is guided by Sunan Kudus. The potential rival to Raden Patah is Ki Ageng Pengging who is the son of Dipati Jayaningrat by a daughter of Brawijaya. Ki Ageng Pengging's spiritual advisor is Pangeran Siti Jenar.

Siti Jenar forms a group of four pupils: Ki Ageng Pengging, Ki Ageng Tingkir, Ki Ageng Butuh, and Ki Ageng Ngerang. Ki Ageng Pengging has a son who is given the name Krebet by Ki Ageng Tingkir who predicts a great destiny for him. In the unfolding of the narrative, Krebet who is also known as Jaka Tingkir becomes Adi

Wijaya, the founder of Pajang, the kingdom that provides the transition from Demak to Mataram. Before this can occur, however, the differences between Demak and Pengging must play themselves out.

Raden Patah becomes angry because Ki Ageng Pengging has not visited him in Demak to show obeisance and Sunan Kudus becomes suspicious of the secret learning that Ki Ageng Pengging has obtained from Siti Jenar. Eventually, Sunan Kudus is sent to visit Pengging where he engages Ki Ageng in a test of his secret knowledge and of his allegiance. In the end, Sunan Kudus kills Ki Ageng Pengging.

Ki Ageng Pengging's orphaned son, Jaka Tingkir, is adopted by the widow of Ki Ageng Tingkir, but when he grows up, he is sent to Ki Ageng Sela and becomes his devoted student. It is here that the dynastic lines of Pengging and Pajang become intertwined with the line of Mataram.

Ki Ageng Sela is the grandson of Raden Bondhan Kejawan who was given the name Lembu Peteng by Ki Ageng Tarub. Lembu Peteng marries Nawang Sih and has two children, a boy named Getas Pandhawa and a girl, who marries Ki Ageng Ngerang, another of the pupils of Siti Jenar. Getas Pandhawa has seven children, a son, Ki Ageng Sela, and six daughters.

12. *Jaka Tingkir and the Rise of Pajang*

According to the narrative, the reason that Jaka Tingkir was sent to be raised by Ki Ageng Sela was because he was too prone to practise asceticism in the mountains and forests among unbelieving ascetics who knew nothing of Islam. For this reason, the good widow of Ki Ageng Tingkir sends Jaka Tingkir to be taught by Ki Ageng Sela who adopts him as his beloved grandson. But Ki Ageng Sela continues to train him in ascetic practice. They spend seven days and seven nights in a hut in a dry rice field northeast of Tarub. Each has a dream that foretells the future. Ki Ageng Sela dreams that he goes to a forest to clear it but finds Jaka Tingkir has already cleared it for him. Jaka Tingkir dreams of the moon coming down upon him.

Ki Ageng Sela then instructs Jaka Tingkir that he must go to do service in Demak; he also tells him that in the future, one of his descendants will succeed to Jaka Tingkir's high office. Jaka Tingkir accepts this as a destined eventuality.

Before he sets off for Demak, Jaka Tingkir returns to see his stepmother at Tingkir. His stepmother orders him to help two servants who are weeding a dry rice field. There, while Jaka Tingkir is in the rice field, Sunan Kalijaga appears holding his staff. Kalijaga addresses him familiarly telling him to cease his weeding and go immediately to Demak because he is to be a future ruler of Java.

Jaka Tingkir's arrival in Demak coincides with the death of the Sultan who is briefly succeeded by his second son, Sabrang Ler, who soon after dies without issue. Raden Trenggana, the former Sultan's fourth son, becomes the Sultan of Demak. Sultan Trenggana favours Jaka Tingkir and makes him the chief of his special soldiers known as the Tamtama.

A considerable portion of the next segment of the *Babad* narrative is concerned with the various adventures of Jaka Tingkir. As chief of the Tamtama, Jaka Tingkir has the task of selecting exceptional individuals to join the Tamtama. All candidates must prove their powers by fighting a bull and killing it with a blow to the head. Jaka Tingkir kills one ugly candidate who wants to join the Tamtama and for this offence is sent into exile by the just Sultan Trenggana.

In exile, but expecting to be forgiven his crime, Jaka Tingkir wanders through a great forest and there encounters his father's fellow pupils, Ki Ageng Butuh and Ki Ageng Ngerang who take him in and continue his instruction. When eventually Jaka Tingkir is neither forgiven nor recalled to Demak, he returns to Pengging and goes to sleep beside his father's grave. During his meditation, he hears a voice that instructs him to go south to the village of Getas Aji to serve Kyai Buyut Banyu Biru. There Jaka Tingkir meets Ki Mas Manca, another descendant of the rulers of Majapahit who has been adopted by Kyai Buyut Banyu Biru. Kyai Banyu Biru informs Manca that he is to serve Jaka Tingkir who will eventually become the ruler of Java at Pajang.

Kyai Banyu Biru instructs both Jaka Tingkir and Manca together. He tells them that they must go to meet Sultan Trenggana on the mountain, Prawata, and he gives Jaka Tingkir the means by which he can regain royal favour. Kyai Banyu Biru assigns Ki Mas Manca, his brother, Ki Wuragil, and his nephew, Ki Wila, to accompany Jaka Tingkir. This group of four, which is formed on Kyai Banyu Biru's instruction, will eventually become one of the core groups of the court of Pajang.[12] When Jaka Tingkir is restored to royal favour, he returns to Demak as the chief of the Tamtama.

---

[12] At Kedung Srengéngé, on his way to meet Sultan Trenggana at Prawata, Jaka Tingkir overcomes the Bau Reksa, the Lord of the Crocodiles, who then pledges his

Shortly after the return of Jaka Tingkir, Sultan Trenggana journeys to Cirebon to invite Sunan Kalijaga to come to reside in Demak. Sunan Kalijaga moves to Adi Langu, outside of Demak. Adi Langu remains thereafter Sunan Kalijaga's permanent residence where, according to the narrative, he continues to teach the religion of the Prophet, attracting many students.

Jaka Tingkir marries a daughter of Sultan Trenggana who elevates him to Bupati and grants him land at Pajang where he builds his kraton. When the Sultan of Demak dies, Jaka Tingkir as Sultan of Pajang is recognised as the ruler of Java. All who oppose Pajang are defeated; only Jipang, ruled by a grandson of the first Sultan of Demak, continues to oppose Pajang. The sons of Sultan Trenggana, including Pangeran Prawata, Sultan Trenggana's eldest son, accept Pajang's overlordship.

13. *Ki Ageng Sela and the Foreshadowing of Mataram*

The narrative at this stage becomes far more detailed. The *Babad* narrative dealing with the period from the establishment of Pajang to its conquest by Mataram is much longer than the narrative that covers the period from the rise of Pajajaran to the fall of Demak. In the narrative of Pajang, Sunan Kalijaga's role in guiding the rise of Mataram becomes ever the more prominent.

At a point in the narrative that marks the transition of rule from Demak to Pajang, the narrative relates various short episodes in the life of Ki Ageng Sela. All of these episodes function as foreshadowings.

In the first episode, Ki Ageng Sela tries to join the Tamtama. He fights and kills the bull to qualify but turns away, as he says, to avoid being splattered with the animal's blood. This is considered a sign of fear. Shamed at his rejection, he attacks the kraton of Demak but his horse is struck with arrows shot by the Sultan. He is thus driven off. The Sultan states that Ki Ageng Sela can never be ruler but he does not know what will happen in the future.

The second episode is more curious and would seem to be a

---

loyalty and provides an escort of forty crocodiles to draw Jaka Tingkir's raft upriver. The group stops briefly to see Ki Butuh and Ki Ngerang and during the night a light is seen to come from the northwest and to descend upon Jaka Tingkir while he is asleep on the raft in the river. Ki Ageng Butuh wakes Jaka Tingkir to tell him that the circle of light of Demak has shifted to descend upon him.

demonstration of Ki Ageng Sela's powers. Ki Ageng Sela is working in a rice field when lightning appears to him in the form of an old man. He captures this lightning-man and takes him to the Sultan of Pajang who sets him in an iron cage and orders that no one provide him with water. An old lady, who is the old man's wife, appears and gives him a coconut shell with water, at which the thunder sounds, the cage melts and the lightning forms disappear.

The third episode concerns a *wayang* puppeteer named Ki Bicak whom Ki Ageng Sela kills because he covets his beautiful wife. After he has killed Ki Bicak, Ki Ageng Sela takes his wife, his puppets and his gongs. He loses interest in the wife but asks permission of Sunan Kalijaga to make the gongs special heirlooms. When they are beaten and give forth their full sound, this will be a sign that a battle will be won; if they give no sound, this will be a sign that a battle will be lost.

Yet another episode concerns an attack on Ki Ageng Sela by someone who is running amok. The attack occurs while Ki Ageng Sela is planting squash. At the time, he is wearing a cloth of flowered silk but without a belt. In the field, Ki Ageng Sela trips over a squash vine and his cloth comes undone. He is therefore forced to stand naked when the madman attacks him. He kills the attacker with one blow but then proclaims that henceforth none of his descendants may wear a similar cloth, nor may they plant or eat squash.

None of these brief accounts advances the narrative nor are they explicable on their own except in so far as they explain the origins of the particular, distinctive traditions of the Mataram court and its regalia.

Ki Ageng Sela has seven children, six girls and a boy. His second daughter is Nyai Ageng Saba and his only son, the youngest of the seven children, is Kyai Ageng Ngenis. Little is related in the narrative about this generation; rather it is the next generation on which the narrative focuses.

Kyai Ageng Ngenis' son is Kyai Pamanahan who marries the daughter of his father's sister, Nyai Ageng Saba. Nyai Ageng Saba's youngest son is Kyai Juru Martani. Juru Martani is thus both cousin and brother-in-law to Pamanahan. Kyai Ageng Ngenis also adopts a close relative, a boy called Ki Panjawi. These three boys form an inseparable group. All three go to study with Sunan Kalijaga who invites the Sultan of Pajang to join them as a brother. Kyai Ageng Ngenis takes up residence in Lawiyan (Lawean), dies and is buried there.

14. *Rival Groups in the Struggle for Rule*

The groupings of genealogically related individuals become more complex as the narrative continues. In Pajang, three groups are formed, each with the Sultan of Pajang as a crucial member.

The first group is that formed at Kyai Banyu Biru's insistence. It consists of the Sultan together with Ki Mas Manca, Ki Wuragil and Ki Wila. Ki Mas Manca becomes the Patih (chief administrator) of Pajang and adopts the name, Manca Negara; Ki Wuragil and Ki Wila both become Bupati (senior courtiers).

The second group is that formed around Sunan Kalijaga. It consists of the Sultan together with Ki Pamanahan, Ki Panjawi and Juru Martani. Both Ki Pamanahan and Ki Panjawi are adopted as "elder brothers" to the Sultan of Pajang and are given the responsibility to lead the Tamtama. Only Juru Martani is given no responsibility, although he continues to support Pamanahan and Panjawi. These four students constitute a group like the one that was formed earlier around Siti Jenar consisting of the Sultan's father, Ki Ageng Pengging, together with Ki Ageng Tingkir, Ki Ageng Butuh, and Ki Ageng Ngerang.

The bond between the Sultan of Pajang and Ki Pamanahan is further strengthened by the Sultan of Pajang's adoption of Ki Pamanahan's second son, Raden Bagus, as his oldest son. This son is given the name Raden Ngabehi Lor-ing-Pasar and eventually is made the commander of the Tamtama. This son, who will become known as Senapati, will succeed the Sultan of Pajang and establish the rule of Mataram.

Finally a third group is formed around Sunan Kudus. This group consists of the Sultan together with Pangeran Arya Panangsang of Jipang, a grandson of the first Sultan of Demak, and Pangeran Prawata who is also called Sunan Prawata, the son of the second Sultan of Demak. It is within this group that the next struggles arise.

From among his pupils, Sunan Kudus favours Arya Panangsang and he persuades Arya Panangsang to kill Sunan Prawata. Sunan Prawata's wife and the husband of Sunan Prawata's sister, Ratu Kali Nyamat, are also killed. In response, Ratu Kali Nyamat ascends to the hilltop of Dana Raja, removes all her clothes, and becomes an ascetic, vowing that she will not wear clothes again until Arya Panangsang is killed and promising to give all her possessions to the person who kills him.

Sunan Kudus next persuades Arya Panangsang to kill the Sultan of Pajang. When Arya Panangsang sends men to stab the Sultan while he is sleeping, the Sultan remains completely unharmed and in fact gives a reward to his attackers warning them never to attempt to kill him again. His reputation for mystic power is only enhanced by the incident.

Sunan Kudus then arranges a meeting in Kudus between Arya Panangsang and the Sultan. The Sultan goes to Kudus accompanied by his troops and by Ki Pamanahan and Ki Panjawi. At their meeting, the Sultan allows Arya Panangsang to see one of his *kris* but protects himself with a more powerful *kris*. The result is a stand-off.

The Sultan and Ki Pamanahan then go to pay a visit to Ratu Kali Nyamat and with Ki Pamanahan's help, Kali Nyamat succeeds in persuading the Sultan to kill Arya Panangsang. Just as Kali Nyamat has offered all her possessions and those of Sunan Prawata to whoever kills Arya Panangsang, the Sultan offers the realms of Pati and Mataram to whoever will carry out this task for him.

Ki Pamanahan, Ki Panjawi, Juru Martani and the young Raden Ng. Lor-ing-Pasar form a group of four—the core group of Sesela—to carry out the Sultan's wishes. By sending a message purporting to be an invitation from the Sultan of Pajang to single combat, they lure Arya Panangsang in battle alone. In the struggle, Raden Ng. Lor-ing-Pasar stabs and kills Arya Panangsang with the pike, kyai Plèrèd, the gift of Brawijaya to Raden Bondhan Kajawan. Since Raden Ng. Lor-ing-Pasar is still a young boy and has already been adopted as the Sultan's son, Juru Martani then advises Ki Pamanahan and Ki Panjawi to claim to have killed Arya Panangsang and thus request the offered reward. They do this and the Sultan immediately grants Pati to Ki Panjawi and promises Mataram to Ki Pamanahan.

The Sultan orders Ki Pamanahan to inform Ratu Kali Nyamat of the death of Arya Panangsang. Kali Nyamat offers Ki Pamanahan all sorts of rewards but he accepts only two rings and some of Kali Nyamat's serving girls. These gifts he offers to the Sultan who refuses them, except for one young girl whom he entrusts to Ki Pamanahan until she is of marriageable age. Later Raden Ng. Lor-ing-Pasar sleeps with this girl but the Sultan forgives him his offence. He marries and has a child by her, Raden Rangga.

15. *Sunan Giri, Sunan Kalijaga and the Bestowal of Mataram*

After waiting for some time for the Sultan to bestow Mataram on him, Ki Pamanahan leaves court and goes to the village of Kembang Lampir where he becomes an ascetic. There Sunan Kalijaga goes to meet him and brings him back to court and offers to ask the Sultan on his behalf why he has not fulfilled his promise. In approaching the Sultan, Sunan Kalijaga invokes the brotherhood of the common tutelage of Pajang and Pamanahan under his direction. In reply, the Sultan tells them of Sunan Giri's prophecy that whoever holds Mataram will rise up and become a greater ruler than Pajang.

To allay the Sultan's fears, Sunan Kalijaga makes Ki Pamanahan swear an oath that if he contemplates becoming the ruler of Mataram and overthrowing Pajang, he will have no success. The oath, however, includes the statement that whatever happens later must depend on God's will. In response to the oath, the Sultan grants Ki Pamanahan the realm of Mataram which consists largely of forest. Ki Pamanahan takes the name, Ki Ageng Mataram. He and his family depart the court to make their way to Mataram.

Later the *Babad* relates, as a kind of retrospect, the incident involving the prophecy of Sunan Giri. This incident occurred when the Sultan journeyed to Giri to obtain the approval of the Sunan for his assumption of the Sultanate. At the gathering of all the lords of Java, Sunan Giri turned to Ki Ageng Mataram and prophesied that his descendants would rule over all the inhabitants of Java including Giri itself.

16. *Ki Ageng Karang Lo, Ki Ageng Giring and Ki Ageng Mataram*

Two incidents during the founding of Mataram are related as of special significance. At Taji, Ki Ageng Karang Lo offers food to Ki Ageng Mataram's group as they journey to Mataram. He is invited to join them and at the river Ompak they meet Sunan Kalijaga who is bathing in the river. Sunan Kalijaga instructs Ki Ageng Mataram that Ki Ageng Karang Lo's descendants will live in the midst of Ki Ageng Mataram's descendants without titles or signs of privilege.

Ki Ageng Mataram continues his ascetic practices in forests and mountain tops hoping to bring about the prophecy of Sunan Giri. He goes to visit another ascetic who is his friend, Ki Ageng Giring.

Ki Ageng Giring is a palmtapper who taps coconuts for their juice (hence he is also known as Ki Ageng Paderesan). While he is at work in one of his coconut trees, he hears a voice speaking to him. It tells him that whoever drinks all of the juice from one young coconut in the tree will have descendants who become the rulers of all of Java.

Ki Ageng Giring stops his work, plucks the coconut and takes it home with him. Rather than drink the juice immediately, he decides to leave it on a platform above his hearth and to cut some wood to work up a thirst to be able to drink all the juice of the coconut. Just after he leaves, Ki Ageng Mataram arrives and asks for a drink. When he can find nothing else to drink, he takes down the coconut and, despite the objections of Ki Ageng Giring's wife, he drinks the juice of the coconut in one go. When Ki Ageng Giring returns, he is overwhelmed. He tells Ki Ageng Mataram what the voice foretold and begs Ki Ageng Mataram repeatedly to allow his descendants to rule after Ki Ageng Mataram's descendants. Ki Ageng Mataram steadfastly refuses Ki Ageng Giring's requests and relents only after the seventh request by saying he knows not what will happen in the future.

In time, Mataram grows prosperous. On his death bed, Ki Ageng Mataram names Raden Ng. Lor-ing-Pasar as his successor and instructs Juru Martani to look after his children and his children to obey Juru Martani.

Juru Martani goes to Pajang to announce Ki Ageng Mataram's death. The Sultan concurs in appointing his adopted son, Raden Ng. Lor-ing-Pasar, as successor in Mataram and he bestows upon him a new name, Senapati-ing-Alaga Sayidin Panatagama. He tells Juru Martani that Senapati need not pay a visit of obeisance in his first year because he must bring order to Mataram, but that the Sultan will expect a visit in the second year of his lordship. The whole of the next portion of the *Babad*, which is almost as long as all of the preceding narrative, is concerned with the exploits of Senapati and his establishment of Mataram's rule over all of Java.

17. *Sunan Kalijaga and Senapati-ing-Alaga*

As relations become strained between Pajang and Mataram, Juru Martani and Senapati agree to seek God's will on what to do. Juru Martani proposes that Senapati go to the sea to pray while he climbs

Mt Merapi to pray. On the seashore, Senapati's prayer to Allah causes a great storm that heats the sea's waters and forces Nyai Rara Kidul, the goddess of the southern ocean, to beseech Senapati to have pity on her and to cease his disturbances. She assures him that his descendants will be the rulers of Java and will have the protection of her spirit forces. Senapati falls in love with Nyai Rara Kidul and accompanies her to her sea palace. There, for three days and three nights they make love and Nyai Rara Kidul instructs Senapati on how to be the ruler of humans and spirits. He then returns arriving on shore at Parang Tritis where he immediately encounters Sunan Kalijaga deep in prayer. Sunan Kalijaga counsels him not to be overconfident in his mystic power and might but rather, if he wishes to be ruler, to be obedient to God's commands. They then go to Mataram where Sunan Kalijaga urges him to build an outer brick wall around Mataram for protection and then marks out for him the lines along which he is to build this wall.

Pangeran Benawa, the son of the Sultan and therefore, by the rules of adoption, also the younger brother of Senapati, goes to visit Mataram and is well received. He assures his father that Senapati has no intention to overthrow Pajang, but the Sultan's other councillors warn him to distrust Senapati. Eventually Pajang's army moves to attack Mataram. They camp at Prambanan. Juru Martani urges Senapati to pray to God but also to call the Nyai Rara Kidul and the guardian spirit of Merapi to come to Mataram's aid. As they pray, a storm arises and Merapi begins to burn; stones rain down upon the land and the southern mountains become a sea of fire. Kyai Bicak's gongs of war—part of the Mataram regalia from Ki Ageng Sela—sound continuously.

The Sultan flees with his army, telling his councillors that they must not struggle against Senapati because he is destined to be the successor of Pajang. The Sultan makes his way in the night as far as the tomb of the Muslim saint of Tembayat. There he is denied entry and is told by the custodian that this denial signifies that he no longer has God's permission to be ruler. He therefore sleeps outside in the Bale Kencur and the next day, on his return to Pajang, he falls ill.

The Sultan again tells his followers and his son, Pangeran Benawa, not to oppose Senapati who will be his successor. Senapati with some of his horsemen comes to the Mayang on the outskirts of Pajang and sends *selasih* flowers as a sign of his affection. At night, while Senapati is praying, his *jinn familiar*, Juru Taman, appears and asks whether he should go and kill the Sultan. Senapati tells the *jinn* that he will not request the *jinn* to do so but he will not forbid him either. The *jinn* goes to the Sultan and descends upon his chest and he dies. When Senapati hears of the death of the Sultan, he goes immediately to Pajang to mourn his death, as a son would for his father.

It is at this point that Sunan Kudus once more intervenes on behalf of Demak. At a gathering after the funeral of the Sultan of Pajang, he urges that the Adipati of Demak, the Sultan's son-in-law by his eldest daughter, be chosen as his successor. Juru Martani advises Senapati to avoid a quarrel and the two return to Mataram.

Demak's impositions upon Pajang cause unrest and Pangeran Benawa, who has been made Adipati of Jipang, invites Senapati to join him in overthrowing his brother-in-law. The two meet at Weru and many of Pajang's soldiers desert to their cause. Only the troops from Demak oppose Senapati who captures the palace and sends the Adipati of Demak with his family back to Demak. Although Pangeran Benawa offers him the rule of Pajang, Senapati insists that his younger brother Benawa become Sultan. For his part, he asks for three pieces of regalia, the gong kyai Sekar Delima—originally the gift of the ruler of Cempa to Brawijaya—the special bit for a horse, kyai Macan Guguh, and the saddle, kyai Gatayu. Senapati asserts that he is destined to rule from Mataram. Within a year, however, the Sultan Benawa dies and a younger brother of Senapati, Pangeran Gagak Baning, is appointed as Adipati of Pajang, thus ending the dynastic line of Pajang.

From Mataram, Senapati sends a message to Sunan Giri requesting confirmation of his prophecy. Sunan Giri replies that if Senapati wishes to confirm that it is God's will that he become the ruler of Java, he has only to begin his campaign for the conquest of east Java since Sunan Giri's prophecy stated that the world would be turned upside down and that Giri itself would be conquered by Mataram.

Senapati begins his campaign against east Java in the month of Muḥarram.[13] When his army is arrayed against the armies of east Java led by the Pangeran of Surabaya, Sunan Giri sends a message

[13] Muslims are enjoined not to make war, except in self-defence, during the month of Muḥarram. Senapati asserts his action in marching on east Java during this month is to commemorate the first journey that he and the Sultan Pajang made to visit Sunan Giri.

that Mataram and Surabaya must choose between "content and vessel": Surabaya chooses "content" and Senapati chooses "vessel". Sunan Giri then reveals that "vessel" signifies the right to land and state; "content" refers to the population. By this division of authority, the conflict between the two is resolved. In the kinship idiom that is adopted between them, Senapati becomes the elder brother, Surabaya the younger brother.

This prepares the way for a resolution of the dynastic struggles within the *Babad*, the transference of the single most important piece of regalia to Senapati, and finally his exercise of rule over Java. This critical point in the *Babad* is reached in the struggle over Madiun and appropriately it involves the final appearance of Sunan Kalijaga in the narrative.

A son of the last sultan of Demak, appointed as *bupati* of Madiun by the Sultan of Pajang, assumes the leadership among the lords of east Java. Together they prepare to overthrow Mataram. Senapati realises that his army is no match for the assembled armies of east Java and so he sends a beautiful woman from the court to the court of Madiun to convince its lord that Senapati is about to submit to Madiun. This she does successfully and the *bupati* of Madiun releases the other armies and sends them home. In the meantime, Juru Martani—now with the title Adipati Manda Raka—urges Senapati to seek Sunan Kalijaga's assistance.

Senapati goes to Adi Langu and asks Sunan Kalijaga for kyai Gundil or Anta-Kusuma, the cloth prepared from the heavenly packet containing the prayer mat and the mantle of the Prophet bestowed upon Sunan Kalijaga in the mosque at Demak. Kyai Gundil is the final gift that Sunan Kalijaga gives to Mataram. This cloth, which confers invulnerability, has been destined to be worn only by the rulers of Mataram. With this gift, Senapati takes his leave of Sunan Kalijaga and returns to the battle.

Senapati puts on kyai Gundil and orders his troops to attack the unwary army of Madiun. The lord of Madiun flees with his family leaving only his daughter, Retna Jumilah, in the inner precincts of the palace. The beautiful Jumilah has vowed she will only marry a man who shows no wound when he is stabbed by her knife. When Senapati penetrates the inner palace, she confronts him with a sacred *kris*, Gumarang. He tries to woo her but she tells him she will accept him only if he shows no effect from the cut of the *kris*. She attempts to wound him but Senapati remains unharmed. Senapati then takes her as his wife and the *kris* is given the new name, kyai Gupita.

Senapati's marriage with a woman from the dynastic line of Demak unites the two lines separated by a fierce rivalry from the time of Brawijaya. His adoption by the Sultan of Pajang had already reconciled and united the separate lines of Mataram and Pajang. Thus, in genealogical terms, Senapati succeeds in joining the three dynastic lines that derive from Majapahit. (See Figure 2)

Senapati's conquest of east Java, whose first step is the conquest of Madiun, fulfils the prophecy of Sunan Giri while the gift of kyai Gundil from Sunan Kalijaga confers on Senapati a piece of truly royal regalia associated with the Prophet. The *Babad Tanah Jawi* continues its narrative of the rulers of Java but from Senapati the dynastic line of Mataram is established as the single ruling line of Java.

18. *Conclusion*

The *Babad Tanah Jawi* has to be recognised as an exceptional literary work. Read as a genealogical narrative, the first half of the *Babad* has in fact a remarkably coherent structure, perhaps too coherent to be considered as an evidential history. It is also a work that provides a religious justification for the rulership of Java.

The *Babad Tanah Jawi* is also one of the most important initial sources for a succession of other *Babad* that retell the early history of Java. It is particularly instructive to consider the different ways in which subsequent *Babad* represent the genealogies of the rulers and Muslim saints of Java.[14]

It is evident that many sources for the *Babad Tanah Jawi* were originally oral narratives. One of the most remarkable features of Jawa is that these oral traditions continue to be told to this day. They are still recounted by the custodians of the sites on Java where these events occurred and where the figures in these narratives are buried. It is still possible to record the oral narratives of Java's past at precisely those sites that are identified as significant by the *Babad Tanah Jawi*.

From this perspective, in providing a guide to some of the most significant sites on the island of Java, it also provides a means of interpreting what remains at these sites. Since many of these sites

---

[14] See Fox 1991:24–33.

Figure 2

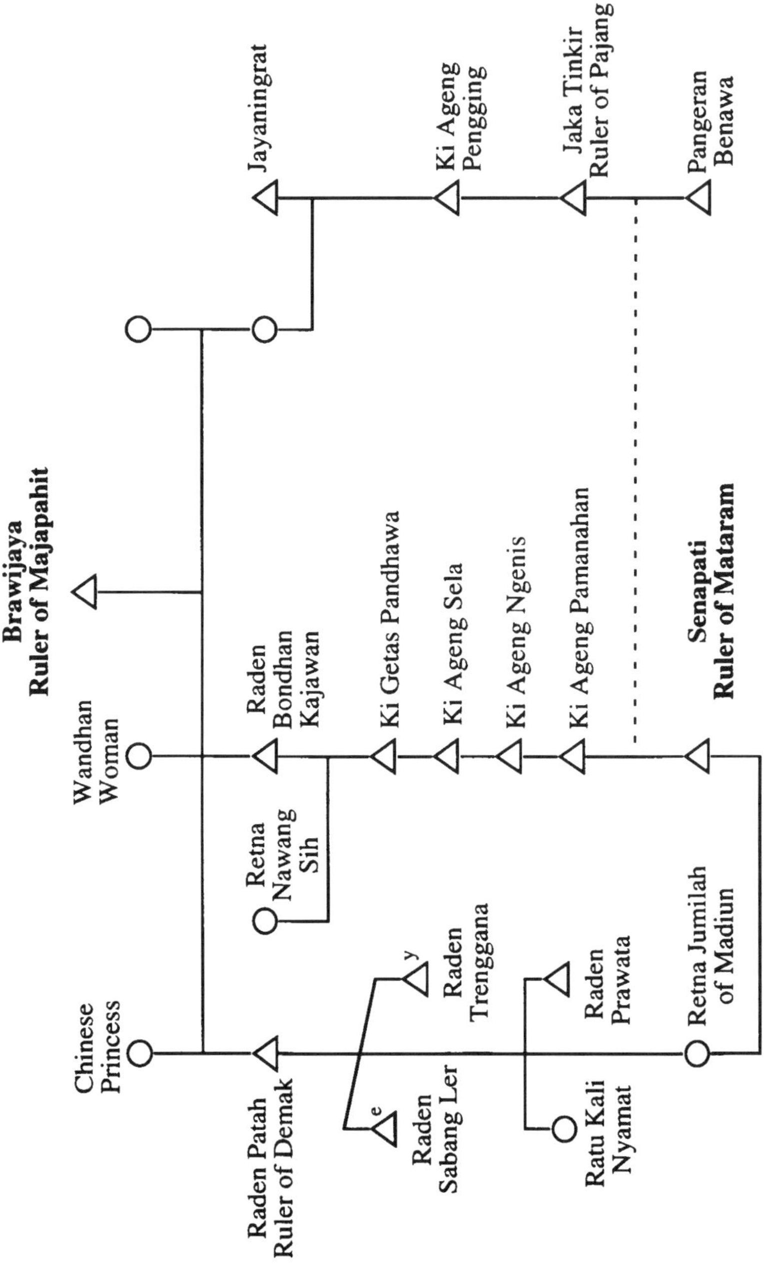

BRAWIJAYA TO SENAPATI:
THE RESOLUTION OF DYNASTIC DIFFERENCES THROUGH SENAPATI

are tombs, the *Babad* offers identification for those who are buried in them. For the Mataram dynasty, the *Babad* recounts the burial of Ki Ageng Sela at Sela and Ki Ageng Ngenis in Laweyan. It also identifies the burial site of Senapati "to the south of the mosque" of Mataram and "at the foot end of the grave of his father" in what is now Kota Gede.

At present, at this tomb complex, there are hundreds of graves crammed into a limited space. In the main mausoleum are the graves of more than seventy of the closest of Senapati's relatives. These graves are arranged in rows that represent different generational levels as they might be represented in a kinship chart.

The senior generation is represented by Nyai Ageng Ngenis, Senapati's grandmother, whose husband is buried at Laweyan. In the next generation are Ki Ageng Mataram (Ki Pamanahan) and his wife, Nyai Ageng Mataram, Senapati's parents. Also on this same level are the graves of Juru Martani, Senapati's uncle, and Nyai Ageng Pati, the wife of Ki Panjawi, another uncle. Senapati is buried at the next level below his father's grave and beside the grave of his brother, Pangeran Gagak Baning, and in a row with his other brothers. Below him are his oldest son, Raden Rangga, and the son who succeeded him, Pangeran Seda-ing-Krapyak. To one side at an intermediate level are the two women of the Demak dynasty: Ratu Kali Nyamat and Ratu Retna Jumilah, Senapati's wife. Figure 3 presents yet another genealogical representation of the Mataram dynasty and its founding relations for which the *Babad Tanah Jawi* provides the narrative.

Figure 3

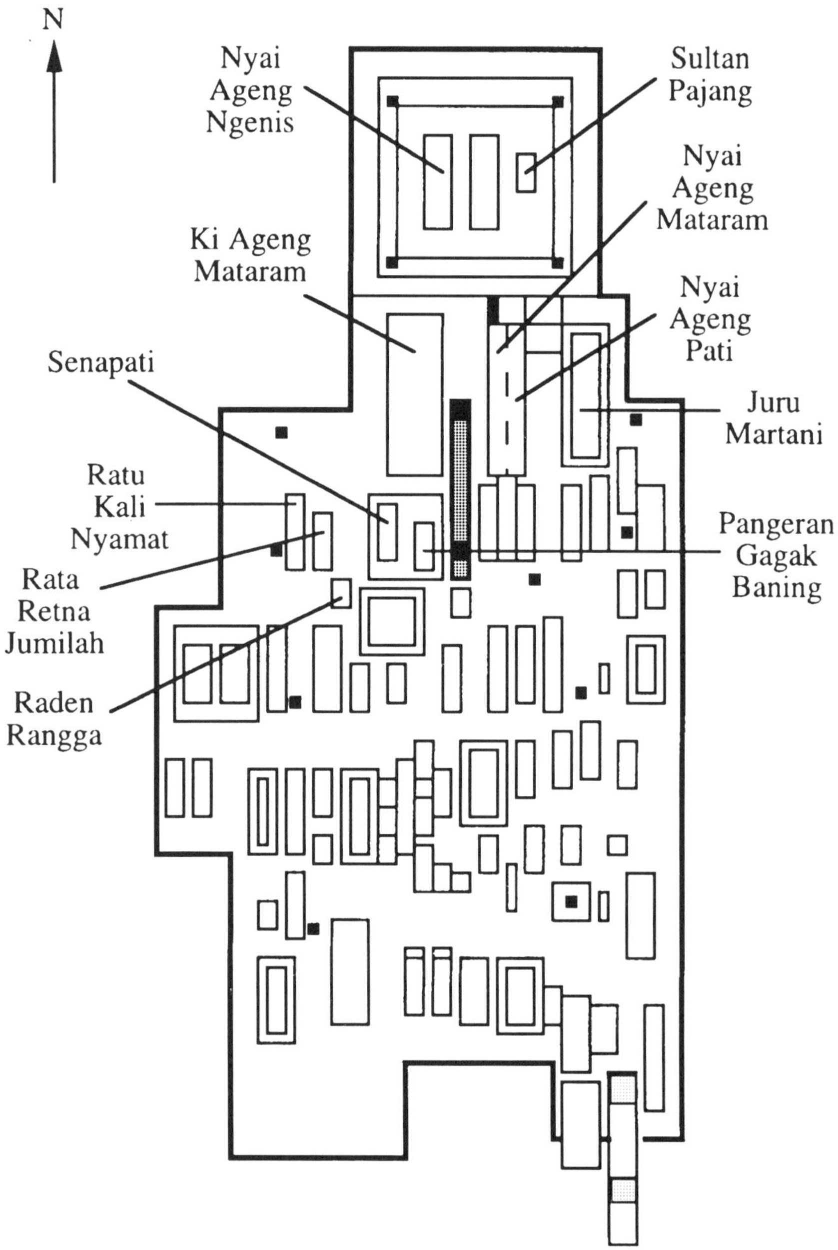

PASAREYAN KOTA GEDE

FROM *ŚAKTI* TO *SHAHĀDA*

The Quest for New Meanings in a Changing World Order

S. Supomo

1. *From Parwa to Jarwa*

There are a number of events which are of great significance to the Javanese people, but as far as its literary history is concerned none is more important than the one that took place at the *kraton* of king Dharmawangśa Tĕguh, a ruler of an East Javanese kingdom, from 14 October to 12 November 996. For "one month minus one evening" people gathered at the court to hear the first reading of what was apparently the first completed Old Javanese prose rendering (*parwa*) of the fourth book of the *Mahābhārata*, the *Wirāṭaparwa*. That the king took great interest in the efforts of rendering the *Mahābhārata* into Old Javanese is evident from the fact that not only was he the patron of the whole undertaking of "rendering Byāśa's thought into Javanese" (*mangjawakĕn Byasāmata*), but also that he himself assiduously attended all the sessions, except for one, when he was "prevented by other affairs".[1]

The importance of Dharmawangśa's meritorious deeds in sponsoring the writing of the *parwa* for the development of Javanese literature and Javanese culture in general is quite evident—more than half of the narrative poems (*kakawin*) which have come down to us have heroes and heroines from the *parwa*.[2] Moreover, the epics must have also been a favourite source of wayang stories (*lakon*). This is already evident from the Sangsang inscription (dated 907), in which we read that a wayang performance of the story of *Bhīmayakumara*

[1] Supomo 1972; Zoetmulder 1974:95.

[2] See Pigeaud 1967–80:I, 157–197 and Zoetmulder 1974. Of the 18 books of the *Mahābhārata* and seven of the *Rāmāyaṇa*, ten *parwa* have come down to us, nine from the former and one from the latter. In addition, four other *parwa* from the *Mahābhārata* may also have been completed, but were lost sometime after the composition of the *Bhāratayuddha kakawin* in 1157 (Supomo 1993:4–37; Zoetmulder 1974:68–100).

(probably based on an episode from the *Wirāṭaparwa*) as well as a recital of the *Bhīmakumara* and *Rāmāyaṇa* stories were held to celebrate the granting of freeholds to the monasteries of Hujung Galuh and Dalinan.[3] It is interesting to note that a *lakon* from the more Hinduistic *Mahābhārata* was chosen for a celebration in a Buddhist monastery. This indicates that by that time such *lakon* must already have been accepted by the population in general, regardless of their religious affiliation.

Nor did the appeal of the epic-based narratives diminish when the seat of power moved back to central Java in the sixteenth century. There are only a handful of Old Javanese works that survived the upheavals following the demise of the last Hindu-Buddhist kingdom of Majapahit, yet the influence of these works is found in almost all aspects of Javanese cultural life. As is to be expected, most of these works are either directly derived from or somehow related to the *Mahābhārata* and the *Rāmāyaṇa*, such as the *Arjunawiwaha, Bhāratayuddha, Dewaruci*, and the *Arjunawijaya*. These are the *kakawin* which later were rendered into Modern Javanese and known as *jarwa*.[4] According to the eighteenth and nineteenth century sources, long after Islam became the dominant religion in Java and despite the introduction of a number of works from the Muslim world, such as the *Sĕrat Menak* and *Sĕrat Yusuf*,[5] the epic-based *kakawin* and/or their Modern Javanese renderings were still widely read and discussed at gatherings held at royal courts as well as in religious circles. Likewise, the epic-based *lakon* were—and still are—preferred by the general population rather than *lakon* based on Muslim texts, such as *Sĕrat Menak*—just as some nine centuries earlier people in the Buddhist monastery of Dalinan preferred a performance of an epic-based *lakon* and a recital of an episode from the *Wirāṭaparwa* and the *Rāmāyaṇa* to a Buddhist text.

It is also apparent from these eighteenth and nineteenth century works, that it was not uncommon for *ulama* in those days to be well versed in *kawi* works. We read in the *Sĕrat Cabolek*, for instance, that its main protagonist, *Kĕtib* Anom from Kudus "is an *ulama* and in addition is versed in *kawi*". In this respect he is said to be far superior to his antagonist, *Haji* Amad Mutamakin, a mystic who was at the centre of an investigation by the authorities because of his teach-

[3] Sarkar 1972:85–95.
[4] Poerbatjaraka 1952:133–148.
[5] Poerbatjaraka 1952:109–124.

ing which was deemed to be heterodox mystical knowledge and of his disregard for the Law of the Prophet (*sarengat Nabi*).[6] To *Kĕtib* Anom,

> . . . the essence of *kawi* works
> such as the *Bhima Suci* and the *Wiwaha*
> is expressed in many metaphors
> from which the quintessence of mystical knowledge can be mastered
> if the interpreter is penetrating and exact
> And these, just as the book of *Rama* in *kawi*
> are books on ṣūfism.[7]

Indeed, *Kĕtib* Anom seemed so much at home in *kawi* works that when he had to explain new concepts, his natural inclination was to resort to the wayang world. We read in *Sĕrat Cabolek* 9.21, for instance, that in his attempt to explain the four *nafsu* (spirit, passion), he said that

> king Dasamuka is the symbol of
> *nĕpsu luhamah* (greedy desire)
> Kumbakarna is that of *amarah* (the vice of anger)
> Surpakĕnaka is of *supiyah* (a pure desire)
> *mutmainah* (the holy desire)
> is symbolised by Wibisana.[8]

The same device, as Ricklefs[9] has noted, is also used in the *Tuḥfa*, the Javanese version of *al-Tuḥfa al-Mursala ilā rūḥ al-Nabī*. Thus in explaining the concepts of *aʿyān thābitah* and *aʿyān khārijiyya* (i.e. Fixed Prototypes and Exterior Essences) the author illustrated this by using the relation of Wisnu and Krĕsna, of a deity and his incarnation, in *Tuḥfa* 1.12 as follows:

> [Yet those Prototypes] which are within the Knowledge
> are not opposed [to the Essence without] their being the same.
> The relation of Wisnu and Krĕsna
> is an illustration of this,
> for it is Wisnu who is Krĕsna.
> The true Wisnu takes a form becoming manifest in Krĕsna
> and is the reality that is Arya Krĕsna.[10]

---

[6] Soebardi 1975:67.
[7] *Sĕrat Cabolek* 8.6, Soebardi 1975:114.
[8] Soebardi 1975:137.
[9] Ricklefs 1979b.
[10] Johns 1965:34–37.

2. *From Sanskrit to Arabic Verses*

There is also another aspect of the *parwa* which has some bearing on certain types of Javanese literature. One of the characteristics of the *parwa* is the occurrence of Sanskrit quotations, mostly taken from the corresponding passages of the epics, followed by translations or paraphrases in Old Javanese. They often consist of a full *śloka*, i.e. two lines of 16 syllables each, sometimes of only one line, or even less, and then followed directly by a translation or paraphrase of the quoted passage in Old Javanese.[11] The following is an example from the *Wirāṭaparwa*:

> *Yuṣmākaṁ wikramād adya mukto' ham swastimān aham, tasmād bhawanto Matsyānām īśwarāḥ sarwa ewa hi.* Anubhāwa śaktinta kita kabeh, mārga ni nghulun mahurip, wīryaprātapanta sambandha ning agĕsang. Ya ta matang yan prārthana ni nghulun, kita teki rakwa pramāṇa ngke Wirāṭa, sĕmbahĕn de ning sakala Matsyadeṣa.[12]

> *Yuṣmākaṁ wikramād adya mukto' ham swastimān aham, tasmād bhawanto Matsyānām īśwarāḥ sarwa ewa hi.* It is by your beneficial power that I have been rescued, and it is because of your might in battle that I am still alive. It is my request, therefore, that you become the ruler of Wirāṭa, to whom the whole country of the Matsyas will pay homage.

Now and then we find glosses are given to certain words, using the formula *ngaranya*, "its meaning; it means", to separate the Sanskrit words and their Old Javanese equivalents, e.g.

> Śwetawāhana pwa lingnya, nīhan nimitta nikā: *śweta* ngaran ing aputih, *wāhana* ngaran ing kuda. Ya pwa n ikang amatĕk ratha ni nghulun i kāla ning samara, *tenāhaṁ Śwetawāhanah.*[13]

> They call me Śwetawāhana—the reason is as follows: *śweta* means white, *wāhana* means horse. Those are the horses which draw my chariot in battle, *therefore I am He of the White Horses.*

Such quotations are found all over the text, without a definite pattern; the places where they occur seem to have been chosen almost at random, so that it is often impossible to find any reasonable explanation for them. Some quotations may perhaps be explained simply by the author's desire "to throw the story into stronger relief, enliven it and add local colour"; some by the desire "to recapture

[11] Zoetmulder 1974:89–92.
[12] Juynboll 1912:51.
[13] Juynboll 1912:63.

the reader's flagging attention", or even by a most common human weakness: a desire to show off one's learning. As Zoetmulder has pointed out, "Authors of other periods and other lands have used the same device, interspersing their writings or speeches in the vernacular with quotations from a language, only imperfectly known, but surrounded with an aura of learning, holiness or antiquity, such as Arabic or Latin".[14]

Still, quite a number of *śloka* must have been quoted because of their didactic nature, especially those that contain a maxim or a piece of advice on moral conduct. Combined with the belief that it is beneficial to listen to a recitation of the *Mahābhārata*, the quotation of certain passages in their original sacred language must have enhanced the merits of a work which, according to the author of the *Wirāṭaparwa* "is the same as a sacred work, and is exactly like holy water".[15] It is not surprising, therefore, that such a device—of using Sanskrit *śloka* and words followed by its Old Javanese equivalent or its paraphrase—appears regularly in didactic and religious texts, such as the *Ślokāntara*[16] and the *Wṛhaspatitattwa*.[17]

As evident from recent studies by McDonald[18] and Kuntara Wiryamartana,[19] this stylistic feature of the *parwa*, the *ngaranya* formula, is also used widely in the *jarwa*, with the word *tĕgĕse* replacing the Old Javanese *ngaranya*. Such a formula is also a common feature in Muslim religious texts, the only difference is that instead of Sanskrit *śloka* followed by Javanese glosses or interpretations now we have Arabic *lafal* followed by the same. The following is an example from a sixteenth century text:

> E mitraningsun [. . .] Iki si lafale, tingkahing anakseni ing Pangeran, *wa-ashhadu an lā ilāha illā'llāhu, waḥdahu lā sharīka lah(u), wa-ashhadu anna Muḥammadan rasūlu'llāhi*, t(ĕ)gĕse iku ingsun anakseni, kaananing Pangeran, kang anama Allah, kang asifat sadya, langgĕng kĕkĕl, wibuh sampurṇa, purba kadim, sifatira mahasuci, orana Pangeran sab(ĕ)nĕre, anging Allah uga Pangeran kang sinĕmbah, sab(ĕ)nĕre kang agung; kalawan ingsun anakseni yan bagiṇḍa Muhammad kawulaning Allah kang sinihan, ingutus agama Islam, iya iku i(ng)kang tinut dening nabi, wali mumin kabeh.

---

[14] 1974:90.
[15] Juynboll 1912:97.
[16] Sharada Rani 1957.
[17] Sudharshana Devi 1957.
[18] 1983:164–171.
[19] 1990:209ff.

My friends! . . . This is the formula, the way of confessing the Lord: *Wa-ashhadu an lā ilāha illā'llāh, waḥdahu lā sharīka lahu, wa-ashhadu anna Muḥammadan rasūlu 'l-lāh*, i.e. I confess the eternal and immaterial Being of the Lord whose name is Allah. His attributes are everlastingness, omnipotence and priority. There is no Lord but Allah, the object of our devotion, He the truly high. And I confess that our Lord Muḥammad is the chosen servant of Allah, the Apostle of Islam, the first among the prophets, saints and true believers.[20]

3. *The Decline of the Knowledge of Old Javanese*

Nevertheless, despite the high regard that the *parwa* and literary works which are derived or related to them apparently always enjoyed throughout the centuries, with the change of circumstances brought about by the decline and the eventual demise of Majapahit sometime in the 15th century, the kind of literary activities that had produced Old Javanese literature in Java gradually, if not abruptly, also came to an end. While in Bali *kakawin* writing continued to be practised in Java it came to an end with the fall of Majapahit. And with wars being fought incessantly in both central and eastern Java after the fall of Majapahit until the imposition of some kind of peace by the colonial power, not only were new works no longer written, but the old ones were lost as well. Even when there never was any policy of a deliberate burning of the so called *buda* (i.e. pre-Muslim) books by the new converts—as asserted, for instance, in the *Sĕrat Dĕrmagaṇḍul*, which tells us about the burning of books, because "otherwise the Javanese would not have converted to Islam till after a thousand years"[21]—the destruction and the burning of the centres of the many smaller powers, would inevitably have caused the loss of such literary heritage. The fact that only a minuscule fraction of Old Javanese works survived in Java compared to the mass of works that safely found a sanctuary in Bali is a clear indication of the magnitude of the loss of this literary heritage in Java.

Moreover, literary activities in ancient Java were centred in the *kraton*.[22] With either survival or expansion continually occupying their minds, the new class of rulers, even if they had still had an interest in literary works from the *buda* period, obviously would not have

[20] Drewes 1969:38.
[21] Drewes 1966:350.
[22] Supomo 1996.

been able to hold reading sessions at their courts—let alone of the kind that was held at Dharmawangśa's court which lasted for "one month minus one evening". And in the absence of regular reading sessions, the knowledge of Old Javanese gradually would have been lost, and the scribes inevitably would not have been able to maintain the skill needed merely to copy the old manuscripts faithfully. It is hardly surprising, that after successive copying of manuscripts by such copyists, a large number of errors have accumulated in the Javanese tradition manuscripts—which is evident when the readings of the Javanese manuscripts are compared with those of the Balinese. However, such errors in the manuscripts would in most cases have been accepted without any question as correct readings by the next generation of readers. While it may still have been possible for a Balinese traditional scholar to use two or more manuscripts when copying a manuscript, so that "in case of doubtful readings he could compare them and choose the best reading, thus eliminating errors",[23] such a practice may no longer have been possible for Javanese scholars of the 18th and 19th century—for the simple reason that the copies they had were probably the only extant copies available to them.[24]

With the accumulation of errors from one generation of manuscripts to the next, the text obviously became more difficult to comprehend. Nevertheless, if a work still enjoyed a certain degree of popularity, either as a source of narrative or as a piece of guidance for moral conduct, then the book would still be read and copied—readers would just have had to make a bigger effort to find the meaning of the defective passages. Certainly, it was not an easy task. Even without defects, as the language of the *kakawin* was no longer sufficiently understood, their meanings were often too hard to grasp. Even Yasadipura I, arguably the most skilful *pujangga* in writing Modern Javanese works based on *kakawin*, often had to resort to no more than guessing, and at least on one occasion, as McDonald has pointed out,[25] he openly admitted that he was not sure of the correct meaning

---

[23] Robson 1988:15.

[24] *Sěrat Cabolek* 7.7 provides a good illustration. It tells us that when *Kětib* Anom was asked to read the *Bhima Suci*, he "went to fetch a copy of the book *Bhima Suci*, which had not been compared with the original, [because] by mischance the original had been lost" (Soebardi 1975:111).

[25] McDonald 1983:169.

of an expression in a certain context, and therefore suggested that the good readers themselves should decide upon the appropriate meaning. Thus we read in the *Sĕrat Bratayuda* 24.16e–18:[26]

> (16) . . . Then Jayadrata joined the others to see [what happened].
> He went out from the enclosure,
> which was formed by the troops who surrounded him.
> (17) In his movements he was like an *endrajala.*
> Now, *endrajala* has two meanings.
> The first is a thief,
> who stealthily kills a king;
> the second is an arrow which originates from heaven.
> Please try to find [its correct meaning here].
> (18) Whether Sindurja's movements
> may appropriately be likened to an arrow,
> or to a thief,
> the present writer leaves it
> up to those with a noble mind.
> It is not possible to ascribe
> just one meaning to *endrajala.*[27]

While *endrajala* has caused such a problem to Yasadipura I, it is certainly not the most difficult problem he faced, or by any other *pujangga* who wished to render Old Javanese works into Modern Javanese. Defects in certain passages often make them incomprehensible—even to separate one word from the other sometimes becomes impossible. Since obviously one cannot resort to the formula of "let the readers decide the meanings for themselves" all the time, without loosing one's credibility as a *pujangga*, the only recourse left was to use one's imagination and creative power to find an appropriate meaning for the corrupt passage. In many cases, the *pujangga* ended up by creating new meanings far removed from the intention of the original text.

---

[26] Cohen Stuart 1860:62–63. Stanza 18 had been translated by McDonald 1983: 169. The present translation is slightly different from hers.

[27] "In Old Javanese *indrajāla* means 'Indra's net', delusion, spell, deception, trick, stratagem" (Zoetmulder 1982:683). The corresponding passage of the Old Javanese *Bhāratayuddha* (16.5cd) reads: *ndah irika yan katon guṇa Janārdanāngrĕpakĕn aśwa mur kadi kilat/ḍatĕng I harĕp Jayadratha kadîndrajāla haliwat sakeng ripu kabeh* "It was then that the excellence of Kṛṣṇa manifested itself: he let his horses fly as fast as lightning/their knees bent, and passing through the enemies [undetected] *as if by magic*, they reached Jayadratha" (Supomo 1993).

4. *From the "Beautiful Maiden" to the "Scripture"*

One of the best examples of such a process is the "creation" of a book called *sastrajendra*. It has its origin in a corrupt reading which occurs in the *Arjunawijaya*, a *kakawin* written in about 1380 AD.[28] Based on the reading from the more reliable Balinese tradition manuscripts, *Arjunawijaya* 1.11a reads

> *ndan sang paṇḍita dibyacitta wihikan kāryanya sang stryāhajöng*
> (however, the sage of sublime mind knew well the purpose of this beautiful maiden).

This line occurs in the episode in which the demon Sumāli orders his daughter, the "beautiful maiden" Kaikeśī, to offer herself to Wiśrawa, the sage of sublime mind. Sumāli's aim is that his daughter will bear children as powerful as Wiśrawa's son Waiśrawaṇa, so that they will be able to withstand the attack of god Wiṣṇu in a future war. Kaikaśī eventually gives birth to three sons, Daśamukha, Kumbhakarṇa, Wibhīṣaṇa, and a daughter Śūrpaṇakhā.

In a Javanese tradition manuscript, which I call the "Surakarta" manuscript,[29] this line reads

> *ndan sang paṇḍita widyacitta wihikan karyanya sastrahajĕng.*

As I have shown in earlier publications[30] the reading *sastrahajĕng* occurs because of the loss of *saṇḍangan* (diacritical marks in Javanese script), i.e. *cĕcak* ("ng" symbol) in the word *sang, pengkal* ("y" symbol) in *stry*, and the long vowel symbols in *āhajöng*. Such errors are not uncommon in Old Javanese manuscripts, and in general can be attributed to either carelessness (in the case of the loss of *saṇḍangan*) or disregard, or even ignorance of *kakawin* prosody (in the case of the loss of long vowel symbols).

A careful examination of the variant readings of other Javanese manuscripts, however, indicates that the cause of the changes may not be just simple carelessness on the part of a copyist, but also may involve a deliberate choice of the "erroneous" readings. The variant readings from the available Javanese manuscripts suggest that the changes in this line may have happened in at least three stages. The

---

[28] Supomo 1977.
[29] Supomo 1977:83–88.
[30] Supomo 1964; 1977:285–286.

first was the substitution of the word *dibyacitta* of the Balinese manuscripts by *diwyacitta* in the prototype of the Javanese manuscripts.[31] The next stage was a simple error, a metathesis, from *diwyacitta* to *widyacitta*. The line thus read

> *ndan sang paṇḍita widyacitta wihikan kāryanya sang stryāhajöng*

and the meaning changed slightly to "However, the wise sage knew well the purpose of this beautiful maiden". This is probably the reading of the prototype of the Javanese manuscripts (as represented by the readings of the Jakarta manuscript Cod. 219[32] and the "Surakarta" MS). This was followed by the loss of long vowel symbols, which could have happened when the copyist no longer considered the distinction between short and long vowels as an essential element of *kakawin* prosody. The loss of the *saṇḍangan*, such as found in the "Surakarta" manuscript, was the last stage.

Now, since *widya* means "knowledge, science, learning", it may not be too far-fetched to suggest that the loss of *saṇḍangan* was not because of carelessness or negligence on the part of the copyist, but because he believed that *sastra* fitted better with the word *widyacitta*, since both *sastra* and *widya* have the same meaning (science, scripture). Thus even if, like their colleagues in Bali, the Javanese scribes could have had the luxury of having two or more manuscripts to compare their readings, it seems more likely that with the reading *widyacitta* already established, they would opt for *sastra hajĕng* rather than *sang stryahajĕng*. Accordingly, the line, which now reads "*ndan sang paṇḍita widyacitta wihikan karyanya sastra hajĕng*", may be given a new interpretation, such as "And the wise sage knew well the [contents] of the work (book) *sastra hajĕng* (beautiful scripture/science)".

The next development was the use of words such as *ayu* and *arja* which are synonymous with *hajĕng*. Thus we find in the *Arjunawijaya kawi miring*, written by Yasadipura in 1803, that the *sastra hajĕng* is alternately called *sastra arjendra, sastra arjengrat* or *sastra cĕṭa*. It contains the teaching about "the origin of life, the end of life, and the bliss of

---

[31] It is equally possible, however, that it is the Javanese manuscripts which retain the original reading here, since *diwyacitta* is more authentic Sanskrit than *dibyacitta*.

[32] This manuscript apparently belongs to the so-called Mĕrbabu collection, since its catalogue number is under 371 (see van der Molen 1983:117). Moreover, the colophon says that it "was copied at the foot of Mount Pamrihan" (. . . *tĕlas sinurat, jöng ira sang hyang hardhi pamrihan*; Supomo 1977:179). According to van der Molen (1983:78), Pamrihan is the old name of Mĕrbabu.

final emancipation" (*purwakaning dumadi, wasananing dumadi, yuning jiwa muksa*)[33].

Some 25 years later, when Sindusastra wrote a *macapat* version of the Arjunawijaya, the *Sěrat Arjuna Sasrabau*,[34] the book became *sastrajendra*, and was already regarded as "the supreme knowledge" (*pungkas-pungkasaning kawruh*). "Once this science is mastered," Sindusastra explained, "demons, ogres and devils, all the animals of the mountainous forests, if able to comprehend the meaning of the *sastrajendra*, will be redeemed by the gods and will die perfect deaths. Their souls will merge with mortals—mortals who are already superior. If a man comprehends the science, he will merge with a deity when he dies—an illustrious god" (10.32–33).[35] The contents of the book, however, are never fully explained in the *Sěrat Arjuna Sasrabau*, because when Wisrawa was about to reveal the secret of the *sastrajendra* to Sumali's daughter, Sukesi, the whole universe was in such commotion (*gara-gara*) that God Guru was extremely angry. He therefore decided to descend to earth with the intention of preventing the revelation of the secret of the book by entering the body of Wisrawa, while Durga, Guru's consort, entered into Sukesi. Thus tempted, Wisrawa, whose purpose in coming to Ngalĕngka had been to propose to Sukesi on behalf of his son, became enamoured of her and eventually married her.[36]

That the secret of the *sastrajendra* was never revealed apparently did not diminish its popularity. It is repeatedly mentioned in a number of 18th and 19th century books, such as the *Sěrat Cabolang* (canto 177, in which it is called *sěrat jendra ayuningrat*), the *Sěrat Děrmagaṇḍul* (in which it is called *sastra arja ayuningrat* or *sastra rancang*);[37] and the *Sěrat Suluk*,[38] as well as in various wayang stories, such as *lakon Paṇḍu papa*[39] and *lakon Senarodra*.[40]

---

[33] Supomo 1977:285–286; McDonald 1983:275; 372–373.
[34] Palmer van den Broek 1870.
[35] McDonald 1983:254.
[36] *Sěrat Arjuna Sasrabau* 11.13–14.
[37] Drewes 1966:335; 356–357.
[38] Soebardi 1975:38.
[39] Stutterheim 1956a:140. It is clear from the discussion here that Stutterheim's suggestion (1956a:140, n. 94) that *sastraharjendra* in this *lakon* may have derived from the Sanskrit *Rājendraśāstra* or *Indrārjaśāstra*, (which, in the first case, "the same as *rājawidyā* or *rājaçāśtra*, knowledge (book of learning) of the kings") is not acceptable.
[40] Overbeck 1939.

5. *From* Śakti *to* Shahāda

It is clear from this discussion of *sastra jendra*, that even if we accept that carelessness or a misunderstanding of the text by a copyist caused the first changes in the Javanese *Arjunawijaya* manuscript, the next stage is more likely the product of a creative mind. There is yet another factor, however, which probably played an important part in the change from "the beautiful maiden" to "the beautiful Scripture". There is no doubt that whoever first introduced *sastra jendra* to the Modern Javanese version of the *Arjunawijaya* must have known of the existence of another famous "book", mentioned in the *Bhāratayuddha kakawin*. The book, which is referred to as *pustaka*, is called *kalimahoṣadha*. Ironically, the name *kalimahoṣadha* also came into the pages of the *Bhāratayuddha* through a possible misunderstanding of its original source.

The *kalimahoṣadha* is known in the *Bhāratayuddha* as the weapon of Yuḍiṣṭira, the eldest of the Pāṇḍawas. In normal circumstances, the *kalimahoṣadha* has the appearance of a "book bound together with a knot of sparkling jewels" (*pustaka . . . anabhi ratna pradīpta, BY* 9.9) but during the battle the book transforms into a "thunderbolt weapon" (*bajra*). The weapon is considered so powerful, that it is used only once throughout the battle, that is against Śalya, the last commander in chief of the Korawa army, on the very last day of the war. When Śalya, after firing his Rudaroṣa-arrow, has caused such devastation among the Pāṇḍawa army, Kṛṣṇa urges Yuḍiṣṭira to counter Śalya's attack. But being calm and compassionate by nature, Yuḍiṣṭira is appalled at the thought of having to attack his adversary, who is also his uncle. It is only after a strong appeal from Kṛṣṇa that Yuḍiṣṭira finally launches his attack against Śalya. It is also at the urging of Kṛṣṇa that "Yuḍiṣṭira swiftly grasped his weapon, the book Kalimahoṣadha, and transformed it into a blazing lance" (*tan dwa ng sañjata pustaka kalimahoṣadha rinĕgĕp ira/sampun siddha siniddhikāra dadi tomara mangharab-harab, BY* 42.5). Three stanzas later, the fall of Śalya is recounted as follows:

yekā n śīrṇa dinuk ring astra wara pustakamaya lumarap
mabhrâpan maṇi hemadaṇḍa tumanĕm ri ḍaḍa sang ahulun
tan pendah kadi wangkawânginum i rah nṛpati mamulakan
ndah śaktinya tinut ri jīwa nira mantuk ing amarapada

Then he was struck down by the excellent weapon in the form of a book, which was gleaming and luminous, for it was a staff of jewels and gold. It pierced through his breast, and like a rainbow it drank his blood that gushed forth. Such was its power. Śalya's soul then returned to the abode of the gods.

In the corresponding passage of the *Mahābhārata* (9.16.38) we read:

sa dharmarājo maṇihemadaṇḍām
jagrāha śaktiṃ kanakaprakaśam[41]

The King Dharma grasped a lance, shining as gold, with a handle of jewels and gold.

It is clear from this Sanskrit quotation that *śakti* here means a kind of weapon, that is "spear, lance, pike, dart". *Śakti*, however, also means "power, strength", and because this latter meaning is more common in Old Javanese texts, it is not surprising that in the above passage of the *Bhāratayuddha, śakti* is used in this sense. Both in Sanskrit as well as in Old Javanese, *śakti* also has another meaning—which is an extension of the meaning of "power"—that is "energy or active power of a deity personified as his wife".[42] It is from this secondary meaning, that the name of Yuḍisṭira's weapon, *kalimahoṣadha*, i.e. "the great medicine of Kālī", may have derived through the identification of *śakti* with Kālī, the wife of the supreme deity, Śiwa.

The *pustaka kalimahoṣadha* then must have been known in Java long before the "creation" of *sastra jendra*, since the *Bhāratayuddha* is a much older and more famous *kakawin* than the *Arjunawijaya*. Like the content of the *sastra jendra* that apparently has intrigued the Javanese mind since its emergence from a corrupt reading in the Arjunawijaya *kakawin*, the *pustaka kalimahoṣadha* must have raised similar questions in the mind of Javanese people from at least the time the *Bhāratayuddha* was written in 1157. In Bali, the *Kalimahoṣadha*, known as *Kalima usada*, is appropriately the name of one of the two great handbooks on magic and incantations with reference to medicine—the other being *Buddha Kĕcapi*[43]—as well as the name of a compendium of religious speculation.[44] It is not possible to know with certainty from these Balinese manuscripts, whether these works originated from Java or from Bali, but if such works already existed in Java they apparently were lost without leaving any trace.

---

[41] Dandekar 1961.
[42] Monier-Williams 1964:1044; Zoetmulder 1982:1607.
[43] Goris 1937:282–284.
[44] Pigeaud 1967–80:I, 59.

In any case, at least early in the 19th century the Javanese, who by then had embraced Islam for more than four centuries,[45] had found a new meaning for the *kalimahoṣadha*. Just as the story of the revelation of the *sastra jendra* by Wisrawa found its way into the encyclopaedic *Sěrat Cabolang-Cěnṭini*, so did the story of revelation of the "true" meanings of the *kalimahoṣadha*. As recounted by a certain *kyai* Rasika, the *juru kunci* "cemetery caretaker" of Glagahwangi,[46] the story is as follows:

After the death of his brothers and other relatives, Yuḍisṭira, who wishes to join them, goes to the realm of the gods with his material body (II.45.16: *muksanya mring kaendran, dalah ing saraganipun*). He asks God Guru the reason why he cannot *sirna* (vanish), although, like all his brothers, his wife and his mother, he also had entered into the fire. God Guru, however, advises him that he should return to the world of men because those who die must leave their bodies behind, and only those who have assumed their incorporeal body may ascend to the great heaven. So he returns to the world and tries to take his life by jumping into the ocean, but still he fails to die. After six hundred years at the bottom of the sea, the God gives him the message, advising him to perform asceticism (*martapa*) in a forest called Glagahwangi, in the Majapahit region. It is there that he will die. Thus Yuḍisṭira leaves the ocean and performs asceticism at Glagahwangi, an awe-inspiring forest, always shrouded in mist. Near the end of the Majapahit period, the council of *wali* (*sanggyaning kang waliyolah*) wishes to establish a *kraton* at Glagahwangi, to be known as the kingdom of Demak. In order for the forest to be cleared quickly, thousands of people are mobilised, but to no avail—trees which are felled in the morning, grow luxuriantly again in the afternoon, and vice versa. After having been told of what happened, *Sunan* Giri summons *Sunan* Kalijaga and orders him to supervise the clearing of the forest. When he arrives at the edge of the forest, *Sunan* Kalijaga says his greeting in Arabic, "*assalam-ngalaikum*", and the mist which is shrouding the forest disappears at once. He then enters the forest and there he sees "a big, tall man, radiating a brilliant aura, who is

---

[45] We do not know the exact date of the coming of Islam to Java, but there is evidence indicating that by the fourteenth century there was already a Muslim community, perhaps even including members of the royal family, who lived—and died and were buried—in or near the capital of Majapahit (see de Graaf and Pigeaud 1974:19–21; Ricklefs 1979:102–104; 1984:11–12).

[46] *Sěrat Cabolang*, Part II, 45.22–47.6.

about three times the size of present-day man", sitting under a banyan (*waringin*) tree. Kalijaga approaches him, addressing him politely, but the man, who is none other than Yuḍisṭira, does not reply, but only stares at him. So, Kalijaga says to himself "Probably this is a *buda*-man", and so he addresses him in *buda* language, asking him who he is and why he looks so sad. Yuḍisṭira now replies, also in *buda* language, telling Kalijaga that he is Yuḍisṭira from Ngamarta of the *buda* era, when people still embraced *brahma* religion. Then, when Kalijaga accuses him of being the cause of the failure of his people to clear the forest, Yuḍisṭira explains that he is there merely to perform asceticism with the purpose of seeking the way to death, and that the reason he cannot die is because at his coronation he was given an amulet in the form of a book, called *kalimasada*, by the Great God (46.17: *dipun paringi, jijimat dening dewa gung, nama kalimasada, ingkang ugi awarna pustaka jamus*). Kalijaga asks him about the contents of the book, but Yuḍisṭira replies that he dares not even open the book, let alone know its contents. And so Kalijaga asks him if he would allow him to read it. After receiving permission from Yuḍisṭira, Kalijaga reads it, and tells its contents to Yuḍisṭira. "It is called *kalimasada*," says *Sunan* Kalijaga, "because it is truly *kalimah sahadat*" (46.24: *mila ran kalimasada, kalimah sahadat yekti*). Then Kalijaga explains that *kalimah sahadat* is "the origin of the True Knowledge" (*babon ngelmi sajati*), which came from the Prophet, the beloved of the Great God. And those who have mastered the meaning of the *kalimah sahadat*, will find inner peace, so that they may die a perfect death (*sagĕd sampurneng pĕjah*). Delighted by this revelation, Yuḍisṭira readily accepts the teachings of Kalijaga and becomes a Muslim. To show his gratitude for the teachings, Yuḍisṭira gives Kalijaga a palm-leaf manuscript (*kropak*), which contains three wayang pictures of Baladewa, Krĕsna and Wĕrkudara, as well as two *lakon*, namely the story of the marriage of Arjuna and Sumbadra and the *Bratayuda* (*Sunan* Kalijaga later creates wayang based on these three wayang pictures). After explaining the contents of the *kropak*, Yuḍisṭira dies. His body is buried under the tree where he performed asceticism with a sign of a gravestone engraved with his name, *kyai* Yuḍisṭira. It is still there today, a very long gravestone, said *kyai* Rasika, at the head position (?) in the mosque of Demak (47.9: *lastantun tĕkeng samangkin, neng lon-ulon masjid Dĕmak*).

An interesting variation to this *Cabolang* version of the *kalimasada* legend is found in what we may call the Gunung Lawet version.

According to this version, as recorded by Knebel more than 90 years ago, after explaining to Yuḍisṭira that his talisman is really the *kalimah sahada*, *Sunan* Kalijaga advises him to embrace Islam. Yuḍisṭira, however, refuses, the reason given to Kalijaga is that because whenever he invokes God Guru, there is always a salutary effect that makes him powerful (*digdaya*). Kalijaga therefore challenges Yuḍisṭira to pit their supernatural power one against the other. Yuḍisṭira accepts the challenge, and with the power of his imagination he creates eggs, piling them up so high that the top reaches heaven. Kalijaga then takes off his slipper, throws it to the sky, knocking down and breaking all the eggs. Witnessing the power of the slipper, Yuḍisṭira asks for Kalijaga's forgiveness, saying, "I admit that I have been defeated, and that my supernatural power (*kasĕkten* and *kadigdadayan*) is inferior to yours. . . ." Thus, Yuḍisṭira is converted to Islam—indeed, he is made a *wali* by *Sunan* Kalijaga, known as Seh Jambukarang. He then dies, and his body is buried at the summit of Mount Lawet which is situated in the Banyumas region, Central Java. According to Knebel's report, the cemetery of Mount Lawet is regarded by many as more sacred than any other in the region, and every Monday and Wednesday people come from far and wide to make a pilgrimage.[47]

It is clear from the Mount Lawet version then that *Sunan* Kalijaga, who had mastered the *kalimah sahada*, was considered to have had more *kasĕkten* than Yuḍisṭira, who, although possessing the book, did not understand it because he dared not open it. Even invoking God Guru apparently was not much help to him. The legend therefore provides a good illustration of the proposition that Javanese rulers were attracted to Islam—as their ancestors had been to Hindu and Buddhist cults in the early centuries of our era—primarily because they regarded it as a means of tapping another source of supernatural energy.[48] By reciting Arabic verses one may acquire spiritual power much more efficaciously than invoking the deities from the Hindu and Buddhist pantheons using Sanskrit *mantras*.

It is obvious, however, that despite some differences, the two versions of the *kalimasada* legend must ultimately have derived from one origin, since they both agree on the main point, namely that it was

[47] Knebel 1903:363–369. According to another legend, as told in the Leiden manuscript, LOr 7576, Yuḍisṭira's body was buried in a village called Wiraca, at the foot of Mount Lawu (Pigeaud 1967–80:II, 455).

[48] Ricklefs 1979b:104.

Sunan Kalijaga who finally revealed the meaning of Yuḍisṭira's *kalimasada* as *kalimah sahadat* and that by this revelation Yuḍisṭira was able to die and go to heaven. The next question that may be asked is why *Sunan* Kalijaga? If, as the Gunung Lawet version suggests, it is because Kalijaga's supernatural power played an important part in the conversion of Yuḍisṭira, then many other *wali* would have been able to fulfil such a role as well. As Ricklefs points out, there are many wondrous tales about "the *walis'* ability to walk on water, to change rice to sand or, rather profitably, earth to gold".[49] So why not *Sunan* Bonang, for instance, whose supernatural power, according to the *Babad Tanah Jawi*, was the main factor in Kalijaga himself eventually becoming a *wali*?[50] Why is it that the unknown author(s) of this legend chose him to reveal the meaning of *kalimasada*? The answer, I believe, may have to do with the name of Kalijaga. According to the *Babad Tanah Jawi*, he was the son of Tumĕnggung Wilatikta of Majapahit. His name before he became a *wali* was Said[51]—no doubt a Javanised form of Arabic *shāhid*. Now, an early Muslim text, using the *tĕgĕse* formula which we have noted before, explains the meaning of *sahid* in this way: *Tĕgĕsing sahadat iku sahid, tĕgĕsing sahid iku saksi*, that is "*Sahadat* (Arab. *shahāda*, 'testimony', 'confession of faith') means *sahid* (Arab. *shāhid*), and *sahid* means witness".[52] The choice of Kalijaga, who was also known as *Mas* Said, to reveal the true meaning of *kalimasada* and to witness the reading of the *kalimah sahadat* by Yuḍisṭira seems to be a most appropriate one.

There is, however, also another explanation that may account for the crucial role that *Sunan* Kalijaga played in the final release of Yuḍisṭira's suffering from this mortal world. While it is obvious from the discussion above that the talisman *kalimasada* itself has its origin in the *kalimahoṣadha* of the *Bhāratayuddha*, the story of Yuḍisṭira's wandering in search of a way to die has no bearing whatsoever on the *kakawin*. Its relation with the *parwa*, however, is unmistakable, if only because the name Yuḍisṭira ultimately must have had its origin in the *Mahābhārata*. Moreover, according to *Kyai* Rasika of the *Sĕrat Cabolek* the story is based on a wayang story (II.45.26: *criyos paḍalangan ringgit*), and as I have mentioned earlier, the *parwa*-based *lakon*

49 1974:5.
50 Olthof 1987:21–22.
51 Olthof 1987:21.
52 Drewes 1978:54.

were—and still are—preferred by the general population to *lakon* from any other sources.

Looking at the *parwa* as possible sources for the *kalimasada* legend, then, the answer is certainly not hard to find, because the story of the last days of the Pāṇḍawas *is* only found in the last two books of the *Mahābhārata*, namely the *Prasthānikaparwa* and the *Swargarohanaparwa*.[53] Although there are obvious differences between the *kalimasada* story and the *parwa*, similar elements are found in both, which may not be attributed to mere coincidence. Thus in both stories, Yuḍiṣṭira is said to enter heaven with his body (*Prasthanikaparwa*: *mulih ring swargaloka mwang śarīra nira*;[54] *Sĕrat Cabolang* II. 45.26: *muksanya mring kaendran, dalah ing saraganipun*). In both stories, Yuḍiṣṭira then leaves heaven, although for different reasons. In the *parwa* it is because he wished to be united with his brothers and Dropadī who were temporarily put in the place of the damned, while in the *Sĕrat Cabolang* because a human being was not allowed to enter heaven with his material body, but only with his incorporeal body. In both stories, Yuḍiṣṭira finally succeeded in returning to heaven, although the means to achieve it were different. Yet even in these vastly different endings of the two stories, we may find a fine thread that somehow connects them. We read in the *Swargarohanaparwa* that in order to be able to leave hell and return to heaven, Yuḍiṣṭira with his brothers and Dropadī had to purify their bodies in the holy river Ganggā (*madyus ri sang hyang Ganggā*).[55] And we know from the *Babad Tanah Jawi* that before obtaining his *wali*-hood *Mas* Said also had to perform asceticism, that is purify himself, in the river (*kali*) Jaga—hence his name Kalijaga.[56] So, it may be not too far-fetched to suggest that for a creative Javanese author(s), who after all had created a *ngelmu Sastrajendra* out of badly corrupt manuscripts, it would not have been too difficult to relate the purification story of Yuḍiṣṭira and that of Kalijaga, and then to create a single story in which Yuḍiṣṭira, instead of being purified by the holy *kali* Gangga, was purified by the holy Kalijaga.

---

[53] Juynboll 1893; Zoetmulder 1963:168–182; 1974:81–83.
[54] Zoetmulder 1963:172.
[55] Zoetmulder 1963:182.
[56] Olthof 1987:22.

ISLAM AND THE REIGN OF PAKUBUWANA II, 1726–49

M.C. Ricklefs

Islamic issues do not loom large in the major works on Javanese history, particularly the history of the courts of Java. Modern-day perceptions of Javanese society tend to see it as consisting of two cultural variants which are at least in tension with one another and at times in conflict. These are a Javanist variant which retains cultural forms of largely pre-Islamic inspiration, for which the term *abangan* is employed, and the more self-consciously Islamic variant, whose adherents are variously labelled *Muslimin, putihan* or *santri*. The courtly elite of Java are commonly seen as the bearers, indeed the principal definers, of the Javanist variant. But this view of Javanese society—for all its relevance to the last 150 years or so—is an anachronism if applied to pre-nineteenth-century Java. This writer has never seen signs that such categories existed in the seventeenth or eighteenth centuries and, as will be seen below, has found evidence in the reign of Pakubuwana II (1726–49) that the *kraton* could be an Islamising force.

Pakubuwana II came to the throne in 1726 at the age of sixteen.[1] The dominant figure in *kraton* religious and cultural life in his first years appears to have been his grandmother Ratu Pakubuwana. She was probably born c. 1660 and had been a powerful person throughout the reign of her husband Pakubuwana I (1704–19). She seems to have had authority in such supernatural matters as the holy regalia (*pusaka*) and an interest in pious Islamic legends. In 1715 she composed or sponsored the composition of a *Sĕrat Menak* MS, containing highly mythological tales surrounding Amir Hamza, the uncle of the Prophet Muḥammad.[2]

In 1729–30, the septuagenarian Ratu Pakubuwana, who was completely blind by this time, sponsored the composition of a series of pious Islamic works which included three of supernatural potency.

---

[1] What follows is an overview of the evidence and arguments concerning Islam to be found in my forthcoming study of the reign of Pakubuwana II, *The seen and unseen worlds in Java, 1726–49: History, literature and Islam in the court of Pakubuwana II.*

[2] Perpustakaan Nasional MS KBG 613. See Poerbatjaraka 1940:30.

The first, *Carita Sultan Iskandar*, was begun on 30 September 1729.[3] It describes itself as a text from Arabic sources (*tafsir*) originally translated into Javanese from a Malay version in the time of Sultan Agung (1613–46). Indeed one can identify its ultimate origin in the Qur'anic story of Alexander the Great. The text says that Ratu Pakubuwana sponsored it and goes on to establish her extraordinary spiritual status. She is said to be beloved of God, already to have received the intercession of the Prophet, to be guarded by angels and blessed by an unnamed holy sage, to be gentle, just, devoted to religious instruction and in awe of her ancestors. Finally she is described as the amulet (*jimat*) of all the people of Java; i.e. their supernatural protection against all harm. Her *Carita Sultan Iskandar* is said to have been composed so that it could become a *pusaka* and God is asked to ensure the continuity and increasing greatness of her royal grandson. This was, thus, a potent act by a lady who claimed special spiritual standing.

The second book, *Carita Nabi Yusuf*,[4] was commenced on the day when the previous text was finished, 25 October 1729. This is a version of the Javanese romance of Joseph in Egypt, based on the Qur'anic version of that story. Ratu Pakubuwana's *Yusuf* opens as does her *Iskandar*, making the same spiritual claims for her. There is a strong probability that this *Yusuf*, too, goes back to a version from the time of Sultan Agung, but the evidence for this is problematic and cannot be analysed fully here. The supernatural potency of the *Yusuf* text is perhaps echoed in the continuing ritual significance of present-day performances of *Yusuf* in places like Banyuwangi.[5]

The most extraordinary of Ratu Pakubuwana's books was entitled *Kitab Usulbiyah*,[6] the writing of which was begun on 26 December 1729. It also seems to derive from a text done in the time of Sultan Agung. Its opening is briefer than those found in the previous two works, but more explicit about the book's purpose. Ratu Pakubuwana is said to be blessed and loved by God, to have received the intercession of the Prophet, to be watched over by angels. The reason for the writing of *Usulbiyah* was "her desire to make perfect (*sampurna*) the reign of her royal grandson. For her sun, indeed, rests upon the

[3] Radyapustaka MS no. 262 carikan.
[4] Radyapustaka MS no. 261 carikan.
[5] See Arps 1992, esp. 150–155.
[6] Radyapustaka MS 263 carikan.

mountaintops, for she is already old and is nearing perfection". Thus the spiritual power of the old queen's work was directed to the goal of perfecting the reign of Pakubuwana II.

The story itself concerns some of the most important figures in Islamic hagiology. Whereas Ratu Pakubuwana's *Iskandar* and *Yusuf* can be seen to derive ultimately from Qur'anic stories, *Usulbiyah* seems to be more original. Central to the tale is an encounter upon the earth between Jesus and Muḥammad for which there is certainly no Qur'anic authority. This story, like those of the other two works, purports to take place in a mythological Middle East which is unmistakably located in Java. God, Jesus and Muḥammad all reign in the style of a Javanese monarch.

The lengthy colophon at the end of *Usulbiyah*[7] confirms its supernatural potency. It says that if *Usulbiyah* were taken to war it would lead to victory in battle and the submission of enemies. Writing out *Usulbiyah* was equivalent to going on the pilgrimage to Mecca a thousand times in a day or reciting the Qur'ān a thousand times in a day and night. Anyone who kept *Usulbiyah* would be watched over by God and 7,700 angels, freed from witchcraft and evil spells or other adversity. The beneficent power or blessing (*sawab*, from Arabic *thawāb* merit, etc.) of the book was greater than the falling rain or all the palm-leaves in the world or all the sands of the sea, because of its mystical knowledge (*elmu*). If an infidel owned the book that person would become a Muslim. A vehement person who read it would become patient, a severe person calm in speech, an ignorant person learned, for the book revealed what was behind the screen of mystical knowledge. Finally, the creator of the work was said to be protected by it, to be shaded by God as if by a thousand umbrellas and to have received the perfect mercy of God, who ordered angels to watch over that person (implicitly Ratu Pakubuwana). This was clearly meant to be a book of extraordinary supernatural potency, the purpose of which was to perfect the reign of the young Pakubuwana II. It was explicitly equated with the Qur'ān and said to contain God's words.

Ratu Pakubuwana's final text—or at least the last work to survive—was a sort of Javanese doctrine of Sufi kingship, called *Suluk Garwa Kancana*.[8] This, too, appears to derive from the court of Sultan

---

[7] Ibid. 42–45.
[8] Ibid. 60–61.

Agung. Here the king was admonished not to be deceived by the courtiers who surrounded him but to turn away from the world and to practise piety, eschewing sexual pleasures. He should have constant struggle as his citadel, the contemplation of God as his weapon and steadfast trust in God as his vehicle. The scriptures were to be his followers, piety his bow, *dhikr* his quiver and the Qur'ān his arrows. Because of his pious heroism, he was shown divine grace and installed as king with new raiment: *Khak* (Reality) as his crown with *tarekat* (the Sufi path) as its crest and *sarengat* (the law) as his lower garment. *Suluk Garwa Kancana* thus wove together Islamic mysticism and martial values to produce an ascetic ideal of monarchy. This was a Javanese version of the "greater Holy War" (*al-jihād al-akbar*) of Sufism, the war for purity against the lower self.

The surviving historical evidence does not allow one to say with confidence what Pakubuwana II made of his grandmother's admonitions and supernaturally charged works of piety. In the early 1730s there is, however, some evidence of the king demanding greater piety from his subjects. He banned gambling (except for cock-fighting) in 1731[9] and himself attended Friday worship in the public mosque at Kartasura in 1732, a very rare event.[10] There are also grounds for thinking that the tale in *Sĕrat Cabolek* of religious controversy presented to the king for judgement refers to events which actually took place at court c. 1731.[11] So it is reasonable to think that the Islamising thrust of Ratu Pakubuwana's view of kingship found support at court, and that it continued to do so after her death in January 1732.

After the exile of the *Patih* (chief administrator) Danurĕja in 1733 the most influential courtier was Dĕmang Urawan, cousin and brother-in-law to Pakubuwana II. This man is depicted in much of the Javanese and VOC (Dutch East India Company) records as an evil influence over the king and the kingdom. The VOC found him arrogant and uncooperative. Other courtiers were fearful and jealous of his power and condemned his homosexuality. Yet some evidence survives to suggest that there was much more to Urawan than this.

---

[9] Coster, Kartasura, to Coyett, Semarang, 6 November 1731, in VOC 2203 (OB 1732). (All VOC . . . (OB . . .) references are to sources in the Algemeen Rijksarchief, The Hague.)

[10] *Babad Sangkala* (LOr 4097), 69; Duirvelt, Kartasura, to Coyett, Semarang, 22 July 1732, in VOC 2257 (OB 1733).

[11] This is discussed at length in Ch. 4 of my forthcoming book (see note 1 above).

In *Sĕrat Cabolek*, it is said that the other courtiers feared Urawan but then discovered, to their surprise, that he was good-hearted and well-read in Islamic literature.[12] Two surviving MS volumes strengthen this depiction of Urawan. One, a MS of the Staatsbibliothek in Berlin, was copied for Urawan (by then named Purbaya) in 1736–7.[13] This is a collection of texts of lexicographical, didactic, legal and romantic character in both Modern Javanese and Old Javanese. The presence of the Old Javanese *Nītiśāstra* in this MS shows that the elite of Kartasura continued to patronise pre-Islamic Javanese literature as well as Modern Javanese works of more obviously Islamic inspiration such as *Johar Sah*, a romantic story set in the Middle East, which is found in Urawan/Purbaya's volume.

A second MS volume seems also to have belonged to Urawan/Purbaya. In this case the MS (in the India Office Library)[14] is undated but it names its owner as Purbaya and this was probably the Urawan/Purbaya of Pakubuwana II's time. The first part of this MS consists of religious texts in Arabic with interlinear Javanese translations. Among them is the anonymous mystical treatise *Kitāb Majnūn Allāh*. It is evidently this work, called *Maljunah*, in which a Javanese chronicle depicts Urawan/Purbaya's sister, the queen Ratu Kĕncana, reading in her sleeping-chamber c. 1731.[15] The second part of the volume consists of mystical texts in Javanese alone. These include texts on the seven grades of emanation, prayer, the four stages of the Sufi path, the mystic unity of *kawula* and *gusti*, the apostles (*wali*) of Islam in Java, and so on.

Thus the most powerful courtier of the period c. 1731–8 was evidently a patron of literature, including Islamic mystical literature. He was supported in this by the *Patih* (1733–42) Natakusuma, who was brother-in-law to both Urawan/Purbaya and the king. From his embassies to Batavia Natakusuma brought back to Kartasura two new religious figures. In 1735 he was accompanied by one Kyai Haji Mataram, whose origin is unknown. In 1736 Pakubuwana II made him a senior religious figure in the court.[16] In 1737 an Arab *sayyid*

[12] Soebardi 1975:99.

[13] Or. fol. 402, described in Pigeaud 1975:226–227.

[14] Arab. 2446 (Loth 1047), described in Ricklefs and Voorhoeve 1977:56–57 and (on the basis of the photocopy in LOr 12,588) in Pigeaud 1967–80:IV, 87–90.

[15] *Babad* 1939–41:XXI, 52–3.

[16] Duirvelt, Kartasura, to Duyvensz, Semarang, 19 May and 20 April 1736, in VOC 2391 (OB 1737).

named ʿAlwi came back with Natakusuma from Batavia.[17] Both Ky.H. Mataram and Sayyid ʿAlwi appear to have wielded considerable influence at court. The Europeans later identified them as two of their principal enemies.

Urawan/Purbaya fell from his position of influence over the king after his sister and protector, the king's wife Ratu Kĕncana, died after giving birth to a stillborn child in early 1738. Late in that year his enemies at court and the VOC forced Pakubuwana II to turn him over to be exiled. This left a legacy of royal bitterness towards the Company which would later contribute to bloody conflict. Natakusuma remained at court, despite the Europeans' wish to lay hands on him as well. Although he was not as forceful a character as Urawan/Purbaya, it seems that he continued to groom Pakubuwana II as a pious Muslim monarch, along with Ky.H. Mataram and Sayyid ʿAlwi.

By 1739 Pakubuwana II was as well placed to be the Sufi Susuhunan as he would ever be. He was his own man, free of the domination of his dead wife, dead grandmother, exiled Patih Danurĕja and exiled favourite Urawan/Purbaya. He had around him people of evidently lesser influence but who nonetheless promoted his piety: Natakusuma, Ky.H. Mataram, Sayyid ʿAlwi, and perhaps others. The VOC was of little significance in the court's affairs at this time and therefore did not limit the king's room for manoeuvre. This was true in economic and political affairs and, of course, even more true of cultural affairs.

At this time Pakubuwana II seems to have been a king who was anxious to ensure the moral purity of his court. The son of the *Pĕngulu* (the chief religious official) and a royal concubine were executed for an affair late in 1738. Then the *Pĕngulu's* wife was accused of having known of this liaison and of teaching the royal concubines "scandalous histories and ditties". So she, the *Pĕngulu* and all the rest of their family were banished from the court.[18] The king also took action against notorious homosexuals at the court, notably his younger brother Pangeran Blitar. He was banished in 1739 to the Pajimatan mosque at the foot of the royal gravesite at Imagiri, where he was impris-

[17] Crul, Semarang, to Duirvelt, Kartasura, 12 Apr. 1737; Duirvelt, Kartasura, to Crul, Semarang, 22 Apr. 1737; both in VOC 2418 (OB 1738).

[18] Duirvelt, Kartasura, to Crul, Semarang, 19 Jan. and 19 Feb. 1739, in VOC 2449 (OB 1739); *Babad Sangkala* (LOr 4097), p. 91; *Babad* 1939–41:XXII, 25.

oned in a stockade with only women in attendance.[19] When he reoffended after being pardoned eight months later, Blitar was banished again to Imagiri and his lover was killed, his head impaled on a stake in the marketplace as a warning to others.[20]

Public display of Pakubuwana II's piety combined with emulation of the greatness of Java's past culminated in a grand tour to Mataram in September 1739. The king was accompanied by a VOC escort which left a graphic account of his progress.[21] He set off wearing Dutch garb of black velvet with gold braid, white leather gloves, hose and shoes, with a walking stick in his hand. On his head he wore "a massive golden crown". This appears to have been the golden crown of Majapahit, an object of considerable ritual significance which was, so far as is presently known, last seen on this occasion.[22] Pakubuwana II travelled in "an elevated and beautifully made buffalo cart", just as four hundred years before the Majapahit king Hayam Wuruk (Rājasanagara, reigned 1350–89) had conducted his royal progresses in buffalo carts decorated with gold.[23] A later VOC report says that Pakubuwana II's carts were made of ivory and were 200 years old.[24] The Susuhunan's brothers rode with him in his cart. They were preceded by other buffalo carts, a royal elephant, four state-horses with yellow trappings, 200 pikemen in yellow uniforms, 700 musketeers in scarlet, and the ladies of the court in five closed conveyances. Then followed pikemen estimated by the VOC to total 20,000 in number and a thousand musketeers, uniformed in red, yellow and blue tunics and hats, marching in rank and file and carrying 150 silk banners and flags. This great spectacle would have been accompanied by the sounds of multiple *gamĕlan* orchestras.

Pakubuwana II's purpose in going to Mataram was, according to

[19] Duirvelt, Kartasura, to Crul, Semarang, 2 Nov. 1739 (2nd letter of the day), in VOC 2478 (OB 1740). Duirvelt says only that Blitar was banished to a small temple at the foot of the hill; the Pajimatan mosque is clearly meant. For an account of Imagiri, with a useful map of the site, see Prawirawinarsa & Jayengpranata 1921:4–5.

[20] Van Velse, Kartasura, to Visscher, Semarang, 28 June and 15 Oct. 1740, in VOC 2512 (OB 1741).

[21] The following account of the visit to Mataram rests upon Nieuwenhuijsen, dagregister 16 Sept.–10 Oct. 1739, in VOC 2478 (OB 1740). See also *Babad* 1939–41:XXII, 26–32.

[22] For reference to this crown in the period before 1726, see Ricklefs 1993: index s.v. Majapahit.

[23] *Nāgarakātāgama* cantos 18–38; see Pigeaud 1960–63.

[24] Baerenclouw, dagregister 5 July–12 Aug. 1740, in VOC 2512 (OB 1741).

the Surakarta Major *Babad*, twofold: to pay his respects at ancestral graves and to pursue his pleasures.[25] He hunted and entertained himself in a beautifully constructed bamboo residence at Garjitawati (present-day Yogyakarta). It was all grand and pious at once. But it was not the ascetic piety promoted in Ratu Pakubuwana's books. And as an act of state, as a deployment of the supernatural powers of royalty in this world, this great spectacle was a failure. The Surakarta Major *Babad* describes dreadful omens in the capital of Kartasura during the king's absence in Mataram: blood appeared upon the doors and walls of houses and deformed banyan fruit and bananas were seen.[26] The kingdom was indeed approaching crisis as the court's factions drew apart into ever more hostile configurations, a threatening process which Pakubuwana II was unable to control.

In October 1740 a massacre of Chinese in the VOC capital at Batavia marked the outbreak of the conflict known as the Chinese War (1740–3). Locally domiciled Chinese along Java's *pasisir* (coast) overran several VOC posts and laid siege to the VOC coastal headquarters at Sĕmarang.[27] In the opening months of 1741 it seemed possible that the VOC could be expelled from Java's coastal territories by the Chinese and the local people who sided with them. It was necessary for Pakubuwana II and his increasingly factionalised court to determine how to respond to these circumstances. Suddenly there were issues in the phenomenal world which urgently required greater attention. Naturally the courtiers continued to compose works of mystical speculation[28] but these did not, on the evidence, prove to be of much use in guiding their deliberations about the bloody affairs of this world.

Pakubuwana II now faced the most difficult and crucial decision of this reign. There is a lengthy court debate on this matter described in the Surakarta Major *Babad*.[29] This account clearly contains some chronological confusion but probably depicts at least the main lines of division. Coastal and eastern regional lords argued that the king

---

[25] *Babad* 1939–41:XXII, 26: *prĕlu angujung luluhurira, ing Magiri Pasar Gĕdhe, myang Panitikanipun, Girilaya karsanira Ji, asasamben cangkrama.*

[26] *Babad* 1939–41:XXII, 32.

[27] Vermeulen 1938; Blussé 1986: Ch. 5; Remmelink 1994:125 *et seqq.*

[28] See the India Office Library MS Jav. 30, in which texts *A* and *B* (ff. 1–83) are *suluks* carrying a date equivalent to 27 Oct. 1740. This MS appears to be of *kraton* origin.

[29] Ricklefs 1983.

should back the VOC. Tirtawiguna, a powerful courtier and reputedly a great writer,[30] but evidently a person who had little sympathy for the king's more enthusiastically Islamic advisers, remained silent in the court debate. The *Patih* Natakusuma urged Pakubuwana II to back the Chinese against the Europeans. In the end, it was the latter view which prevailed.

On 20 July 1741, the Javanese attacked the VOC garrison of over two hundred men at Kartasura.[31] In the initial attack several VOC officers, including the commander Captain Johannes van Velsen, were wounded and about thirty-five were killed. About eighty Javanese died, among them several leading figures in court affairs. The VOC survivors repulsed the Javanese, who proceeded to besiege the fortress for nearly three weeks. During this time the garrison were told that the king and his court would do them no harm if they converted to Islam. On 10 August the garrison surrendered. They were ordered to accept conversion through circumcision or die. Most chose to live. Van Velsen was killed by the Javanese. Here was the ultimate Islamic *persona* of Pakubuwana II: the conquering, converting warrior of the faith.

It is noteworthy that one of the ways in which the court commemorated this attack was by composing works of Islamic mysticism. Two texts entitled *Kitab Daka* and *Kitab Fatahurrahman* contain mystical teachings of a kind found widely in Javanese *suluk* literature: the unity of *kawula* (servant) and *gusti* (lord), the fourfold Sufi path, the seven grades of emanation of Wujudiyya, and so on. The two works clearly belong together and are evidently of *kraton* origin.[32] At

---

[30] Winter 1911:354 and 359.

[31] The following account rests upon the three eyewitness records in Leupe 1864; documents in VOC 2548 (OB 1742) from 9 Aug. to 12 Dec. 1741; Batavia to H. XVII, 6 Nov. 1741, in de Jonge & van Deventer 1862–1909:IX, 387–8, 392; *idem*, 6 Dec. 1741, in ibid. 400–1; van Velsen et al., Kartasura, to Sĕmarang, 23 July 1741, in VOC 2549 (OB 1742) (a letter which Sĕmarang did not receive until it was brought out by the survivors of the attack); *Babad Kraton* (British Library Add. MS 12320), ff. 642r.–655r.

[32] The MS is India Office Library Jav. 83 (IO 3102), described in Ricklefs & Voorhoeve 1977:70. The works of concern here are texts *A* and *B*. Texts *C–I* are in different hands, falling into two groups which evidently belong together (*C–E* and *F–I*).

I have examined the MS directly, but have studied *Kitab Daka* primarily *via* an unpublished transcription by J. Soegiarto entitled "Manuscript uit Londen van Indian [sic] Office Library no. 3102 Shattariya tracts," IOL MSS Eur. D. 518. *Kitab Fatahurrahman* is contained in Soegiarto's transcription as well, but is found more conveniently in transcription with an English translation in Drewes 1977:52–87. It seems reasonable to accept a *kraton* origin. The reference at the end to the *rusake*

the end of the second of them is found a date equivalent to 14 August 1741, just after the VOC in Kartasura had surrendered. The manuscript concludes with the words, "This was written was at the time of the Dutch-Javanese destruction".[33]

Unfortunately for Pakubuwana II in his guise as the fearsome enemy of infidels, he had chosen to join the battle against the VOC just as the tide of war was about to turn. The number of besiegers around Sĕmarang grew to an estimated 40–50,000 Javanese and 3,500 Chinese with over fifty pieces of artillery.[34] The company brought in reinforcements by sea so that by November 1741 there were over 3,400 VOC troops in Sĕmarang. When they went over to the offensive in November they discovered, to their own surprise, that the besieging army scattered before them.[35] Meanwhile, forces of the Company's ally Cakraningrat IV of West Madura were sweeping through East Java.

The signs were unmistakable that Pakubuwana II had been disastrously wrong to attack the Company, so he now undertook a *volte-face* which was at least as disastrous: for him, for the court of Kartasura and perhaps for the prospects of a more consciously Islamic style of

Walonda-Jawa of 1741 (see the following note) certainly suggests a *kraton* setting. The other texts bound in the volume with these texts include a Shaṭṭariyya *salsilah* (spiritual genealogy) which goes down to *Kanjĕng Pangeran Pakuningrat ing Ngayogyakarta Adiningrat* and *Kanjĕng Raden Ayu Kilen ingkang garwa Kanjĕng Sinuhun Sultan Pakubuwana* [sic] (text *F*, 47–50), suggesting that the whole collection was kept in court circles. It was probably acquired by Colin Mackenzie at the sack of the Yogyakarta *kraton* in 1812. A substantial number of his Javanese MSS derived from that episode (see Ricklefs & Voorhoeve 1977:xxvi). The other IOL MSS from Kartasura employed in this study also almost certainly derived from the plundered Yogyakarta *kraton* library.

33 Drewes 1977:87, Canto III (Sinom): *18. mantuning sĕrat tinĕdhak, Sĕnen-Wage surya nĕnggih, Dumadilakir wulanya, tanggal ping kalih Jimakir, taune duk tinulis, angkaning taun ingitung, sewu nĕm atus warsa, sawidak lan tigang warsi, duk tinulis rusake Walonda-Jawa.* Drewes did not recognise the error in the date here. The text gives Mon.-Wage, 2 Jumadilakir, Jimakir 1663, which he merely equates (3) to AD 1738. But AJ 1663 was a *Dal* year. Clearly Jimakir AJ 1666 (= AD 1741–42) is meant. The reference to the "Dutch-Javanese destruction" makes this certain. I take the correct date to be Mon.-Wage, 2 Jumadilakir, Jimakir 1666, equivalent to 14 Aug. 1741.

34 Batavia to H. XVII, 6 Nov. 1741, in de Jonge & van Deventer 1862–1909:IX, 392, 404; Verijssel & Theling, kort bericht, Sĕmarang, 14 Dec. 1743, in Arsip Nasional Solo 42, "Rapport Verijssel & Theling 1743".

35 Sĕmarang krijgsraad, 1 Nov. and 5 Nov. 1741, in Arsip Nasional Java N.O. Kust 388, "Resolutien krijgsraad 1741–1742"; Batavia to H. XVII, 6 Dec. 1741, in de Jonge & van Deventer 1862–1909:IX, 391–392, 399–401, 403, 404. Even shortly before the breaking of the siege, the VOC at Sĕmarang were still very doubtful of success against the besiegers; see Mom to Verijssel & Theling, Sĕmarang, 30 Oct. 1741, in Arsip Nasional Java N.O. Kust 388, "Resolutien krijgsraad 1741–1742"; Batavia to H. XVII, 6 Dec. 1741, in de Jonge & van Deventer 1862–1909:IX, 399.

kingship in Java. Within weeks of its breaking of the siege of Sĕmarang, the VOC received letters from Pakubuwana II's mother Ratu Amangkurat and then from the king himself seeking reconciliation with the Europeans.[36] The 177 survivors of the Company's Kartasura garrison were reassembled from the villages in which they had been placed and were allowed to return to the north coast in January 1742.[37] According to *Babad Kraton*, it was Ratu Amangkurat and, in particular, Tirtawiguna who pushed the king into this reversal of policy.[38]

The Chinese and the many Javanese who had joined with them against the Europeans, fighters who had thought Pakubuwana II to be on their side, now saw him seeking rapprochement with the Christian Company. They turned angrily against him and the war against the VOC thus also became a rebellion against the king. In the eyes of those rebels who were devout Muslims intent on Holy War, the ruler was no doubt seen as an apostate. The VOC, however, was still stuck in a defensive posture on the *pasisir* and did not have the means to march into the interior to defend the king—whom, in any case, it hardly trusted.

In the early months of 1742 the rebels proclaimed their own rival king. This was a youth descended from the line of Amangkurat III (reigned 1703–8), whose throne had been usurped by Pakubuwana II's grandfather with the support of the VOC. The young man employed several titles, the best known being Sunan Kuning. It may well be that he could still claim greater legitimacy than the usurping line which was then occupying the throne of Kartasura with such flamboyant incompetence.

Pakubuwana II sent Tirtawiguna to Sĕmarang to act as his representative with the VOC. The Company sent a small detachment of eight men commanded by Captain Joan Andries Baron van Hohendorff to Kartasura in March 1742. The Patih Natakusuma was sus-

[36] Ratu Amangkurat, Kartasura, to Verijssel, Theling & Steinmetz, Sĕmarang, rec'd 25 Nov. 1741; Pakubuwana II, Kartasura, to Batavia, 22 Siyam Jimakir (1666) (1 Dec. 1741), rec'd 21 Dec. 1741; both in VOC 2549 (OB 1742).

[37] Wiltvang et al., Kartasura, to Sĕmarang, 23 Dec. 1741 and 1 Jan. 1742; Verijssel, Sĕmarang, to Batavia, 20 Jan. 1742; Ratu Agĕng Amangkurat, Kartasura, to Theling & Steinmetz, Sĕmarang, 14 Dulkangidah AJ 1666/21 Jan. 1742; Verijssel, Theling & Steinmetz, Sĕmarang, to Batavia, 4 Feb. 1742; Verijssel, Theling & Steinmetz, Sĕmarang, to Ratu Agĕng Amangkurat, Kartasura, 28 Jan. 1742; all in VOC 2549 (OB 1742).

[38] British Library Add. MS 12320, ff. 674v.–682v.

pected—probably correctly—of being secretly in league with Sunan Kuning's rebels. On 18 June he entered the VOC fortress in Sĕmarang for consultations and was arrested in accordance with Pakubuwana II's wishes.[39] He was exiled to Sri Lanka. Thus was removed from the innermost circle of the court the last Javanese figure who seems to have shared the self-consciously Islamising ideal of kingship.[40]

The rebellion now culminated in the conquest of Kartasura itself. On 30 June 1742, as rebel forces burned and plundered the capital city and broke through into the court, Pakubuwana II took flight with his young son (the future Pakubuwana III) and Capt. van Hohendorff. The women of the court and its many treasures fell to the rebels. "Sacks of money, packs with gold and silver, gold betel sets, chalices and other priceless objects" were lost.[41] The princes and dignitaries of the realm scattered: some fled into the countryside, some took refuge with the VOC at Sĕmarang, some stayed in Kartasura and submitted to Sunan Kuning, some later rallied to Pakubuwana II. Naturally many Javanese saw the hand of God in this great debacle. The writer of *Babad Kraton* observed, "This was God's dispensation, for it was the decree of the All-Disposing that the retribution of the Immaterial should fall upon the Javanese, employing the Chinese as the means".[42]

Pakubuwana II was excluded from his court for five months. At first he travelled through wild country east of Kartasura in the company of van Hohendorff, then he settled down in Panaraga under the protection of local lords. Van Hohendorff left the king and returned to the coast via Surabaya on 10 August 1742. During this time in the wilderness, the king of course sought spiritual guidance and support. But now there was little sign of the Islamising style of earlier years.

The most significant episode in the wretched king's search for supernatural support was his encounter with the spirit of Mt. Lawu,

---

39 Batavia to H. XVII, 5 Dec. 1742, in de Jonge & van Deventer 1862–1909:IX, 416–417.

40 It should be remembered particularly that it was Natakusuma who brought both Sayyid 'Alwi and Ky.H. Mataram to Kartasura. No Javanese sources survive, however, which enable one to be as confident of his views as is the case with Ratu Pakubuwana or Urawan/Purbaya.

41 Van Hohendorff & Hogewits, eerbiedig bericht, Sĕmarang, 25 Aug. 1742, in Gijsberti Hodenpijl 1918:599–600.

42 British Library Add. MS 12320, f. 713v.: *sampun dilalah, pan takdir ing Yyang Widi, pamalĕse Yyang Sukma prapta wong Jawa, Cina kinarya margi.*

called Sunan Lawu. Of course this tale may be a later courtly fiction about Pakubuwana II's time in the wilderness, composed some time before the text of the Surakarta Major *Babad* was finalised in 1836. But it is at least as likely that the tale was told at the time and was both a tool for reassembling the defeated king's followers and, very probably, an account of an experience which Pakubuwana II regarded as real. It is important to note that nowadays beliefs about Sunan Lawu have a distinctly non-Islamic, indeed anti-Islamic, flavour, although one need not assume that this must always have been so. Sunan Lawu is said to be the spirit of the last king of Hindu-Buddhist Majapahit and not to care for devout Muslims. It is said to be taboo to speak the name of Allah while climbing Mt. Lawu; explicitly sexual jokes and foul language are regarded as more appropriate.[43]

According to the Surakarta Major *Babad*,[44] Pakubuwana II engaged in fervent ascetic practices in search of supernatural support, and ordered his followers to do likewise. One night, as the king was sleeping in the open air, a wind rose gently and then became a gale, in the midst of which Sunan Lawu appeared to him. This king of the spirits (*ratuning dhĕdhĕmit*) was of terrifying size, with his lower garment (*kampuh*) flung across his shoulder. He told the wretched Pakubuwana II not to grieve so, for he would help him to reconquer Kartasura. But the king must marry Sunan Lawu's daughter, a graceful and beauteous spirit maiden.

The king was speechless. "Is this the assistance of the All-Disposing God?", he asked himself, "for it is a spirit which has come". But he decided that nothing was forbidden to serve as a means to dispense God's grace, so he accepted Sunan Lawu's offer and married his daughter, who came to him the following Friday. She told him that spirit armies would come to his assistance in battle. And when at last he was restored in Kartasura, she said, "then I, my lord, and all the spirit warriors will be in the forests by day but will guard you at night".

Kraton Islam of Pakubuwana II's time admitted pre-Islamic culture, but Sunan Lawu may have stretched the capacious boundaries of Javanese Sufism beyond their natural limits. In *Sĕrat Cabolek* the defender of Islamic orthodoxy says that Old Javanese classics are

---

[43] Adam 1938:97–101.
[44] *Babad* 1939–41:XXVIII, 4–7.

works of Islamic mysticism.[45] Similarly, the *měnthek* (tungro virus) king, a spirit which damages rice fields, tells Prince Mangkubumi that since the time of the Prophet Muḥammad there have been Islamic spirits as well as those who come from devils.[46] In Ratu Pakubuwana's *Kitab Usulbiyah*, Muḥammad wears an object which seems clearly to be the golden crown of Majapahit.[47] But none of these inclusions of pre-Islamic knowledge, forces and symbols involves a figure so connected with primitive carnality and (at least in more recent times) such specifically anti-Islamic concepts as Sunan Lawu.

There is also a pious Islamic legend about Pakubuwana II's time in the wilderness, but its antiquity is open to question. The famous Islamic school (*pesantren*) of Tĕgalsari, near Panaraga, is said to have been founded by a holy hermit living at the foot of Mt. Wilis called Kyai Agung Kasan Bĕsari. Pakubuwana II is said to have sought Kasan Bĕsari's spiritual support and, after eventually regaining his throne, to have rewarded Kasan Bĕsari by making Tĕgalsari the cradle of Islam in the realm. This story, deriving from Tĕgalsari, was first recorded—so far as this writer is aware—in a Dutch publication of the 1870s.[48] The chronicle source consulted for this period—the Surakarta Major *Babad* which is preserved in a recension completed in 1836—makes no mention of Kasan Bĕsari but tells instead of Pakubuwana II indirectly contacting a different holy hermit of Mt. Wilis named Ṿmbahan Sĕkondha.[49] This figure said that the king should turn over authority to his Crown prince, who should be called Bauwarna, a name from the pre-Islamic Panji stories. Pakubuwana II is renamed Brawijaya, the name ascribed to the kings of Majapahit, including the final one who is supposed to have become Sunan Lawu. So again one encounters pre-Islamic referents and is left wondering whether the later nineteenth-century story of Kyai Agung Kasan Bĕsari can be a version of the Ṿmbahan Sĕkondha story, purged of its pre-Islamic details and polished with Muslim piety.

The rebel Sunan Kuning was expelled from Kartasura at the end of November 1742, not by Pakubuwana II's forces but by Madurese forces of Cakraningrat IV. The latter despised Pakubuwana II so much that he proposed to the VOC that he should be killed as an

---

[45] Soebardi 1975:14.
[46] *Cabolek* 1885:89.
[47] Radyapustaka MS no. 262 carikan, 34.
[48] Fokkens 1877.
[49] *Babad* 1939–41:XXVIII, 22–24.

example to disloyal kings. The Madurese refused Pakubuwana II permission to reoccupy his own court. The Europeans, however, remained committed to Pakubuwana II, who in his desperation promised them anything they might wish.[50] Not until 21 December 1742 was the king escorted back into his court by a VOC column which had reached Kartasura. By that time the Madurese had thoroughly plundered whatever had remained after the Chinese sack of the capital five months before.[51]

The kind of pious Islamic magic represented by Ratu Pakubuwana's books of 1729–30 was tried once more, but not in the camp of Pakubuwana II. Rather, in the temporary rebel headquarters of Sunan Kuning in Mataram, a woman of the court wrote out a new recension of *Kitab Usulbiyah* in May 1743.[52] It proclaims itself to be a weapon whose supernatural power (*sakti*) would guarantee victory if carried into battle by a believer. But it failed to do this, just as Ratu Pakubuwana's recension had failed to make perfect her grandson's reign. Sunan Kuning was expelled from his temporary refuge by a thousand VOC soldiers in early June 1743, and the rebellion collapsed soon thereafter.

So Susuhunan Pakubuwana II was restored to his throne. But he could hardly claim now to be the pious Sufi monarch which Ratu Pakubuwana and others had tried to make of him. Whether or not his supposed contact with Sunan Lawu exemplifies a turning towards more indigenous, less Islamic, powers, certainly he had now abandoned the anti-VOC cause, in which Islamic sensibilities had played a leading role, and was instead the abject protégé of the Europeans. He soon surrendered his religious mentors Ky.H. Mataram and Sayyid 'Alwi to the VOC for exile.[53] Both VOC and Javanese sources picture the king hereafter as relying above all upon the advice of the Capt. van Hohendorff, who commanded the Company's garrison at the court.

In the final years of Pakubuwana II's reign, there is no evidence

---

[50] CN IV, Madura, to Verijssel, Theling & Steinmetz, Sĕmarang, 3 Sawal Alip (2 Dec. 1742), rec'd 8 Dec. 1742, in VOC 2588 (OB 1743); Batavia to H. XVII, 5 Apr. 1743, in de Jonge & van Deventer 1862–1909:IX, 422–3, 424; Verijssel & Theling, kort bericht, 14 Dec. 1743, in Arsip Nasional Solo 42. *Babad* 1939–41: XXVIII, 54–71, describes the Madurese advance upon and conquest of Kartasura. According to this account (ibid. 65), Kuning's forces were afflicted by eye disease as was promised by Sunan Lawu's daughter.

[51] Steinmetz, Kartasura, to Batavia, 24 Dec. 1742, in VOC 2588 (OB 1743).

[52] Sonobudoyo MS PB A.109.

[53] Verijssel & Theling, kort bericht, Sĕmarang, 14 Dec. 1743, in Arsip Nasional Solo 42.

of the pious Islamising seen in court circles in the years before 1742. It is interesting that chronicle accounts of the decision to abandon the battered court of Kartasura and to move to the new *kraton* of Surakarta (occupied in early 1746) report the existence of a prophecy that if the new court were east of the Sala River, the Javanese would adopt the pre-Islamic (*buda*) religion again.[54] Although the historical interpretation of such prophecies is always difficult, these reports suggest that perhaps some courtiers felt the court now to be so far from Islamic commitment that de-Islamisation was conceivable.

A fuller interpretation of the significance of Pakubuwana II's reign within the history of Islam in Java must await this writer's book on that reign. Readers familiar with the scholarly literature on the Javanese courts from the seventeenth century to the present will realise that this period appears to stand out as an exception. In no other king's reign does the literature discuss the presence of an influential Islamising elite at the centre of court affairs. Rather, the courts seem to have been somewhat indifferent to Islamic piety at best and its enemy at worst. So perhaps in the reign of Pakubuwana II, one sees the high-water-mark of Islamisation in *kraton* circles. Perhaps the abject failures and disasters of this reign discredited Islam as a central ideology and a source of spiritual power within the *kraton* elite. But it is also possible that future research will show scholarly studies of Javanese history in other periods to have undervalued the influence of Islam in court circles. Only more research will resolve this matter satisfactorily.

It is in any case clear that the existence of two contending cultural streams within Javanese society, a Javanist and an Islamic stream, and certainly the perceived dominance of the former in *kraton* affairs, is historically contingent. It is not some primordial state of affairs within Javanese society, but rather the product of specific historical circumstances. For some fifteen years of the reign of Pakubuwana II, the style of the Javanese court was that of pious mystic Islam. This was one of the principal causes of a decision to go to war against the Europeans. These observations have consequences for understanding the past, present and future of Javanese—or more broadly Indonesian—society. Anyone, for example, who might wish to argue that radical Islamic politics cannot develop in Indonesia because of the strength of Javanism might do well to consider the reign of Pakubuwana II.

---

[54] *Babad* 1939–41:XXXI, 6–7; Yasadipura I, 1937–39:I, 9.

PANCASILA PLUS, *PANCASILA* MINUS

Ann Kumar

A major focus of the political controversies of the first half of the 1980s was the position of *Pancasila*, the Five Principles that form the philosophical foundation of the Indonesian state. These principles were first defined by Sukarno in an extempore speech before the Investigating Committee for the Preparation of Independence on June 1, 1945.[1] The five principles in the order they are given by Sukarno are:

1. Nationalism.
2. Internationalism.
3. Representation, mutual consultation and consensus.
4. Social justice.
5. Belief in the One God.

These five principles were subsequently written into the preamble to the Constitution, and after the change from Sukarno's "Old Order" to Suharto's "New Order" retained and indeed increased their significance as a focus of political debate. In March–April 1980 Suharto made two outspoken speeches in which he said, inter alia, that the Indonesian armed forces (ABRI) would never allow *Pancasila* and the Constitution of 1945 to be changed and if forced to they would take up arms. He referred to earlier armed challenges to constitutional rule and the established state ideology, not only Communist ones against which he had made common cause with Muslim groups and whose threat was frequently referred to in his political statements, but this time also Islamic ones. He also made a strong attack on the policies of the political parties, accusing them of promoting "*Pancasila* Plus", that is, *Pancasila* plus another ideology as distinct from "pure" *Pancasila*. This accusation seemed to be aimed primarily at the Development Unity Party (*Partai Persatuan Pembangunan*, generally known as the PPP). In reply K.H. Anwar of *Nahdatul Ulama* (one of the component

[1] The speech is translated in Feith and Castles 1970.

organisations making up the federal-style PPP) posed the question of whether in *Pancasila* democracy everyone had to be a "yes-man". The Minister for Internal Affairs, Amir Machmud, responded with severe criticism of anyone who criticised government policy, questioning their loyalty to *Pancasila.*

Early in May, a response to the statements of the President and government came in the form of the "Petition of the 50", which was signed by a number of prominent Indonesians. The petitioners deplored Suharto's implication that polarisation was developing between people who stressed the imperishability of *Pancasila* and those who wanted to change it, perhaps causing social conflicts by doing so. They accused Suharto of incorrectly interpreting *Pancasila* so that it could be used to threaten his political opponents, saying that the founders of the Indonesian Republic had intended the *Pancasila* to be a uniting, not a divisive ideology. Thirdly, they saw in Suharto's speeches a justification of a campaign by the authorities to paralyse systematically the 1945 Constitution using the *Sapta Marga* or the Soldier's Oath as an excuse. They deplored Suharto's invitation to the armed forces to take sides. Fifthly, they criticised the impression that Suharto had given that some people considered themselves personifications of the *Pancasila* so that any criticisms of them were to be regarded as criticisms of *Pancasila* itself. Finally they expressed their concern about Suharto's statement that there were subversive and armed activities being prepared for the forthcoming elections.

The government in response suppressed reporting of this petition in Indonesia and subsequently withdrew all government facilities from the petitioners. In a speech commemorating the introduction by Sukarno of *Pancasila,* Sjarifuddin Zuhri joined the debate, claiming that the Muslims could not be labelled *Pancasila*-plus: after all ABRI also had the *Sapta Marga* as well as *Pancasila.* On June 10th Amir Machmud responded by saying that there were some people who "wanted to use Parliament for political manoeuvring". This was the beginning of a prolonged and heated controversy, with the government insisting on the necessity for all political and other organisations to accept *Pancasila* as the "sole foundation" (*azas tunggal*). When in September 1984 the PPP finally did so, there were headlines proclaiming that the party had "abandoned Islam".[2]

---

[2] Useful summaries of political events are to be found in the *Review of Indonesian and Malaysian Affairs* (Sydney University) for the relevant years.

In all this, the Islamic parties were seen as trying to add something to a document which many scholars have seen as a defeat for Islam and a triumph for non-Islamic forces—hardly surprising considering that Sukarno's speech was intended to counter the idea of Indonesia becoming an Islamic state. Yet I believe we miss important dimensions of *Pancasila* if we focus solely on the speech's function as a strategic countering of Islamic claims to provide the sole ideological basis of the Indonesian state. If we look at the text of the speech, the first two principles are respectively the national unity of Indonesia and the principle of internationalism. Sukarno then goes on to say:

> And now, what is the third principle? It is the principle of *mufakat*, unanimity, the principle of *perwakilan*, representation, the principle of *permusjawaratan*, deliberation among representatives. The Indonesian state shall not be a state for one group although that group be the wealthy. But we shall set up a state of "all for all", "one for all, all for one". I am convinced that an absolute condition for the strength of the Indonesian state is *permusjawaratan/perwakilan.*[3]

Here we have three concepts recruited from the Islamic world; and in the fourth of the five principles, social justice or *keadilan sosial*, another is added. At least two of these concepts, *musyawarah* and *mufakat*, had earlier been canvassed by Sukarno in the influential Muslim magazine *Pandji Islam.*[4] In an article on the difference between fascism and the Indonesian approach, he wrote:

> The Indonesian spirit is a spirit that, in keeping with *traditional customs* (consider Minangkabau or village meetings in Java), is a spirit fond of "mufakat" or consensus, and of "mushawarah" or deliberations, and which is taught by *Islam too* to be devoted to "mufakat" and "mushawarah"—*Wa amruhun sjura bainahum! Wa sjawirhum fil amri!*—while the spirit of fascism is a spirit leaving everything to the will of just one man, to the spirit of "individualism", the spirit of tyranny, the spirit of dictatorship!

In the *Pancasila* as we know it today, the principle of humanitarianism or internationalism is qualified by the phrase "just and ethically founded" (*adil dan beradab*) in the latter term a further borrowing from the Muslim vocabulary.

---

[3] Translation from Feith and Castles 1970:44.

[4] In 1940: this article is reproduced in Sukarno 1964:589f.

1. *Java's Dual Tradition: Left and Right, Indic and Islamic*

In this paper I would like to show that these concepts laid down in the *Pancasila* added radically new perspectives to Indonesian political thinking. I shall use a reading of a work from the 1820s that provides a magisterial exposition of the old, dominant, sophisticated Javanese political tradition. This is the *Sasana Sunu* of the famous philosopher-poet Yasadipura II.[5]

This text deals with personal morality, in particular, the morals and manners appropriate for the *priyayi*, the administrative elite, and with political and social values. The two are not unrelated, since it is clear that the health of the polity is seen by Yasadipura II as resting primarily on the personal qualities of the upper class: in this respect his program of moral instruction resembles the old-fashioned moral education of the English elite. In the instructions he gives to the young *priyayi* that he addresses, the place of Islam appears to be a major one. He says in the strongest terms that one must observe the *Shariah*, and condemns those mystics (*ahlul hakekat*) who say that nothing is forbidden[6]—a reference to the heterodox but nevertheless widespread Sufi belief, represented by the mystic al-Ḥallāj and his Javanese counterpart Seh Siti Jĕnar,[7] that for those who have reached the ultimate state of enlightenment (that of oneness with Reality, *hakekat*, from Arabic *ḥaqīqa*), the prescriptions and prohibitions laid down by the Law for ordinary mortals are no longer binding. This seems a very orthodox position, especially when combined with the text's saturation with Arabic words. It would be easy to go through it picking these out, defining and using them as evidence of the preeminent position already achieved by Islam at this time. In one sense this would be valid, and in parts of the text a strongly Islamic posi-

[5] Canto and stanza numbers and references are based on the printed text, which is the edition published in Yasadipura II 1980. Unfortunately, as is often the case in this otherwise valuable series of text editions, the manuscript on which it is based is not noted. The manuscript version transcribed by me is LOr 1806 from the Leiden University Library Oriental collection. This was clearly the same text as the printed one, though there were occasional differences in the number of stanzas per canto and variations in wording throughout. Of the two texts, the manuscript version had a greater number of corruptions.

[6] Canto II, stanza 21.

[7] Both of whom were put to death for allegedly spreading heretical teachings. For a brief account of the theological and political rationale for al-Ḥallāj's condemnation and execution in 931, see Macdonald 1926:183–86. On the condemnation of Siti Jĕnar see Soebardi 1975:35.

tion is indeed taken. Canto II, for instance, advises the young men who are addressed in the text to follow the *shariah*, to know *sunah, fardu, wajib, batal*, and *kharam*,[8] and the Five Pillars; and to take care not to be *kafir, fasik*, or *musyrik*, i.e. infidels, heretics, or apostates.[9] It also admonishes them against laughing at people performing the *salat*, and saying *arak* is *halal*, which struck this reader as perhaps a momentary descent from the elevated tone that distinguishes most of the text into the real world of youth.

In general, however, Islamic concepts are combined with or glossed by Javanese ones, and the overall framework seems clearly Javanese rather than Islamic. The exemplary works which the author advises his young audience to read are a mixture of Islamic and pre-Islamic works: the *Nitipraja, Wulangreh, Pranitisastra*, and Old Javanese *Ramayana*, all works from or based on the Hindu-Javanese tradition[10] with the exception of the *Wulangreh*, which was written by Pakubuwana IV. Versions of the *Pranitisastra* were written in 1796 by Yasadipura I and in 1808 by Yasadipura II himself.[11] In Canto V, Yasadipura II adds the *Kisangsul Ambiya* (*Qiṣaṣ al-anbiyā'* or Stories of the Prophets: a Javanese version is attributed to Yasadipura I)[12] and *Kitab Insan Kamil* (*Book of the Perfect Man*, i.e. a life of Muḥammad, of which there are numerous Javanese versions) are commended for the instruction they provide on the manifold ways in which the devil tempts mankind. Like the recommended books, the personal examples cited are also mixed, ranging from the Prophet and Moses to exemplary figures from Javanese versions of Indic myths.

The commendation of restraint in food, drink, and sleeping, however, leads up to a eulogy of *tapa* (verse 14), a Sanskrit borrowing in one sense but nevertheless perhaps the most enduringly Javanese of spiritual values, showing the characteristic Javanese prizing of restraint and self-denial in all things, whether food, drink, or sleep, as a way of acquiring spiritual power. Yasadipura II writes: "He

8 Muslim canon law divides actions into five classes, i.e. obligatory, recommended, permitted/indifferent, disapproved, and forbidden. The terms *farḍ* and *wājib* are used for the first category, and *ḥarām* for the last. *Sunna* is a term used for old custom or usage, which Muslims are counselled to follow in preference to innovation (*bid'a*). See Macdonald 1926:183–86. *Batal* is from the Arabic *bāṭil*, meaning legally void.

9 Arabic originals: *kāfir, fāsiq* and *mushrik*.

10 Canto III stanzas 3–4.

11 The first was a Kawi-miring version, the second a Kawi-jarwa: see Poerbatjaraka 1957:148.

12 See Winter 1911:354.

who has great abilities, he who has supernatural power, and he who becomes a *priyayi*, all have their roots in *tapa*. Every great matter has its origins in *tapa*, which is followed by happiness. Even if one is very able, and even if one becomes a *priyayi*, if this does not originate in *tapa* it is riches from the devil."[13] Even if the devil has the ability to confer supernatural power, the power one obtains from him lasts only a moment, and later one will be powerless against the wise and knowledgeable.

Tapa on its own can be translated as "penance" but is often elaborated into the compound *tapa-brata*, penance through self-mortification and abstinence.[14] In the *Sasana Sunu* as in other Javanese works, *tapa* is frequently glossed as "death in life" (*mati ana sajroning ngurip*), and the young *priyayi* are advised not to concern themselves about whether their life will be long or short: what should occupy their thoughts is to *live as if they were dead.*[15] In another place[16] *tapa* is coupled with *tobat* from the Arabic *tawba* (repentance) and the young *priyayi* are advised to prepare themselves for the fact that no-one remains in a high position forever and that they should meet this contingency with *tobat* and *tapa*, the most efficacious way to restore their rank.

We have seen above how Yasadipura's language and his prescriptions for reading matter and personal exemplars show the duality of Java's religious tradition. In Canto XI verses 17–19 (dealing with the duties of a *Mantri* in the ruler's service) it is consciously formulated as consisting of a left and a right-hand branch. From the left side, a *Mantri* must know about *Janaloka, Ngendraloka*, and *Guruloka*: the first is the place of humans, and knowing about it means knowing the proper behaviour and activities of humans (*tatakramanipun, pakariyane ing manungsa*). *Ngendraloka* is where Batara Endra has his *kraton*, and knowing *Ngendraloka* means knowing the *tataning panĕmbahing dewa* (the proper arrangements for the veneration of the gods). The third, *Guruloka*, is the place of Batara Guru or Sang Hyang Pramesthi (Girinata), and knowing *Guruloka* means knowing the *sĕmbah mring Hyang Girinata* (the act of homage paid to Hyang Girinata). From the right side a Mantri must know about *sarengat* (the *Shariah*), *tarekat*, and *kakekat*, the three stages of enlightenment for a Muslim who takes the path of

[13] Canto VII, stanza 14.

[14] See e.g. Rani 1957, section 25, where *tapa* and *brata* come at the top of the list of the Ten Best Things.

[15] Canto I, stanza 10.

[16] Canto XI, stanza 7f.

joining a mystic order (*tarekat*) in order to attain knowledge of the ultimate Reality (*kakekat* or *hakekat*, Arabic *ḥaqīqa*). So it seems that the parallel is that observance of the Islamic Law (*sarengat*) belongs to the province of humans, the path of the *tarekat* raises one to the world of the Gods, and knowledge of ultimate Reality to that of the highest Godhead.

Elsewhere, Yasadipura says that one should take direction from a teacher and that both the "left" and the "right", i.e. the Hinduized and Islamic traditions, can provide a good path for one.[17] In the Javanese classificatory system, left is usually ranked higher than right: is Yasadipura II making a point about the relative ranking of the Indic and Islamic heritages of the Javanese by assigning the Indic to the left-hand side?

As is not uncommon in works devoted to the instruction of the young, much of the time the author is dealing with prohibitions. Canto II deals with the concept of *ĕndĕm*, "intoxication". There are numerous different sorts of *ĕndĕm*, as follows. Firstly, strong drink is to be avoided because of its effect on behaviour, making the drinker over-confident and ill-mannered, turning his attention from God and his religion—and also because it means one destroys one's own body. Also reprehensible is excess preoccupation with fine clothes, thinking oneself as exquisite as Arjuna or Panji (described as a common fault with young people who do not realise that true beauty is of the heart), as well as intoxication with pleasure and sleeping. Next comes intoxication by *hawa nafsu* (passion) which drives one to unreasonable anger with others for the slightest offence; and intoxication through desiring something beyond all reason. It is interesting that whereas the Arabic word *nafs* means something equivalent to "soul",[18] in Java its derivatives *nafsu* and in common speech *nĕsu* have come to mean passion of an undesirable and baneful character, and in particular the passion of anger—yet another example of the dangers inherent in focusing on the Arabic word rather than on the Javanese concept that it expresses.

---

[17] Stanzas 17–21.

[18] It is used for the translation of this concept from the Greek philosophers: personal communication, Dr T. Street. The baneful effects of *hawa nafsu* are also foregrounded in one of the works of the famous Raja Ali Haji of Riau (c. 1809–c. 1870), which particularly castigate the qualities of contentiousness, arrogance, stubbornness, and the desire for self-aggrandisement. See Andaya and Matheson 1979:108–128. The work in question is the *Kitab Pengetahuan Bahasa*, see p. 118.

In the same Canto, stanza 24 speaks out against opium: it is not the man that consumes opium, but opium that consumes the man (*dudu wong kang mangan apyun, apyun kang mangan janma*). It is an offence against the *Shariah*; however, it is permitted, according to the *Kitab Sarahbayan*,[19] to use a little opium in a fever medicine. Stanza 27 deals with gambling, also forbidden by the law, and together with opium-smoking the most usual reason that people take to crime, according to Yasadipura II. Stanza 28 advises against putting too much credence in the 30-*wuku* system,[20] which is used to predict the future life of a new-born baby in detail, since believing in what is predicted causes our perceptions to alter and we really seem to perceive that it has come about. On the other hand, the sciences of mysticism,[21] astronomy (*falak*) and astrology (*nujum*) come from Arabia, where they were known as *ʿilm al-falak* and *ʿilm al-tanjīm* respectively, and from the Prophet (and are therefore acceptable).

Related to the concept of *ĕndĕm*, is that of *pakarĕman*, which might be translated as "infatuation" or "attachment". These include love of wealth (*karĕm dunya*), whose baneful consequences are illustrated in the story of the *kaum desa* Ki Nurngali[22] a friendless man who tried to "dam up" his wealth, against the advice of the *Panitisastra*, and ended up by being killed for it. The fact that the person chosen to exemplify the dangers of not allowing wealth to flow freely is a village Muslim official is consonant with the frequent depiction in Javanese texts of *santri* as stingy.[23] In another work, the *Wicara Kĕras*, Yasadipura II again condemns love of money, which is only permissible if it is used to finance the state or the army or given to the poor and deserving—again regarding money as something that should not be "dammed up".

Canto V adds *sabeng wanadri* or *samodra*, (making trips to the forest

---

[19] Although the second part of the title of this book (*kitab*) seems to be Arabic *bayān*, exposition or commentary, the compound *Sarahbayan* is not an Arabic construction. I am not sure which work is meant; one guess might be the *Bayān al-sirr* (see Kumar 1985:65) but this is a compendium relating to mysticism, and it seems more likely that some other commentary, relating to practice, is meant here.

[20] The *wuku* calendar is an indigenous Javanese calendar that was used for everyday purposes such as determining market days, but also for predicting the fate of individuals according to their date of birth. For the latter purpose it is still, like Western astrology, quite popular.

[21] The term used is *iladuni*, presumably a contraction of *ʿilm ladunī* knowledge imparted directly by God through mystic intuition, a Ṣufi concept.

[22] Canto III, stanza 32f.

[23] See e.g. Drewes 1978:37.

or sea) and *kasektin* (supernatural power) to the list of undesirable attachments. As well as these numerous prohibitions, the text puts great emphasis on correctness in all areas of deportment—as for example in the following areas:

Clothing. Here again[24] Yasadipura displays the enormous attention to detail found in other sections. He lays out the intricate, worldly-rank-and-occasion-oriented rules governing the choice of batik pattern and other aspects of Javanese clothing. Even here, however, the influence of Islam is apparent, in this case in Yasadipura's commendation of the practice of the *ulama* of dressing themselves as if they were dressing a corpse—which is in fact a very different attitude to clothing from the careful distinctions of pattern and style of Javanese, and especially court Javanese, attire that he has just been laying down.

Friendship. Canto V gives advice against making friends with those who are *bodo* (brainless) or *tanpa budi* (ill-bred) or *tan rahayu* (malevolent, evil) or *tan bisa ing sastra* (illiterate) or *pasĕk* (heretics—from the Arabic singular *fāsiq*) or *drĕngki* (envious, ill-wishing) as well as positive recommendations about making friends with those who are *bĕrbudi* (well-bred), *wicaksana* (wise), *sujanma kang gĕḍe ngamalira/ngamal saleh* (good people who are pious and full of good works). Conversely, as a friend one has a duty not to reveal other people's secrets, and to be steadfast (*mantĕp*) in friendship.

Eating. Canto VI gives detailed instructions for the etiquette to be followed here. Muḥammad ate only once a day, at mid-day, and always said *bismillāh* before and *al-ḥamdu li'llāh* after eating. In addition, one must follow the Yudanagara,[25] being polite and neat, sitting in the proper fashion, not with the feet out or the knees up, and not talking while eating. One should offer food politely to guests, and not urge them to talk; nor should one ever finish eating before they do. As a guest you must similarly be well-behaved and not criticise what you are offered either out loud or internally. This is reinforced

[24] Canto III stanzas 6–25.

[25] This is a story centring on the characters Koja Jajahan and a king, intended to provide lessons on statecraft. It seems that Yasadipura regards it principally as a source of instruction on manners, however.

by the story of Moses who while on a journey with the *umma* prayed for food from heaven on condition that no one should criticise it: when some did presume to say that there was one defect, in that there were plenty of side-dishes but no fresh vegetables, it all disappeared into the heavens again. When your wife serves you food at home, do not wolf it down or criticise it if it is not to your taste—a few tactful words afterwards about what you like are enough. Don't regard cooking as a trivial matter—it is our link to life. Do not be gluttonous, or you will die young. Be moderate in everything. Carrying out *tapa* for the whole of your life brings many benefits. Do not get into the habit of having an early morning meal, this will darken your heart and dull your wits. If you eat until you are sated, you will be irritable and sleepy, your sharpness of mind will be dulled. Eating to satiety is only appropriate for those who do heavy work such as lifting and ploughing—such people are described as *bangsa badan* (physical people)—not for *priyayi* who have to use their minds and hearts: they are the *bangsa ati* (spiritual people).[26]

Sleeping, going out, staying in. Canto VII gives detailed prescriptions on these matters, laying down the proportion of the day it is right to spend sleeping (eight hours in total) and explaining how Allah descends in the last third of the night (*lingsir wĕngi*)[27]—a Muslim belief, not an older Javanese one—at which time one should, if possible, wake up. Earnest prayers (*salat kajat*) at *lingsir wĕngi* of *malĕm Jumungah* (the eve of Friday) will be granted. Yasadipura II points out the bad effects of sleeping when the sun is up, or taking too long an afternoon sleep except occasionally when one is very tired. The direction in which one should sleep is towards the west, the *kiblat* (*qibla*), like a dead man, and sleeping towards another direction has a baneful effect on one's livelihood, friendship, or health.

Receiving guests (Canto VIII). Standards of reception required for everyday acquaintances and for guests from afar differ: the former may be idle callers who disturb one's official work, the latter must be well received, even if you have to pawn your ceremonial lance to provide refreshments, for this is the *adat* of all Javanese. If you receive

[26] Stanzas 28–29.
[27] *Lingsir wĕngi* is one of the traditional Javanese divisions of the night, usually given as from midnight or 1 a.m. to 3 a.m., but sometimes as from 2 a.m. to 6 a.m.

a visitor who is of superior rank, you must receive him with due ceremony and sit before him in the proper fashion, with bowed head and hands resting in your lap, speaking softly, and taking care not to appear above yourself. The old must be well received, but those who are old and wise must receive superior distinction. If a *fakir* comes and asks something from you, give it without delay if you have it—in this way you will not cut off God's mercy, for our livelihood has its origins with God. Envoys must be shown the same distinction and honour as their masters when they visit you. If you have to give a message to an envoy, make it as short as possible so that no confusion will arise.

Speech (Canto IX). This section begins with an injunction to avoid *tĕkabur/kibir* (overweening conceit) *ujub* (the desire to impress), *riya* (the desire for praise and prominence), *sumungah* (boastfulness), *duraka* (speaking ill of others) and *dora* (lying)—note the complex range of Javanese, Sanskrit, and Arabic terms for the faults of mankind. By speaking ill of others you add their sins to your own; by lying you darken your heart: it is as if your house was in darkness and you had no lamps to light it and guard your possessions. In addition, lying will make your rank (*darajat*) decline and you will sink to the most lowly station. Don't criticise people, don't speak without a reason, don't tell jokes or pointless or irreligious stories, or speak for the sake of speaking, don't be given to joking (*sĕsĕmbranan*) which will destroy the gracious and winning modesty and reserve (*kajatmikan*) you should have and also wipe out your store of *tapa brata*, causing a decline in your rank. Good-Fortune (*Kī Bĕgja*) will desert you and Ill-Luck (*Kī Cilaka*) be with you day and night.

Since speech is an activity involving other people of different kinds and conditions, Yasadipura II goes on to give the guidelines the young *priyayi* should observe. When conversing in a large gathering do not be the first to speak and do not hasten to draw the discussion to a conclusion: this should be left to the most senior person. Observe the Yudanagara.[28] Even when speaking with those whose rank is higher than yours, you must weigh their utterances so as to decide whether they come from the evil passions and devils (*hawa nĕpsu kalawan ĕblis*), from the angels or from Adam: what is inspired by the first group

---

[28] See above n. 25.

must be rejected, that which comes from either of the last two is equally good. Lastly, he gives advice on how to respond if your Monarch (*gusti*) asks your opinion: answer according to your knowledge, and give examples. If your Monarch should be of an opinion which will lead to his shame, it is your duty to prevent this happening: to be an accomplice in reprehensible deeds is not true service, and those who think that it is do not truly love their Monarch but are simply desirous of praise and vainglorious (*yen gustinira arsa/pikir ingkang nĕmpuh/sanadyan tumibeng nisṭa/tumurunga milya anut anglabuhi/aywa mĕngĕng ing cipta/yeku dudu pasuwitan kaki/pan sayĕktining wong asuwita/ingkang mangkana pikire/pikir suwitan iku/wĕtune tan ngeman ing gusti/amung mburu aleman/anjurung kumlungkung*).

1.1 *Perspectives on Society*

The *Sasana Sunu* does not use a word that could be considered an equivalent of this concept, focusing instead on the moral formation of the elite. But it seems to me that there is an emergent conceptualisation of society as something broader than the ruler-subject relationship; and certainly ethnographic material from this period provides striking evidence of the complex organisation of Javanese regional society and the formidable socialisation of the Javanese.[29] Canto X, in laying down the proper behaviour for young *priyayi* as they receive appointments, provides some insights on how society was perceived to be organised, and, to a lesser extent, on how it really operated. It begins by advising the young men not to complain if they are appointed to a low post such as a village *bĕkĕl*.[30] If that is their lot, they must master the requirements of the job, set out under the headings *saguna*, *satata*, and *satau*. *Saguna* means knowing all about the farmer's equipment: harrow, plough, sickle, crowbar, different types of axes and hoes, adzes and choppers, as well as about livestock. They must also work diligently in the fields, and not relax their efforts; when they have a good harvest they must

[29] See Kumar 1996 ch. 3.

[30] Court-based appanage holders left the administration of the populations assigned to them in the hands of local tax-collectors called *bĕkĕl* who gathered the land-rent (*pajĕg*) and some other taxes, of which they received a percentage. For the most part they were from the upper echelon of village society and on the lowest rung of the hierarchy of officials under the appanage system: see diagram in Carey 1986:69.

surrender the correct amount to their superior as tax when it is due. If their land is taken away from them they must not resist and fight.[31] Yasadipura II says that if the young men behave in this way they will be despised and cut off from the *priyayi* class. *Satata* means knowing the ways of the farmers, providing the *santri* with rice-fields, and not taking any part of the *zakat* and *fitrah.*[32] They should also appoint as a *kabayan*[33] someone who is strong and of good character.[34] They should build a fence around the village and be hospitable to visitors. *Satau* means maintaining the *adat* of the villages of the area[35]—and not setting up your own *adat.* They should not allow bad people to gather in their area; and should govern the common people (lit. little people, *wong cilik*) in such a way that they know what they are doing. If there is a thief among them, forgive him, but if he does not stop his evil-doing drive him away so that he does not contaminate others. Set up a mosque and see that everyone goes there on Fridays:[36] If the population is strong in *ibadah* (observance of the rules of Islam) there will be few who fall into evils such as

[31] Carey notes that on the replacement of the appanage holder in the royal capital, an all too frequent occurrence usually entailing the appointment of a new *bĕkĕl,* it often happened that the current *bĕkĕl* would abscond with the cash advances from the cultivators or refuse point blank to make way for the new appointee. This was the most frequent cause of the numerous "village wars" (*prang desa*) which plagued the countryside of south-central Java at this time and which one Dutch traveller referred to as being almost a daily occurrence in the years immediately preceding the Java war (Carey 1986:76).

[32] Paying *zakat* (*zakāt*) is one of the five pillars of the faith, and there are precise specifications about the types of property subject to *zakat* and the rate to be paid. The *zakat* money is used for the poor, slaves, debtors, travellers, and those in the service of God. *Fitrah* (*fitra*) is a charitable contribution usually of about a *gantang* of rice made by every member of the mosque congregation at the end of the fasting month, for the purpose of allowing the poor to celebrate the great annual festival at the end of the fast. It is also known as *zakat badan* to distinguish it from the true *zakat* levied on property. Participation by *priyayi* in the collection and particularly in determining the distribution of these religious contributions opened opportunities for misappropriation, and there were occasions when members of the *santri* community complained that officials had acted improperly in this way. See Kumar 1996:44.

[33] An official in the village government.

[34] Here the printed text reads "who does not smoke opium" instead of "of good character".

[35] Referred to as the *mancapat/mancalima,* four-sets and five-sets, since villages were traditionally conceptualised in groups of four, at the compass points, around a centre. This four-five compass classification is very old and is depicted in textile patterns, and correlated with colours and the five days of the market week.

[36] Note the assumption in this passage that the rural areas to which the *priyayi* would be posted could be assumed not to have mosques.

gambling and opium-smoking. Remember that poverty[37] is the root of crime. Once again, there is an emphasis on what we would term the social benefits of a strong religious commitment among the village population.

Yasadipura next lays down the right way to serve at the capital (*nagari*) for those who are appointed there. They must be diligent (*taběri*, a word that occurs frequently in this type of discussion). If they have not yet been granted rice-fields (as appanage lands), they should not reveal a desire for them but reconcile themselves to living in the *pasewanan*.[38] They should be humble in their dealings with their fellow *priyayi*, and be very attentive to the instructions of their superiors, outwardly and inwardly. They must remember that the Monarch is the representative of God, and that he will be just to his subordinates.[39] Towards one's fellows in service one should not be too quick to criticise, and one should sincerely commiserate with them when they incur their master's anger: one day it may be your turn, and your companions in service are like your brothers (in such a situation).

Yasadipura then deals with the rank-order of those to whom one owes the deepest respect (in Javanese, those who are *siněmbah*, i.e. receive the act of homage). First is the ruler; second your parents; third your parents-in-law; fourth your *guru*; and fifth your older brothers. *Mantri* must pay this respect to *Tumenggung*s, and *Tumenggung*s in turn to those of the blood royal (*santana*). With this last, unelaborated statement Yasadipura II brings us up against one of the central principles of Javanese society: the concept that descent, or to use the old-fashioned term blood, was of central importance in the formation of a man, and that royal blood conferred a social rank higher than any other—and in fact sprang from spiritual pre-eminence. The ruler's close relatives, the *santana*, rank above those who have risen to high rank, that of *Mantri* and *Tumenggung*, in the service of the

---

[37] I.e. from gambling and opium-smoking?

[38] The *pasewanan* is a *pěnḍapa* (pavilion) in the palace forecourt, used for audiences. The implication is probably that one should be prepared to put in time at court, perhaps as a lowly *magang*.

[39] The gloss given for "just" is forgiving, long-suffering, benevolent, indicating the reliance on an outstanding ruler to see justice done which is also evident in the messianic movements centring around the installation of a Just King (*Ratu Adil*). In the many Javanese discussions on kingship, kings are traditionally classified as low, middling, and outstanding (*nisṭa, madya*, and *utama*), a classification that goes back to Sanskrit texts from the Old Javanese period.

ruler and the state. Yasadipura II justifies this reverence by reference to the *dalil*[40] which commands us to revere Allah and His Messenger, and those who have government over us. The canto ends with the instruction to the young men that when they become *priyayi* they must put to use four *budi*: those of the *priyayi*, *santri*, *sudagar* (merchants) and farmers (*tani*). *Budi* is an untranslatable, much-used, word meaning, in this instance, the best normative conduct of the four groups named, who may perhaps be compared to the "estates" of French society of the *ancien régime*. The *budi* of the *priyayi* is to maintain the proprieties and good forms of social intercourse, not to behave in a common way, to dress appropriately, to be rather frugal in respect to food, to be careful and precise, to treat other people's opinions nicely, to be able to get people to work together, not to be afraid of suffering a personal loss, to be intelligent and civilised in action and thought (readers will appreciate how closely the work's emphasis on abstinence, restraint, understated refinement, cultivation, moral rectitude, the ability to work well with others and the observance of detailed rules concerning dress, speech, etc. are related to this idea of the *priyayi* code). The *budi* of the *santri* is to be pure and holy, to multiply the works of Allah and give thanks to Him. The *budi* of the farmer is to work long and hard at all sorts of work, heavy and light. He is never envious or given to talking about other people's affairs, never presumptuous or arrogant. He is steadfast (*mantĕp*, another concept on which great value is placed) and in earnest and stout-hearted about his work, not given to time-wasting and shirking. Finally the farmer is *tĕmĕn*, which can be translated as "sincere" or "honest" but has the interesting twist of being used of the attitude of inferiors towards their superiors.[41] Thus the young *priyayi* whom Yasadipura II addresses should imitate the humble farmer in being *tĕmĕn* in their work for the ruler: it is inconceivable that the ruler should be asked to display the same quality towards them.[42] The *budi* of the merchant is to be calculating, economical and careful and treat his undertakings with respect. So the task of the *priyayi* therefore is to combine the special code of his own estate, the purity of

---

[40] A legal proof, in this case one of the texts from the Qur'ān or *Ḥadīth* in which Muḥammed exhorts his followers to obedience to him and to those in authority over them. An example is *sūra* 4:59, which reads: "You who believe! Obey God, obey the Messenger (Muhammad), and those in authority among you!".

[41] I owe this insight, among many others, to Dr S. Supomo.

[42] Moertono 1963:97.

the *santri*, the earnest application of the farmer, and the careful calculation of the merchant.

Canto XI deals with the responsibilities of high officials, *Mantri* and *Bupati*, and the highest of all, the *Patih*, and their all-important relationship with the Monarch. When speaking of the *Patih* Yasadipura II uses the well-known Javanese trope of the *kris* and the sheath: the *Patih*, the sheath, must follow the shape of the *kris*, the Monarch; and if the *kris* fits well into its sheath, the state will be safe from all evils and the sharpness of the *kris* will not be in evidence.

Cantos XII–XIII deal with the question of what causes a decline in one's rank, and the flight of one's *wahyu*, the last a concept of absolute centrality to the *Sasana Sunu* which will be defined below. The first cause of a decline in rank Yasadipura describes is taking food from the mouths of the poor (the *wong cilik*), who have so little and whose life is so hard. It seems to me that in its emphasis on the treatment due to *fakir* who visit one, in the emphasis on seeing that the *zakat* and *fitrah* reach their proper destination (see above), and in this statement about one's moral responsibility to the poor, we see how Islam has reinforced the strong Javanese sense of responsibility to those below one, rather than the equally strong Javanese emphasis on responsibility, of a different kind, to those above one in the social hierarchy.

Following the *hawaning ati* (passions of the heart) instead of *wajib* (duty) will certainly have a bad effect on one's *wahyu*. Building an excessively large and fine house is another thing that can only cause a decline in one's fortunes. Stories from both the left (*pangiwa*) and the right (*panĕngĕn*) traditions prove this: the strong and wealthy *danawa* (demons of the *Mahābhārata* stories depicted in *wayang*) and the Arabian kings who constructed palaces rivalling heaven all came to bad ends. If you do your work well you will get real praise from your Monarch, whereas even if you have a fine house, if your work is behind-hand and full of mistakes you will certainly arouse his anger. Yasadipura II lists the signs that a man's *wahyu* is about to leave him: if he is repeatedly warned not to do something, but nevertheless goes ahead and does it, or if he wrongs or mistreats someone despite attempts to restrain him. Here *wahyu* is described as being like the soul, very pure and, if one could see it, like a clear light, shining like the moon. "Small *wahyu*" (*wahyu alit*) is like a clear star. If it is asked to be party to a bad deed, it becomes disturbed and angry, and then appears dull and dirty. It will certainly flee elsewhere, since there is no lack of places for it to perch. It will seek a heart that is pure and wise, fortunate and sage, for there it will be cared for. To keep your *wahyu* is difficult, but becomes easier with practice. You must be watchful and mindful, remembering God and his commands, doing good in the world. You must reduce your eating and sleeping, in order to obtain rank. Be familiar with Javanese and Arabic literature. Know the Islamic Law, and the established *adat* and customs. Be steadfast without anxiety. Associate with those who may not be clever but are charitable to the poor and needy (*pěkir miskin*). Good deeds are a part of a shining *wahyu*, the sign of God's love.

This is the most extensive definition of the central concept of *wahyu* and those who have it provided by Yasadipura II.[43] In Javanese literature, kings are generally depicted as the principal vehicles of *wahyu*. A Javanese Babad dealing with the Chinese War that began in 1740 tells how when Mangkuněgara I was born the reigning king's *wahyu* moved from him to Mangkuněgara's mother, so that the baby was born with a special glow, and many interpreted this to mean that he would become a great leader in war:[44] we saw above this understanding of *wahyu* as a physical manifestation of light (a star, a ball of light) in the *Sasana Sunu*. Although the word is from the Arabic *waḥy* and means "revelation" it has become naturalised in Java to such an extent that there is a popular *wayang lakon* centring on the struggle between the Pandawas and Korawas for the *wahyu*, which underlines its association with royalty, legitimisation and the right to power already suggested by the story about the birth of Mangkuněgara I. As the concept is presented in Yadadipura's *Sasana Sunu*, it appears not as an exclusive attribute of prophets or the ruler but as a quality which all members of the elite can aspire to possess, and which has a sort of Indic, *karma*-like quality in that it is increased or decreased by good or bad deeds. In other words, the Javanese governing class has appropriated (not to say pirated) and redefined a term which in the rest of the Muslim world is identified with the Prophets (*nabi*, from Arabic singular *nabī*, plural *anbiyāʾ*) and above all with Muḥammad and the revelations made to him by God and recorded in the Qurʾān. They were not content to claim the lesser

[43] Yasadipura also speaks of *wahyu jali*, which is presumably from the Arabic *jalī* (evident, manifest, brilliant) from a base meaning "to shine, to be brilliantly evident".

[44] See Remmelink 1990:218. See also Kumar 1982:364.

form of illumination (*ilham*—Arabic *ilhām*) possessed by the *wali* (saints, friends of God—Arabic singular *walī*, plural awliyā'), but put themselves into the category of the Prophets, so much nearer to God.[45]

* * * * *

Islam has, therefore, a prominent but by no means exclusive position in the moral formation of the Javanese elite as laid down by Yasadipura II in this work. This is clear from the status given to the Left-hand tradition, the Hindu-Javanese, alongside the Right-hand, the Islamic, and the great prominence given to the practice of penance (*tapa*), the cultivation of death-in-life, from this Left-hand tradition. It will also be noted that Islamic concepts such as *adil* (*'adl*) and *wahyu* (*waḥy*) have been reinterpreted in such a way as to make them consistent with, and supportive of, the hierarchical structure of Javanese society, organised beneath the high centre of the king.

Apart from recognising the Left-hand or Hindu-Javanese tradition as being equally as important as the Islamic one, Yasadipura II puts great value on Javanese-ness. He repeatedly advises that Java's *adat* should be maintained, not changed, and that the young *priyayi* should not invent their own *adat*. He is, however, aware that certain important parts of Javanese *adat*, are actually contrary to Islam. Thus Canto XII, verses 22–32, counsels against an idolatrous deification or anthropomorphism of *krisses*, using material from both the Left- and Right-hand traditions. The point made is that the power of *krisses* is only an external one (*wasiyat lair*) as is evident from the cases of Siyung Wanara of Pajajaran in the Babad story[46] and Aswatama and the magic weapon Cundamanik.[47] It is much better to have inner spiritual power (*wasiyat ati*), as in the case of Sunan Giri, the *wali* who

---

[45] See Macdonald 1926:281.

[46] Siyung Wanara (later title, Arya Banyak Wiḍe) was the son of a ruler of Pajajaran whose father attempted to put him to death as a baby because of the prediction of a holy-man the father had unrighteously murdered. Siyung Wanara became a *kris*-smith (*panḍe*) of great supernatural power and imprisoned his father in an iron cage, subsequently becoming king of Pajajaran himself. The most accessible version of the Babad story is found in the edition of the Meinsma version by Olthof 1941:13–17.

[47] The story of Aswatama (Sanskrit Aśwatthāmā) occurs in the *Bhāratayuddha* section of the *Mahābhārata*. In it, Aswatama seeks to defeat the God Krĕsna (Sanskrit Kṛṣṇa) and the Pandawa (Paṇḍawa), who have come to take his magic jewel, by loosing the world-shaking fire-arrow Brahmaśirah. Krĕsna counters this weapon with one of his own, the Śirśāntyani, and so Aswatama has to surrender his jewel and is punished with 1,000 years torment and disgrace for loosing this dreadful weapon: See Supomo 1993: Canto 51, 157f. and 251f.

when his state was attacked by the heathen forces of Majapahit threw down the pen he was using, which thereupon changed into a *kris* that on its own put the Majapahit army to flight. The veneration of the supernatural potency of *krisses* deplored by Yasadipura II is still by no means a thing of the past in Javanese society today. Stanza 33 says that, according to a prohibition of the ancestors, the *gamĕlan* should not be used at the *mamantu* (wedding) ceremony, and in fact the *gamĕlan* is prohibited by our religion (i.e. Islam). However, it is allowed (according to established custom) at the *tĕtakan* or *khitanan* (circumcision) and *tingkĕban* (seven-month ceremony for pregnant women) and in fact, though rather ostentatious, is in common use, especially among the king's courtiers. If you are in this position, when the *gamĕlan* begins to play you should say a prayer to God and to the ancestors who have made the prohibition, asking their forgiveness and permission to listen to the *gamĕlan*; and six days or a week beforehand you should make an offering in a secluded spot asking for a sign that your request is granted.

1.2 *Kingship*

A central pillar of Yasadipura II's program of instruction is his strong support for a hierarchical, king-centric polity, where subjects seek salvation by serving (*ngawula*) their king, which is for them a religious observance. In this all-pervasive hierarchy, the highest rank is determined by blood descent, with the ruler at the very top, followed by those of royal blood, the *santana*, followed by the four estates of society, of which that of *priyayi* is higher than those of *sudagar, santri*, and *tani*. These differences of rank, as well as the very important internal differentiation among different ranks of *priyayi*, are marked in every detail of speech, dress, and deportment. The Arabic terms *drajat* (*daraja*) and *kurmat* (*karāma*) are mustered for support and legitimisation of this hierarchy, and the supreme spiritual value is serving the ruler. As far as this last is concerned, in Canto IV stanzas 35–9 Yasadipura II says that carrying out your allotted tasks in the service of the Monarch can be compared to prayer (performance of the five daily prayers—Indonesian *salat*, Arabic *ṣalāt*); your Monarch is the true *Kalifah*—a sentiment that puts serving the ruler on a par with serving God. By contrast, Islamic political philosophers generally stress—while enjoining the obedience of his subjects to the king—the king's subordination to the Law in this life and subjection to divine judgement in the next. Indeed, it is not infrequent to find statements that the pious man should not associate with courts or serve kings.[48] In an Islamic work on kingship, the *Taj us-Salatin*—the Javanese version of which is attributed to Yasadipura I[49] and which would therefore have been well known to Yasadipura II—the king is depicted as personally responsible on the day of judgement for any hardship or oppression his subjects suffer. If he does not serve them well, the pains of hell are his reward. In this text the exemplary stories of good kings portray them as spending their nights going around their realm disguised in common clothes, finding out the sufferings of the least in the kingdom and carrying on their own shoulders sacks of food for the unfortunate.[50] Though from pre-Islamic times Javanese works on kingship lay great stress on the king's responsibility for the material welfare of his subjects, neglect of which will lead to his downfall (whereas in the Islamic text it imperils his *salvation*), going around the kingdom in rags like a coolie hardly seems congruous with the Javanese ideal of royal dignity and aloofness.

Thus at this period Javanese kings retained their old central position and derived from Islam both confirmation of their martial role[51] and the light of prophecy (*wahyu*), by appropriation. As we have seen, the hope for and dispensation of justice is also appropriated to kings.

* * * * *

Contrasting *Pancasila* with the *Sasana Sunu*, we can see that old concepts have disappeared and new ones have taken their place; and that even though Arabic words are used in both cases, there has been a quantum shift in the conceptualisation of the political order as a whole. Somewhere between the time of Yasadipura II and 1945, Islam has helped to bring about a revolution in Indonesian social and political thought, introducing a whole swathe of new concepts. These concepts relate to the collegial and the procedural, rather than to the hierarchical, personal, and patrimonial. Also, these new concepts flowed from Islam into the mainstream of political thinking at a time that is rightly regarded as the darkest part of the colonial night for Islam, a time of political impotence.

---

48 See e.g. Lambton 1981:285.

49 See Winter 1911:352.

50 See the 7th chapter of this work, of which three editions are fairly accessible, i.e. Bukhari 1966; Jusuf 1979; and Bokhāri 1878.

51 Dealt with in another of Yasadipura II's works, the *Wicara Kĕras*.

Yasadipura II's political viewpoint reflects the old world of Kingship and service by an elite with a special moral claim to their position of guardianship of the voiceless "little people". This claim is justified by an extraordinarily rigorous program of moral training, by the performance of *tapa*, and by an unself-seeking, intelligent, and laborious service of the ruler (*ngawula*) all of which leads to the bestowal of *wahyu*. Javanese tradition stresses the development of certain personal qualities, both in the ruler and in his servants. Islam, though it is also interested in personal virtue, introduces more of a focus on the collective, society. In the *Sasana Sunu* ideas with a communal or social aspect are already beginning to be evident (see the stress on the socially beneficial outcomes of *ibadah*—Arabic: *ʿibāda*). By the time of the *Pancasila*, however, the focus on society has been made explicit through the widespread currency of the term *masyarakat*, replacing the focus on the ruler. The old concept of service to the ruler has been replaced by the concepts of consultation (*musyawarah*) and consensus (*mupakat*). The governing elite are no longer there by virtue of *tapa* leading to the bestowing of *wahyu*, but because of their function of representation (*perwakilan*) and representation not of kings or princes but of the common people—the *rakyat*. This also is a new term, replacing Yasadipura's *wong cilik* (little people). It has made possible the abstract form *kerakyatan* to stand as the indigenous equivalent of "democracy" in the constitutional preamble and elsewhere, whereas the associations of *wong cilik* would not have allowed this. These Arabic terms and others are also enshrined in the new nation's most important political institutions, such as the *Dewan Perwakilan Rakyat* (Indonesian parliament), and the *Majelis Permusyawaratan Rakyat* (People's Consultative Assembly, which elects the President and sets the broad outlines of state policy).

Only in the *Pancasila*'s stress on the superordinate position of wisdom in the words *hikmat kebijaksanaan*, an Arabic-Sanskrit compound such as occur frequently in the *Sasana Sunu* and other works of this period, and which contains in the modern Malay form *bijaksana* the quality of *wicaksana* which the *Sasana Sunu* praises,[52] do we find an echo of the old justification of the special position of a morally cultivated elite. This concept of the need to modify democracy by the leadership of the wise was elaborated by Ki Hadjar Dewantoro into a proposal for a notably paternalistic polity in his *Demokrasi dan*

---

[52] *Wicaksana* was also the cognomen of one of the Sunans of Surakarta.

Leiderschap. However, the special status of royal blood and the division of society into estates have disappeared (unless one takes the functional groups of the New Order as a descendant of the latter). Another bridge between the world of Yasadipura II and that of Sukarno is in the value placed on justice, but the former sees justice as a function of royal benevolence, whereas though Sukarno does refer to the old belief in the *Ratu Adil*, the Just King, he reinterprets this as a search for *social* justice based on economic equality.

Thus, it seems that if one may not have *Pancasila plus* Islamic concepts, *Pancasila minus* Islamic concepts would have some very large holes in it. It is notable that the *Pancasila* contains almost nothing in the way of terms derived from European languages, with the exception of the adjective *sosial* (and I would not be at all surprised if this owes its presence simply to the awkwardness of an adjectival form of *masyarakat*). Of course it would be naive to assume that because there are no Dutch- or English-derived words, there is no influence of Western thought. But neither should we assume that the Arabic terms are used only as the best available translations of Western concepts.

Early in this century, Tjokroaminoto's *Islam dan Sosialisme* assessed the political ideals of Islam in terms of how far they conformed to the western formula of Liberty, Equality, and Fraternity: it is time now, surely, to look at Islam in its own terms. A fuller study than has been possible in a paper of this length would look at the way in which the terms discussed here were used in other Islamic societies, not in order to impose a sort of Arabic essentialism on their specifically Indonesian usage and context, but to develop some comparisons that might be illuminating. Even more importantly, it should look at the history of the usage of these terms in the Indonesian media over the period between Yasadipura II and Sukarno. This would involve inter alia a better knowledge of the Islamic presses that developed in 19th-century Java,[53] as well as the leading role of Islam in popular education.

* * * * *

[53] I owe this suggestion to Dr Ian Proudfoot.

2. *Conclusion*

The earliest Western view of Indonesia was of a provincial form of exogenous great civilisations—first and most notably the Indic, and later and to a lesser degree the Islamic. Van Leur later claimed not only that Indonesians were selective in what they borrowed, taking only what fitted in with existing structures and values, but also that the externally-derived elements remained a thin and flaking glaze. Yasadipura II's analysis, in which Arabic-derived terms like *wahyu, kurmat, darajat,* etc. are used to confirm established Javanese ideas about the king-centric, personal/patrimonial, hierarchical polity ruled by a morally-legitimated aristocracy suggests a deeper and more dynamic mixing, though one in which indigenous values are still dominant. But the terms used in the *Pancasila* and related texts, with their shift towards a collective, collegial, abstract, procedural, institutional and relatively egalitarian ethos reveal a more open and dynamic engagement with Islam. From the perspective taken here, it seems that Indonesians neither abdicated their judgement before Islam nor took only what confirmed existing arrangements, but rather drew from Islam those skills and concepts that were needed at different times. For it is clear that needs varied greatly from time to time, and that the history of the interaction of the Javanese and Islamic traditions is a dynamic and complex one. Islam has been used as a resource in many different ways. Some of these were quite utilitarian, as for instance the adoption of Islamic medical skills.[54] Others related to more abstract ideas. in which it is evident that there has been a long dialogue between indigenous Indonesian and Islamic concepts. In this paper I have shown how at one point in time Islamic concepts such as *wahyu* were used to buttress royal power and social hierarchy, and the moral claim of an elite to wise governorship of society. The martial tradition of Islam also reinforced the military tradition of Javanese kingship, though in other realms Islam had already introduced new perspectives and ideas. Later, the *Pancasila* text reveals an important new development towards a focus on society, not the king, and on

[54] The Pangerans of Kadilangu, an Islamic "theocracy" on the north coast, were the personal physicians of the Sunans of Surakarta, for instance, and there are many instances in Javanese and Malay literature of conversion to Islam of a ruler being the consequence of a cure successfully effected by a Muslim from overseas. In the colonial period, Muslim "dignitaries" were used as vaccinators. The importance of healing for conversion has already been pointed out by A.H. Johns (1961:15).

the institutional, collegial, procedural and widely participatory polity rather than on the moral formation of an elite (though, as we have seen, echoes remain of the claim of the wise to govern). Islamic concepts (but new and different ones) have once again been recruited, so that a *Pancasila minus* Islam is hardly conceivable.

This dialogue with Islam has been an extremely intelligent and fruitful one, but Western scholars have in general notably failed to recognise this adequately. There has been a dominant tendency to try to infer from the record of historical events large and ill-defined abstractions about the reasons for the acceptance of Islam,[55] as in the debate about whether political or economic motives (inseparable in any case) were more important. The political and religious writings of Indonesians themselves, as the small selection used here reveals, are a much more reliable and illuminating basis for such judgements.

[55] More recently, an attempt to generalise from anthropological evidence has been made by Reid (1984) who argues that the success of Islam owes much to its ability to cater for pre-Islamic feasting of the dead. Reid argues on the basis of evidence from Toraja, Sumba, Philippine and other societies that this was the central feature of pre-Islamic religion in South-East Asia and that "The extravagant feasting which non-Muslim parts of the archipelago associate pre-eminently with death-rituals, was transferred among Muslims to weddings" (16). Whatever the case in Torajaland etc., this is clearly wrong for Java, where the wedding ceremony with its Javanese (i.e. not Indic or in any way imported) mythology is *the* central rite of Javanese religion from court to village. It may be that the polluting character of death led to the rituals associated with it being hived off to foreign religions, first Hinduism and then Islam, whereas the marriage ritual (like rituals of pregnancy and rice cultivation) retained its Javanese character throughout.

MUSLIM CREATIVE COMMERCIAL MINORITIES

Some Examples c. 1800–1950

Christine Dobbin

Whatever may be said about Islam and its relationship to a capitalist sector in the heart land of the Middle East at particular periods of time,[1] Islam found itself fully capable of adjusting to the "spirit of capitalism" in the European empires on the periphery of the Islamic heartland. The Dutch in the East Indies, the British in India and the French in Algeria all made use of minority groups to establish their commercial supremacy from the very commencement of their empires in particular port cities. The attempts of the British in Bombay and the Dutch in Batavia to attract Parsis and Chinese respectively into their commercial sphere are well known.[2] Muslim minorities were equally attracted to the opportunities European empires opened up. This paper deals with three in particular: the Isma'ilis in Western India and East Africa, the Mizabis in Algeria and the Baweanese in Java.

The main thrust of the paper is to investigate what were the particular characteristics which enabled these Muslim minorities to take advantage of the new opportunities introduced with European rule. Two, the Mizabis and the Isma'ilis, originated in homelands that were marginal, extremely dry and subject to harsh conditions of existence, the Mizabis in a group of oases in the south of Algeria and the Isma'ilis in the treeless, barren region of Kutch, Western India. The Mizabi oases nevertheless stood astride important desert trade routes, and Kutch also had a sea coast enabling its inhabitants to seek their fortunes elsewhere, including East Africa. The Baweanese inhabited a small island 120 km north of Java, with insufficient rice land and a tradition of sea-going. All three groups were strongly attracted to their own form of Islamic belief and practice. The Mizabis were Ibadites, following a highly particularistic doctrine and rules for

---

[1] For still the best discussion of this subject, see Rodinson 1974.

[2] Dobbin 1989:110–111.

living. The Ismaʿilis espoused a highly syncretistic form of Shiʿism, with many Hindu practices and unique institutions for worship. The Baweanese practised an extremely orthodox form of Sunni Islam, characterised by sending as many young men as possible to the leading religious schools of Java.

Although these groups did not comprise the great middlemen minorities used as partners by the European powers, they formed intermediate minorities and an investigation of some of the theoretical issues related to these minorities adds something to the debate on Islam and capitalism. In many ways the three communities to be discussed here, operating their business life in the form of commercial diasporas stretching over considerable geographic distance, provide examples of a theme Max Weber turned to immediately after he wrote *The Protestant Ethic and the Spirit of Capitalism.* Maxime Rodinson calls the Mizabis "the Puritans of Islam",[3] but Max Weber in 1906 after a visit to the United States turned instead to the theme of sectarianism and capitalism. In *The Protestant Sects and the Spirit of Capitalism* he stressed the role of particular religious institutions in the businessman's undertakings. Referring to the Baptist church, he writes:

> Admission to the congregation is recognised as an absolute guarantee of the moral qualities of a gentleman, especially of those qualities required in business matters. Baptism secures to the individual the deposits of the whole region and unlimited credit without any competition. He is a "made man". Further observation confirmed that these, or at very least similar phenomena, occur in the most varied regions. In general, *only* those men had success in business who belonged to Methodist or Baptist or other *sects* or sectlike conventicles. When a sect member moved to a different place, or if he was a travelling salesman, he carried the certificate of his congregation with him, and thereby he found not only easy contact with sect members but, above all, he found credit everywhere. . . . It is crucial that sect membership meant a certificate of moral qualification and especially of business morals for the individual.[4]

It is, then, not Puritanism which is the key here, but the existence of a diaspora of commercial entrepreneurs with a distinctive identity, bound to one another as a moral community with common values and principles.[5] Like Protestant sectarianism, certain forms of Islam can further this identity.

---

[3] Rodinson 1974:115.
[4] Weber 1948:305.
[5] Cohen 1971:267.

1. *The Isma'ilis*

The Indian group which dominated the British push into East Africa in the late nineteenth century were the Isma'ilis (commonly called Khojas) of Kutch and Bombay. These imperial collaborators had a history of adapting to challenge, whether geographical, religious or political. Kutch had a unique geographical location, treeless and barren but with an extensive coastline and well-established ports which gave an opening into the world of the Gulf and East Africa. Famine and recurrent scarcity gave birth to a mentality favouring outmigration and also favouring trade, both by sea and by land.[6]

A mentality open to change also favoured change in the religious sphere. Kutch was very open to Islamic conversion and gradually gained a high percentage of Muslims in the population. In 1821, and for the rest of the century, it was stated that more than one third of the population was Muslim.[7] The form of Islam brought to Kutch was highly suited to local beliefs, where there was a tradition of worshipping local saints and a belief in divinely reincarnated human teachers according to the spiritual needs of the time. Isma'ili missionaries in the fourteenth and fifteenth centuries gained their first success among the commercial caste of the Lohanas, followers of the Hindu god Vishnu. The missionaries represented a Shi'a sect, the Shi'a Imami Isma'ilis, which believed in a divinely inspired and infallible *imam*. These doctrines proved congenial. The ideas concerning the *imam* were acceptable and the Shi'a practice of *taqiyya* or permissible dissimulation of belief in difficult situations meant that Hindu beliefs and practices could be retained by converts.[8] The Isma'ilis, then, possessed a dual identity through which their commercial concerns could only prosper.

Further, they possessed a unique Islamic institution. From the beginning the missionaries established Isma'ili religious lodges, the so-called *jamatkhana*,[9] where prayer and community administration were conducted. A mixture of religious beliefs prevailed in the *jamatkhana*, but administrative matters gradually evolved in a particular form. From the very earliest days Isma'ilis were exhorted to save their money

---

[6] *Gujerat State Gazetteers: Kutch District* 1971:116–118.
[7] Ibid. 115.
[8] Ibid. 128–129. Also Enthoven 1920:217–27 and Morris 1958:458–459.
[9] Enthoven 1920:221.

in order to pay the tithe and also other minor contributions to their revealed *imam* living in Persia. The tithe was paid every month, while there were also occasionally extraordinary levies on Isma'ilis' possessions. Although these funds were often spent on improvements for the Isma'ili community in the place of collection, they were regarded as the personal property of the *imam* and were controlled by his agents. These agents also advised on the *jamatkhana*'s election of a *mukhi* (treasurer) and *kamaria* (accountant). The *jamatkhana* also served as a council hall, where members voted on issues placed before them and were theoretically equal and at liberty to speak on any issue.[10]

Bombay was the home of India's commercial minorities. Like the Parsis from further south, by the early nineteenth century so many Isma'ilis had migrated from Kutch that Bombay had become their headquarters. By the 1840s it contained about 2,000 of them, mostly small traders selling parched rice but with some engaged already in more profitable ventures.[11] Common practice was to purchase items from the internal trade of Kutch, such as pulses, cloth and cottonseed, and sell them to wholesale traders in port towns and in Bombay. Gradually certain Bombay Isma'ilis expanded their commerce to more profitable items such as ivory, opium and silk, following other communities into the China trade.[12] By the 1850s certain Isma'ilis in Bombay had reached the position of *shetias* (leading merchants) and one, Habib Ibrahim, was already a shareholder in Bombay's first cotton mill.[13]

The newly acquired wealth of the community led to a series of schisms, in which those who were prospering tried to break away from their Persian *imam*, first of all declaring they were truly Sunnis and later adopting the Shi'a Twelver (Ithnā 'asherī) faith.[14] But the core of the community remained faithful to its peculiar doctrines and was strengthened when its spiritual leader, endowed with the title Aga Khan by the Persian Shah in 1834, arrived in Bombay in 1845 after political trouble in his homeland. From that time on the Aga Khan began to exert his spiritual authority very close to home, and his divine guidance was recognised by his followers. At the same

[10] Ibid. 221–222, 228–230.
[11] Perry 1853:113–114.
[12] *Gazetteers* 1971:290; Enthoven 1920:230.
[13] Dobbin 1989:20.
[14] Ibid. 114–15; Penrad 1988:232; Rizvi and King 1973:12–13.

time, to put matters on an even surer footing, it was also recognised by the British courts. The Aga Khan received a warm reception from the British establishment in Bombay and his followers gradually felt they no longer had need to practise concealment. Those Isma'ilis who wished to move away from the Aga Khan's authority and proclaim themselves Sunnis continued to challenge him, the outcome being the great Aga Khan case of 1866. The court determined that the community consisted of Shi'a Imami Isma'ilis bound by ties of spiritual allegiance to the hereditary *imam* of the Isma'ilis, who had absolute legal ownership of communal property.[15]

The Isma'ilis now possessed a set of institutions which served them well in their major economic enterprise, their collaboration with the British in the opening up of East Africa. In this enterprise, although other Indian communities were involved, theirs was the major contribution. Communal life in East Africa revolved around the *jamatkhana*, in which individuals and families were able to compete for power and prestige and were encouraged to look outside the community in order to increase their prosperity and their chance of dominance within it.[16] This competition also encouraged social mobility, as group loyalty placed emphasis on hiring from within the community, thus ensuring that it was entrepreneurial talent rather than social status which was offered business opportunities. A successful information network produced not only intense rivalry but also diffusion of information and access to credit, encouraging creative entrepreneurial behaviour.[17] Finally, of course, there was the role of the Aga Khan. The religious flexibility of earlier years, suitable to the beginning of entrepreneurial endeavours in Bombay, gave way to a clear identity and the acceptance of firm guidance which proved well suited for the Isma'ilis' East African commercial endeavours.

Kutchi vessels had a long history of trade with East Africa, but Isma'ili merchants were only actually present there from the early nineteenth century, particularly after the Imam of Muscat had moved his capital to Zanzibar in 1840. They were the agents of business houses in Kutch or Bombay and traded largely in ivory, gum-copal, slaves and British iron and printed cottons. Before long trade in Zanzibar was monopolised by several families and the Isma'ili agents,

---

[15] *Judgement* 1866: *passim*.
[16] Penrad 1988:231 and 233.
[17] Papanek 1972/73:19.

often poorly paid, went on to open commercial branches along the Swahili coast. With increasing British protection in the region, they were encouraged to finance caravans of Arab-Swahili traders and Europeans and then by the 1860s, to make their own first voyages into the interior and to establish posts on caravan routes. There they offered financial services, bartered cloth, wire and pearls for ivory, rhinoceros horn, ambergris and slaves and attached themselves to important personalities for protection.[18]

Some of these Ismaʿili agents became immensely successful merchants. Taria Topan, for example, arrived in Zanzibar in the 1840s to join his father. By the late 1860s he began to finance ventures to the interior, placing as his agents on the coast members of his family or other Ismaʿilis. On his return to Bombay in the 1880s he started new ventures to China, largely in tea and opium, and used his African earnings to finance these. The Ismaʿili community served him well. In 1852, at only the beginning of his commercial career, he was chosen *mukhi* of the Zanzibar *jamatkhana*, an indication of his commercial acumen, while on his return to Bombay he was made a member of the council charged with looking after the interests of the third Aga Khan in his minority.[19] Other successful merchants pushing into the interior were similarly active in their home *jamatkhana*.

The partition of Africa drew attention to the interior and other Ismaʿilis elaborated appropriate business techniques for their advance. Allidina Visram, the best known at the turn of the century, arrived in Zanzibar in 1877 from Kutch as a young apprentice to an old-established firm. Soon, working from the coast, he opened stapling posts in the interior, where imported goods could be sold for ivory and skins. But the opening of the Uganda railway in 1901 diverted his attention from the old caravan routes towards Uganda and Kenya, where he worked in partnership with the advancing British by establishing *duka* or shops which also operated as banking facilities and which encouraged the sale—and therefore production—of agricultural products such as groundnuts, chillies, sesame seed and cotton. Allidina Visram, by the early twentieth century, had established a mercantile empire of *duka*, bazaars and trading centres throughout East Africa, his thirty major branches stretching from Bombay through Mombasa and Bagamoyo deep into the interior. About 1909 he

---

[18] Penrad 1988:223 and 229.
[19] Ibid. 224–225.

entered industry, investing in furniture manufacturing and then in factories using local materials such as sesame seed and copra. Ultimately he entered the fledgling Uganda cotton industry, establishing a cotton ginnery at Kampala in 1912–14 which, together with another ginnery established by a Bombay firm in 1914, laid the foundations for the Indian role in the Uganda cotton industry.[20]

Allidina Visram's empire was based on the use of Isma'ili institutions. Those Isma'ilis, whether relatives or others, who were lower in the socio-economic scale were invited from India to staff his shops. These small, semi-independent *dukawallahs* ran the shops and acted as his agents, receiving supplies from him and providing him with local produce to sell on the international market. The agent was tied to the wholesaler not as an employee but by the granting of credit. His aim, of course, was to establish his own shop and to bring out fellow Isma'ilis in turn to act as agents.[21] Isma'ili solidarity—despite individual commercial rivalries—was based largely on the evolution of the role of the Aga Khan since the great law case of 1866. The third Aga Khan, who succeeded in 1885, had a British upbringing and a talent for organisation. The Isma'ilis retained their *jamatkhana* in East Africa, but because the Aga Khan had become enormously personally wealthy, the contributions raised were often used for the welfare of the community, for setting up Isma'ilis in business and the provision of food and shelter. The Isma'ili law of inheritance further assisted families to maintain their capital, diverging as it did from the more fragmentary dispensation of true Islamic law.[22]

The Aga Khan (d. 1957) established a number of institutional changes for the Isma'ilis of East Africa. He took pride in what he called the community's "fluidity", which was coupled with the unassailability of his own position.[23] Hence there developed, above the local *jamatkhana*, a system of regional councils, beginning with the Zanzibar Isma'ili council at the turn of the century. It has been pointed out that these organisational forms have been advantageous for the Isma'ilis' business dealings. From the beginning intense competition for control of the institutions has taken place among the richest families, meaning that those who were able to maintain themselves

[20] Ibid. 227–229; Mangat 1968: *passim*.
[21] Mamdani 1976:80–81.
[22] Trimingham 1964:107–108.
[23] Khan 1954:185–187.

in the system were generally the shrewdest business people, who then provided advantages for the rest of the membership.[24] The Aga Khan, who first visited East Africa in 1899, explained the economic benefits of his reforms:

> In Africa, where I have been able to give active help as well as advice, we have put the finances of individuals and of the various communities on a thoroughly safe basis. We established an insurance company—the Jubilee Insurance, whose shares have greatly increased in value. We also set up what we called an investment trust, which is really a vast association for receiving money and then putting it on loan, at a low rate of interest, to Ismaʿili traders and to people who want to buy or build their own houses.[25]

The Ismaʿilis, then, accepted institutions which incorporated many forms of Western political and business methods and yet which grew out of their traditional organisation and their relations with the *imam*. The Aga Khan, as virtually a British aristocrat, could give his followers certain advantages under a British colonial administration, and in this way persuaded them to accept his religious reforms and the imposition of Western customs.[26]

The final point to note is that the Ismaʿilis evolved beyond commercial entrepreneurship to Weber's "rationalised capitalistic enterprise", with its concomitant disciplined labour force and regularised investment of capital. This took place both in India and in East Africa. In Bombay the Ismaʿilis continued to be important in the cotton mill industry, although from time to time some families broke away from the Aga Khan and declared themselves Sunnis or Twelvers.[27] In India, and later in Pakistan, they continued to form a financial and social self-help network which provided loans to Ismaʿili businessmen to assist them in their endeavours.[28]

Similarly in Uganda Ismaʿilis moved into manufacturing through cotton, which was required to reach a particular quality in order to act as a market substitute for American cotton. Emphasis on quality led to government regulations which were prejudicial to the existence of small, technically unsophisticated hand-ginning enterprises. In 1914 Allidina Visram and collaborators established the first Indian-

---

[24] Morris 1958:465–471.
[25] The Memoirs of Aga Khan 1954:188.
[26] Morris 1958:462 and 466.
[27] Dobbin 1972:156; Gordon 1978:42 and 59.
[28] *The Economist* 14 November 1987.

owned cotton ginnery. The outbreak of the first World War saw capital flowing into Uganda from Bombay textile interests, and the establishment of Allidina Visram's second ginnery. Small Indian ginners, including Isma'ilis, also flowed up-country, becoming so-called middlemen ginners with capital provided from India. In 1925, out of a total of 114 ginneries of all sizes, 100 were owned by Indians.[29] In addition to Isma'ili institutions, family solidarity provided the basis for manufacturing enterprises in cotton, sugar, sisal and timber and a number of Isma'ili families developed their industrial potential in the period up to the second World War.[30] With no good cause to welcome the modern world, as Gellner remarks, theirs was a "brilliant *economic* performance".[31]

2. *The Mizabis*

An ideological minority with similar "creative" capacities to the Isma'ilis is represented by the Mizabis of southern Algeria. The challenge of the Mizabis' environment was severe. The Mizab valley lies in an arid limestone plateau about 350 miles south of Algiers and contains five small cities with, at the beginning of the nineteenth century, a Berber-speaking population of about 20,000. With no productive resources, the valley's inhabitants lived partly by date cultivation made possible by a complex system of irrigation occupying a large part of the population. The foundations of this society go back nearly a millennium, and trade had always provided a supplementary form of income. The valley itself by the sixteenth century had grown into an important northern Saharan market and the Mizabis participated in the caravan trade to various regions of northern Africa. Receiving wool and meat from their nomad transporters, the Mizabis provided storage facilities and certain staple and luxury goods.[32]

It is not clear when the Mizabis turned towards the north for their trade. Holsinger argues that from the seventeenth century there were increasing strains on the ecology of the valley, necessitating the

[29] Mamdani 1976:73–75, 86–92; Mangat 1969:89–90.
[30] Mangat 1969:136–139.
[31] Gellner 1981:104.
[32] Holsinger 1980:61–64; Bourdieu 1958:43–44.

creation of two new towns and breeding increased competition between settlements. Groups then travelled to Algiers to engage in commerce and return with adequate profits to impose their will in whatever dispute might be underway.[33] They were able to take advantage of opportunities offered by the Ottoman occupation, just as the Ismaʿilis, well before European control, had associated themselves with the ruling families of Muscat and then Zanzibar. Initially they sold dates in Algiers and, by the eighteenth century, their colony there was well known for its butchers' shops, flour mills, bakers' shops and public baths. Mizabis were also active in the vegetable trade and small currency exchange. In 1775 they were 800 in number.[34]

The Mizabi trade diaspora spread to other cities of northern Algeria. In Algiers they were organised in a way which enabled them to operate more successfully, as an independent corporate body governed by an *amin*. The Ottoman *deys* of Algiers recognised them as a separate and alien trading community, with equivalent privileges to other separate communities such as European Christians and black Africans. Their commercial privileges in such activities as flour milling and baking amounted to monopolies. Of course individual members of the corporation varied in wealth and influence, but there was a general solidarity of privilege surrounding them and by the turn of the nineteenth century the members of the Mizabi corporation in Algiers were regarded as belonging to the bourgeoisie. The corporation was the leading one of thirty-two in the city; it was the richest and lent funds to the Ottoman governor himself.[35]

One of the reasons for the attraction of the Mizabi diaspora to the newly Ottoman cities of the north was the latitude they were given to practise their own form of Islam. In Algiers they had their own mosque in one of their mills outside the city, and they did not frequent public mosques.[36] The Mizabis were Ibadis, one of the few remaining North African communities of the Ibadiyya, a Muslim fundamentalist sect dating from the first Islamic century and once prevalent in the Maghrib. The Mizabi Ibadis had migrated to their valley in the tenth and eleventh centuries as a means of escaping persecution. Their religion represented elements of a puritanical re-

[33] Holsinger 1980:64–65.
[34] Ibid. 66; Capot-Rey 1953:164.
[35] Curtin 1984:50; Holsinger 1980:67–68.
[36] Holsinger 1980:72.

action against the prosperity of the first Islamic caliphate and they preached a return to the communal ideals of the Qur'ān as embodied in the life of the Prophet and practised in the early Islamic community. To preserve themselves they, like the Isma'ilis, practised *taqiyya* or concealment. Bourdieu calls them the "Puritans of Islam", elaborating on their egalitarianism, their belief in works and purity of conscience as a necessary adjunct to faith, their rejection of saint worship and their high moral standards. In their valley, they lived apart and defended their religious exclusiveness.[37]

But Rodinson claims that it is not any marked originality of the Mizabis' religious doctrine which explains the success of their commercial activities:

> The secret of their special economic dynamism is to be found only in their situation as an ideological minority, their will to maintain a particularism based on a very strong cohesion. This will to cohesion leads to special importance being accorded among them to the clergy, the experts in religious law, who closely watch over the moral conduct of their flocks, their austerity in morals, and so forth, and this ensures that they will not let themselves be drawn into indolence, dissipation or extravagance. Here we see a phenomenon which, characteristic of ideological minorities, is found elsewhere in Islam for example, among the Isma'ilis, not to speak of what happens in other religions. Schumpeter has stressed the role played by "creative minorities".... It is not in ideas that the initial cause of the attitude in question is to be found, but in the social situation of the group. And this shows that the ideas of Islam on economic life, or on the conduct of man in general, are not in the least opposed to an orientation of activity in the direction of capitalism.[38]

The interplay of both an ascetic style of life and an existence as part of a commercial diaspora exhibiting the solidarity of strangers can help to explain the commercial success of the Ibadi Mizabis in northern Algeria. From the inherent tension arises their creativity and it is not necessary to find a solution to this creativity in one or the other factor exclusively. Work may indeed have been regarded as a religious act and duty and the ideal man distinguished by his moral qualities and his disdain for luxury, leading to capital accumulation as an end in itself.[39] Equally, however, the Mizabis were highly organisationally suited to operate as a commercial diaspora. In the Mizab

---

[37] Bourdieu 1958:44–45; Holsinger 1980:61–63; Gibb and Kramers 1961:561.
[38] Rodinson 1974:116.
[39] Bourdieu 1958:52–53.

itself the *azzāba* or council of *ʿulamāʾ* exercised a formidable role, responsible for the right conduct of the present generation, for the literary and further education of the succeeding one and for providing a model to all by living lives of probity and austerity. This control extended to the diaspora and legal matters were settled internally, away from the public courts.[40]

Within the diaspora, the cohesion expressed in life in the Mizab valley was retained, partly by customs which demanded periodic return and emphasised group solidarity. Women were forbidden to leave, which preserved the community by preventing a permanent exodus. Moreover, their weaving of wool products provided basic capital. In the northern cities, mutual aid and solidarity operated between members of the same city or clan, and this could be converted into a commercial agreement, a buying cooperative or a joint stock company. The preferred pattern, however, was to employ family members, either sons or nephews, and much of the profit would be returned to family members still living in the Mizab, the business entrepreneurs active in Algiers being satisfied with a very small margin. The mosque—set apart from other mosques—saw the exchange of information concerning prices and profits, and newcomers could be given help to set up in business.[41]

Other factors also operated to promote commercial success. Religious requirements promoted literacy and the community enjoyed a long tradition of literacy and respect for learning, permitting a merchant in the north to have good communication lines with an associate elsewhere. Merchants could also keep their own account books, allowing for a high level of complexity in commercial affairs. Solidarity in the northern cities was aided by experience of a shared way of life in the Mizab. The Mizabis knew an urban desert society in which cooperation was highly valued, in order to manage a complex system of water distribution. The solidarity engendered by coping with this task was transferred to northern enterprises, where learned ingenuity and industriousness were transformed into commercial success.[42] Moreover, the Mizabis in northern Algerian cities represented an archetypal stranger community, both near to and remote from the society in which they lived, exemplifying "that synthesis of nearness

[40] Holsinger 1980:71.
[41] Bourdieu 1958:53–54.
[42] Holsinger 1980:73.

and distance which constitutes the formal position of the stranger".[43] The stranger, as Simmel describes him, is then ideally suited to intermediate trade. The Mizabis, moreover, were Berbers and not Arabs, their doctrinal peculiarity separating them as well from other Berbers.[44]

In the last days of Ottoman rule in Algiers the Mizabis were reported to be much favoured as commercial collaborators and operated as the principal agents in the trade of Algiers with the interior. In addition to the businesses they had built up over a long period, the Mizabi corporation provided meat to the Janissaries.[45] The French conquest saw the maintenance and continuation of Mizabi collaboration, with considerable Mizabi fortunes being made in new enterprises as older ones declined. Even with French abolition of the corporations in 1868, the Mizabis continued to function unofficially as corporations due to their strong group solidarity; they maintained their commercial prominence in urban retail trade into the twentieth century, their numbers slowly increasing in the cities of the north.[46] By the 1950s they had become financiers, specialising in big business and high finance, while in the Mizab valley itself each city conducted numerous business enterprises spanning the trans-Saharan trade routes.[47]

Unlike the Ismaʿilis, the authorities exercising social control over the Mizabis did not operate to promote the adoption of a Western identity. By the early twentieth century more than one-sixth of the male population of the Mizab valley was absent in the north at any one time. The mechanisms functioning to preserve Mizabi identity in the north became more and more rigid. Councils of Ibadi *ʿulamāʾ* functioning in the valley itself interpreted written codes containing the principles of Ibadi jurisprudence. These codes covered both public life and private morals, and provided formidable punishments. Mizabi values were upheld throughout the diaspora and religious law intruded on every act of life, fostering group solidarity to an extreme degree. Drinking, smoking, music and dancing were prohibited, along with any kind of conspicuous consumption. Exclusiveness was considered a virtue and the preservation of the home culture a moral

[43] Simmel 1950:404.
[44] Weeks 1978:103.
[45] Holsinger 1980:69.
[46] Rodinson 1974:115; Holsinger 1980:70.
[47] Bourdieu 1958:45–46; Bourdieu 1962:52–53.

obligation. As with the Aga Khan, but to different effect, no important decision, civil regulation, new prohibition, or sanction against a serious crime, could be taken without the intervention of a council of *ʿulamāʾ*.[48] The laity was in all matters subordinate, and in this way the Mizabi business elite of Algeria retained a unique identity which set it apart from the rest of society while at the same time contributing to its success within that same society. Bourdieu has penetrated the essence of their commercial creativity:

> . . . their world of values is organised around two opposite poles: the domain of the secular, the economic life, and the domain of the sacred, the religious life. A real consciousness of this distinction on the part of the Mozabites can alone explain the fact that fierce resistance, obstinate and scrupulous particularism, and a touchy self-loyalty can coexist with a cautious desire for evolution, an attempt at compromise and planned development. . . . The maintenance of stability, far from excluding change, presupposes the capacity to modify oneself to adapt to new situations. But these adjustments (for which theological justification is found in the concepts of *taqiyya*, prudence, and of *kitmān*, the act of veiling, which authorise the Mozabite to dispense with the prescriptions of religion in cases when threatened with damages) must be accompanied either by a clear or an obscurely felt awareness of the values and norms whose permanence must be maintained at all costs, as opposed to those which can be modified or reinterpreted in order to assure the stability of the really important values. It is in this context that the material success of the Mozabites and their almost miraculous adaptation to forms of economic activity that are foreign to their strict tradition take on their full significance.[49]

3. *The Baweanese*

The commercial achievements of the Baweanese—a small community from an island 120 kilometres north of the northern coast of Java—in late nineteenth-century Javanese business life were remarkable. They were to be found conducting successful enterprises in Surabaya, Gresik, Banyumas, Kedu, Madiun and Kediri. In certain areas they posed a successful challenge to the Chinese and entered into direct relations with European firms for the supply of cloth, their main article of commerce. They travelled widely throughout Java with their cloth, textiles, calicoes, knitwear, flannel and sheets. Much

---

[48] Bourdieu 1958:45 and 48–49; Curtin 1984:51.
[49] Bourdieu 1962:54.

later, Geertz found them to be the dominant Javanese traders in Modjokuto, competing strongly with the Chinese and living together with the Arabs in the *kauman* (mosque quarter) of the town.[50]

This Baweanese commercial success developed, like that of the Mizabis, from two interlocking aspects of Baweanese existence. The island of Bawean was mountainous and limited in its rice lands, only enough rice being produced to feed the population for four months of the year. Trade, based initially on an extensive fishing industry, provided the solution to scarcity. Travel, too, led to a particular attachment to Islamic orthodoxy and to the interweaving of a form of Islam, based on frequent journeys to *pesantren* and to make the *haj*, with commercial undertakings.[51]

The Baweanese from the seventeenth century rose to a series of new commercial challenges. The first scientific investigation of the island, undertaken in 1803, reported that one-third of the entire male population was absent for almost the whole year in Java or the Malay peninsula, leading to the conclusion "that this nation was pre-eminently inclined to keep changing dwelling-place. . . ."[52] Taking fish to the north Java coast opened up lines of communication to other commercial enterprises, in particular the salt trade operating out of Surabaya, Gresik and Bangkalan. Salt was shipped into Bawean by Baweanese vessels from Gresik and Bangkalan and then re-shipped throughout East Java, where a considerable Baweanese trading network was built up. Furthermore a large proportion of the salt was carried into the Javanese hinterland by way of small roads and navigable rivers, resulting in a certain measure of Baweanese commercial penetration of the interior.[53] This nascent commercial diaspora was reinforced from the mid-eighteenth century by Baweanese involvement in opium-smuggling networks on the north Java coast, run by both official Chinese opium farmers and by clandestine dealers.[54] Opium was shipped to the island from all over the archipelago, and then transhipped to the coast between Rembang and Tuban, where numerous Chinese smugglers lived. Smuggling routes then ran inland to Surakarta and Yogyakarta by way of Blora and Wirosari or, from Japara, via Kudus. The Baweanese in this way gained knowledge of

---

[50] Geertz 1960:132–133; Fernando and Bulbeck 1992:70; Dobbin 1991:119.
[51] Dobbin 1991: *passim*.
[52] de Jonge and van Deventer 1888: Vol. 13, 159.
[53] Knaap and Nagtegaal 1991:150 and 155.
[54] Dobbin 1991:121.

the interior trade routes and familiarity with Chinese trade patterns.[55]

As with the Mizabis, there were other factors particular to the Baweanese island villages which pre-adapted the society to commercial success in late nineteenth-century Java. The land tenure system pertaining since at least the eighteenth century meant that land was a commodity and heirs could sell land. The end result was the creation of a large class of landless individuals in most villages, together with the existence of certain villages which had no rice fields whatever. Trade was the only way out, and successful trading ventures opened up the possibility of the purchase of land. But the prestige attached to land as an investment had a further deleterious effect on agriculture. Constant fragmentation made it difficult to carry out farming on a cooperative basis or to arrange an adequate water supply, with the result that more and more potentially productive land was withdrawn from use and the pressure to succeed by working or trading outside the island became stronger. Alternatively, villages could adapt to the lack of rice land by specialising in particular items which could be exported. The capital accumulated, whether from areca nuts, *areng* sugar or pandanus mats, assisted Baweanese commercial success in Java.[56]

Baweanese Islam was adapted to commercial requirements. Success in the *rantau* had a religious as well as a temporal dimension. The island was fully converted by at least the eighteenth century and soon had a reputation for extreme orthodoxy. In an 1819 report it was noted that Bawean possessed 109 *langgar* or prayer houses used for religious instruction, usually attached to individual homes. Commercial wealth made it obligatory to fund such buildings, and often the instructor as well. Further, many Baweanese children were furnished with considerable sums of money to set off to further their education in north Java *pesantren*, returning after two to three years.[57] Commerce and the journey in search of religious knowledge were intertwined. By the nineteenth century the *haj* had taken on a key role in the formation of the Baweanese personality. By the middle of the century no other district in the whole of the Netherlands Indies produced as many pilgrims as did Bawean; each year between 75 and 100 pilgrims left for Mecca and of the 35,000 inhabitants in 1874, approximately 1,000 were *haji*s, including a number of women.

[55] van Waeij 1875:173–175; Baud 1853:94–98 and 104–105 and 118–120.
[56] Dobbin 1991:122–123.
[57] van der Chijs 1864:230–231.

Individuals who had undertaken the journey four or five times were encountered.[58]

Not only did saving for the *haj* mould the personality in the direction of care and frugality. The care with savings was an important contributory factor to later commercial success on Java, as considerable capital formation—an average of fl. 400 to fl. 500 for each traveller at the start of the twentieth century—was tied up in the pilgrimage. Success in the *haj* enterprise led to more confidence in penetrating Javanese commercial networks, and a tangible response in terms of trust and credit from other merchants.[59]

It was success in the *rantau* which was the very goal of Baweanese Islamic life, and declining opportunities in Java after the 1930s led to the search for other economic niches, particularly in the Malay peninsula. Baweanese creative entrepreneurship then consisted in adopting strategies of expansion and contraction as circumstances required, based on a religious life which combined careful orthodoxy with relentless seeking.

4. *Conclusion*

Maxime Rodinson concluded in *Islam and Capitalism* that it was not ideas which informed the entrepreneurial activities of creative minorities but rather "the social situation of the group".[60] He argued, for example, that the Ibadis of the Mizab did not hold a religious dogma exhibiting marked originality as compared with Islam in general: rather, as already noted, the secret of their special economic dynamism was to be found only in their situation as an ideological minority, their will to maintain a particularism based on a very strong cohesion.[61]

But there is another aspect to be considered. It was in this context that Joseph Schumpeter introduced the notion of "creative minorities", entrepreneurial groups whose qualities paralleled those he observed in the individual entrepreneur, qualities marked by "the joy of creating, of getting things done, or simply of exercising one's energy and ingenuity. . . . Our type seeks out difficulties, changes in

[58] Wiselius 1874:442.
[59] Dobbin 1991:123–124.
[60] Rodinson 1974:116.
[61] Ibid. 115–116.

order to change, delights in ventures".[62] The argument of this paper has been that the creativity of these three Muslim commercial minorities has wellsprings both in their religious experiences and in their organisational life. Their religious existence has been one of adaptability, of "getting things done", of accommodating constantly to each new political or social challenge.

Nowhere is this more clearly expressed than with the Ismaʿilis, who transformed themselves from Hindus into Shiʿite Muslims when a new religious configuration was presented to them, learned to conceal their allegiance and to masquerade as Sunnis, and gradually agreed to adopting a highly Anglicised style of life painted over their adherence to their creed and their supreme *imam*. The Mizabis and the Baweanese too evolved religious responses to the situations in which they found themselves. The Mizabis gradually fixed upon an elaborate set of rules, derived from their heterodox faith, which stood them in good stead as a commercial diaspora. The Baweanese derived their extreme orthodoxy from the custom of visiting distant religious schools, and Mecca itself. Travel for religious purposes underpinned business life and commercial journeys.

Organisational life, too, was creative and innovative, in comparison with the mass of Muslim societies. The Ismaʿilis preferred their *jamatkhana* to a mosque; financial arrangements and internal competition for influence promoted business success. The Mizabis preserved their identity far away from home through the mechanism of their home based councils of *ʿulamāʾ*, who interpreted written codes covering both private and public life; every act of life could be intruded upon and the solidarity of the diaspora was thereby maintained. The Baweanese on Java had their *pondok* where commercial intelligence was exchanged and a life of extreme modesty and considerable orthodoxy could be followed.

The creative commercial minority, then, is a group characterised by "deviating conduct".[63] As entrepreneurs they are businessmen with particular psyches, obsessed by the effort to do something new and the need to bring to birth a new combination, conceived in "mental freedom".[64] In the case of Muslim creative commercial minorities, the transmission of Islam has led to delight in doing.

---

[62] Schumpeter 1949:93; Schumpeter 1943:132; Rodinson 1974:116.
[63] Schumpeter 1949:86.
[64] Ibid.

AL-MANĀR AND AHMAD SOORKATTIE

Links in the Chain of Transmission of Muḥammad 'Abduh's Ideas to the Malay-Speaking World

Jutta Bluhm-Warn

In 1930 Sheikh Muhammad Basyuni Imran, Imam of Sambas, Borneo, wrote to *al-Manār*,[1] an Egyptian Islamic reform magazine, requesting its editor, Rashīd Riḍā, to approach al-Amīr Shakīb Arslān (1869–1946) to answer the following questions:

- What are the causes that led Muslims, especially we Muslims of Java and the Malay Archipelago, to be weak and in a state of decadence in both the temporal and religious spheres of life? Yet God says in the Qur'ān (*Sūra* 63:8): "But honour belongs to God and His apostle, and to the believers. . . ." But where is the honour of the believers today?
- What are the causes which greatly advanced Europe, America and Japan? Is it possible for Muslims to reach their level of advancement if they emulate these causes whilst adhering to their own religion?[2]

A reply from al-Amīr Shakīb Arslān, a renowned writer and defender of Islam who came into contact with Muḥammad 'Abduh in 1889, was subsequently published in three parts in *al-Manār*.[3] On the premise of the Qur'anic verse (*Sūra* 13:11): "Verily, never will God change the condition of a people until they change it themselves", Arslān argues that it is the Muslims themselves who must strive for a religious renaissance by exerting effort to: establish independence from colonial rule; change the Muslim fatalistic attitude to life; seek the benefits of knowledge and science; and find a rational midway between the ultra conservative Muslims who cling to blind dogmatism and

---

[1] Published in Cairo in 35 volumes from 1898–1936.
[2] *Al-Manār* XXX1, 5, 1930:353–354.
[3] *Al-Manār* XXX1, 5, 1930:355–370; XXX1, 6, 1931:449–464; XXX1, 7, 1931:529–539.

obscurantism and the ultra modern sophists who disown their religious and cultural identity.

Such introspection and search for a solution to the ills of Muslims by initiating a change from within the Muslim community is thematic in the Islamic reform movement of the twentieth century and consonant with the Qur'anic exhortation in *Sūra* 13:11: "Verily, never will God change the condition of a people until they change it themselves". It was in a similar vein of introspection that Muḥammad ʿAbduh, leader of the reform movement in Egypt (1849–1905), poses the rhetorical question in his work *Sunan Allāh fī 'l-umam*: "What is the cause of the decline and decadence of the Islamic nation? Has God let us down after promising us prosperity?"[4] ʿAbduh concludes that a nation only declines after its deviation from the legally binding precedents (*sunan*) which God prescribed. God does not change the honour, power and well being of a people until these people change what is in their souls with respect to reason and veracity. For ʿAbduh, the means to achieve an Islamic renaissance lay in the all embracing principle: the restoration of Islam and the reform of Muslims. ʿAbduh envisaged that this could be achieved by:

- Purification of Islam from all accretions (*bidaʿ*) and a return to pristine Islam based on the Qur'ān and *sunna*;
- Liberation of Islam from the blind acceptance of the dogmas of former scholars (*taqlīd*);
- Reopening the doors of independent reasoning (*ijtihād*) to enable Islam to respond to the exigencies of modern life;
- Reformation of Islamic education to accommodate secular subjects and methodology; and
- The revival of Arabic language sciences to facilitate interpretation of the Qur'ān and *sunna*.

The letter sent by Imran is indicative of the dialogue that had been established between the Islamic reform movement of the Malay-speaking world and *al-Manār* magazine, mouthpiece of the Egyptian reform movement led by ʿAbduh.[5]

Al-Manār appears to have been reasonably well circulated in the Malay-speaking world through a variety of means. In Indonesia it

[4] ʿAbduh 1965:153–155.
[5] Bluhm 1983:35–42.

was smuggled in via the port of Tuban in East Java where there was no customs supervision.[6] Pijper, the Adviser of the Dutch Government for native and Arabic matters, created no censorship problems for Ahmad Soorkattie al-Ansarie, founder of the *al-Irshad* movement in Indonesia, who freely received shipments of *al-Manār* and other Arabic books.[7] Another avenue was through the circulation of personal copies of *al-Manār* obtained by *hajis* returning from the pilgrimage to Mecca. Nevertheless, it seems that *al-Manār* may not have been readily accessible to all readers in the Malay-speaking world as among the correspondence that was sent to *al-Manār* there are several requests that Riḍā not refer to previous editions of *al-Manār* as the writer may have difficulty in obtaining that particular edition. This may account for the fact that hand written extracts from *al-Manār* were circulated among groups and that Riḍā noted in an obituary to Sayyid Muhammad ibn Aqil ibn Yahya, of the *al-Imam* periodical, that he took trouble to circulate *al-Manār* in Singapore, Java and all of the Indonesian archipelago.[8]

The respect with which *al-Manār* was received in the Malay-speaking world and the influence that it exerted in this region is apparent in three reform magazines: *al-Imam; al-Munir*; and *Azzachierah al-islamijah. Al-Imam* was published in Singapore between 1906 and 1908, originally under the editorship of Tahir Jalaluddin. This magazine reflected the reformist ideas of *al-Manār* as well as its predecessor magazine, *al-ʿUrwa al-wuthqā*.[9] Articles from both these reform magazines were translated into Malay and published in *al-Imam*. Similarly, *al-Munir*, founded by Haji Abdullah Ahmad and published in Padang from 1911 to 1916, cited the opinions of *al-Manār* and translated and published several of its articles in Malay. *Azzachierah al-islamijah* was published in Arabic and Malay in Jakarta in 1923 under the editorship of Ahmad Soorkattie. It styled itself on *al-Manār* in format and content.

During the period of its publication (1898–1936) *al-Manār* published 26 articles and some 135 requests for legal opinions (*fatwā*) from the Malay-speaking world. The articles consist of announcements, letters commenting on various matters related to the homeland;

---

[6] Ali 1971:9.
[7] Personal interview with Professor G.F. Pijper, the Netherlands, 1983.
[8] *Al-Manār*, XXX11:238–239.
[9] A magazine published by al-Sayyid Jamāl al-Dīn al-Afghānī and Muḥammad ʿAbduh, March–October 1884, in eight issues.

letters commenting on previous articles published in *al-Manār*; and letters requesting and furnishing advice on specific issues. This material provides interesting insights into the Malay-speaking Muslims' concept of themselves, their perceived role within the international Muslim reform movement of the early twentieth century, and reflects the concomitant internal religious and social tensions arising from their growing religious, political and national consciousness.

The requests for legal opinions sent to *al-Manār* can be broadly categorised into: general theological issues and those pertinent to the ideology of the Islamic reform movement such as *ijtihād* and *taqlīd*; issues related to the new economic environment such as mortgaging real estate, life insurance and bank interest; issues related to technological advances such as the use of telegraphs, photography and listening to the Qur'ān on phonograph; issues related to patriotism and nationalism; and controversial issues such as the principle of parity of birth (*kafā'a*).

This correspondence from the Malay-speaking world attests the legitimising role *al-Manār* played as a source of authority on Islamic canonical law; adviser and commentator on Muslim affairs; and arbiter and reconciler in controversial matters. It was in this role and capacity that *al-Manār* promoted the reformist ideas of ʿAbduh. More importantly, it presented the ideas of ʿAbduh in a synthesised and easily digestible form and gave its readers access to his works which may have otherwise been inaccessible to many readers. It was perhaps due to the geographical isolation of the Malay-speaking world from the great centres of Islamic learning and the fact that there was no comparable centre of Islamic learning, such as al-Azhar, in the region, that Muslims in the Malay-speaking world turned to *al-Manār* as a source of religious authority. Interestingly, *al-Manār* not only established a dialogue with the reform movements in the Malay-speaking world, but also those who opposed it and thereby provided a forum for debate.

A debate which was echoed in the pages of *al-Manār* and which had wide theological, social and political implications for the Muslim community in the Malay-speaking world centred on three leading Islamic personalities: Ibn Ḥajar al-Haythamī; Ibn Taymiyya, and Abū Sufyān Muʿāwiya. This debate provides contextual material for establishing the types of ideas which filtered down to the Malay-speaking world and the way in which these ideas were argued and presented by *al-Manār*.

Foremost in the debate stands the figure of Ibn Ḥajar al-Haythamī (1504–1567) an Egyptian Shāfiʿite. It was particularly among the *Sayyids* of the Hadhrami community in the Malay-speaking world that Ibn Ḥajar was ardently supported. His main work, *Tuḥfa al-muḥtāj ilā sharḥ al-minhāj*,[10] a commentary on al-Nawawī's (1233–1278) *Minhāj al-ṭālibīn*,[11] provides a theological basis and rationale for the *Sayyids*' claim that they are the descendants of Prophet Muḥammad through Fāṭima's son Ḥusayn and consequently that the principle of *kafā'a* be interpreted to support their ascriptive system of social stratification. This ascriptive system operates through and is largely maintained by the ruling of hypergamous marriage, namely, that the daughter of a *Sayyid* may only marry a *Sayyid*.[12] In *Tuḥfa al-muḥtāj ilā sharḥ al-minhāj*, Ibn Ḥajar states that there are four degrees of genealogy with regard to the observance of *kafā'ah* in marriage: at the lowest end, non-Arabs are not equal in status to Arabs; and at the highest end, the descendants of Fāṭimah, the *Sayyids*, are higher in status than the rest of the Muslims.[13]

However, this prescription relegated the non-Arab Muslims, the Jawi in the Malay-speaking world, to the lowest level of status in the hierarchy. As such it was in fundamental contradiction with the egalitarian spirit of Islam upheld by the Islamic reform movement and with the aspirations and vision of the nationalist movements. On the other hand, defence of Ibn Ḥajar's stance was vital to the *Sayyids*' struggle to maintain their position of status and privilege in the Malay-speaking world in the face of increasing contention and debate with the Islamic reformists.

The second Islamic personality in the debate, Ibn Taymiyya (1263–1328), was a Hanbalite scholar of Damascus. He and his student Ibn Qayyim al-Jawziyya (1292–1356) had a formative influence on Muḥammad ʿAbduh, particularly with regard to his espousal of the right to apply independent reasoning (*ijtihād*) and analogy (*qiyās*) to deduce judgements, his appeal for a return to the Qur'ān and *Sunna* and his fervent attack on accretions in religion (*bidaʿ*). The *Sayyids* maintained that Ibn Ḥajar considered Ibn Taymiyya an heretic and wrote his famous polemical work *al-Fatāwī al-ḥadīthiyya*[14] against him.

In *al-Manār*[15] the writer M.M. from Batavia, complains that people canonise Ibn Ḥajar and they give precedence to what he says over

---

[10] GAL: S11, 527.
[11] GAL: S1, 496.
[12] Bujra 1967:355–375.
[13] Cited, *al-Manār*, V111, p. 581.
[14] GAL: S11, 528.
[15] *Al-Manār*, X11, 8, 614–623.

what God, His Messenger and his Companions and Followers say. The writer notes that among those who defame Ibn Taymiyya is Sayyid Uthman ibn Aqil[16] from Java. As a conciliatory gesture, *al-Manār* responds that the accusations brought against Ibn Taymiyya are due to lack of understanding rather than bad intentions. *Al-Manār* notes that Ibn Ḥajar falsely attributed to Ibn Taymiyya that he said that God is the Cause of events, that the Qur'ān is created, that the world is eternal in nature and the Agent, and that the Messenger has no glory. *Al-Manār* points out that the works of Ibn Taymiyya, such as *al-Tawassul wa'l-Wasīlah*,[17] are replete with the opposite of these allegations and states that it is inclined to believe that Ibn Ḥajar either heard these allegations and believed them, or that these allegations were interpolated into his writings. *Al-Manār* points out that more authoritative scholars, such as Ibn Ḥajar al-ʿAsqalānī in his *Ṭabaqāt al-ḥuffāẓ*,[18] have refuted such allegations against Ibn Taymiyya.

In *al-Manār*[19] the writer S.Y. in Singapore, complains that the people of Hadhramaut venerate Ibn Ḥajar who defames and curses Ibn Taymiyya. In its reply, *al-Manār* explains that Ibn Ḥajar is tradition bound to the Shāfiʿite legists, yet, his books are the best books of the later Shāfiʿite authors, however, they do not reach the standard of the books of al-Nawawī,[20] al-Māwardī[21] and al-Ghazālī. *Al-Manār* concludes that it considers the downfall of Ibn Ḥajar to be his book *Taṭhīr al-lisān wa'l-janān*.[22]

The third personality, Abū Sufyān Muʿāwiya, was also linked to the *Sayyid* dispute. The charge brought against Muʿāwiya by the *Sayyid*s was that he refused to acknowledge ʿAlī as Caliph and after a protracted battle usurped his position as Caliph. ʿAlī belonged to the Prophet's clan of Hāshim and he had married the Prophet's daughter, Fāṭima, and it is through her son, Ḥusayn, that the *Sayyid*s trace their descent. The *Sayyid*s therefore owe allegiance to ʿAlī by virtue of their lineage affiliation. However, the greatest charge brought against Muʿāwiya from various groups within the Islamic community, including ʿAbduh, Riḍā and his Salafiyya movement, is that Muʿāwiya

---

[16] Snouck Hurgronje 1892–93:CV–CXI.
[17] GAL: S11, 100; S11, 119.
[18] GAL: S1, 159 and 291–292 and 359–360.
[19] *Al-Manār*, XIII, 2, 108–111. Other letters from Malay-speaking world on this topic are in XII, 12, 953–55nd XII, 2, 104–108.
[20] GAL: S1, 496.
[21] GAL: S1, 668; S1, 483.
[22] GAL: S11, 527.

effectively dismantled the caliphate system by transforming it into a kingship (*mulk*) as he had arranged prior to his death that power be transferred to his son.

Requests to resolve the disputes surrounding Muʿāwiya's right to usurp the caliphate from ʿAlī and whether it is acceptable to curse him were raised in several letters to *al-Manār* from the Malay-speaking world.[23] This was a sensitive issue for *al-Manār* which followed an orthodox line in this matter. Riḍā's book *al-Khilāfa aw al-imāma al-ʿuẓmā*,[24] in which he advocates the retention of the caliphate, was published in part in *al-Manār* volumes 23 and 24. ʿAbduh went as far as maintaining that the preservation of the Ottoman Empire is the third article of belief after belief in God and the Prophet because it protects Islam and its domains.[25] In his work *Risāla al-tawḥīd*, ʿAbduh partly attributes the disintegration caused by the death of the third Caliph, who damaged the structure of the caliphate irreparably, to the development of rival schools on the caliphate as well as forgers of the Traditions.[26] *Al-Manār* therefore calls for the unity of all Muslims and advises Muslims to abandon discussion of this issue which has been one of the most divisive issues in Islamic history.

A contemporary figure from Batavia who evoked much local controversy and was the subject of numerous requests for advice from *al-Manār*, was that of al-Sayyid Uthman ibn Abd Allah ibn Aqil ibn Yahya al-Alawi. He was born in Batavia of Hadhrami parents and was an orthodox scholar who studied law in Hadhramaut and Mecca. He was friend and assistant to Snouck Hurgronje, Advisor on Native and Arabic Affairs to the Dutch East Indies Government, who appointed him honorary government advisor.[27] In 1914 he received a medal of recognition for service to the Dutch government. It was Sayyid Uthman's liaison and cooperation with the Dutch that was criticised in a number of letters written to *al-Manār* from the Malay-speaking world.[28]

Sayyid Uthman's works, which he published on his own lithographic press, were also a source of contention. In *al-Manār*[29] S.M.M.

[23] *Al-Manār*, VIII, 625–631; IX, 3, 212–213; XII, 12, 953–955 (two letters); and XIII, 5, 399.
[24] Riḍā 1922.
[25] Riḍā 1908:339.
[26] ʿAbduh 1966:11–12.
[27] Snouck Hurgronje 1894:285–303.
[28] *Al-Manār*, 11, 1899:670–71; 11, 43, 1900:661–663; and 11, 45, 1900:717–719.
[29] *Al-Manār*, XII, 11, 871–873.

in Batavia requests that Riḍā review the enclosed treatise, *Jamʿ al-nafāʾis* by Sayyid Uthman, which deals with education and the improvement of schools. The writer to *al-Manār* feared that the ideas expressed in this work may impede the religious educational renaissance in progress in Java. Riḍā responded to this request in *al-Manār*[30] with a detailed comment on Sayyid Uthman's treatise. This provided *al-Manār* with an opportunity to advance its ideas on the reformation of Islamic education, a topic central to ʿAbduh's reformist vision.[31]

Sayyid Uthman's treatise consists of less than twelve pages dealing with knowledge, education, the school and expenditure on education. The general thrust of the treatise is a reaction against imitation of western methods of organisation and curricula in education. Sayyid Uthman bases his argument on two *ḥadīth*: "He who imitates a people, then he is one of them" and "Whoever loves a people is assembled with them on the Day of Judgement in Hell". On the premise of these two *ḥadīth* Sayyid Uthman argues that it is unlawful to imitate or make use of any Western ideas, and in the case of education, to model and organise Muslim schools and their curricula according to Western schools. Riḍā retorts that these two *ḥadīth* do not substantiate his argument as their chain of transmission is weak and their true purport does not support his claim. Riḍā points out that Sayyid Uthman is unqualified in the science of the *ḥadīth*, lacks powers of reasoning, opposes *ijtihād* and supports *taqlīd*, which is not in accord with the true spirit of Islam, and his lack of knowledge of the Arabic language is obvious as his treatise is replete with errors. Riḍā advises the Muslims of Java not to pay attention to this treatise nor to any other works by Sayyid Uthman. He encourages the Muslims of Java to go ahead and select teachers proficient in both the religious and temporal sciences for their schools.

In his comment to a letter from Muhammad ibn Hashim Tahir in Palembang, Sumatra, Riḍā states that in the first three years of its publication, *al-Manār* received many articles detailing the oppression of Holland and noting that Sayyid Uthman was an assistant and advisor to the Dutch Government and spied against the Muslims. Despite the numerous letters *al-Manār* did not publish them for fear that it may have been prompted by bias and rivalry. However, Riḍā admits that, "*al-Manār* could no longer remain silent after reading

---

30 *Al-Manār*, XIII, 1, 60–63.
31 ʿAbduh 1965:98–112; Riḍā 1908:364–381.

his treatises which he printed and spread among the Muslims to the deterrence of Islamic reforms and reformers. . . ." Riḍā concludes with a vitriolic attack against Snouck Hurgronje denouncing him as an enemy of Islam and a hypocrite who embraced Islam and spied on the Muslims in Mecca. Then, as advisor for Muslim Affairs for the Dutch Government he used Sayyid Uthman for the oppression of Muslims and obstruction of their progress.[32]

Another work by Sayyid Uthman which caused some controversy was his work *al-Naṣā'iḥ* which Riḍā states was probably written in response to the legal opinion issued by *al-Manār* which was not in favour of the permissibility of cursing Muʿāwiya.[33]

A key link in the transmission of ʿAbduh's ideas in Indonesia was Ahmad Soorkattie al-Ansarie who was born in the Sudan in 1872. He left the Sudan in 1896 to undertake the pilgrimage and stayed on to study in Medina, unable due to the Mahdist revolution to pursue his father's wish that he study at al-Azhar in Cairo. He studied in Medina for four years and then in Mecca for eleven years where he became the favourite student of his teachers, especially Shaykh Muḥammad ibn Yūsuf al-Khayyāṭ, a Meccan, who once lived in Malaya and occasionally visited East Sumatra. He received the highest certificate (*al-shahāda al-ʿālimiyya*) of the Government in Istanbul for religious teachers and began teaching in Mecca in 1908 at the Ḥaram al-Mālikī.[34] At that time Mecca was under the rule of Sharīf Ḥusayn who was opposed to the ideas of ʿAbduh. However, Soorkattie received smuggled editions of *al-ʿUrwa al-wuthqā* and *al-Manār* and secretly circulated these magazines to his students and lectured about them. He also corresponded with Riḍā at this time.[35]

At the request of *al-Jamʿiyya al-Khayriyya*, more widely known as *Jamiat Khair*, Soorkattie came to Java in 1911 in the capacity of inspector of the *Jamiat Khair* schools in Jakarta. *Jamiat Khair* was established in 1901 by a group of ʿAlawites and non-ʿAlawites in response to an offer in 1897 by the Consul General of Turkey in Jakarta to provide scholarships from the Ottoman State for Indonesian students

---

[32] *Al-Manār*, XIV, 10, 761–766.

[33] *Al-Manār*, XII, 12, 953–955; VIII, 625–631—Awd ibn Juman Saidan in Singapore requested a legal opinion on cursing Muʿāwiya.

[34] A handwritten Arabic manuscript on the biography of Ahmad Soorkattie courtesy of his nephew Muchtar Luthfi al-Anshary, 9–14. Refer also O'Fahey & Abu Salim 1992/93:68–72.

[35] Personal interview with Muchtar Luthfi al-Anshary, Jakarta, 1983.

to study in Istanbul. The *Jamiat Khair* organisation saw its role as providing elementary religious education and for its students on scholarship to further their studies in Istanbul. However, Soorkattie's involvement with *Jamiat Khair* was short-lived. In 1913 Soorkattie went to Solo and stayed at the house of Sheikh Awad ibn Sunkar, Captain of the Arabs. By chance the conversation turned to the question of a *sharifah* who had become the mistress of a Chinese man. Soorkattie suggested they collect money in order to support her. No one was prepared to do so. Then Soorkattie suggested that she be married to any willing Muslim, as there is no legal objection to such a marriage provided that her parents consent to it. This legal opinion, which did not acknowledge the *kafāʾa* principle, caused a rift between Soorkattie and *Jamiat Khair* who ordered Soorkattie to leave the country.[36] However, Ahmad Dahlan, Oemar Said Tjokroaminoto and Haji Agus Salim urged Soorkattie to stay and continue his work towards Islamic reform. So in 1913 Soorkattie established *Jāmiʿa al-Iṣlāḥ waʾl-Irshād al-ʿArabiyya*, more commonly known as *al-Irshad*, and opened a school in Batavia.

However, the *kafāʾa* issue did not subside. In 1915 Soorkattie wrote *Ṣūra al-jawāb*, which generated a considerable number of polemical works, as documented by Schrieke.[37] *Ṣūra al-jawāb* was written in reply to an inquiry from the editor of the newspaper *Soeloeh Hindia* concerning an article this newspaper had published in Number 2 page 2, 28 October 1915. The article in question was written by an ʿAlawite from Pekalongan and dealt with the issue of marriage between a *sharifah* and a non-*sharif*. At first Soorkattie declined to make any comment on this article, which was clearly directed at him, because he felt that the writer was fanatical and had overstepped the bounds of fair mindedness and had failed to observe the etiquette of debate. However, since the editor had made an inquiry concerning this article, Soorkattie felt morally obliged as a scholar of Islam to state his case. Soorkattie's reply was subsequently published in 1915.[38]

In *Ṣūra al-jawāb* Soorkattie interpreted the principle of *kafāʾa* in marriage in terms of the parity of means of livelihood, compatibility of the spouses in terms of moral, intellectual and general character traits, and harmony in conjugal life. These practical considerations

[36] Al-Bakrī 1936:256.
[37] Schrieke 1920:189–240.
[38] Soorkattie 1915.

were to be taken into account in order to prevent an ill-matched marriage which would lead to loss of respect and discord between the spouses. Soorkattie does, however, make provision for these practical considerations to be waived on the basis of *maṣlaḥa* (that which is beneficial) in cases where the woman who is of legal age consents to marriage, aware of the shortcoming of her suitor, since she may see in him other qualities or merits which compensate for the loss in material or social status. He concludes that if a woman, her closest guardian or guardians, agree to marriage with a Muslim and the dowry is fixed and unconditional and consent is obtained in the presence of two witnesses, then the marriage is valid without taking into account any further considerations. No consideration is given to parity of descent and lineage. In fact, Soorkattie does not even make the distinction of a marriage between a *sayyida* and a non-*sayyid*, but refers only to marriage between two Muslims. As proof that lineage and descent were not a consideration for eligibility for marriage at the time of the Prophet, Soorkattie enumerates eight examples where marriages were concluded without regard for tribal affiliations, clan or social and economic status. Soorkattie further argues that since all believers agree that the origin of mankind is traceable to Adam, logically there can be no superiority of one person over the other by mere virtue of lineage and descent. Rather, superiority among the believers is based on moral excellence which is measured by one's piety, knowledge and good deeds, as supported in the *ḥadīth*: "No one has superiority over another except in matters of religion and pious deeds". Soorkattie carries his argument to its logical conclusion: if we all originate from Adam and Noah and descent itself determines superiority, then there would be no vile or sinful people among mankind. Since this is not the case, then the claim of the *Sayyids* is untenable. In a style and tone reminiscent of ʿAbduh's work, *al-Islām wa'l-radd ʿalā muntaqidīh*,[39] Soorkattie draws the conclusion:

> . . . the statement that some people are superior to others due to their blood and flesh relation, without taking into consideration their deeds and knowledge, and ascribing this statement to the noble Law, sullies it with that which is inconsistent with its principles, and is provocative of a major conflict between it and reason, reason which God has made the criterion of all things.[40]

[39] ʿAbduh 1909.
[40] Soorkattie 1915:17.

The interpretation of *kafā'a* which Soorkattie advances in *Ṣūra al-jawāb* follows much the same line of argument which Riḍā had earlier advanced in a legal opinion he issued in *al-Manār* in 1905[41] and which was subsequently approved by ʿAbduh.[42]

An important link that was forged in the transmission of the ideas of ʿAbduh was the relationship between Ahmad Soorkattie and Ahmad Dahlan, founder of the *Muhammadiyyah* movement which was established in 1912. The relationship between the two leaders is not well documented; however, an overall picture can be pieced together.

In 1911 Soorkattie and Dahlan met on a train in Java and a conversation between the two ensued when Soorkattie noticed Dahlan reading ʿAbduh's work *Tafsīr al-Manār* which was not well known in Indonesia at that time. The two leaders found common ground in their ideals and both promised to work for the spread of the teachings of ʿAbduh in their respective communities. Their relationship did not end there. According to *al-Haqq* magazine, Soorkattie was one of the people who inspired the *Muhammadiyyah* movement and from the outset made suggestions for developing the movement.[43] Pijper notes that when Dahlan was establishing the *Muhammadiyyah* he consulted with Soorkattie.[44] The respect with which Soorkattie was held as an Islamic scholar is evident from the fact that Dahlan became his private pupil and that the *Muhammadiyyah* sought the advice of Soorkattie when they required an official definition of the term *al-sharīʿa* (Islamic Law).[45] In an eulogy for Soorkattie, the *Muhammadiyyah* states that he provided continued support and assistance to the *Muhammadiyyah* by his views, opinions and collection of monetary assistance, especially from *al-Irshad*.[46]

Soorkattie was a teacher-reformer whose main focus was on bringing about a reform of Muslims through education. By 1935 *al-Irshad* had established some thirty schools throughout Java. The schools were organised along modern lines into grades and levels with boys and girls being taught in the same class. Modern subjects were intro-

[41] *Al-Manār*, VII, 10. The *fatwā* issued by Riḍā was published in al-Bakrī 1936, including the counter *fatwā* sent to *al-Manār* by Sayyid ʿUmar ʿAṭṭās who based his argument on the work of Ibn Ḥajar al-Haythamī, *Tuḥfa al-muḥtāj ilā sharḥ al-minhāj*.

[42] *Al-Manār*, VIII, 583–584.

[43] *Al-Haqq* no. 4, 1932.

[44] Pijper 1977:106.

[45] Personal interview with Prof. Haj M. Rasjidi, former student of Soorkattie, Jakarta, 1983.

[46] Manuscript on the biography of Ahmad Soorkattie, 24.

duced such as science, geography, physical education, history and modern languages such as Dutch, English and Malay. The organisation and curriculum of these schools were in accord with ʿAbduh's stance on education and indeed, his works such as *Risāla al-tawḥīd, Tafsīr juzʾ ʿamma* and *Tafsīr al-Manār* were studied.[47]

An insight into the reformist ideas that were promulgated through the *al-Irshad* schools can be gained from Soorkattie's major work *al-Masāʾil al-thalāth.* This work deals with the three issues: *al-ijtihād* and *al-taqlīd; al-sunna* and *al-bidaʿ*; and visiting graves, intercession and mediation. In this work Soorkattie sought to demonstrate that Islam and its practices are coterminous with reason and rationalism and that the Qurʾān as the divine word of God is relevant to all people through all ages, as advocated by ʿAbduh.[48]

A catalyst in the spread of ʿAbduh's ideas was the arrangement that existed between *al-Irshad* and the *Muhammadiyyah,* whereby graduates from *al-Irshad* schools became cadres of the *Muhammadiyyah* working in its branches throughout Indonesia. How many graduate students from *al-Irshad* schools did become cadres of the *Muhammadiyyah* under this arrangement I am unable to establish. However, in several interviews with former students of Soorkattie this arrangement was verified.[49] Foremost among those *al-Irshad* graduates who were specifically sent to *Muhammadiyyah* to assist in giving lectures, teaching and proselytising throughout Indonesia are Yunus Anies, leader and adviser of the *Muhammadiyyah* from 1959 to 1968,[50] and Iskandar Idries. Idries is the author of several books on the exegesis of the Qurʾān[51] and together with Muchtar Luthfi el-Anshary, the nephew of Soorkattie, he was a member of a project team, established in 1975 under the auspices of the Indonesian Council of Ulama, to revise and improve on the translation of the Qurʾān into Bahasa Indonesia by

---

[47] Personal interview with Muchtar Luthfi al-Anshary, Jakarta, 1983; Yunus 1979:307–315; and Pijper 1977:114.

[48] Manuscript on the biography of Ahmad Soorkattie, 46–66. This work was also published by Muḥammad ʿAbdullah al-Sammān, Dār al-ʿItiṣām, n.d.

[49] Abdullah Baraba; Hussain al-Bakri; and Muchtar Luthfi el-Anshary (Jakarta 1983).

[50] 1959–62 principal adviser of *al-Haqq* magazine; former head of PUSROH *Islam Angkatan Darat.*

[51] His works include: *Tafsier Hibarna,* I–V, Ekonomu, Bandung, 1951; *Tafsier Muchtasar,* I–III, Yayasan Sosial Islam, Jakarta, 2nd edition, 1967; *Tarjamah Djuz Amma,* NV Fajar Nusantara, Bandung, 5th edition, 1968; *Tafsir Juz Amma,* NV Fadjar Nusantara, Bandung, 5th edition, 1960.

H.B. Yassin.[52] Other graduates of the *al-Irshad* who became cadres of the *Muhammadiyyah* include Professor Farid Ma'ruf, K.M. Muhammad and Muhammad Ma'shum.

In this way *al-Irshad* "tapped into" the *Muhammadiyyah*, the largest populist Islamic movement in Indonesia. The impact that the combined reform movements of *al-Irshad* and the *Muhammadiyyah* had as a dynamic force, whose appeal to the masses raised, at least, the awareness and consciousness of the basic ideas and principles advocated by Muḥammad 'Abduh, cannot be over-estimated.

[52] H.B. Yassin, *al-Quranu'l-Karim—Bacaan Mulia*, Yayasan, Jakarta, 1942. The revised edition of this translation of the Qur'ān was published in 1982. In the introduction by al-Anshary, he notes that the project team referred to *Tafsīr al-Manār*.

KAUM MUDA AND *KAUM TUA* IN WEST JAVA

The Literary Record

WENDY MUKHERJEE

The historical facts of the coming of Islamic reform from Egypt to the Malay-Indonesian archipelago are well known to scholars of Indonesian Islam. Johns asserts that "the impact of Muḥammad ʿAbduh's ideas marks a new chapter in the history of Islam" there.[1] These ideas, imported from the Middle East early this century by students studying at al-Azhar in Cairo, reading the magazine *al-Manār*, and by pilgrims in touch with reformist scholars among the long-term residents of the *Jawah* community at Mecca gave rise to the reformist movement referred to as the *Kaum Muda*. The propagation of *Kaum Muda* ideas through the efforts of reformist religious teachers and the social repercussions of the movement's engagement with traditionalists, the *Kaum Tua*, have also been studied: standard references[2] convey a picture of bitter debates, personal antagonisms and no small measure of conscience-searching among the religious learned. Pamphlet warfare also played an important role.

Johns has summarised Muḥammad ʿAbduh's programme under four main points: "the purification of Islam from corrupting influences and practices; the reformation of Muslim education; the reformation of Islamic doctrine in the light of modern thought; the defence of Islam".[3] Elsewhere he adds: "a restoration of the primal understanding of the Qur'ān from beneath centuries of interpretation and the elimination of the Sufi brotherhoods".[4] The full range of these ideas, although thinly in evidence, is represented in a number of works of the early modern Sundanese fiction of West Java. By this phrase I mean works both in prose, novels, and in the long narrative verse form of the *wawacan* appearing in print from the first decade of the century up to the close of the colonial period in 1942.

---

[1] Johns 1980a:177.
[2] Hamka 1967; Federspiel 1970; Abdullah 1971; Roff 1974.
[3] Johns 1987b:410.
[4] Johns 1987a:15.

Occasionally membership of either a traditionalist or modernist camp may be discovered within the lives of Sundanese writers. The two most highly acclaimed pre-war authors were *Kaum Tua.* D.K. Ardiwinata (1866–1947), who wrote the first Sundanese novel, *Baruang Ka Nu Ngarora* (Poison To Our Youth) published in 1914—a work which is as important in the Sundanese literary canon as Marah Rusli's *Siti Nurbaya* (1922) in the Indonesian and Syed Sheikh al-Hadi's *Faridah Hanom* (1925–26) in the Malay—condemned the *Kaum Muda* in pamphlets for their desertion of their own culture in favour of the ways of the West.[5] Ardiwinata was the founding chairman of the *Paguyuban Pasundan* (The Pasundan League), set up in 1914 as a Sundanese equivalent of the Javanese cultural organisation *Budi Utomo* (Noble Endeavour) and was active in a number of smaller conservative aristocratic and Islamic organisations as well. Mohammad Ambri (1892–1936) was a member of a *tarekat* and was a practising *dukun*, a traditional psycho-medical healer, which indicate his *Kaum Tua* orientation. Both writers published their works through the colonial government press, Balai Pustaka.

Conversely, *Kaum Muda* affiliations can be detected for Achmad Bassach (d. 1930), who wrote novels of social protest under the pen name of "Joehana" and was a member of the Communist mass organisation, the *Sarekat Rakyat.* Although his novels do not advocate religious reform, Bassach[6] turned his hand to the Sundanese translation of a Malay work of Qur'anic exegesis by A. Hassan, the leader of the Bandung-based reformist association the *Persatuan Islam* (The Islamic Union).[7] The political polarisation of the conservative *Kaum Tua* writers on one side and of radical *Kaum Muda* on another should not be lost on us; it is a fact of life of the Indonesian nationalist movement of the mid 1920's. Selections from another Marxist-*Kaum Muda* text appear below.

The above are extreme cases however, and quite rare. Most traditionalist-modernist dialogue is represented by a diffuse scattering of ideas, not a complete apology for either programme. Realist fiction in the archipelago came into being under the influence of European ideas of individualism, commercial endeavour and education, while the appearance of the novel genre itself is an index of the modern

[5] Ardiwinata and Mangkoe Pradja 1910.
[6] Bassach 1929a, 1929b.
[7] Federspiel 1970.

spirit.[8] Many of these texts were prefaced with a wish for progress for the Sundanese people, and all commended the benefits of a modern Western style schooling to the young. Secular, modernising intentions could be consciously held by an author alongside a generally traditionalist religious position, and this seems to have been the main pattern of inspiration in the writing of early Sundanese fiction.

It is generally accepted that a *cause célèbre* in the matter of a marriage was the first indication of the influence of *Kaum Muda* ideas in the archipelago. This event occurred in Singapore in 1905, in the form of a marriage contracted between a Hadhrami Arab *sharifah* (a woman of the Prophet's line) and "an Indies man" not of her community. It was reported in *al-Manār* that a *fatwa* had had to be obtained from Cairo ratifying the marriage, apparently from Rashīd Riḍā himself, which offended traditional Hadhrami social norms. It was hypergamous, a mesalliance which violated the principle of *kafā'a*, that there should be social equality between the partners.[9]

The Singapore case was a sign of the times and an example of a trend spreading among the indigenous communities of the archipelago. New pressures towards inter-class marriages, and the reform of marriage itself under *sharī'a* law, were felt increasingly in the prewar period, with the extension of general secular education and the propagation of nationalist ideals. In West Java, another factor of class instability lay in the rising competition between the nobility who traditionally manned the native branch of the colonial civil service, and the lower ranks of new professionals, better trained along Western lines. While it was not the key issue of their reforms, the *Kaum Muda* turned their eye on injustices in the implementation of family law by the traditionalist *ulama*, advocating greater freedom for women within Islam and a more humane application of the conditions of marriage.[10]

1. Kaum Tua *Morality and Sundanese Novels*

From the appearance of the first Sundanese novel in 1914 up to the close of the colonial period in 1942, *Kaum Tua* stories predominate

---

[8] Johns 1979a:2 and 31.
[9] Federspiel 1970:62; Noer 1980:72; Bluhm 1983:37.
[10] Hamka 1967:113–119; Bluhm-Warn in this volume.

as a type. These novels are morality tales, turning on the perfidy of one of the partners. The plots begin with a betrothal or an established marriage, which is destroyed when one of the partners proves unfaithful. The wronged party is faced with a choice: to assuage his/her pain by taking to vice and pleasures, or to meet the loss with patient forbearance. The errant party enjoys his/her new union for a time, then the force of morality, under the narrator's hand, takes hold. The initial act of perfidy leads to new vices. Both parties of the new union begin to suffer under an accumulation of their vices—gambling, spendthrift ways, theft, further perfidy. Ends awaiting men are gaol, and women, common prostitution. To both men and women, there awaits also destitution, bringing public shame, illness and death. Suicide is a frequent plot solution. Meanwhile, the individuals who have been virtuously patient are rewarded with a new, happy and socially respectable union.

The goal presented in the novels is the maintenance of happy marriage:

> This the elders say: "husbands and wives must be in harmony, in water sharing one pool, on land sharing one hollow, as one in the bitterness and in the sweetness (of life). . . ."[11]

A young woman is advised:

> There is no-one else to whom you can commit yourself but to your husband, who replaces your father and your mother.[12]

and

> To be unfaithful to her husband, this is the worst thing that a woman can do.[13]

while a husband must provide financially for his wife, be honest with her in all his dealings, be understanding and compassionate and guide her with discretion.[14]

A well-developed system of tropes of Islamic ethical terms attests to a *Kaum Tua* influence from the Islamic schools, the *pesantren*, upon the works. These appear at crucial stages in the plot, mostly in the form of admonitions conveyed in conversations between characters.

---

[11] Ardiwinata 1966:34.
[12] Ibid. 31.
[13] Ibid. 35.
[14] Ibid. 42–44.

They also may be proclaimed by the narrator in formal prologues and epilogues set aside from the story proper.

The tropes are as follows: all narrated events are deemed to occur under the working of fate (*kadar*) or of divine providence (*takdir*). Temptation to evil (*gogoda*) occurs as part of *kadar* and cannot be avoided in life, but in response to temptation, the individual may choose either the way of patient resignation (*sabar tawakul*) or to follow Satan's prompting and give rein to desires (*turut napsu amarah*). While virtue consists of the undifferentiated quality of patience, the vices are many. They are codified under the rubric of the Seven "M" Sins after the initial letter of their names, the *Mim Pipitu*: opium-smoking (*madat*), sexual wantonness (*madon*), gambling (*maen*), thieving (*maling*), the drinking of alcohol (*minum*), gluttony, including a love of all material pleasures (*manganni*) and evilsaying (*mada*).[15] The didactic closure of the texts evident in the strong plot solutions makes clear the message of virtue rewarded and all vices punished.

2. *Novels About Arranged Marriage*

How different is the atmosphere of the novels about arranged marriage, in which the moral teaching of centuries is brought to nought by psychological studies of the effects of unwished-for unions. An arranged marriage condemned young people, as Johns puts it, "to live out their lives in anguished submission"[16] or, as in the Sundanese stories, it could drive them to all the vices warned against by the *Kaum Tua* and lead to the same didactic endings as just described. All novels about arranged marriage raise a protest against the practice.

The *Kaum Muda* lent its influence to objections to arranged marriage in fiction. The early Indonesian and Malay novel traditions begin with plots about arranged marriage: *Siti Nurbaya* and *Faridah Hanom*, in which prevailing traditional social conditions crush the idealistic protagonists and over which they display exemplary virtue and eventually prevail respectively. It can be no coincidence that such novels arose in areas where the *Kaum Muda* was first active, among the Minangkabau of Sumatra and in the cosmopolitan city of Singapore.

[15] Ardiwinata and Mangkoe Pradja 1910.
[16] Johns 1979a:7.

Novels about arranged marriage in Sundanese follow various plot lines. First, heroines from aristocratic families fall in love with young men without rank. They are forbidden to marry and other matches are arranged, with unhappy consequences on the lives of all the young people involved. Second, there are representations of marriages arranged for financial reasons, in which a daughter is given to an older man, a rich *haji* or a trader, to release her father from debt, as we find in *Siti Nurbaya.* A third category, of most interest here, includes works about marriages arranged for class interests, to preserve an aristocratic pedigree, which are successfully *averted.* These novels carry an explicit expression of the *Kaum Muda* argument on *kafā'a.*

3. Kaum Muda *Ideology on Marriage*

Under Shafi'ite jurisprudence, which governs the Muslim communities of the Indonesian archipelago, young women could not enter a marriage in their own right. Marriage was contracted for them, the signatories of the contract being the groom and the bride's representative, her *wali,* usually her father or an elder male kinsman. Once a marriage had been contracted on her behalf, the hapless girl had little recourse but to resign herself to the match.

A Qur'anic justification is given for this. The arranging of a marriage by parents was predicated on the equality of the partners. Love and happiness were understood to follow automatically between the partners if *kafā'a* was met. The verse adduced is *Sūra al-Nūr,* 24:26.[17] Arberry's rendering of this verse runs:

> Corrupt women for corrupt men,
> and corrupt men for corrupt women;
> good women for good men,
> and good men for good women-
> these are declared quit of what they say;
> theirs shall be forgiveness and generous provision.[18]

But an argument against *kafā'a* can also be found. The verse adduced is *Sūra al-Nisā',* 4:1, which states that the whole of mankind is of a single descent (in the commentary, the line of the Prophet Adam)

[17] Joenoes 1961:374–375.
[18] Arberry 1964:355.

and hence no rank or other division among people is recognised.[19] This is rendered as follows:

> Mankind, fear your Lord, who created you
> of a single soul, and from it created
> its mate, and from the pair of them scattered
> abroad many men and women.[20]

4. Kaum Muda *Ideals Construe Plot*

Bapa Mami's *Wawacan Juag Tati* (The Verse Tale of Lady Tati) (1923) best expounds the *Kaum Muda* position on arranged marriage. With its negligible narrative content, this short work in verse comes close to being a pamphlet. Juag Tati, the protagonist, stems from a family of aristocrats fallen on hard times; as a young woman, she had been obliged to marry an untitled merchant for wealth rather than rank. The son of this mixed union, Ujang Atang, is of the *santana* or intermediate rank, but his father's money has made it possible for him to be sent to Batavia to be educated to enter the civil service. The question here is not the forcing of Ujang Atang into a marriage not of his choosing, but rather to prevent him from marrying a commoner with whom he has fallen in love. Juag Tati insists that the girl, Nyi Acih is unsuitable because she is "*lain babad, lain tanding*" (no match for him, and not his equal).[21] She offers the standard argument for an arranged marriage: that there must be *kafā'a*. Ujang Atang is furious, responding with the *Kaum Muda* argument that refutes the notion of *kafā'a*:

> All mankind are the descendants of Adam. In my case, both my mother and my father have their own lineage, the one from servant, the other from master. I don't need to bring all this up again, for there's no benefit in it, it only leads to heart-ache.
>
> Commoners are oft descended of nobles, and nobility sprung from the little people: some people bear titles through their mothers, some only through their fathers. You will surely see, mother, that it's not good to make an issue of this matter, for it's only so that you can talk badly about Acih.[22]

---

[19] Joenoes 1961:64–65.
[20] Arberry 1964:72.
[21] Mami 1923:14 and 26.
[22] Ibid. 27.

While the tension in Juag Tati's household mounts, she is visited by Raden Ijroi, the son of the Chief Cleric of Wanasuka, Garut. Raden Idjroi is dismayed by the unhappiness Juag Tati is causing and informs both young people that they do not need the presence of a *wali* to ratify their marriage contract, but that they might legally act on their own initiative.[23] When still they waver, Raden Ijroi calls in his father, who gives a *fatwa*—as Rashīd Riḍā and Ahmad Soorkattie had done—in favour of the union.[24] This advice, of course, is tantamount to refuting the authority of the *ulama*, an application of ʿAbduh's first reform.

We meet the same argument in a short romantic novel, *Manehna Geus Nekad* (The Obstinate Regent) by S. Goenawan, published by the *Pembatjaan Rakyat* (People's Press) in Bandung in 1924. Similarly constructed like a pamphlet, this work appeared in simultaneous Sundanese and Malay versions. Its author was a member of the Communist Party of Indonesia who also ran the press. We should not wonder that a religious argument is brought into the text, since for a time there were close connections between the *Kaum Muda* and radical politics. The novel dates from that moment when Communist fortunes were allied to the life of the nationalist mass organisation, the *Sarekat Islam* (The Islamic Union) before its ranks were split in 1925 and resulted in the expulsion of the "red" Marxist wing from the Islamic "green".

Enden Mutiara, daughter of the "Regent of B.", is in love with Urip, a man of the people, a junior clerk and the son of a carpenter. She attempts to put off a marriage arranged by her parents to a young nobleman. Her mother tries to persuade her to give up the idea of marrying Urip but Mutiara defends her choice, using the arguments of her teacher of Qur'anic recitation. Mutiara says:

> Why, Mother, why must you differentiate between people? Is it because he is not a *Raden*, an *Aom*, not a *Raden Mas* and not even a *Mas*[25] that he is to be looked down upon? Or is it that you're afraid your own status will go down if you have a simple *Si* for your son-in-law? Does the honour or lowliness of humankind under heaven depend only on whether one has a title or not . . .?
>
> Some time ago, my Qur'ān teacher told me that all human beings are the descendants of Adam, that means one heritage, and I remember

[23] Ibid. 21 and 28.
[24] Ibid. 40.
[25] *Raden, Aom, Raden Mas, Mas*: feudal titles; *Si* indicates one of the common people.

> that you yourself, Mother, once said the like to me. Now you prove that what you told me is not true any more, since you're differentiating between people. Why must there be differences? Were there two Adams, Mother, a *Raden* Adam and a *Si* Adam? If that's the case, where's the truth in what you once said about people being descended of one line? Which side are you on, then, making out that Urip is tainted because he doesn't have a title?[26]

Mutiara is willing to back her convictions with action. Ready to die rather than be married to a man other than Urip, she takes poison, but is saved by the quick ministrations of a Dutch doctor. After a brief convalescence in hospital, Mutiara's father, the Regent relents and the marriage of the two young people goes ahead. This brief work was able to convey a message as acceptable to the *Kaum Muda* as it was to the Marxist doctrine of class warfare.

We now turn to motifs within novels as indices of *Kaum Tua* and *Kaum Muda* ideas.

5. *Anti-Sayyid Sentiments*

On the reformist list of issues to be addressed was the question of the veneration of the *sayyids*, or *Habib*, Arabs claiming descent from the Prophet through his daughter Fāṭimah. The practice of the *taqbil*, kissing the hand of the *sayyid*, and other outward forms of respect were deplored by the *Kaum Muda*.[27] The question of *taqbil* appears in an incident in M.K. Hardjakoesoema's *Wawacan Pareumeun Obor* (The Verse Tale of the Dimming of the Lamplight) (1928). The title is an idiom meaning "the loss of all family relationships", which encapsulates the action of the story: a young village man's discovery of his lost family tree and his resuming of his rightful place within a noble family.

The father of a poor peasant family in the Priangan dies suddenly; the young son, Salim goes to Batavia and finds work in a Dutch household. He studies and joins the native civil service, rising to high rank and dying in happy old age, pensioned and with many descendants. With his rationalism and his optimism, Salim is the ideal *Kaum Muda* hero, although the text as a whole maintains a balance between modernising and traditionalist sympathies. Parallel to the

[26] Goenawan 1923:11–120.
[27] Federspiel 1970a:64–68; Noer 1980:77.

Bildungsroman structure is Salim's reunion with his lost family. His father had quarrelled with his first wife in Banten and sought the anonymity of village life, re-marrying and settling in the Priangan. After a persistent search, Salim is able to reunite his village mother and his sister with their aristocratic relatives.

In the extract below, Salim has just come to Batavia to seek his fortune. Following his mother's wishes, he visits a saint's grave in Luar Batang near the city. With him is his best friend, the titled boy Encep Tarlan. The visit to a saint's grave is a feature of traditional Islam in the archipelago, as is the making of vows, *kaul*, and the distribution of alms which complete the ritual. For the *Kaum Muda*, this practice could too easily lead to *shirk*.[28] Salim refuses to pay the customary homage to an Arab boy asking for alms. There is a hidden irony in the mention of Luar Batang, however. The grave located there is that of one Habib Husein Alaidrus.[29] The venerated saint whose grave Salim was willing to visit was, as were many, a *sayyid*.

> On the completion of their orisons and thanksgivings, the two young men come out of the grave-site. Beggars have gathered there. Young Salim digs into his pockets and gives them all something, and Master Tarlan likewise. They offer alms befitting their vows. Meanwhile there appears on the scene an Arab boy, claiming to be a *Habib*, with his hand outstretched for alms.
>
> Master Tarlan proffers ten cents, but the boy does not withdraw his hand, so he receives another five, and young Salim stands motionless, staring at the *Habib*, looking him up and down. Salim glares at him, not paying any heed. Then rather than retreat, he hastens his stride and goes on ahead of Master Tarlan.
>
> When they have fallen back into step with each other again, Master Tarlan asks Salim why he didn't give anything to the *Habib*, for it is incumbent upon everyone to give alms to those of the Prophet's line and to ask for their blessing. Young Salim replies:
>
> "That is indeed so, but on the other hand, if he were truly of *Habib* blood-line, he would not have behaved so. As for those who play such a fraudulent game, it is unseemly behaviour for persons of sound body. Now that one just now bore no infirmities, rather what he did was an insult to the Prophet.
>
> Wasn't that proof enough of someone without shame, not to accept what was offered him, and to demand more of you? That was the mark of a low spirit. I do not believe it's right to give to the likes of that. Even though his *Habib* lineage be impeccable, if he displays such unfitting conduct, I'll not do him any honour."[30]

---

[28] Hamka 1967:99; Johns 1993c:26.
[29] Kostiner 1984:220ff.; Noer 1980:67.
[30] Hardjakoesoema 1928:43–44.

The novel as a whole, however, is socially conservative, for Salim's egalitarian sentiments are not matched at other levels in the story. There is still a belief in a nobility of the blood: his best friend is an aristocrat and Salim himself is a nobleman whose origins have been lost. His success in life as a government official is precisely what would have been his due, had he been raised within his true station from the start.

6. *Dukun*

Once, recourse to a *dukun*, or traditional healer, was universal in the Indonesian archipelago. In the colonial cities of Java, the *dukun's* reputation as a physical healer had declined with advances in tropical medicine, introduced by the medical services of the colonial government, but his reputation for powers to guide or influence the course of human affairs, especially matters of the heart, lived on. The *dukun* could dispense charms and spells which were especially useful in matters of love. He had also become a practitioner of "white magic", able to summon up spirits to some good purpose. Such practices were not considered to be antithetical to religion by the *Kaum Tua*, being an old accommodation by Islam in the archipelago, and one which Johns reminds us is by no means an exclusively Indonesian phenomenon.[31] For reformist thinkers, however, trust in the *dukun* represented one of a whole host of attitudes to be labelled as superstition (*takhayul*) or accretions (*khurafat*) deserving of purification.

I found four Sundanese novels featuring *dukun*, and in three out of these four, traditionalist attitudes prevail. The figure of the *dukun* enters the main action: the protagonist seeks the *dukun's* help and it is his ministrations which precipitate central events in the story. The representations of *dukun* perhaps give an archaic image of Indonesian society in the 1930s, for while we can find pamphlets written against the crafts of the *dukun* outside of fiction, the Sundanese novels treat them ambiguously, putting only the force of fate, *takdir*, above their powers.

In R. Memed Sastrahadiprawira's *Jodo Pakokolot* (Matched in Maturity) of 1930, Raden Suria-Sungkawa and Enden Ratna-Wulan are

[31] Johns 1993c:4–5.

not permitted to marry because although he is titled, he has not yet found work. Ratna-Wulan is married off to a man of high public rank. The disappointed Suria-Sungkawa follows a *dukun's* instructions to steal his beloved's detachable hair-bun in order to produce love magic which will return her affections to him. He bungles his attempt at theft, is arrested and thrown into gaol. The humiliation drives him to live as a recluse in the mountains. Fate later reunites the lovers after the sudden illness and death of both Ratna-Wulan's husband and her young son.

In M.K. Mangoendikaria's *Wawacan Siti Permana* (The Verse Tale of Siti Permana) of 1936, a village maiden of great beauty marries the man of her choice, the son of the village headman. The son of the local district official, who has become enamoured of her beauty, enlists the aid of a *dukun*, Ki Abdulkarim whose spell makes possible the abduction of Siti Permana and her immurement in the official's residence. When Ki Abdulkarim dies, the spell is broken. Permana shakes off its effects and her husband, Mas Prawira, who has gone temporarily mad with grief over the loss of his bride, comes to his senses and is able to reclaim her.

It is Moh. Ambri who gives the most developed picture of the role of a *dukun*. The most celebrated Sundanese writer of the pre-war period, Ambri maintained a lifetime interest in matters mystical; he was a member of a *tarekat* and a practising *dukun*, reputed to possess healing powers and able to perform exorcisms, mainly of nuisance spirits of place. His fiction reports on the psychological and spiritual life of the Sundanese.

His 1935 work *Lain Eta* (Not The One), is a novel about an arranged marriage, set among the Muslim nobility of the conservative city of Cianjur. The heroine Neng Eha, daughter of the *Kalipah* (Assistant Chief Cleric) of the Mosque administration is not permitted to marry Juragan Mahmud, the young man with whom she is in love because he does not bear a title. A marriage is arranged to her father's kinsman, Raden Mantri, a high civil official. The Mantri is middle-aged and has a brood of unruly children from a previous marriage. He cherishes Eha but she despises him in return. There are a number of emotional crises in the novel as the passionate and intelligent Neng Eha is reduced to spiritless resignation to what life has dealt her. First is Eha's parting with her first suitor, Mahmud; second, her sexual capitulation to her husband after having refused to join his bed for some months after the wedding (which encounter leaves her bitterly disappointed) and third, a desperate visit to a *dukun*. Neng Eha has begged her aunt, Juragan Teja, to take her to a *dukun* to find some means to alienate her husband's affections so that he will repudiate her. She has run away from him several times, again refused him his rights of consorting, and has forsaken the marriage in every way possible. The Mantri, however, insists on reconciliation and will not grant Eha a divorce.

The *dukun's* refusal to help Neng Eha rid herself of her despised husband confirms her in a path of flagrant infidelity. Her father disowns her. She takes up with a young man who resembles her lost Mahmud, living openly with him in his house in Bandung; she contracts typhoid and goes through a long convalescence. Finally, seeing no other way open to her, Neng Eha begs forgiveness of her father for her actions, is reconciled with him and returns to live in his house.

The *dukun*, Mang Okom is presented in a conventional portrait: he is an old man living in mean material conditions outside the limits of the city, yet he handles Neng Eha's distress with sympathy and sophistication. He does not admit Eha's case to lie beyond his powers, and gives her to believe that he can help her. A true doctor of the psyche, he divines correctly the nature of the relationship between the Mantri and Eha and will not risk incurring the sin of intervention in another man's marriage. The measures he prescribes for Neng Eha to change her husband's heart (fasting and praying) are therefore impossibly rigorous; they are in effect intended to be a deterrent to her purpose. In the end, we know that Mang Okom will not help Eha as she would wish. In a supremely tactful course, he commits her situation to the will of the Almighty.[32]

In M.K. Hardjakoesoema's *Wawacan Pareumeun Obor*, mentioned above, we find a rare statement against *dukun* in pre-war Sundanese fiction. The young hero, Salim berates his mother for using the services of a mid-wife *dukun* in the delivery of her second child. This again is a minor incident in the novel, but it is also the first indication of Salim as a rationalist hero, a boy of sharp and inquiring mind. Nyi Patimah is a simple, quiescent village woman who sees no harm in maintaining the customs of the past. Salim questions the *dukun's* performance and the elaborate appurtenances of her craft.

[32] Ambri 1935:48–50.

He is made the mouthpiece of *Kaum Muda* ideology, and although there is no mention of the terms *takhayul*, nor of *khurafat*, Patimah's explanation that the practices are "from our ancestors and our forbears from Buddhist times" leaves no doubt as to what is intended:

> Patimah is cared for as is the custom. When the mid-wife's work is done, she lies back, resting on pillows, with legs extended, her brow anointed with a black medicinal paste.[33] The child has been swathed and is nursed against its mother's breast. A standing lamp gives off a glow from beside her and an incense burner throws out varied stripes of light.
>
> The mid-wife sprinkles water upon the censer, walking back and forth around the house. The aroma rises up in drifts. A container of turmeric stands by Patimah's side, little pouches of herbs lie scattered around her and threads of cotton are strung about, to vouchsafe the mid-wife's efforts.
>
> Nyi Patimah opens her mouth to speak, indicating that she wants Salim to fetch her a drink from the water flask, and Salim busies himself in serving his mother. Muttering all the while about the mid-wife's ministrations, he says: "Ah, what's the use of all this?"
>
> His mother answers gently, "Indeed, my son, this has been common practice from our ancestors and our forbears, that when a woman gives birth, she must be attended in this way. I myself don't understand how it all came to be. It seems it dates from Buddhist times, and so has passed down to us today. I have done it because it's customary."
>
> Then Salim replies: "But if you don't understand it, what's the use of it? Why do you go along with all this paraphernalia?" His mother answers with a smile, "It's true what you say, my son, but you must give some thought as to how you might be hurting others.
>
> If we find fault with what's a common belief and does no harm and causes us no disadvantage, even though we feel it's unnecessary in a religious sense to perform such practices, and though we follow like buffaloes, it's hard to stop uninformed people."
>
> Whereupon Salim falls silent, shifting about as if in confusion. In her heart, Patimah bears guarded praise for her son for having the inclination to put his mind to such things, and she knows that later on, he will become a man of discernment, because he has shown himself keen to inquire into all matters.[34]

Within the next few pages of the work, the ideological balance swings back in favour of a traditionalist view. A community of pious Muslim women is identified, and through them a reference to the *Kaum Tua* is made. For all their simplicity, the village women are kindly and of good faith and although Nyi Patimah has just become a widow and she and her children are now left destitute, there follows a moment

[33] *Turmeric paste*: a natural disinfectant as well as a decorative balm in rituals of purification.

[34] Hardjakoesoema 1928:16–17.

of comfort for her. The custom of giving a feast, *sidekah*, after the delivery of a child is a traditionalist one, as is that of reciting from the Stories of the Prophets. The lyricism of the natural description softens the harshness of Salim's criticism of the mid-wife who has attended his mother. The event takes place on the evening of the day after Nyi Patimah has given birth:

> By chance it is a night of the full moon, whose light floods over all, lighting up the earth and gladdening human hearts, even of those in sorrow. A cool breeze has arisen, and drifts over the flower gardens.
>
> The women approach arm in arm, going at a leisurely pace, by the light of the newly-risen moon, apparelled in fresh clean clothes. They emerge from the stillness, moving in perfect comportment, for these are pious women, and so they arrive at Patimah's house.
>
> Inside, preparations have been made and mats have been spread on the floor. Before the guests seat themselves, the mid-wife bustles about, setting the mats in order and inviting the guests to sit down. The women settle themselves in a row, encircling refreshments standing ready. The village headman's wife speaks up: "Come, Bibi Erum, begin the reading straight away. It's already late." So Erum's voice rises in song.
>
> Her voice carries on the breeze, accompanied by the clear sound of someone playing a flute. The tune falls pleasantly on their ears as she reads with correct phrasing and pausing, at a lively pace, and Bibi Erum alternates singing with Miss Ni'ah. Those listening give it their full attention, for they are all women well versed in religion.
>
> Tonight the acts of the Prophets are being sung about, and in between the verses, there are passages rendered in ordinary language. Thus they recite and re-tell, so that all that is read out is perfectly comprehended. The headman's wife leads the performance, narrating in perfect order, and in the end it comes out well and the task is expediently executed.[35]

In this essay, I have restricted my comments to the most visible literary representations of *Kaum Muda* and *Kaum Tua* ideas; in fact, to little more than checking against a list, among a number possible, of *bida*ᶜ or "deviations" proscribed by the Reformist programme.[36] However, Johns,[37] in an analysis of just such one visible issue—the rejection of the use of the *usalli*, the statement of readiness preceding the ritual prayers—has recently demonstrated how it flags the broader weight and significance of reform. Beyond the minutiae of juristic argument lay the larger moral dimensions of the challenge of reform and traditionalist responses. This brief discussion of Sundanese realist fiction of the pre-war period offers some notion of the human concerns around *Kaum Muda* and *Kaum Tua* among the Muslims of West Java.

---

[35] Ibid. 18.
[36] Hamka 1967:98–100.
[37] Johns 1993c.

"FUNDAMENTALISM" RECONSIDERED

Towards the "Reactualisation of Islam"

CLIVE S. KESSLER

1. *Introduction*

The phenomenon generally known, and usually misrecognised, as Islamic "fundamentalism" consists, in the many countries where it is found, of a variety of efforts towards the "re-realisation" of Islam. This endeavour is not, as a frequently bestowed characterisation suggests, one of religious "revivalism". This label, as its critics persistently protest, would wrongly imply that Islam had somehow been dead or dying before the Islamic movement's late twentieth-century efflorescence. Nor, they insist, can the Islamic movement be appropriately typified as one simply of "renewal", the renovation of a faith that had somehow become old-fashioned, out-of-date, or obsolete. How, they ask, could this possibly be true of a faith, born of the final divine revelation, that is to be for all time? The Islamic movement, as such critics insist, is one not of revivalism or even renewal but rather of "reactualisation". Long neglected—its authentic essence preserved only as an ideal by a faithful few—Islam is now to be implemented comprehensively and, as a totality, at last made real.[1]

In its various and even contrary forms throughout the Muslim world, the movement displays not so much a common appearance or goal or even outward direction but a common underlying impetus, a generating and activating impulse. The differing forms that this impulse takes are no less diverse than the specific contexts from which those movements emerge and the particular local accents lent to the articulation of their Islamist agendas. They are movements, or a loose family of movements, seeking not a selective affirmation of "fundamentals" nor the "revival" of a moribund faith but to reactualise—to endow, in the circumstances of our time, with new expression and a new form—an enduring but at times overshadowed, even neglected or suppressed, or at best a hitherto only partially achieved ideal.

---

[1] This is the central insistence, for example, of Muhammad Abu Bakar, signalled in the title of his award-winning collection of essays (1989).

These movements are seeking ways to implement anew and reactualise a cherished and, to its adherents, a permanently valid and binding ensemble of religious ideals: those that derive from the revelations made to Muḥammad during the course of his prophethood together with the related, subsequently formed moral and cultural values to which those ideals gave rise and which for a while gloriously animated what was to become known, in its period of growth and ensuing stasis and even eclipse, as Islamic civilisation. They pursue the realisation or reactualisation within the socio-political world of the late twentieth century and beyond of an historic, religiously-informed civilisational ideal: an ideal which (in the eyes of virtually all Muslims, not just the movement's zealots, supporters, and fellow travellers) emerged within history, immediately transformed and thereafter shaped human history, and then somehow—during a traumatic era of foreign domination—lived on in history within a trajectory of world development that for a while somehow abandoned it or, for reasons that puzzlingly resist satisfactory explanation, refused its divinely assured charter of determinative primacy.

The challenge that, in all its various forms, the movement faces and the objective that it seeks to realise is simply how, once again, to express that ideal within history, here and now and into our common global future, and to restore Islam's historical primacy, its ethical and civilisational as much as its (in the narrower Western sense) "religious" centrality. Instead of having their history written, as for centuries too much of it was, by others, how might Muslims—and through them Islam itself—recapture the ability not only to begin writing their own history but once more that of all humankind? Islam might and should serve as the framework for a universal human future, the Islamic activists are convinced; the question is how.

The similarities among these various modern, contending Islamist social movements are generated from the restless and varied exploration of this deeper dynamic. In all its various forms, this pursuit of Islamic "reactualisation" seeks an overdue rendezvous with universal human destiny, a renewed contemporary historical pertinence, and with it also historical vindication—through a struggle to achieve the institutional embodiment of enduring ideals within the modern social and political order of humankind. It is this history-reaffirming search that makes these movements (if we are to avoid the contested and misleading terms "fundamentalism" and "revival") movements of Islamic reassertion and resurgence. For their adherents, the rendezvous with history—Islam's reassertion of its universal historical significance—

is also a rediscovery and reaffirmation of authentic Islamic identity, a resurgence of its people as avowed Muslims on the stage of world history.

2. *Reactualising Islam: Three Scenarios*

Various options for "reactualising" Islam are identifiable. Among them, three major trends or possibilities—distinctive modalities of Islamic action—are prominent. What differentiate them are the kinds of measures—their combination and the priorities among them—for Islamization that they use and the focus or emphasis of their deployment. While all the three main identifiable tendencies of the movement are concerned, as they understand it, with the project of "Islamization"—or the contemporary reactualisation of authentic Islam—they vary in their approach, their tactics, and in their choice of strategic focus for their Islamising efforts.

Islamization measures may be directed at four levels or targets: at people, as actual or prospective Muslims; at society and its cultural values; at the law and legal system more broadly; and at the state itself. Accordingly, while the boundaries between them are fluid and not absolute, three different modalities of Islamic activism may be identified on the basis of their choice and preferred combination of measures: those that focus primarily on people, with some emphasis on social values and culture at a more general level; those that are concerned primarily with imbuing social and cultural values with a greater Islamic content or emphasis, while also carrying this concern forward to some degree into the area of legal values, processes, and institutions; and those that, while regarding all four levels or dimensions as important, give priority to the creation of an Islamic state and the top-down Islamization of formal legal codes and procedures (and which accordingly urge the implementation of *shariʿa* law as state law, or at least reform of existing law along increasingly *shariʿa*-based lines, as the means for a comprehensive Islamic transformation including the reorientation of people, society, values, and culture).

2.1 *Communitarian Reinvention*

In its clearest form, the first strategy in effect seeks to reinvent, as they are imagined, the Muslims of the seventh century and to make them a model for emulation in the twentieth and beyond. It seeks, in effect, to reactualise what is imagined as the paradigmatic Islamic society, namely Medina at the time of the Prophet Muḥammad. Some of those in Southeast Asia who favour this imagined option seem content simply to affect this archaic, Arabizing "lifestyle"—the men often adopting white or green robes and turbans and upholding polygamy as a practice favoured by the Prophet himself (while, shrouded in flowing black, the women of this tendency reportedly subscribe to these domestic arrangements with varying degrees of enthusiasm). But while it is easy to scorn these efforts as some contrived twentieth century pantomime performance of a simplistically imagined seventh-century reality (not unlike many of the crudely-made Egyptian movies on classical Islamic historical themes that are at times shown on Malaysian television), there is often an impressive moral seriousness to many of them.

This strategy or modality of Islamic action and reactualisation is one essentially of retreat: of opting out of modernity and turning one's back on its pursuit in favour of what is seen—and also appeals—as a simpler, pristine, and authentic Islamic way of life. Energetically committed, in its own terms, to worldliness, it rejects the modern world and its developmental trajectory for a different path and direction. If the Prophet Muḥammad was the *insān kāmil*, the model or exemplary human being, then how better might one ever aspire to live than by seeking to imitate and approximate to the life-pattern of this paragon? Attempting, to the extent still possible, to live his kind of life in our times is, for them, a way of being close to the Prophet himself, of experiencing in one's own life the authentic and formative moment of Islam. As a turning away from the modern world and also in its association with Medina—a replication of the Prophet's own move there from worldly and compromised Mecca, imitating his impetus towards the full realisation of the Islamic revelation in the intense community life of Medina—this modality of Islamic action is not simply retreat but also *hijra*: that paradigmatic form of Muslim action, a journey or quest, a venture in which physical movement symbolises human and moral transformation.[2]

While many of this tendency are rejectionists in full retreat from modernity, this is not true of them all. In fact, the most conspicuous

---

[2] On *hijra* as a paradigmatic mode of Islamic action, see Kessler 1992:147–153, esp. pp. 148–149.

and controversial manifestation of this tendency in Malaysia in recent times has been the *Dar-ul-Arqam* movement, which combined the outward appearance of this kind of retreat from the workaday world with a variety of almost Gandhian strategies for "people-based" self-help and grass-roots economic development. The movement as a collective maintained an extensive range of enterprises and commercially-based service activities that deeply involved its members in mundane entrepreneurial action and committed them energetically and industriously to worldly pursuits.

To the extent that movements of this kind simply opt out of development and modernity, they may go against a modern government's sustained developmental push but are no threat to it. Whatever their religious and cultural interest, they are therefore of only marginal political significance. As for *Dar-ul-Arqam*, with its combination of retreat from and recommitment of its followers to the world of material pursuits and well-being, it was no threat to government economic or social policy. There was much in it that a modern government might admire—especially a government urging its people to become self-reliant, and not to base their hopes for economic improvement on never-ending official assistance or the provision of projects and opportunities. But the *Arqam* movement became an object of official concern and frequently voiced displeasure and condemnation—and ultimately of proscription—on religious grounds, because of the movement's markedly heterodox beliefs and their capacity, in the opinion of the government and its religious officials, to undermine orthodox faith.

Proponents of this first tendency place priority on the Islamization of people, their lives and values and personalities. Some are concerned with the propagation of Islam among non-Muslims and securing their conversion. But most groups within this tendency aim at the Islamization of the members of the Muslim *umma* itself: at calling them back to a largely forgotten faith and misunderstood practice through intense participation in a frequently communitarian way of life. The slogan "Let us be Muslims!"—Mawdudi's call[3] to Muslims to rediscover and reacquaint themselves with their ancestral faith and to endeavour to begin living it out in full seriousness—captures their essential strategy and impetus.

---

[3] Mawdudi 1985.

2.2 *Absorption of Islamic Values or the Implementation of Islamic Law?*

In today's Islamist rivalries, adherents of that first, somewhat quietist modality stand largely on the sidelines. The principal political struggle in the contemporary Islamic world is between the exponents of the second and third approaches. In Malaysia that struggle is expressed in the rivalry between the United Malays National Organisation (UMNO), and the UMNO-led *Barisan Nasional* government, and Parti Islam Se-Malaysia (PAS), the leading Malay-based opposition party. Broadly committed to a gradualist approach towards Islamization, UMNO is challenged by PAS which, especially since the accession to power within it in the early 1980s of a new cohort of Islamic activists, uncompromisingly pursues an Islamist agenda. In the northeastern state of Kelantan where it wields local power, PAS seeks not merely to exemplify the thoroughgoing approach to Islamization but, in microcosm, to "showcase" its appeals and feasibility. While the UMNO gives prime emphasis to the Islamization of Malaysian society via the absorption of core Islamic values into its governing institutions and processes, the PAS scenario is one of Islamising the state directly, most immediately through the implementation of the *sharīʿa* as—or as the basis of—modern Malaysian state law.

Modern Malaysian politics, including conflicts over Islamization and the UMNO's struggle with PAS, need no detailed account here.[4] But the consequences of that struggle for the nature of the Malaysian state and its legal system deserve some analytical examination. For although UMNO and PAS have pursued and broadly exemplify two different strategies of Islamization, the boundaries between these approaches, as already noted, are neither solid nor absolute. Moreover, the very conflict between UMNO and PAS over the years has only further blurred the differences between the two approaches. A certain fuzziness, or apparent lack of precise delineation of official state policy, may often result from a government's need to accommodate diverse, even competing interests. Among the circumstances that have made the pursuit of clear and unambiguous policies difficult, of particular significance here has been the UMNO's need to ensure that it is neither ideologically outflanked by its Islamic critics, in PAS and also outside it, nor loses control to them of its ability to

[4] For an overview, see Means 1991.

set the national agenda of Islamization and regulate the momentum of its implementation. UMNO accommodation to these constraints and the resulting occasional imprecision or apparent inconsistency of government policy towards Islam have themselves had certain implications for the nature of the state and society in Malaysia that deserve attention.

The UMNO has been determined to pursue accelerated economic growth and thereby to modernise Malaysian—and, centrally within it, Malay—society. In doing so, it has been opposed by and, in direct political terms, has successfully resisted PAS, its main rival for political support within the ascendant Malay component of Malaysia's electorate and population. In opposing a rival fully committed to the cause of Islamization and impelled by the vision of a *shari'a*-centred state and legal system, UMNO can afford to make no concessions to PAS's claim that it alone embodies the political cause of Islam. The cumulative effect of UMNO's determination not to be outbid by the more insistent or thoroughgoing Islamizers has been the growing rapprochement of the second approach with the third, even its unacknowledged if incremental capitulation to the latter's tenor and demands. PAS's approach, and the UMNO's reluctance to be left exposed as it seeks to stand aside from its rival's more direct approach to Islamization, has threatened over time to make UMNO Islamic policy hostage to PAS rhetoric and strategy.

For, no matter how far—willingly or with prudent reluctance—the UMNO goes, so long as its objectives are more restrained in implementation and less ambitious in scope than PAS's, it can always be outbid by PAS. It must, in the midst of political competition, always seek to differentiate itself and its approach from that of PAS; but, to the extent that it succeeds, every such effort at differentiation only provides PAS with leverage over it. Yet, even if it were at any point to abolish that gap by embracing fully the PAS position, PAS always has the option, often taken in the past, simply to increase its demands and once more outbid UMNO, thereby further raising the stakes in the ideological battle over Malaysian Islamization. Cumulatively, this has not only shaped UMNO policy towards Islam, bringing it closer to that of PAS. By affecting the policy and strategic action of the nation's governing party, it has also affected the character of the state and its legal system, bringing them some way towards PAS's requirements.

From outside government, Malaysia's Islamic opposition party has in this way exerted a significant influence upon the UMNO as an instrument of Islamization. The dynamic of its political competition with PAS has led the UMNO over time to redefine its Islamic policies: the gradual adoption of a number of Islamization measures has incrementally shifted UMNO's focus from the inculcation of Islamic values to the enactment and enforcement of selected legal provisions drawn from the *shariʿa* legal tradition. Respecting the religious freedom of Malaysia's non-Muslim citizens, the UMNO-led government has quite scrupulously insisted that these provisions apply only to Muslims in the country. Even so, these developments pose some fundamentally important issues about the character of the Malaysian state and the direction of its further development.

Often, these measures introduced by UMNO have involved the enactment, through legislation as statute law, of selected elements drawn from the *shariʿa* legal tradition. As a result of this process of the elaboration and growing implementation of substantive Islamic law, the state's Muslim and non-Muslim citizens have become increasingly subject to the enforcement of somewhat different legal systems and, in time, are coming to inhabit rather distinct and divergent socio-cultural spaces. The state has increasingly developed a distinctly different attitude towards and interest in these two contrasting categories of citizens. While it is by no means indifferent to its non-Muslim citizens, the state is not greatly interested in their private lives or conscience and only requires them to be publicly law-abiding; but it is intensely concerned with the intimate life and even private religious conscience of its Muslim subjects, requiring of them a kind of moral conformity and obedience that far exceeds simple outward compliance with the legal conventions of modern civil society. The Muslim citizen's relation to and experience of the state become increasingly distinct and divergent from the non-Muslim's.

As a result of the concern of the state, under pressure from PAS, to make its Muslim citizens increasingly subject to the advancing requirements of Islamic law, the state is in effect creating amongst its people two increasingly divergent categories of citizenry. But these measures for the selective enforcement of certain *shariʿa* provisions do not only constrain Malaysia's Muslims and thereby establish a dichotomy between the everyday life-worlds of its Muslim and non-Muslim people. In addition to reshaping Malaysian society, they thereby also reshape the Malaysian state itself.

Since colonial times, but markedly in the years since the emergence of the modern Islamic movement in Malaysia during the 1970s, the state has in this way played a crucial role in giving the force of statute law to elements drawn from the intellectual tradition of Islamic legal culture. It is through its own civil legislative processes that the Malaysian state increasingly chooses to authenticate and enforce, as enacted statute law, selected elements drawn from the Islamic legal tradition. This process not only has profound implications for the standing and tenor of Islamic law in Malaysia. Its deepening and intensifying involvement in this process of lending its own authority to the implementation of selected provisions of the *shariʿa* law tradition also has important consequences for the state itself. What is involved here is much more than any simple opposition or balance or distinction, as a number of legal scholars seem to hold, between so-called "civil" and "religious" law. No such simple distinction may any longer be drawn, precisely because of the pre-eminent role played by the civil processes of the state in giving those elements that it chooses to recognise from the *shariʿa* tradition the standing and force of statute law, state-enacted and state-mandated.

What is significant here is the historical and political basis of that recent *shariʿa*-based modification in the nature of the Malaysian state. In the early years of his prime ministership, the emphasis in Dr Mahathir's policies in this area was upon Islamic values: upon intensifying public and private commitment to Islamic values among the nation's Muslim, especially Malay, citizens and, by that means, upon the "absorption"—or assimilation by moral osmosis—of broad Islamic values of potentially universal appeal, albeit cast in Malay Muslim terms, into the structure and institutions and processes of the state. Over the 1980s and beyond, the emphasis has shifted. The approach has become far more legally oriented. This shift—and the consequent blurring in the Malaysian context of the distinction between the "Islamization of people and values" approach and the sterner "Islamization of people and their culture and social values under the state through the enactment of *shariʿa*" approach—has been the result of the UMNO's continuing political struggle with PAS. UMNO anxieties towards and accommodation of PAS as the "pacemaker" of Malaysian Islamization have resulted in a creeping if often imperceptible capitulation on many issues to the PAS approach and project.

But whether it is given eagerly by a *shariʿa*-minded party such as PAS or more reluctantly by a party primarily concerned with economic growth—or as a result of the competition between parties of those two kinds—the greater weight and prominence thereby given to the *shariʿa* has one clear consequence: the increasing centrality and power as well of the *ulama* as an "estate" of broad social authority, based upon their expertise in and custodianship of traditional religious knowledge, most notably of Islamic legal culture. And where Arabic—the language of the Qurʾān and of Islamic high culture including legal knowledge—is not the dominant language of a nation's civilisation and region, the power that the *ulama* may exert through the special legal expertise that they claim is enhanced by their similar near-monopoly over the knowledge of classical Arabic, command of which, they aver, is essential to accurate human understanding of the divine Qurʾanic word and the system of law issuing from it.

In this way, in circumstances such as those of contemporary Malaysia, the actions of a governing party centrally and pragmatically committed to economic rationalism and growth may, even inadvertently, promote the cause of a resurgent clericalism—a clericalism that is only rendered invisible to most who are subjected to it by the familiar and often repeated insistence that in Islam, unlike Catholicism, there is no clergy to interpose itself between the believer and the Almighty. Prompted by understandable and quite urgent political pressures, the ambiguities of UMNO policy towards Islamization have begun to have long-term structural implications—through the state-supported role of the state-supporting *ulama*—for the Malaysian state. In particular, the influence within the state, and upon society generally, of certain understandings of the Islamic legal tradition—and of its pre-eminent and zealous custodians among the *ulama*—has increased enormously. In their zeal, the *ulama* see any questioning of their own claims to an exclusive role in religious and legal interpretation as a repudiation of the *shariʿa* and its requirements, even as an attack upon Islam itself: for them, in effect, mere opposition to the clerisy is itself heresy.

3. *Ijtihadic Islam: A Fourth Option?*

In addition to the three broad modalities or scenarios for the "reactualisation" of Islam noted above, there is in fact a fourth: one that represents a rather different manifestation of the same underlying impulse to give expression, form, and pertinence to Islam within the modern world. But, while arising from the same sources, animated by the same impetus, and therefore generically part of that same contemporary Islamic movement, this fourth approach is not recognised as part of it. Far from being simply ignored, this venture in the contemporary reactualisation of Islam is in fact rejected by the mainstream Islamic movement and often condemned by it as one of Islam's principal and most dangerous enemies.

While the position known over the last century as "Islamic modernism" has been overwhelmed by a resurgent neo-traditionalism and has even itself become a beleaguered tradition, there are those in the Muslim world today, including Malaysia, who in effect seek to implement in today's terms and under today's conditions the same kind of Islamic agenda that was pursued at the onset of the modern period by such pioneers of Islamic modernism as Muḥammad ʿAbduh. Their approach is moral, cultural, ethical, and civilisational. They focus not upon law or the state nor upon the traditions and idealised practices of the first *umma* in Medina but upon what they understand as the core values of the Qurʾanic revelation. They are not so much "fundamentalists" or "scripturalists" as Islamic "essentialists". For them, the inner impulse of Islam and its historical call is moral, energetically activist, rational, egalitarian, and emancipatory. It is a call to and of a faith that is grounded in the connection between reason and the knowledge that it yields, a far-reaching compassion, and a consistent demand for justice. These are values that, for them, are both enduring and modern, Islamic and universal.

The challenge facing modern Muslims, for them, is to be both modern and Muslim, to participate in both Islamic civilisation and the world of modernity, to pursue and promote modernity within Islamic culture and beyond it on an Islamic basis: not simply, that is, by modernising Islamic civilisation but also by bringing Islam and its distinctive contribution to bear within an emerging worldwide, universal human culture of modernity.

Their position is that the Qurʾān and its message speak directly to humankind; that, using their divinely endowed reason that differentiates responsible humans from animals and those who act only from base impulses, modern people are able to understand, in its powerful directness and austere ethical simplicity, the Qurʾanic message and its moral imperatives; and that today's Muslims can and must strive, through the use of their capacity for autonomous moral reasoning and their own independent judgement, to give modern social expression and form to the Qurʾanic vision.

Their position is a kind of moral and cultural as well as religious equivalent to "zero-based budgeting". Instead of being obliged to take on, with all its accumulated anachronisms and ambiguities, its irrelevancies and embarrassments, the entire post-Qur'anic legacy of Islamic civilisation, they are ready to wipe the historical board clean and start anew. They do not propose to discard wholesale all that the history of Islamic civilisation has bequeathed to today's believers, but they insist on the right and obligation of modern Muslims to review that legacy critically, to decide how its historical evolution is to be understood, and to choose on that basis which parts of it are to be reappropriated into contemporary Muslim life and thought, and how. That is, they do not repudiate history, only the dubious historical assertion that what prevailed contingently in the past necessarily remains obligatory and legitimating in the present.

They wish instead to go back to the Qur'anic essentials, to explore and seek to apply them in a modern way within their own lives. Without repudiating Islamic civilisation and its legal-centred intellectual culture in its entirety, "root and branch", they wish to address and draw upon their Islamic heritage critically, creatively, and with a selectivity born of intellectual fastidiousness. Not unmindful of the past but not subjugated to it either, they would actualise, even in ways that were never previously possible in Islamic and human history, the core Qur'anic vision. They wish to address Islam's founding Qur'anic impulse from the basis of today, their efforts unmediated and unconstrained by any reverential obligation towards what emerged as historical Islam in the intervening period.

While the orthodox *ulama* treat much of what Islamic civilisation yielded—and especially its accumulated legal traditions and culture in which the *ulama* elaborated upon the meaning of the Qur'ān—as canonical, immutable, and enduringly binding, the new modernists insist upon the historicity of the Islamic tradition including the entire body of *sharī'a* law itself (that is, the *fiqh*, including, but not only, the so-called *hudud* punishments). To the *ulama* (no matter how selective they must be in their actual if unacknowledged intellectual practice, and however contingent historically their own interpretations must therefore necessarily be), whatever has throughout history entered into the Islamic legal and theological tradition avowedly remains ever binding thereafter, not subject to abrogation; for the new modernists, Islamic culture in its entirety, and especially its legal forms and expression, must be understood historically, assessed critically, and modified or set aside if found wanting.

For the *ulama*, therefore, the accumulated *sharīʿa* becomes, in effect, an intrinsic part of the divine revelation which it interprets. For the modernists, it is a human construct—the product of people whose understanding, no matter how capable they were, was limited by the circumstances of time and place—and one which therefore needs to be approached critically. To the traditionalist *ulama*, this position is not merely error but intellectual and moral deviation. For the modernists, the *sharīʿa* not only can be subjected to revision and thoroughgoing reformulation; it positively requires such treatment.

Just as the classical scholars elaborated and "actualised", as best they could, Islam in their time, so too can and must modern Muslims in these times reactualise Islam in currently appropriate terms and relevant forms, not limited by any obligation to preserve or adhere to what were merely a previous generation's necessarily imperfect human measures to realise a timeless ideal. Indeed, far from the Medinan moment or that of the classical *ulama* being a privileged or paradigmatic one, the emergence of the modern world (the new modernists maintain) has now created a context more appropriate to the historical realisation of the Qur'anic vision than any that ever existed before: a modern culture has emerged that is congruent at last with Islam's always modern ethos, and a universal human civilisation commensurate with Islam's universalistic aspirations. If so, the limited past cannot dictate to or restrict a present more pregnant with possibilities for authentically actualising Islam; rather, the present, and the Islamic future to which it is a bridge, will illuminate and clarify a more heroic but necessarily narrower past in which the Islamic vision first entered human history. For the modernists, the Prophet was a human being through whom a divine message was given, addressed to the people and in the circumstances of that time. Everything else about Islam other than the divine message itself is a human construct, is characterised by circumstance, is historically contingent and conditioned or marked by its historicity.

For the orthodox *ulama*, in contrast, it is not just the Prophet's message in the Qur'ān that is sacred. So too, and in effect no less so, are the *sunna* (exemplary lived practice) including the *ḥadīth* (anecdotal reports of the life and sayings of the Prophet which are seen as amplifying the Qur'ān), as well as the *sharīʿa* itself as a body of

Qur'anically-derived divine law built by the *ulama* upon their own interpretation of the Qur'ān and *ḥadīth*. To the modernists this position entails an unwarranted "sacralisation" of the *sunna* and *ḥadīth* and of the historically evolved, humanly produced, and also politically conditioned *sharīʿa*—a sacralisation which, to put the matter starkly, approaches idolatry. It treats as divinely authoritative something of purely human origins and making.[5]

This critical approach of the new modernists yields what is clearly an Islam of and for the intellectual, the modern intellectual, and those similarly educated and inclined professionals who see themselves as part of the worldwide project and culture of modernity. To the three mainstream trends within the Islamic movement they are, of course, mere secularists, lost and misguided Muslim souls who have been culturally and morally uprooted, contaminated by "Orientalism", afflicted with what the Iranian publicist Jalal Al-e Ahmad termed the painful *dis*"orientation" of "occidentosis" or "West struckness".[6]

What the members of this newer generation of contemporary modernists are urging is, in fact, the reopening and renewal of *ijtihad*, of informed independent judgement and moral reasoning, on a prospectively universal and even communitarian or collective basis within the *umma*—not as a privilege, prerogative, or monopoly (as the traditionalists would have it) of the orthodox *ulama*. Theirs might be characterised as an "ijtihadic"—an unconditionally and universally ijtihadic—Islam.

Such an approach is hardly a universally welcome one within today's worldwide Muslim *umma*. It would clearly bypass, and suspend the continuing obligatoriness of, the entire accumulated weight of Islamic culture (including traditional Islamic legal culture) of which the *ulama* see themselves as custodians and over which they claim a monopoly expertise. Moreover, by asserting the direct accessibility of the essential Qur'anic message to the responsible and enquiring Muslim mind, this ijtihadic approach would undercut the claims of the *ulama* to play a decisive role as indispensable intermediary-interpreters between the faithful and the sacred texts through which the Almighty has been and is to be known.

Not surprisingly, therefore, this thoroughgoing ijtihadic approach is one that is reviled by the orthodox *ulama* and their followers. There

---

[5] A position outlined with impressive precision by Larif-Béatrix 1994.
[6] Jalal Al-e Ahmad 1984.

is no doubt that this revulsion against the new modernists is genuinely experienced, on their part, by the *ulama* as a justified and righteous as well as the required response of the learned to those who would damage what they understand as Islam itself. But it is also clear, often quite explicitly to the *ulama* themselves, that—by devaluing their own religious expertise and eroding their own exclusive role and consequent rights as authorised interpreters of divine intentions and requirements—the ijtihadic approach of the modernists and their call for unconditional or universal *ijtihad* are a direct assault on their own position and social authority.

The point is sharply encapsulated within the argument of one such *alim* in a television debate: the *ulama* are the heirs of the Prophet (*ulama adalah pewaris Nabi*), he asserted, and since the Prophet was the legislator in his own time, his heirs and successors, today's *ulama*, should exclusively exercise in the present the state's legislative and legal-interpretative functions. "We in Malaysia are fortunate," he continued. "We have our freedom [*merdeka*], we have the Qur'ān, we have the *sunna*, and we have the *ulama*. What more could we possibly want or need?" Those who want to bypass the *ulama*, their expertise and prerogatives and to interpret the Qur'ān for themselves in the light of their own powers of human reason confuse themselves and others, he insisted; they are dangerous and must be opposed. In their righteous indignation at the ijtihadic modernists, the *ulama* are in that happy position where they can simultaneously defend their own interests, pride, and passions as well as the principles and dignity of Islam itself.

4. *Unrecognised Affinities?*

The characterisation just offered of a "fourth option" or approach in Islamization—of what is here termed "ijtihadic Islam"—can be applied to a number of small but significant movements in different Muslim countries, and to what is therefore a significant intellectual tendency throughout the Muslim world.

To draw this general intellectual portrait of this tendency and offer some account of the common underlying logic and historical sensibility that informs the thinking of these new modernists serves two purposes. First, it provides some comparative context, within an overview of the situation of contemporary Islamic politics and Muslim thought, within which such scattered groups can be placed and better understood. Seen in this way, they are not peculiar phenomena, aberrant groups deserving marginalisation because of their differences from mainstream Muslim socio-political thought. Set in this wider context they can be more appropriately appreciated: as early, possibly significant, manifestations of a major worldwide trend or intellectual tendency in contemporary Islam.

Second, to see the their arguments and these ijtihadic tendencies in worldwide contemporary Islam in this way—as the exploration of a fourth variant or progressive option within the broader movement of Islamization or "Islamic reactualisation"—is to underline a point that may come as no less surprising to the modernists than it will to their critics among the *ulama*. In this light, the new modernists—against whom the mainstream Islamization movement often aims its heaviest rhetorical artillery—surprisingly represent not something extrinsic to that mainstream's own concerns but a different approach to the same objective, an alternative component of the same project.

If the advocates and partisans of mainstream Islamization could only learn to understand the new modernists—and also themselves—in this way, the prospects of a truly revitalising dialogue within contemporary Islamic civilisation would be greatly enhanced. Those who really seek the reactualisation of Islam and the renewal of its intellectual and civilisational vitality will need to engage together in that kind of debate: to see in their rivals and hear in their rivals' arguments sometimes puzzling reflections and echoes of themselves.

5. *An Afterword*

On two occasions (including the conference held to honour him), Tony Johns heard verbal presentations of the argument offered here, and in his characteristically polite but forthright fashion distanced himself from it. In particular, he upheld, on grounds of the legitimacy of the past and of tradition, the claims of the *ulama* as an estate to exercise, on behalf of the entire *umma* and at its head, an exclusive right of interpretation through the exercise of *ijtihad*. The counter-position, he averred, was one that could not be properly put within Islam on traditional grounds. Quite so; but it has nevertheless been put—notably, in Malaysia and elsewhere, by a number of groups, including some members of the Malaysian *Sisters In Islam* group. As Norani Othman put it in a volume published not long after the conference in honour of Tony Johns was held,

> Contrary to the urgings of individual moral autonomy and responsibility (*taqwa*) that characterise Qur'anic Islam, Malaysian Muslims are routinely cautioned . . . not to question the knowledge and authority of the *imam* and *ulama*. Deference to them is made the sign of piety and the proof of faith.
>
> Yet . . . as part of their efforts to fashion an Islamic culture of modernity, forward-looking Muslims in Malaysia—and elsewhere in the worldwide *umma*—will have to devise and make use of new methods of sociolegal and religious reasoning. Renewal (*islah*) and innovation (*tajdid*)—in general an Islamic culture of modernity that is congruent with the Islamic principle of a reasoned participatory activism—will require action on a basis that goes beyond conventional understandings of *ijtihad*.
>
> The new understanding of *ijtihad* presumed by the idea of an Islamic culture of modernity entails a dual recognition: of the moral autonomy and responsibility of the thinking Muslim individual; and of the need for the process of "ijtihadic" reasoning in which those individuals are involved to be conducted not anarchically but in a dialogical or communitarian manner within the *umma*.
>
> This is not a proposal for "disenfranchising" the *ulama*. Rather, it is an argument that, consistent both with the spirit of modernity and the central principles of Islam in its formative moment, the *ulama* must democratise their procedures and practice.
>
> That is, they must learn to exercise their own *ijtihad* in cooperative engagement together with the "laity" or ordinary members of the *umma*.
>
> Their own continuing role will depend upon their learning to do so as part of a common endeavour to give expression to the enduring principles of our common faith: in ways and forms, including within forms of sociolegal reasoning and through the devising of legal institutions, that are appropriate to the dignity of modern believers and the times in which we all now live.[7]

To end this tribute to Tony Johns on a note of courteous disagreement is not to be churlish. On the contrary, the greatest tribute that one may pay to another scholar is to engage seriously with his ideas and to make explicit where, and why, we ourselves differ from them. This contribution is offered in that spirit, one which we both—in the great traditions of intellectual disputation of all the three great Abrahamic faiths—can readily recognise.

[7] Othman 1994a:152–153.

BIBLIOGRAPHY

Abbreviations

ANU	Australian National University
ANUA	Australian National University Archives
BKI	*Bijdragen tot de Taal-, Land- en Volkenkunde*
EI[1]	*The Encyclopaedia of Islam.* Leiden & Leipzig 1913/1938.
EI[2]	*The Encyclopaedia of Islam.* New edition. Leiden 1960/–.
ER	*The Encyclopaedia of Religion.* New York 1987.
GAL	Brockelmann, C., (1949) *Geschichte der Arabischen Litteratur.* Leiden.
IBLA	*Institut des belles lettres arabes*
IJMES	*International Journal for Middle Eastern Studies*
IKIP	Institut Keguruan dan Ilmu Pengetahuan (Teacher's College)
JMBRAS	*Journal of the Malayan [Malaysian] Branch, Royal Asiatic Society*
JRAS	*Journal of the Royal Asiatic Society*
JSEAS	*Journal of Southeast Asian Studies*
MIDEO	*Mélanges de l'Institut dominicain d'études orientales*
SEI	*The Shorter Encyclopaedia of Islam.* Leiden 1961.
SOAS	School of Oriental and African Studies
TBG	*Tijdschrift voor indische Taal-, Land- en Volkenkunde, uitgegeven door het Bataviaasch Genootschap van Kunsten en Wetenschappen*
ZDMG	*Zeitschrift der deutschen morgenländischen Gesellschaft*

ʿAbd al-Jabbār, *al-Mughnī fī abwāb al-tawḥīd wa'l-ʿadl.* 15 vols. Edition: Ḥusayn et al. 1959–65.

——, *Mutashābih al-Qur'ān.* 2 vols. Edition: Zarzūr 1969.

——, *Uṣūl al-Khamsa.* Edition: D. Gimaret 1979, in: *Annales islamologiques* 15:79–96.

ʿAbdallāh ibn Fūdī, (1963) *Tazyīn al-waraqāt.* Edition and translation: M. Hiskett. Ibadan.

ʿAbduh, M., (1909) *al-Islām wa'l-radd ʿalā muntaqidīh.* Cairo.

——, (1965[r]) *Durūs min al-Qur'ān.* Cairo.

——, (1966[r]) *Risāla al-tawḥīd.* Egypt.

Abdullah, T., (1971) *Schools and Politics: the Kaum Muda Movement in West Sumatra, 1927–1933.* Ithaca.

Abdulrazak, F.A., (1990) "The Kingdom of the Book: the history of printing as an agency of change in Morocco between 1865 and 1912", doctoral thesis, Boston University.

Abu Bakar, M., A. Kaur, and A.Z. Ghazali, (1984) *Historia: Essays in Commemoration of the 25th Anniversary of the Department of History, University of Malaya/Esei-Esei Memperingati Ulangtahun Ke-25 Jabatan Sejarah Universiti Malaya.* Kuala Lumpur.

Abu-Manneh, B., (1990) "*Khalwa* and *Rābiṭa* in the Khālidi suborder", in: Gaborieau, Popovic and Zarcone 1990:289–302.

Abū Rashīd al-Nīsābūrī, *al-Tawḥīd.* Edition: Abū Rīda 1969.

——, *al-Masā'il fī 'l-khilāf.* Edition: Ziyāda and Sayyid 1979.

Abun-Nasr, J., (1965) *The Tijāniyya.* Oxford.

Adam, L., (1938) "Geschiedkundige aanteekeningen omtrent de Residentie Madioen II: Bergheiligdommen op Lawoe en Wilis", in: *Djawa* 18, 97–120.

Adams, C.C., (1968[r]) *Islam and Modernism in Egypt.* Cairo.

Ahmad, N., (1976) "Development of Printing in Urdu 1743–1857", MPhil thesis in the School of Library, Archive and Information Studies, University College, London.

——, (1985) *Oriental Presses in the World.* Lahore.

Ahmad, Q., (1966) *The Wahhābī Movement in India.* Calcutta.

Albin, M.W., (1981) "Iraq's first printed book", in: *Libri* 31, 167–174.
——, (1985) "Islamic Book History: Parameters of a Discipline", in: *Bulletin of the International Association of Orientalist Librarians* 26–27, 13–16.
——, (1988) "An Essay on Early Printing in the Islamic Lands with special relation to Egypt", in: *MIDEO* 18, 335–344.
Algar, H., (1990) "Political aspects of Naqshabandi history", in: Gaborieau, Popovic et Zarcone 1990:123–52.
——, (1992) "Shaykh Zaynullah Rasulev: the last great Naqshabandi shaykh of the Volga-Urals region", in: Gross 1992, 112–133.
Ali, A.M., (1971) *Modern Islamic Thought in Indonesia.* Yogjakarta.
Alter, R., (1981) *The Art of Biblical Narrative.* New York.
Ambri, M., (1935) *Lain Eta.* Batavia.
Āmidī, ʿAlī b. ʿAbī ʿAlī al-, *Al-Iḥkām fī uṣūl al-aḥkām.* Pr: Cairo. 1967.
Andaya, B.W., and V. Matheson, (1979) "Islamic Thought and Malay Tradition: the Writings of Raja Ali Haji of Riau (ca. 1809–ca. 1870)", in: Reid and Marr 1979:108–128.
Andaya, L.Y., (1987) "Malay Peninsula", in: *EI²* vol. 6, 232–39.
Anon., (c. 1600) *Tafsir Surat al-Kahf. Camb. MS Or. Ii.6.45.* Cambridge University Library.
——, *Babad Tanah Jawi.* 31 vols. Edition: Batawi Sentrum 1939–41.
——, *Djidwal memindahkan tahoen Djawa dan ʿArab ketahoen Maséhi.* Edition: Batavia-Centrum 1932.
——, *Serat Cabolek . . . anggitanipun abdi-dalĕm bujongga Kraton ing nagari Surakarta Adiningrat . . .* Edition: G.C.T. van Dorp 1885. Sĕmawis.
——, *Sĕrat Cabolang,* microfilm of Leiden MS, Cod. LOr 6678 a–e, in: Pigeaud 1968:405.
Ansari, S., (1992) *Sufi Saints and the State Power: the Pirs of Sind, 1843–1947.* Cambridge.
Anṣārī, Abū ʾl-Qāsim al-, [a] *Al-Ghunya fī uṣūl al-dīn.* Istanbul: MS III Ahmet no. 1916.
Arberry, A.J., (1964) *The Koran Interpreted.* Oxford.
Ardiwinata, D. and M.S. Mangkoe Pradja, (1910) *Buku Piwuruk Budi Utomo Tina Bab Mim Pipitu.* Bandung.
Ardiwinata, D.K., (1966[r]) *Baruang Ka Nu Ngarora.* Batavia.
Aristotle, *Metaphysics.* Edition: Jaeger 1957.
Arps, B., (1992) *Tembang in two traditions: Performance and interpretation of Javanese literature.* London.
Asani, A.S., (1993) "Folk romance in Sufi poetry from Sind", in: Dallapicola and Zingel-Ave Lallemant 1993:229–237.
Ashʿarī, Abū l-Ḥasan al-, *Maqālāt al-islāmiyyīn.* Edition: Ritter 1929–1930.
——, *Kitāb al-Lumaʿ.* Edition: R. McCarthy 1953, in: *The Theology of al-Ashʿarī.* Beyrouth.
Attas, S.M.N. al-, (1971) "Indonesia: iv History (a) Islamic period", in: *EI²* vol. 3, 1218–1221.
Aubin, F., (1990) "En Islam Chinois? quels Naqshabandis", in: Gaborieau, Popovic et Zarcone 1993:491–572.
Avery, P., (1991) "Printing, the Press and Literature in Modern Iran", in: Fisher 1968–91: vol. 7 ch. 22.
Avicenna, *Ilāhiyyāt al-Shifāʾ.* Edition: Anawati 1960.
Baalbaki, R., (1979) "Some aspects of harmony and hierarchy in Sibawayhi's grammatical analysis", in: *Zeitschrift der arabischen Linguistik* 2, 7–22.
Baghawī, al-Farrāʾ al-, *Maʿālim al-tanzīl.* Edition: Sawār 1987.
Bai Jianmin, (1958) *Qurʾān (Chinese Translation).* Taipei.
Bakar, M.A., (1989) *Penghayatan Sebuah Ideal: Suatu Tafsiran Tentang Islam Semasa* (Realizing an Ideal: An Interpretation of Contemporary Islam). Kuala Lumpur.
Bakri, S. al-, (1936) *Taʾrīkh Ḥaḍramawt al-siyāsī,* vol. 2. Cairo.
Bāqillānī, Abū Bakr al-, *al-Tamhīd.* Edition: McCarthy 1957.
Barnett, S. and J. Fairbank, (1985 eds.) *Christianity in China; Early Protestant Missionary Writings.* Cambridge MA.

Bassach, A., (1929a, trans.) of A. Hassan's *Al-Boerhan: Kitab Fiqh*. Bandung.
——, (1929b, trans.) of A. Hassan's *Al-Foerqan: Tafsir Qoer'an*. Bandung.
Baud, J.C., (1853) "Proeve van eene Geschiedenis van den Handel en het Gebruik van Opium in Nederlandsch Indie", in: *BKI*, 1.
Baysal, J., (1981) "Turkish Publishing Activities before and after the New Alphabet", in: *Anatolica* 8, 115–127.
Benjamin, S.G.W., (1887) *Persia and the Persians*. London.
Bennigsen, A., (1964) "Un mouvement populaire au Caucase au 18e siècle: la guerre sainte du sheikh Mansur, 1785–1791", in: *Cahiers du Monde Russe et Soviètique* 2, 159–205.
Berg, C.C., (1938) "Javaansche Geschiedschrijving", in: Stapel 1938:5–148.
Berkes, N., (1964) *The Development of Secularism in Turkey*. Montreal.
——, (1969) "Ibrāhīm Müteferriḳa", in: *EI²* vol. 3, 996–998.
Bernand, M., (1986) "Ḳiyās", in: *EI²* vol. 5, 238–242.
Bettelheim, B., (1976) *The Uses of Enchantment: The Meaning and Importance of Fairy Tales*. New York.
Bianchi, X., (1843) "Catalogue générale des livres arabes, persans et turcs, imprimés à Boulac", in: *Journal asiatique* 4/2, 24–61.
——, (1859–63) "Bibliographie ottomane, ou notice des ouvrages publiés dans les imprimeries turques de Constantinople, et en partie dans celle de Boulac, en Égypte, depuis les derniers mois de 1856 jusqu'à ce moment", in: *Journal asiatique* 5/13 (juin 1859), 519–555; 5/14 (oct.–nov. 1859), 287–298; 5/16 (oct. 1860), 323–346; 6/2 (août.–sept. 1863), 217–271.
Bloget, H., (1893) *The Use of Tien Chu for God in Chinese*. Shanghai.
Bluhm, J.E., (1983) "A preliminary statement on the dialogue established between the reform magazine al-Manār and the Malayo-Indonesian world", in: *Indonesia Circle* 32, 35–42.
Blussé, L., (1986) *Strange Company: Chinese settlers, mestizo women and the Dutch in VOC Batavia*. Dordrecht and Riverton.
Bokhāri de Djohōre, (1878) *Makōta Rādja-Rādja, ou la Couronne des Rois*, (ed. Aristide Marre). Paris.
Bourdieu, P., (1958) *Sociologie de l'Algerie*. Paris.
——, (1962) *The Algerians*. Boston.
Brass, P.R., (1974) *Language, Religion and Politics in North India*. Cambridge.
Brenner, L., (1988) "Concepts of *ṭarīqa* in West Africa: the case of the Qādiriyya", in: O'Brien and Coulon 1988.
—— and M. Last, (1985) "The role of language in West African Islam", in: *Africa* 55, 432–446.
Browne, E.G., (1914) *The Press and Poetry of Modern Persia*. Cambridge.
Brunschvig, R., (1971) "Logic and Law in Classical Islam", in: von Grunebaum 1970:9–20.
Buhl, F., (1961) "Ḳur'ān", in: *SEI* 273–286.
Bujra, A.S., (July 1967) "Political Conflict and Stratification in Ḥaḍramaut", in: *Middle Eastern Studies* 3, 4, 355–75.
Bukhari al-Jauhari, (1966) *Taj Us-Salatin*, (ed. Khalid Hussain). Kuala Lumpur.
Bulliet, R.W., (1987) "Medieval Arabic *Ṭarsh*: A Forgotten Chapter in the History of Printing", in: *JAOS* 107.3, 427–438.
Butt, A.R., (1988) "The Nineteenth Century Book Trade in Sind", doctoral thesis, University of Wales, Aberystwyth.
Butterworth, C., (1987) "Medieval Islamic philosophy and the virtue of ethics", in: *Arabica* 34, 220–250.
Capot-Rey, R., (1953) *L'Afrique Blanche Française. Tome Second: Le Sahara Français*. Paris.
Caresajee, R., (1958) "The printing press in Bombay: 1780", in: Priolkar 1958: ch. 5.
Carey, P., (1986) "Waiting for the Just King: The Agrarian World of South-Central Java from Giyanti (1755) to the Java War (1825–30)", in: *Modern Asian Studies* 20.1, 59–137.
Chaidar, (1978) *Syech Nawawi al-Banteni*. Jakarta.

Chappell, W., (1970) *A Short History of the Printed Word.* New York.
Clancey-Smith, J.A., (1986) "Saintly lineages, border politics, and international trade: Southeastern Algeria and the Tunisian Jarid, 1800–1881", PhD Dissertation, University of California, Los Angeles.
Clayer, N., (1994) *Mystiques, état et société: les Halvetis dans l'aire balkanique de la fin du 15e siècle à nos jours.* Leiden.
Cohen Stuart, A.B., (1860) *Brata-joeda: Indisch-Javaansch heldendicht.* Verhandelingen van het Bataviaasch Genootschap van Kunsten en Wetenschappen 27–28.
Cohen, A., (1971) "Cultural strategies in the organization of trading diasporas", in: Meillassoux 1971.
Cowan, C.D. and O.W. Wolters, (1976 eds.) *Southeast Asian History and Historiography: Essays presented to D.G.E. Hall.* Ithaca.
Crabbs, J.A., Jr., (1984) *The Writing of History in Nineteenth-Century Egypt: A Study in National Transformation.* Cairo.
Cragg, K., (1988) *Readings in the Qur'ān.* London.
Crites, S., (1989) "The Narrative Quality of Experience", in: Hauerwas and Jones 1989:65–88.
Curtin, P.D., (1984) *Cross-Cultural Trade in World History.* Cambridge.
Dallapicola, A.L. and S. Zingel-Ave Lallemant, (1993 eds.) *Islam and Indian Regions.* Stuttgart.
Dandekar, R.N., (1961) *The Śalyaparvan: being the ninth book of the Mahābhārata, the great epic of India.* Poona.
Davis, E., (1983) *Press and Politics in British Western Punjab 1836–1947.* Delhi.
de Graaf, H.J., (1965) "Later Javanese Sources and Historiography", in: Soedjatmoko et al. 1965:119–136.
—— and Th.G.Th. Pigeaud, (1974) *De eerste Moslimse vorstendommen op Java: studiën over de staatkundige geschiedenis van de 15de en 16de eeuw.* 's-Gravenhage.
de Jong, F., (1987) "Muṣṭafā Kamāl al-Dīn al-Bakrī (1688–1749): revival and reform of the Khalwatiyya?", in: Levtzion and Voll 1987:117–132.
de Jonge, J.K.J. and M.L. van Deventer, (1862–1909 eds.) *De opkomst van het Nederlandsch gezag in Oost-Indië: Verzameling van onuitgegeven stukken uit het oud-koloniaal archief.* 16 vols. 's-Gravenhage.
——, (1888 eds.) "Verslag der reis van N. Engelhard . . . 27 Mei 1803", in: *De Opkomst van het Nederlandsch Gezag in Oost-Indië* vol. 13. The Hague.
de Josselin de Jong, P.E., (1986) "Textual Anthropology and History: The Sick King" in: Grijns and Robson 1986:219–232.
de la Lama, G., (1982 ed.) *Middle East I.* Mexico.
Demeerseman, A., (1953) "Une étape importante de la culture islamique: Une parente méconnue de l'imprimerie arabe et tunisienne: La lithographie", in: *IBLA* 16, 347–389.
——, (1954) "Une étape décisive de la culture et de la psychologie sociale islamiques: Les données de la controverse autour du problème de l'Imprimerie", in: *IBLA* 17, 1–48 and 113–140.
Dhahabī, M.Ḥ. al-, (1985) *al-Tafsīr wa'l-mufassirūn.* Cairo.
Diehl, K.S., (1973) "Lucknow Printers 1820–1850", in: Gidwani 1973:115–128.
DiNoia, J.A., (1992) *The Diversity of Religions.* Washington.
Dobbin, C., (1972) *Urban Leadership in Western India: Politics and Communities in Bombay City 1840–1885.* Oxford.
——, (1983) *Islamic Revivalism in a Changing Peasant Economy: Sumatra 1784–1847.* London.
——, (1989) "From Middleman Minorities to Industrial Entrepreneurs: The Chinese in Java and the Parsis in Western India 1619–1939", in: *Itinerario* 13, 1.
——, (1991) "The Importance of Minority Characteristics in the Formation of Business Elites on Java: The Baweanese Example, c. 1870–c. 1940", in: *Archipel* 41.
Drewes, G.W.J., (1966) "The struggle between Javanism and Islam as illustrated by the Sĕrat Dĕrmagandul", in: *BKI* 122, 309–65.
——, (1969) *The admonitions of Seh Bari: a 16th century Javanese Muslim text attributed to the Saint of Bonan.* The Hague.

——, (1977 ed. and trans.) *Directions for travellers on the mystic path: Zakariyyā' al-Anṣārī's Kitāb Fatḥ al-Raḥmān and its Indonesian adaptations, with an appendix on Palembang manuscripts and authors*, in: The Hague.
——, (1978) *An early Javanese code of Muslim ethics*. The Hague.
Duda, H.W., (1935) "Das Druckwesen in der Türkei", in: *Gutenberg-Jahrbuch* 226–242.
Duverdier, G., (1987) "Savary de Brèves et Ibrahim Müteferrika: Deux drogmans culturels à l'origine de l'imprimerie turque", in: *Bulletin du bibliophile* 1987.3, 322–359.
Eaton, R.M., (1978) *Sufis of Bijapur: Social roles of Sufis in Medieval India*. Princeton.
Economist, The, (14 November 1987).
Ellis, N.A., (1955) "Indian Typography", in: Kesavan 1955:10–16.
Enthoven, R.E., (1920) *The Tribes and Castes of Bombay vol. 2*. Bombay.
Fārābī, Abū Naṣr al-, *al-Siyāsa al-madaniyya*. Edition: Najjar 1964.
——, *Kitāb al-Ḥurūf*. Edition: Mahdi 1969.
——, *Mabādi' ārā' ahl al-madīna al-fāḍila*. Edition: Walzer 1985.
Farjenel, M.F. and M.L. Bouvat, (1908) "Un Commentaire Chinois du Quran", in: *Revue du Monde Musulman* 4, 540–547.
Farmayan, H.F., (1968) "The Forces of Modernization in Nineteenth Century Iran: A Historical Survey", in: Polk and Chambers 1968:119–151.
Faroqhi, S., (1976) "The Tekke of Haci Bektas, social position and economic activities", in: *IJMES* 7, 183–205.
Federspiel, H.M., (1970) *Persatuan Islam: Islamic Reform in Twentieth Century Indonesia*. Ithaca.
Feith, H. and L. Castles, (1970) *Indonesian Political Thinking 1945–1965*. Ithaca and London.
Fernandes, L., (1988) *The Evolution of a Sufi Institution in Mamluk Egypt: the Khanaqah*. Berlin.
Fernando, M.R. and D. Bulbeck, (1992 eds.) *Chinese Economic Activity in Netherlands India: Selected Translations from the Dutch*. Singapore.
Fisher, W.B. et al., (1968–91 eds.) *The Cambridge History of Iran*. Cambridge.
Fleisch, H., (1979) "'Illa", in: *EI*² vol. 3, 1127–1129.
Fletcher, J., (1975) "Central Asian Sufism and Ma Ming-hsin's New Teaching", in: Ch'en Chieh-hsien (ed.) *Proceedings of the Fourth East Asian Altaistic Conference*, Taipeh, 75–96.
——, (1977) "The Naqshabandiyya and the *dhikr-i arra*", in: *Journal of Turkish Studies* 1, 113–19.
——, (1986) "Les 'Voies' (*ṭuruq*) soufies en Chine", in: Popovic and Veinstein 1986: 13–26.
Fokkens, F., Jr., (1877) "De priesterschool te Tegalsari", in: *TBG* 24, 318–36.
Fox, J.J., (1980 ed.) *Indonesia: The Making of a Culture*. Canberra.
——, (1991) "Ziarah Visits to the Tombs of the Wali, The Founders of Islam on Java", in: Ricklefs 1991:19–38.
Frank, R.M., (1968) Review of Kholeif 1966 in: *Bibliotheca Orientalis* 25, 229–233.
——, (1978a) "Reason and Revealed Law", in: *Recherches d'islamologie, recueil d'articles offert à Georges C. Anawati et Louis Gardet par leurs collègues et amis* (Bibliothèque philosophique de Louvain, 26): 124–138.
——, (1978b) *Beings and their Attributes, the Teaching of the Basrian School of the Mu'tazila in the Classical Period*. Albany.
——, (1982) "The Autonomy of the Human Agent according to 'Abd al-Ǧabbār", *Le Muséon* 95, 323–355.
——, (1983) "Moral Obligation in Classical Muslim Theology", in: *Journal of Religious Ethics* 11, 205–223.
——, (1985a) "Can God do Wrong?", in: T. Rudovsky (ed.), *Divine Omniscience and Omnipotence in Medieval Philosophy*. Dordrecht: 69–79.
——, (1985b) "Two Islamic Views of Human agency", in: G. Makdisi, D. Sourdel, and J. Sourdel-Thomine (eds.), *La Notion de liberté au Moyen âge*. Paris: 37–49.

——, (1989a) "Knowledge and *Taqlīd*; the foundations of religious belief in classical Ashʿarism", in: *Journal of the American Oriental Society* 109.1, 37–62.
——, (1989b), "*al-Ustādh abū Isḥāq, an ʿaqīda together with selected fragments*", in: *MIDEO* 19, 129–202.
——, (1991/92) "Al-Ghazālī on *Taqlīd*. Scholars, theologians and philosophers", in: *Zeitschrift für Geschichte der Arabisch-Islamischen Wissenschaften* 7, 207–252.
——, (1992) *Creation and the Cosmic System: al-Ghazālī and Avicenna*. Abhandlungen d. Heidelberger Akad. d. Wiss: hist.-phil. Klasse 1992/1.
——, (1994) *Al-Ghazālī and the Ashʿarite School*. Durham.
Frei, H., (1974) *The Eclipse of Biblical Narrative: A Study in Eighteenth and Nineteenth Century Hermeneutics*. New Haven.
Gaborieau, M., A. Popovic and Zarcone, (1990 eds.) *Naqshabandis*. Istanbul-Paris.
Gallop, A.T., (1990) "Early Malay Printing: an Introduction to the British Library Collection", in: *JMBRAS* 63.1, 85–124.
Geertz, C., (1960) *The Religion of Java*. New York.
Geiss, A., (1907–08) "Histoire de l'Imprimerie en Égypte", in: *Bulletin de l'Institut Égyptien*, [I], sér. 5, 1, 133–152; II, sér. 5, 2, 195–220.
Gellner, E., (1981) *Muslim Society*. Cambridge.
Gerth, H.H. and C. Wright Mills, (1948 eds.) *From Max Weber: Essays in Sociology*. London.
Ghazālī, Abū Ḥāmid Muḥammad al-, *al-Mustaṣfā min ʿilm al-uṣūl*. Pr: Būlāq 1322 A.H.
——, *Miʿyār al-ʿilm*. Pr: Cairo 1329 A.H.
——, *Tahāfut al-falāsifa*. Edition: Bouyges 1927.
——, *Iḥyāʾ ʿulūm al-dīn*. Pr: Cairo 1957.
——, *al-Iqtiṣād fī l-iʿtiqād*. Edition: Çubukçu and Atay 1962.
——, *Mishkāt al-anwār*. Edition: al-ʿAfīfī 1964.
——, *Miḥakk al-naẓar fī ʾl-manṭiq*. Edition: al-Naʿsān 1966.
——, *al-Maqṣad al-asnā*. Edition: Shehadi 1982.
——, *Iljām al-ʿawāmm ʿan ʿilm al-kalām*. Edition: al-Baghdādī 1985.
Gibb, H.A.R., (1953) *Muhammedanism*. New York.
Gidwani, N.N., (1973 ed.) *Comparative Librarianship: Essays in honour of Professor D.N. Marshall*. Delhi.
Gijsberti Hodenpijl, A.K.A., (1918) "De zwerftocht van Sultan Pakoeboewana II, na diens vlucht uit den kraton te Kartasoera, op 30 Juni 1742", in: *BKI* 74:562–614.
Gimaret, D., (1974) "Un problème de théologie musulmane", in: *Studia Islamica* 40: 1–73.
——, (1990) *La Doctrine d'al-Ashʿarī*. Paris.
Gladney, D., (1991) *Muslim Chinese*. Cambridge MA.
Goenawan, S., (1924) *Manehna Geus Nekad*. Bandung.
Gonda, J., (1973[r]) *Sanskrit in Indonesia*. New Delhi.
Gordon, A.D.D., (1978) *Businessmen and politics: Rising Nationalism and a Modernising Economy in Bombay. 1918–1933*. New Delhi.
Goris, R., (1937) "The Balinese medical literature", in: *Djawa* 17, 281–287.
Govi, K.M., (1977) "The Genesis and Growth of India's National Bibliography", in: *Libri* 27.2, 165–174.
Graham, W.A., (1987) *Beyond the Written Word: Oral Aspects of Scripture in the History of Religion*. Cambridge.
Grandin, N., (1990) "A propos des *asanid* de la Naqshabandiyya dans les fondements de la Khatmiyya du Soudan Oriental: stratégies de pouvoir et relation maître/disciple", in: Gaborieau, Popovic et Zarcone 1990:621–655.
Grijns, C.D. and S.O. Robson (1986 eds.), *Cultural Contact and Textual Interpretation*. Dordrecht.
Gross, J-A., (1992 ed.) *Muslims in Central Asia: Expressions of Identity and Change*. Chapel Hill.
Gujarat State Gazetteers: Kutch District, Ahmedabad. (1971).
Gutas, D., (1988), *Avicenna and the Aristotelian Tradition*. Leiden.

Gwynne, R., (1990) "The a fortiori argument in Fiqh, Naḥw and Kalām", in: K. Versteegh and M.G. Carter (eds.), *Studies in the History of Arabic Grammar II, Proceedings of the 2nd Symposium on the History of Arabic Grammar, Nijmegen, 27 April–1 May 1987*, Amsterdam, 165–78.
Haafkens, J., (1983) *Chants musulmans en peul: textes de l'héritage religieux de la communauté musulmane de Maroua, Cameroun.* Leiden.
Hadi, S.S.A. al-, (1966[r]) *Faridah Hanom.* Kuala Lumpur.
Haider, S.J., (1981) "Munshi Nawal Kishore (1836–1895): Mirror of Urdu Printing in British India", in: *Libri* 31, 227–237 = *Pakistan Library Bulletin* 12.1 (March), 12–23.
Hallaq, W., (1987) "The development of logical structure in Sunni legal theory", in: *Der Islam* 64, 42–67.
——, (1989) "Non-analogical arguments in Sunni juridical qiyās", in: *Arabica* 36, 286–306.
——, (1990) "Logic, formal arguments and formalization of arguments in Sunni jurisprudence", in: *Arabica* 37, 315–58.
Hamka, (1967) *Ayahku, Riwayat Hidup Dr H. Abd. Karim Abdullah dan Perjuangan Kaum Agama di Sumatera.* Jakarta.
Hammam, M.Y., (1951) "History of Printing in Egypt", in: *Gutenberg-Jahrbuch* 156–159.
Haq, M.E., (1957) *Muslim Bengali Literature.* Karachi.
Hārāsī, al-Kiyā' al- (a), *Uṣūl al-dīn.* MS Dār al-Kutub al-Miṣriyya, *kalām* no. 295.
Harazm, A., (1929) *Jawāhir al-maʿānī wa-bulūgh al-amānī.* Cairo.
Hardjakoesoema, M.K., (1928) *Wawacan Pareumeun Obor.* Batavia.
Hauerwas, S. and L.G. Jones, (1989 eds.) *Why Narrative? Readings in Narrative Theology.* Grand Rapids MI.
Hawting, G.R. and A.Q.A. Shareef, (1993 eds.) *Approaches to the Qur'ān.* London.
Heyworth-Dunne, J., (1940) "Printing and Translations under Muḥammad ʿAlī of Egypt: the Foundations of Modern Arabic", in: *JRAS* 1940, 325–349.
Hirsch, R., (1978) "Scribal Tradition and Innovation in Early Printed Books", in his *The Printed Word: Its Impact and Diffusion.* London: ch. XV.
Hiskett, M., (1975) *A History of Hausa Islamic Verse.* London.
Hitti, P.K., (1960[7]) *History of the Arabs.* London.
Hodgson, M.G.S., (1974) *The Venture of Islam*, vol. 1. USA.
Hofheinz, A., (1990) "Encounters with a saint: al-Majdhub, al-Mirghani and Ibn Idris as seen through the eyes of Ibrahim al-Rashid", in: *Sudanic Africa* 1, 19–59.
Holsinger, D.C., (1980) "Migration, Commerce and Community: the Mizabis in Eighteenth- and Nineteenth-Century Algeria", in: *Journal of African History* 21.1, 61–74.
Hourani, C., (1982) "The Arab Typographical Revolution. The Work of Nasri Khattar", in his *The Arab Cultural Scene, A Literary Review Supplement.* London.
Hourani, G., (1960) "Two Theories of Value in Medieval Islam", in: *Muslim World* 50, 269–87.
——, (1971) *Islamic Rationalism: The Ethics of ʿAbd al-Jabbār.* Oxford.
——, (1975) "Juwaynī's criticisms of Muʿtazilite ethics", in: *Muslim World* 65:161–173.
Hsu, H.C., (1985) "The first thirty years of Arabic printing in Egypt 1238–1267 (1822–1851). A bibliographical study with a checklist by title of Arabic printed works", doctoral thesis, Edinburgh University.
Humphries, C. and W.C. Smith, (1970) *Music Publishing in the British Isles.* Oxford.
Husain, S., (1977) *The Glorious Caliphate.* Lucknow.
Ibn Abī Uṣaybiʿa, *ʿUyūn al-anbāʾ fī ṭabaqāt al-aṭibbāʾ.* Edition: Müller 1882.
Ibn Fūrak, Abū Bakr, *Mujarrad maqālāt al-Ashʿarī.* Edition: Gimaret 1987.
Ibn al-ʿImād, ʿAbd al-Ḥayy, *Shadharāt al-dhahab.* Pr: Cairo 1351.
Ibn Khaldūn, *Al-Muqaddima.* Pr: Beirut 1967.
Ibn Manẓūr, *Lisān al-ʿArab.* Edition: Muhanna 1968.
Ibn Rushd, *Faṣl al-maqāl.* Edition: Nader 1968.
Ibn al-Sarrāj, *Kitāb al-Uṣūl fī 'l-naḥw.* Edition: al-Fatlī 1985.

Ibn Taymiyya, *Risāla al-Furqān*, in *Majmūʿa al-rasāʾil al-kubrā*. Pr: Cairo 1966.

Isfarāʾīnī, Abū Isḥāq al-, *al-ʿAqīda*, in: Frank 1989b.

Israeli, R., (1980) *Muslim China*. London.

—— and A.H. Johns, (1984) *Islam in Asia, Volume II: Southeast and East Asia*. Jerusalem.

Jabartī, ʿA. al-, (1390 A.H.) *ʿAjāʾib al-āthār fī ʾl-tarājim waʾl-akhbār*. Cairo.

Jabre, F., (1959 ed. and trans.), of Ghazālī's *al-Munqidh min al-ḍalāl*. Beirut.

Jackson, S.A., (1993) "From prophetic actions to constitutional theory: a novel chapter in medieval Muslim jurisprudence", in: *IJMES* 25, 71–90.

Jalal Al-e Ahmad, (1984) *Occidentosis: A Plague from the West*, (R. Campbell, trans. H. Algar, ed.). Berkeley.

Jin Yijiu, (1981) "Gulan-jing zai Zhongguo" (Qurʾān in China), in: *Shijie Zongjiao Yanjiu* 1/3, 128–32. (An English version of the same appears in *Contributions to Asian Studies* 17, 1982, 95–101.)

Joenoes, M., (1961[r]) *Tafsir Qur'an Karim Bahasa Indonesia*. Jakarta.

Johns, A.H., (1953) "Nūr al-Daḳāʾiḳ", in: *JRAS*, 137–151.

——, (1955a) "Aspects of Sufi Thought in India and Indonesia at the Beginning of the 17th Century", in: *JMBRAS* 28.1, 70–77.

——, (1955b) "Daḳāʿiḳ al-Ḥurūf by ʿAbd al-Raʿūf of Singkel", in: *JRAS* 1955, 55–73, 139–58.

——, (1957) "Malay Sufism, as illustrated in an anonymous collection of seventeenth-century tracts", *JMBRAS* XXX.2 (no. 178).

——, (1958) *Rantjak Dilabueh: A Minangkabau Kaba. A Specimen of the Traditional Literature of Central Sumatra*. Data Paper 32, Southeast Asia Program, Cornell University.

——, (1959) "The Novel as a Guide to Indonesian Social History", in: *BKI* 115.iii, 232–48. Reprinted in *Cultural Options* (1979), 1–18.

——, (1961) "Sufism as a Category in Indonesian Literature and History", in: *Journal of Southeast Asian History* (Singapore), 2.2, 10–23.

——, (1963) "Genesis of a Modern Literature", in: McVey 1963:410–554.

——, (1964) *Indonesian Studies in Australia: An Open Horizon. An inaugural lecture delivered at Canberra on 30 June 1964*. Canberra.

——, (1965) *The Gift Addressed to the Spirit of the Prophet*. Canberra.

——, (1968) "Introduction", in: Lubis 1968:1–14.

——, (1970–71) "Bahasa Indonesia and Malay Studies at the Australian National University", in: *Abr-Nahrain* X, 26–36.

——, (1976) "Islam in Southeast Asia: Problems of Perspective", in: Cowan and Wolters 1976:304–320.

——, (1979a) *Cultural Options and the Role of Tradition, A Collection of Essays on Modern Indonesian and Malaysian Literature*. Canberra.

——, (1979b) "The Turning Image: Myth and Reality in Malay Perceptions of the Past", in: Reid and Marr 1979:43–67.

——, (1980a) "From coastal settlement to Islamic school and city: Islamization in Sumatra, the Malay Peninsula and Java", in: Fox 1980.

——, (1980b, ed.) *The Qurʾān through fourteen centuries*. Canberra.

——, (1981a) "Joseph in the Qurʾān: Dramatic Dialogue, Human Emotion and Prophetic Wisdom", in: *Islamochristiana* 7, 29–55.

——, (1981b) "Modes of Islamization in Southeast Asia", in: Lorenzon 1981:61–77.

——, (1982) "The Incident of the 'Satanic Verses' allegedly interpolated into sura al-Najm: a psychological interpretation", in: *de la Lama* 1982:145–152.

——, (1987a) "Islam: Genesis, Doctrines and Character", in: *The Australasian Catholic Record* LXIV.1, 3–19.

——, (1987b) "Islam: Islam in Southeast Asia", in: *ER* vol. 7. 404–422.

——, (1988) "Quranic Exegesis in the Malay World: In Search of a Profile", in: Rippin 1988:257–287.

——, (1989) "David and Bathsheba: A Case Study in the Exegesis of Qurʾanic Story-telling", in: *MIDEO* 19, 225–266.

——, (1991) "Reminiscences", unpublished paper presented to Division of Pacific and Asian History, RSPacS, ANU.

——, (1993a) "Islamization in Southeast Asia: Reflections and Reconsiderations with Special Reference to the Role of Sufism", in: *Tonan Ajia Kenkyu (Southeast Asian Studies)* 31.1, 43–61.
——, (1993b) "The Quranic Presentation of the Joseph Story: Naturalistic or Formulaic Language?" in: Hawting and Shareef 1993:37–70.
——, (1993c) "Responses, Reflections and Memories, being comments on papers prepared for the conference, Islam and the Social Construction of Identities: Comparative Perspectives on Southeast Asian Muslims". Draft.
——, (1995) "Sufism in Southeast Asia: Reflections and Reconsiderations", in: *JSEAS*, 26.1, 169–183.
Jomier, J., (1977) "Les *Mafātīḥ al-Ghayb* de l'Imām Rāzī; quelques dates, lieux, manuscrits", in: *MIDEO* 13, 253–290.
——, (1980) "The Qur'anic Commentary of Imām Fakhr al-Dīn al-Rāzī: its sources and its originality", in: Johns 1980b:93–111.
Jourdan, F., (1983) *La Tradition des Sept Dormants*. Paris.
Judgement by the Honourable Sir Joseph Arnould in the Kojah Case, Bombay. (1866).
Jusuf, J., (1979 ed.) *Tajussalatin*. Jakarta.
Juwaynī, Abū 'l-Ma'ālī al-, *al-Irshād*. Edition: 'Abd al-Ḥamīd, 1950.
——, *al-Shāmil fī uṣūl al-dīn*. Edition: el-Nashar 1969.
——, *al-Shāmil fī uṣūl al-dīn, some additional portions of the text*. Edition: R. Frank, 1981, Tehran.
Juynboll, H.H., (1893) *Drie boeken van het Oudjavaansche Mahābhārata*. Leiden.
——, (1912) *Wirāṭaparwa: Oudjavaansch prozageschrift*. 's-Gravenhage.
Kahin, G.McT., (1952) *Nationalism and Revolution in Indonesia*. Ithaca.
Káldy-Nagy, Gy., (1974) "Beginnings of Arabic-Letter Printing in the Muslim World", in his ed. *The Muslim East: Studies in Honour of Julius Germanus*. Budapest.
Kaptein, N., (1993) "An indigenous printer in Surabaya in 1853", in: *BKI* 149.2, 356–361.
Karamustafa, A.T., (1994) *God's Unruly Friends: Dervish groups in the Islamic Later Middle Period, 1200–1550*. Salt Lake City.
Karrar, A.S., (1992) *The Sufi Brotherhoods in the Sudan*. Evanston.
Keasberry, B.P., (1843) *Segala Jenis Hikayat Ilmu Kepandaian*. Singapore.
Kedar, B.Z. and R.J. Zwi Werblowsky, (1996 eds.) *Sacred Space: Shrine, City, Land*. Jerusalem.
Kesavan, B.S., (1955 ed.) *The Carey Exhibition of Early Printing and Fine Printing*. Calcutta.
Kessler, C.S., (1992) "Pilgrims' Progress: The Travellers of Islam", in: *Annals of Tourism Research* 19.i, 147–153.
Khāzin, 'Alā' al-Dīn al-, *Lubāb al-ta'wīl fī mā'anī al-tanzīl*. Pr: Beirut n.d.
Kholeif, F., (1966) *A study on Fakhr al-Dīn al-Rāzī and his Controversies in Transoxiana*. Beirut.
Kindī, Abū Yūsuf al-, *Rasā'il al-Kindī al-falsafiyya*. Edition: Abū Rīda 1950.
Kissling, H.J., (1954) "The Sociological and Educational Role of the Dervish orders in the Ottoman Empire", in: G.E. von Grunebaum (ed.), *Studies in Islamic Cultural History*, the American Anthropological Association, Memoire no. 76, 23–35.
Knaap, G. and L. Nagtegaal, (1991) "A Forgotten Trade: Salt in Southeast Asia, 1670–1813", in: Ptak and Rothermund 1991.
Knappert, J., (1979) *Four Centuries of Swahili Verse; a literary history and anthology*. London.
Knebel, J., (1903) "Desa-legenden", in: *TBG* 46, 363–69.
Köbert, R., (1945) "Gedanken zum semitischen Wort- und Satzbau", in: *Orientalia* (NS) 14, 273–83.
Kostiner, J., (1984) "The Impact of Hadrami Emigrants in the East Indies on Islamic Modernism and Social Change in the Hadramawt during the Twentieth Century", in: Israeli and Johns 1984:206–237.
Kraus, P., (1938) "The 'Controversies' of Fakhr al-Dīn al-Rāzī", in: *Islamic Culture* 12, 131–153.
Kumar, A., (1982) "The 'Suryengalagan Affair' of 1883 and its successors: born leaders in changed times", in: *BKI* 138/2–3, 251–84.

—— and J.H. McGlynn, (1966) *Illuminations: the writing traditions of Indonesia*. Jakarta, New York and Tokyo.
——, (1985) *The Diary of a Javanese Muslim: Religion, politics and the pesantren 1883–1886*. Canberra.
——, (1996), *Java and Modern Europe: Ambiguous Encounters*. London.
Kuntara Wiryamartana, I., (1990) *Arjunawiwaha: transformasi teks Jawa Kuna lewat tanggapan dan penciptaan di lingkungan sastra Jawa*. Yogyakarta.
Lambton, A.K.S., (1981) *State and Government in Medieval Islam: an introduction to the study of Islamic political theory and the jurists*. Oxford.
Lane, E., (1836) *An account of the Manners and Customs of the Modern Egyptians written in Egypt during the years 1833–1835*. London.
Lapidus, I.M., (1967) *Muslim Cities in the Later Middle Ages*. Cambridge MA.
Larif-Béatrix, A., (1994) "Islamic Reform, Muslim Law and the Shari'a State", in: Othman 1994:27–30.
Leemhuis, F., (1991) "A Koranic Contest Poem in Sūrat al-Ṣāffāt", in: G.J. Reinink and H.L.J. Vanstiphout (eds.), *Dispute Poems and Dialogues in the ancient and medieval near east*, Orientalia Lovaniensia Analecta 42, 165–177.
Legge, J., (1832/1971[r]) *The Notions of the Chinese concerning Gods and Spirits etc.* Hongkong.
Leibholt, H., (1991) "Ghazālī and 'Religionswissenschaft'", in: *Asiatische Studien* 45, 19–72.
Levtzion, N., (1977) "North Africa and the Western Sudan from 1050 to 1590", in: Oliver 1977:331–462.
——, (1979 ed.) *Conversion to Islam*. New York and London.
—— and G. Weigert, (1995), "Religious reform in eighteenth century Morocco", in: *Jerusalem Studies in Arabic and Islam* 19, 173–197.
——, (1996) "The Muslim holy cities as foci of Islamic revivalism in the eighteenth century", in: Kedar and Werblowsky 1996.
—— and J.O. Voll, (1987 eds.) *Eighteenth Century Renewal and Reform in Islam*. Syracuse.
Lewis, B., (1967) *The Assassins: A Radical Sect in Islam*. London.
Lombard, D. and J. Aubin (1988 eds.), *Marchands et hommes d'affaires asiatiques dans l'Océan Indien et la Mer de Chine 13e–20e siècles*. Paris.
Lorenzon, D., (1981 ed.) *Religious Change and Cultural Domination*. Mexico.
Lubis, M., (1968) *A Road with no End* (A.H. Johns trans.). London.
Ma Jian, (1981) *Qur'ān (Chinese Translation)*. Beijing.
Ma Song-ting, (1982) "The Translation of the Qur'ān in China", in: *Zhongguo Mu Si Lin* 1, 2–3.
Macdonald, D., (1926) *Development of Muslim Theology, Jurisprudence and Constitutional Theory*. New York and London.
Makdisi, G., (1962/63) "Ashʿarī and the Ashʿarites in Islamic religious history", in: *Studia Islamica* 17, 37–80; 18, 19–39.
Mamdani, M., (1976) *Politics and Class Formation in Uganda*. New York and London.
Mami, B., (1923) *Wawacan Juag Tati*. Batavia.
Manar, al-, (1898–1936) Cairo.
Mangat, J.S., (1968) "Was Allidina Visram a Robber Baron or a skilful and benevolent commercial pioneer", in: *East Africa Journal* V.2, 33–35.
——, (1969) *A History of the Asians in East Africa c. 1886 to 1945*. Oxford.
Mangoendikaria, M.K., (1936) *Wawacan Siti Permana*. Batavia.
Mardin, Ş., (1962) *The Genesis of Young Ottoman Thought. A Study in the Modernization of Turkish Political Ideas*. Princeton.
Margoliouth, D.S., (1938) "Wahhābīya", in: *EI[1]* vol. 4, 1086–1090.
Martin, B.G., (1969) "Notes sur l'origine de la *ṭarīqa* des Tijāniyya et sur les débuts d'al-ḥājj 'Umar", in: *Revue des Etudes Islamiques* 267–290.
Maʿṣūmī, M., (1967) "Imām Fakhr al-Dīn al-Rāzī and his critics", in: *Islamic Studies* 6, 355–374.
Mawdudi, S.A.A., (1985[2]) *Let Us Be Muslims*. (ed. Khurram Murad). Leicester.
McDonald, B., (1983) *Kawi and Kawi Miring: Old Javanese literature in eighteenth century Java*. Canberra. Unpublished PhD thesis.
McVey, R.T., (1963 ed.) *Indonesia*. New Haven.

Means, G.P., (1991) *Malaysian Politics: The Second Generation.* Singapore.
Medhurst, W.H., (1829) *Missionary Herald* 25, 193.
——, (1838) *China: its State and Prospects, with special reference to the Spread of the Gospel.* London.
Meillassoux, C., (1971 ed.) *The Development of Indigenous Trade and Markets in West Africa.* London.
Memoirs of Aga Khan, The, *World Enough and Time*, London. (1954).
Metcalf, B.D., (1982) *Islamic Revival in British India: Deoband, 1860–1900.* Princeton.
Moertono, S., (1963) *State and Statecraft in Old Java: A Study of the Later Mataram Period, 16th to 19th Century.* Ithaca.
Mohl, J., (1853) "Rapport sur les travaux du Conseil de la Société asiatique, pendant l'année 1852–1853", in: *Journal asiatique* 5/2 (août), 171–172.
Monier-Williams, M., (1964[r]) *A Sanskrit-English Dictionary.* London.
Morris, H.S., (1958) "The Divine Kingship of the Aga Khan: a Study of Theocracy in East Africa", in: *Southwestern Journal of Anthropolology* 14, 454–472.
Mutawallī, Abū Saʿd al-, *al-Mughnī.* Edition: M. Bernand (Supplément aux Annales Islamologiques) 1986.
Nawawī al-, *Marāḥ labīd.* Pr: Cairo 1967.
Niebuhr, H.R., (1989) "The Story of Our Life", in: Hauerwas and Jones 1989: 21–44.
Noer, D., (1978 ed.) *The Modernist Muslim Movement in Indonesia 1900–1942.* Kuala Lumpur.
——, (1980) *Gerakan Moderen Islam di Indonesia, 1900–1942.* Jakarta.
O'Brien, D.C. and C. Coulon, (1988 eds.) *Charisma and Authority in African Islam.* Oxford.
O'Fahey, R.S. and B. Radtke, (1993) "Neo-sufism reconsidered", in: *Der Islam* 52–87.
—— and M.I. Abu Salim, (1992/1993) "A Sundanese in Indonesia: A note on Ahmad Surkitti", in: *Indonesia Circle* 59/60, 68–72.
Oliver R., (1977 ed.) *The Cambridge History of Africa.* Vol. 3. Cambridge.
Olthof, W.L., (1941) *Poenika Serat Babad Tanah Djawi Wiwit saking Nabi Adam doemoegi ing taoen 1647,/Babad Tanah Djawi in Proza: Javaansche Geschiedenis.* 's-Gravenhage.
——, (1987[r]) *Babad Tanah Djawi: de prozaversie van Ngabèhi Kertapradja.* Dordrecht.
Oman, G., et al. (1989) "Maṭbaʿa", in: *EI*[2] vol. 6, 794–807.
Othman, N., (1994a) "Epilogue: *Hudud* Law or Islamic Modernity?", in: Othman 1994:147–153.
——, (1994b ed.) *Shari'a Law and the Modern Nation-State: A Malaysian Symposium.* Kuala Lumpur.
Overbeck, H., (1939) "Bima als guru", in: *Djawa* 19, 12–21.
Palmer van den Broek, W., (1869) *Ardjoena-Sasra-Baoe: een Javaansch gedicht.* Batavia.
Pannenberg, W., (1967) *Grundfragen systematischer Theologie.* Göttingen.
Papanek, H., (1972/73) "Pakistan's Big Businessmen: Muslim Separatism, Entrepreneurship, and Partial Modernization", in: *Economic Development and Cultural Change* 21.1, 1–32.
Pavrey, J.D.C., (1933) *Oriental Studies in honour of Cursetji Erachji Pavry.* London.
Pedersen, J., (1984) *The Arabic Book.* Princeton.
Penrad, J.C., (1988) "La presence ismaʿilienne en Afrique de l'est", in: Lombard and Aubin 1988:221–236.
Peron, A., (1843) "Lettre sur les Écoles et l'Imprimerie du Pacha d'Égypte," in: *Journal asiatique* 4/2 (juli–août), 5–23.
Perry, T.E., (1853) *Cases Illustrative of Oriental Life and the Application of English Law to India. Decided in H.M. Supreme Court at Bombay.* London.
Petit, O., (1982) *Présence de l'Islam dans la langue arabe.* Paris.
Pigeaud, T.G.Th., (1960–3) *Java in the 14th century: A study in cultural history.* 5 vols. The Hague.
——, (1967–80) *Literature of Java: Catalogue raisonné of Javanese manuscripts in the library of the University of Leiden and other public collections in the Netherlands.* 4 vols. The Hague and Leiden.
——, (1975) *Javanese and Balinese manuscripts and some codices written in related idioms*

spoken in Java and Bali: Descriptive catalogue, Verzeichnis der Orientalischen Handschriften in Deutschland. Vol. XXXI, Wiesbaden.
Pijper, G.F., (1977) *Studien over de Geschiedenis van de Islam in Indonesia 1900–1950*. Leiden.
Poerbatjaraka, R.M.Ng., (1940) *Beschrijving der handschriften: Menak*. Bandoeng.
——, (1952) *Kapustakan Djawi*. Djakarta.
Polak, E., (1865) *Persien. Das Land und seine Bewohner*. Leipzig.
Polk, W.R. and R.L. Chambers, (1968 eds.) *Beginnings of Modernization in the Middle East*. Chicago.
Poole, H.E. and D.W. Krummel, (1980) "Printing and publishing of music", in: Sadie 1980:15, 232–272.
Popovic, A. and G. Veinstein, (1986 eds.) *Les ordres mystiques dans l'Islam*. Paris.
Prawirawinarsa and Jayengpranata, (1921) *I: Babad alit, mawi rinĕngga ing gambar-gambar sarta kar, II: Jumĕnĕngipun cungkup in pasareyan Kutha Gĕdhe*. Weltevreden.
Priolkar, A.K., (1958) *The printing press in India: Its Beginnings and Early Development*. Bombay.
Proudfoot, I., (1986) "A Formative Period in Malay Publishing", in: *JMBRAS* 59.2, 101–132.
——, (1993) *Early Malay Printed Books*. Kuala Lumpur.
Ptak, R. and D. Rothermund (1991 eds.) *Emporia, Commodities and Entrepreneurs in Asian Maritime Trade c. 1400–1750*. Stuttgart.
Qushayrī, Abū ʾl-Qāsim al-, *al-Fuṣūl fī ʾl-uṣūl*. Edition: R.M. Frank, in: *MIDEO* 16 (1983) 59–94.
——, *Lumaʿ fī ʾl-iʿtiqād*. Edition: R.M. Frank, in: *MIDEO* 15 (1982) 53–74.
Rahman, F., (1960) *Islam*. Chicago.
Rani, S., (1957 ed.) *Ślokāntara: an Old Javanese didactic text*. Nagpur.
Rappoport, A.S., (1995) *Ancient Israel Volume Three*. Myths and Legends. London.
Ras, J.J., (1986) "The Babad Tanah Jawi and its Reliability: Questions of Content, Structure and Function", in: Grijns and Robson 1986:247–273.
——, (1987a) "Betekenis en functie van de Babad Tanah Jawi", in: Olthof 1987: IX–LIV.
——, (1987b) "The Genesis of the Babad Tanah Jawi: Order and Function of the Javanese Court Chronicle", in: *BKI* 143, 343–356.
Ratnam, P., (1972 ed.) *Studies in Indo-Asian Art and Culture*. vol. 1. New Delhi.
Rāzī, Fakhr al-Dīn al-, *Maʿālim uṣūl al-dīn*. Pr: Cairo 1980r.
——, *Mafātīḥ al-ghayb*. Pr: Tehran 1933.
——, *al-Nubuwwāt wa-mā yataʿallaq bi-hā*. Edition: Saqāʿ 1986.
Reid, A., (1984) "The Islamization of Southeast Asia", in: Abu Bakar, Kaur, and Ghazali 1984:13–33.
—— and David Marr, (1979 eds.) *Perceptions of the Past in Southeast Asia*. Singapore.
——, (1993a ed.) *The Making of an Islamic Political Discourse in Southeast Asia*. Melbourne.
——, (1993b) *Southeast Asia in the Age of Commerce, c. 1450–1680*. vol. II: *Expansion and Crisis*. New Haven.
Remmelink, W.G.J., (1990) *Emperor Pakubuwana II, Priyayi and Company, and the Chinese War*. Leiden.
——, (1994) *The Chinese War and the collapse of the Javanese state, 1725–1743*. Leiden.
Ricklefs, M.C., (1974) *Yogyakarta under Sultan Mangkubumi 1749–1792: a history of the division of Java*. London.
——, (1979a) "The Evolution of Babad Tanah Jawi Texts", in: *BKI* 135, 435–454.
——, (1979b) "Six centuries of Islamization in Java", in: Levtzion 1979:101–116.
——, (1983) "The crisis of 1740–1 in Java: The Javanese, Chinese, Madurese and Dutch, and the fall of the court of Kartasura", in: *BKI* 139.2–3, 268–90.
——, (1984) "Islamization in Java: an overview and some philosophical considerations", in: Israeli and Johns 1984:11–23.
——, (1991 ed.), *Islam in the Indonesian Social Context*. Clayton.
——, (1993) *War, culture and economy in Java, 1677–1726: Asian and European imperialism in the early Kartasura period*. Sydney.

Ricklefs, M.C. and P. Voorhoeve, (1977) *Indonesian manuscripts in Great Britain: A catalogue of manuscripts in Indonesian languages in British public collections.* Oxford.
Riḍā, R., (1898–1936 ed.) *al-Manār.* Cairo.
——, (1908) *Ta'rīkh al-ustādh al-imām al-shaikh Muḥammad ʿAbduh.* Cairo.
——, (1922r) *al-Khilāfa aw al-imāma al-ʿuẓmā.* Cairo.
Riddell, P.G., (1984) "The Sources of ʿAbd Al-Ra'ūf's Tarjumān al-Mustafīd", in: *JMBRAS* LVII.2, 113–118.
——, (1986) "Tafsīr al-Qur'ān: Une Ligne de Transmission?", in: *La transmission du savoir dans le monde musulman périphérique* 6, 12.
——, (1989) "Earliest Qur'anic Exegetical Activity in the Malay-Speaking States", in: *Archipel* 38, 107–124.
——, (1990a) *Transferring a Tradition: ʿAbd al-Ra'ūf al-Singkilī's Rendering into Malay of the Jalālayn Commentary.* Berkeley.
——, (1990b) "The Use of Arabic Commentaries on the Qur'an in the Early Islamic Period in South and Southeast Asia: A report on work in progress", in: *Indonesia Circle* 51, 3–19.
——, (1993) "Controversy in Qur'anic Exegesis and its Relevance to the Malayo-Indonesian World", in: Reid 1993a:59–81.
Rizk, N.A., (1978) "The Book Publishing Industry in Egypt", in: *Library Trends* 26.4, 553–565.
Rizvi, S.S.A. and N.Q. King, (1973) "Some East African Ithna-asheri *Jamaats* (1840–1967)", in: *Journal of Religion in Africa* 5.1, 12–22.
Robinson, F., (1991) "Perso-Islamic Culture in India from the seventeenth to the early twentieth century", in: Canfield 1991:104–131.
——, (1993) "Technology and Religious Change: Islam and the Impact of Print", in: *Modern Asian Studies* 27.1, 229–251.
Robson, J., (1979) "al-Baghawī", in: *EI*² vol. 1, 893.
Robson, S.O., (1988) *Principles of Indonesian Philology.* Dordrecht.
Rodinson, M., (1974) *Islam and Capitalism.* Harmondsworth.
Roff, W.R., (1974) *The Origins of Malay Nationalism.* Kuala Lumpur.
Roolvink, R., (1971) "Indonesia, vi. literatures", in: *EI*² vol. 3, 1230–35.
Roper, G., (1982) "Arabic Printing: Its History and Significance", in: *Ur* 1, 23–30.
——, (1988) "Arabic Printing in Malta 1825–1845. Its history and its place in the development of print culture in the Arab Middle East", PhD thesis, School of Oriental Studies, University of Durham, 1988.
Rosenthal, F., (1967²) *Ibn Khaldūn. The Muqaddimah. An Introduction to History.* Princeton.
Roy, A., (1984) *The Islamic syncretistic tradition in Bengal.* Princeton.
Rusli, M., (1974) *Siti Nurbaya.* Batavia.
Sadie, S., (1980) *The New Grove Dictionary of Music and Musicians.* London.
Ṣafadī, Ṣalāḥ al-Dīn al-, *al-Wāfī bi'l-wafayāt.* Edition: Ritter, then Dedering 1931–1959.
Safadī, Y.H., (1981) "Early Arabic Printing", in: *New Books Quarterly* 1.2/3, 26–29.
Sarkar, H.B., (1972) *Corpus of the inscriptions of Java, (up to 928 A.D.),* vol. II. Calcutta.
Sastrahadiprawira, R.M., (1930) *Jodo Pakokolot.* Bandung.
Schacht, J., (1965) "Daḥlān", in: *EI*² vol. 2, 91.
Schimmel, A., (1973) *Islamic literatures of India.* Wiesbaden.
——, (1975) *Classical Urdu Literature from the Beginning to Iqbal.* Wiesbaden.
——, (1976) *Pain and grace: a study of two mystical writers in eighteenth century Muslim India.* Leiden.
——, (1982) *As Through a Veil: Mystical Poetry in Islam.* New York.
——, (1984) *Calligraphy and Islamic Culture.* New York.
Schrieke, B., (1920) "De Strijd onder de Arabieren in Pers en Literatuur", in: *Notulen der Vergaderingen van het Bataviaasch Genootschap,* 58.VI, 189–240.
Schumpeter, J.A., (1943) *Capitalism. Socialism and Democracy.* London.
——, (1949) *The Theory of Economic Development.* Cambridge, MA.
Senefelder, A., (1819) *A Complete Course of Lithography.* London.
Seydou, C., (1973) "Panorama de la Literature Peule", in: *BIFAN* 35, 176–212.

Shackle, C., (1993) "Early vernacular poetry in the Indus valley: its contexts and its character", in: Dallapicola and Zingel-Ave Lallemant 1993:259–289.
Sharar, A.H., (1975) *Lucknow: The Last Phase of an Oriental Culture.* (trans. and ed. E.S. Harcourt and F. Hussain) London.
Sharqawi, E. al-, (1987) "Rāzī, Fakhr al-Dīn al-", in: *ER* vol. 12, 221–222.
Simmel, G., (1950) "The Stranger", in: Wolff 1950.
Snouck Hurgronje, C., (1892–93) "Vier Geschenken van Sajjid Oethman Bin Abdoellah Bin ʿAqil Bin Jahja ʿAlawi beschreven", in: *Notulen Bataviaasch Genootschap,* Bijlage XIV, vols. 30–31, CV–CX1.
——, (1894) "Sajjid Oethman's Gids Voor de Priesterraden", in: *Verspreide Geschriften,* IV. I, 285–303.
——, (1906) *The Achehnese.* (trans. A.W.S. O'Sullivan) Leiden.
——, (1931) *Mekka in the Latter Part of the 19th Century.* Leiden.
Soebardi, S., (1975 ed. and trans.) *The book of Cabolek: A critical edition with introduction, translation and notes; a contribution to the study of the Javanese mystical tradition.* Bibliotheca Indonesia 10. The Hague.
Soedjatmoko et al., (1965 eds.) *An Introduction to Indonesian Historiography.* Ithaca.
Soorkattie, A., (1915) *Ṣūrat al-jawāb.* Surabaya.
Sow, A.I., (1966) *La femme, la vache, la foi: ecrivains et pouvoir du Fouta Djalon.* Paris.
Sprenger, A., (1844) *Catalogue of the Arabic, Persian and Hindústány manuscripts of the Libraries of the King of Oudh.* Calcutta.
Stapel, F.W., (1938 ed.) *Geschiedenis van Nederlandsch Indië,* vol. 2. Amsterdam.
Storey, C.A., (1933) "The Beginnings of Persian Printing in India", in: Pavrey 1933:457–461.
Stutterheim, W.F., (1956a) "An Ancient Javanese Bhima cult", in: Stutterheim 1956b. [= *Djawa* 15 (1935), 37–64].
——, (1956b) *Studies in Indonesian Archaeology.* The Hague.
Subkī, Tāj al-Dīn al-, *Ṭabaqāt al-shāfiʿiyya al-kubrā.* Pr: Cairo 1906.
Sudharshana, Devi, (1957) *Wāhaspati-tattwa: an Old Javanese philosophical text.* Nagpur.
Sukarno, (1964[r]) *Dibawah Bendera Revolusi.* Djakarta.
Suleiman, Y., (1991) "The methodological rules of Arabic grammar", in: K. Dévényi, T. Iványi (eds.) *Proceedings of the Colloquium on Arabic Grammar, Budapest 1–7 September 1991,* Budapest, 351–364.
Supomo, S., (1964) "Sastra Djendra: 'ngelmu' jang timbul karena kakografi", in: *Madjalah Ilmu-Ilmu Sastra Indonesia* 2, 177–186.
——, (1972) "On the date of the Old Javanese Wirāṭaparwa", in: Perala Ratnam.
——, (1977) *Arjunawijaya: a kakawin of mpu Tantular.* 2 vols. The Hague.
——, (1993) *Bhāratayuddha: an Old Javanese poem and its Indian sources.* New Delhi.
——, (1996) "The sovereignty of beauty: classical Javanese writings", in: Kumar and McGlynn 1996:13–32.
Suyūṭī, Jalāl al-Dīn al-, *Kitāb al-iqtirāḥ.* Edition: Qāsim 1976.
—— and Jalāl al-Dīn al-Maḥallī, *Tafsīr al-Jalālayn.* Pr: Cairo 1300 A.H.
——, *Lubāb al-nuqūl fī asbāb al-nuzūl.* Pr: Stamboul 1290 A.H.
——, *Tabaqāt al-mufassirīn.* Pr: Cairo 1976.
Syrdal, R., (1937) "Christ in the Chinese Quran", in: *Muslim World* 27, 72–83.
Ṭabarī, Abū Jaʿfar al-, *Jāmiʿ al-Bayān.* Edition: Shākir and Shākir, n.d.
Thaʿlabī, Abū Isḥaq al-, *Qiṣaṣ al-anbiyāʾ al-musammā ʿArāʾis al-majālis.* Pr: Beirut 1985.
Torrey, C.C., (1967) *The Jewish Foundations of Islam.* New York.
Tregonning K.G., (1962 ed.) *Papers on Malayan History.* Singapore.
Trimingham, J.S., (1964) *Islam in East Africa.* Oxford.
——, (1971) *The Sufi Orders in Islam.* London.
Troll, C., (1978) *A Reinterpretation of Muslim Theology.* New Delhi.
Troupeau, G., (1981) "La logique d'Ibn al-Muqaffaʿ et les origines de la grammaire arabe", in: *Arabica* 28, 242–50.
Twyman, M., (1990) *Early Lithographed Books: a study of the design and production of improper books in the age of the hand press.* London.
van der Chijs, J.A., (1864) "Bijdragen tot de geschiedenis van het inlandsch onderwijs in Nederlandsch-Indie, aan officiële bronnen ontleend", in: *TBG* 14, 212–323.

van der Molen, W., (1983) *Javaanse tekstkritiek: een overzicht en een nieuwe benadering geillustreerd aan de Kunjarakarna*. Dordrecht.
van Donzel, E., (1978) "Khafḍ", in: *EI²* vol. 4, 910–912.
van Ess, J., (1966) *Die Erkenntnislehre des ʿAḍudaddin al-Īcī*. Wiesbaden.
——, (1970a) "The logical structure of Islamic theology", in: Grunebaum 1970: 21–50.
——, (1970b) Review of Kholeif 1966 in: *ZDMG* 120, 374–378.
van Ronkel, Ph., (1987) "Malays: Malay Literature", in: *EI²* vol. 6, 240.
van Waeij, H.W., (1875) "De residentie Rembang", in: *Tijdschrift voor Nederlandsch Indie*, Nieuwe Serie, 4.2, 166–180.
Verdery, R.R., (1971) "The Publications of Būlāq Press under Muḥammad ʿAlī of Egypt", in: *JAOS* 91, 129–132.
Vermeulen, J.Th., (1938) *De Chineezen te Batavia en de troebelen van 1740*. Leiden.
Versteegh, C.H.M., (1980) "The origin of the term 'qiyās' in Arabic grammar", in: *Zeitschrift der arabischen Linguistik* 4, 7–30.
——, (1995) *The Explanation of Linguistic Causes. Az-Zaǧǧāǧī's Theory of Grammar*. Amsterdam.
von Dewall, H., (1857) "[Berigten:] Eene Inlandsche Drukkerij te Palembang", *TBG*, deel 6/n.s. deel 3, 193–198.
von Grunebaum, G.E., (1953) *Medieval Islam*. Chicago.
——, (1970) *Logic in classical Islamic culture*. Wiesbaden.
von Hammer[-Purgstall], J., (1831) *Geschichte des Osmanischen Reiches*. Pest.
von Schlechta-Wssehrd, O., (1853–55) "Verzeichniss der in Constantinopel letzterchienenen orientalischen Drucke und Lithographien", in: *ZDMG* 7, 250; 9, 262, 267.
Voorhoeve, P., (1960) "ʿAbd al-Ṣamad", in: *EI²* vol. 1, 92.
Wāḥidī, Abū ʾl-Ḥasan al-, *Asbāb al-nuzūl*. Edition: Ṣaqr 1969.
Walther, K.K., (1990) "Die lithographische Vervielfältigung von Texten in den Ländern des Vorderen und Mittleren Orients", in: *Gutenberg-Jahrbuch* 223–236.
Wansbrough, J., (1977) *Quranic Studies: Sources and methods of scriptural interpretation*. Oxford.
Watt, W.M., (1988) *Islamic Fundamentalism and Modernity*. London.
Weber, M., (1948) "The Protestant Sects and the Spirit of Capitalism", in: Gerth and Wright Mills 1948.
Weeks, R.V., (1978) *Muslim Peoples. A World Ethnographic Survey*. Westport and London.
Weigert, G., (1985) "Three Bakri *ʿUlamāʾ* in Egypt at the End of the Mamluk and the Beginning of the Ottoman Periods", M.A. Dissertation, The Hebrew University.
——, (1989) "The Khalwatiyya in Egypt in the 18th century", PhD thesis, The Hebrew University.
Weil, G., (1907) "Die erste Drucke der Türken", in: *Zentralblatt für Bibliothekswesen* 24.2, 49–61.
Weiss, B.G., (1992) *The Search for God's Law. Islamic Jurisprudence in the Writings of Sayf al-Dīn al-Āmidī*. Salt Lake City.
Wensinck, A., (1932) *Concordance et indices de la tradition musulmane*. Leiden.
Williams J.A., (1961 ed.) *Islam*. London.
Winstedt, R.O., (1969²) *A History of Classical Malay Literature*. Kuala Lumpur.
Winter, C.F., (1848) *Javaansche Zamenspraken*. Amsterdam.
Winter, C.F., Sr., (1911ʳ) *Javaansche zamenspraken* vol. I, (ed. T. Roorda). Leiden.
Winter, M., (1982) *Society and Religion in Early Ottoman Egypt: Studies in the Writings of ʿAbd al-Wahhāb al-Shaʿrānī*. New Brunswick, N.J.
Wiselius, J.A.B., (1874) "Geschiedkundige en maatschappelijke beschrijving van het eiland Bawean", in: *Tijdschrift voor Nederlandsch Indie*. Nieuwe Serie 3.1, 249–278.
Wittgenstein, L., (1953) *Philosophical Investigations*. New York.
Wolff, K.H., (1950) *The Sociology of Georg Simmel*. New York.
Yasadipura I [ascribed to], (1937–9) *Babad Giyanti*. 21 vols. Batawi Sentrum.
Yasadipura II, R.Ng., (n.d.) *Sana Sunu*. manuscript LOr 1806 of the Leiden University Library.
——, *Serat Sanasunu*. Edition: Sudibjo 1980.
Yunus, H.M., (1979) *Sejarah Pendidikan Islam di Indonesia*. Jakarta.

Zajjājī al-, *Kitāb al-Īḍāḥ fī ʿilal al-naḥw*. Edition: Mubārak 1959.
Zarcone, T., (1993) *Mystiques, philosophes, et franc-macons en Islam: Riza Tevfik, penseur Ottoman (1868–1949), du soufisme à la confrerie*. Istanbul.
Ziadeh, F., (1957) "Equality (Kafā'ah) in the Muslim Law of Marriage", in: *American Journal of Comparative Law*. VI, 503–17.
Zoetmulder, P.J., (1963) *Sĕkar Sumawur: bunga rampai bahasa Djawa Kuno*. II *Korawapāṇḍawacarita*. Djakarta.
——, (1974) *Kalangwan: a survey of Old Javanese literature*. The Hague.
——, (1982) *Old Javanese-English Dictionary*. 's-Gravenhage.
Zwemer, S.M., (1915) "Translations of the Koran", in: *The Muslim World* 5, 244–261.

GENERAL INDEX

ISLAMIC PHILOSOPHY, THEOLOGY AND SCIENCE

TEXTS AND STUDIES

ISSN 0169-8729

8. FAKHRY, M. *Ethical Theories in Islam.* Second expanded edition. 1994. ISBN 90 04 09300 1
9. KEMAL, S. *The Poetics of Alfarabi and Avicenna.* 1991. ISBN 90 04 09371 0
10. ALON, I. *Socrates in Medieval Arabic Literature.* 1991. ISBN 90 04 09349 4
11. BOS, G. *Qusṭā ibn Lūqā's Medical Regime for the Pilgrims to Mecca.* The Risāla fī tadbīr safar al-ḥajj. 1992. ISBN 90 04 09541 1
12. KOHLBERG, E. *A Medieval Muslim Scholar at Work.* Ibn Ṭāwūs and his Library. 1992. ISBN 90 04 09549 7
13. DAIBER, H. *Naturwissenschaft bei den Arabern im 10. Jahrhundert n. Chr.* Briefe des Abū l-Faḍl Ibn al-ʿAmīd (gest. 360/970) an ʿAḍudaddaula. Herausgegeben mit Einleitung, kommentierter Übersetzung und Glossar. 1993. ISBN 90 04 09755 4
14. DHANANI, A. *The Physical Theory of Kalām.* Atoms, Space, and Void in Basrian Muʿtazilī Cosmology. 1994. ISBN 90 04 09831 3
15. ABŪ MAʿŠAR. *The Abbreviation of the Introduction to Astrology.* Together with the Medieval Latin Translation of Adelard of Bath. Edited and Translated by Ch. Burnett, K. Yamamoto and M. Yano. 1994. ISBN 90 04 09997 2
16. SĀBŪR IBN SAHL. *Dispensatorium Parvum (al-Aqrābādhīn al-ṣaghīr).* Analysed, Edited and Annotated by O. Kahl. 1994. ISBN 90 04 10004 0
17. MARÓTH, M. *Die Araber und die antike Wissenschaftstheorie.* Übersetzung aus dem Ungarischen von Johanna Till und Gábor Kerekes. 1994. ISBN 90 04 10008 3
18. IBN ABĪ AL-DUNYĀ. *Morality in the Guise of Dreams.* A Critical Edition of *Kitāb al-Manām*, with Introduction, by Leah Kinberg. 1994. ISBN 90 04 09818 6
19. KÜGELGEN, A. VON. *Averroes und die arabische Moderne.* Ansätze zu einer Neubegründung des Rationalismus im Islam. 1994. ISBN 90 04 09955 7
20. LAMEER, J. *Al-Fārābī and Aristotelian Syllogistics.* Greek Theory and Islamic Practice. 1994. ISBN 90 04 09884 4
22. ADANG, C. *Muslim Writers on Judaism and the Hebrew Bible.* 1996. ISBN 90 04 10034 2
23. DALLAL, A.S. *An Islamic Response to Greek Astronomy. Kitāb Taʿdīl Hayʾat al-Aflāk* of Ṣadr al-Shariʿa. Edited with Translation and Commentary. 1995. ISBN 90 04 09968 9
24. CONRAD, L.I. (ed.). The World of Ibn Ṭufayl. *Interdisciplinary Perspectives on* Ḥayy ibn Yaqẓān. 1995. ISBN 90 04 10135 7
25. HERMANSEN, M.K. (tr.). *The Conclusive Argument from God.* Shāh Walī Allāh of Delhi's *Ḥujjat Allāh al-Bāligha.* 1996. ISBN 90 04 10298 1
26. ABRAHAMOV, B. *Anthropomorphism and Interpretation of the Qurʾān in the Theology of al-Qāsim ibn Ibrāhīm.* Kitāb al-Mustarshid. 1996. ISBN 90 04 10408 9
27. WILD, S. (ed.). *The Qurʾan as Text.* 1996. ISBN 90 04 10344 9

28. RIDDELL, P.G. and T. STREET (eds.). *Islam: Essays on Scripture, Thought and Society.* A Festschrift in Honour of Anthony H. Johns. 1997. ISBN 90 04 10692 8
29. JOLIVET, J. and R. RASHED (eds.). *Œuvres philosophiques et scientifiques d'al-Kindī.* Volume I. *L'Optique et la Catoptrique.* Edited by R. Rashed. 1997. ISBN 90 04 09781 3
30. RUDOLPH, U. *Al-Māturīdī und die sunnitische Theologie in Samarkand.* 1997. ISBN 90 04 10023 7